My young brother

If you read this
we can beat the
Hell out of them.

Your old earts
Agnes & Paul

BRIDGE PLAY
FROM A TO Z

George S. Coffin

Edited with an Introduction by
Guy Ramsey

Dover Publications, Inc.
New York

Published in Canada by General Publishing Company, Ltd., 30 Lesmill Road, Don Mills, Toronto, Ontario.
Published in the United Kingdom by Constable and Company, Ltd., 10 Orange Street, London WC2H 7EG.

This Dover edition, first published in 1979, is a corrected and amended republication of the revised third edition published in 1961, originally published in 1954 by Faber and Faber Limited, London. The author has added the Technical Card-Hand Index from the fourth edition and new bidding for American players; he has also written a new Preface for the Dover edition.

International Standard Book Number: 0-486-23891-1
Library of Congress Catalog Card Number: 79-87810

Manufactured in the United States of America
Dover Publications, Inc.
180 Varick Street
New York, N.Y. 10014

CONTENTS

TECHNICAL CARD-HAND INDEX

INTRODUCTION
by
GUY RAMSEY

Yet another book on bridge? Yes—but this one is different. It is neither a treatise on bidding nor a compendium of problems. It is an exposition of what (if I may be forgiven for saying so) nine out of every ten players lack: the methods of dummy-play and defence which ought to be second nature—the routine which even the routineers of the game ignore through ignorance.

I once watched a quartet in a Pullman carriage; they played every day from Brighton to London and every evening from London to Brighton. You would have thought, would you not, that the rudiments of bridge were familiar to them? Yet, in the course of a single hand I witnessed no fewer than seven mistakes in bidding and nearly double as many errors in play.

I have agonized only too often as dummy on just what my partner (?) was doing with my cards; and seen even more frequently the player opposite me sling away rubber after rubber by a complete disregard of such elementary, commonsensical tactics as this: if you lead a club or a heart, dummy (which you can see) will inevitably win the rest of the tricks; you do not hold a spade—so what should you lead? Yes—the answer is a diamond, for the *chance* (that I hold a winner) is better than the certainty of defeat.

A short consideration of this book—which requires, to get the best from it, careful study—will awaken you to possibilities of improvement of which you never dreamed.

Any practised player will be able to classify, at sight, most of the hands which confront him at the card-table: this one will, obviously, be a run for all available tricks; that, by contrast, involves the

7

INTRODUCTION

strategy of the waiting game; a third is a matter of ruffing, and a fourth requires a prudent husbandry of the trump suit.

To a master-player, a given hand requires little more than recognition: his technique is virtually second-nature. Once he has decided the terms of his problem, the rest is, almost invariably, a matter of routine. But we are not all master-players; and the supreme virtue of this present Coffin *opus* lies in presenting, in separate Files, each identified with a letter of the alphabet, the materials by which the aspirant to mastery may first recognise, and then execute, the best possible manœuvre to achieve success.

While I was in process of editing this manuscript—very considerable, both in quantity and quality—I was dealing with File J for Jettison. A friend, already besotted with bridge—but one whose enthusiasm far transcended his proficiency—looked over some of the hands as he waited for the belated lunch which is the portion of bridge-players' meals. That afternoon, we went to the club and, at one point, he was confronted with these cards:

```
♠ K            ♠ Q J 6 3
♡ Q 5 4 3      ♡ A J 6
♢ A            ♢ K Q 9 7 4
♣ 10 9 8 7 6 4 3   ♣ J
```

He found himself sitting West in a contract of Three Clubs, which would give him rubber; he received from the North hand the lead of a small spade to S's declared suit. He realized that he was sure to lose a spade and a minimum of three club tricks—and the king of hearts seemed, very probably, to be with the man who had bid spades.

S returned a club and N won the ace, shifting, sagaciously, to a low heart. My friend embarked on what, among bridge-players, passes for concentration: this is to say, he lighted a cigarette and drew on it heavily; he sorted and resorted his cards; he consulted the ceiling for inspiration and he asked to be allowed to look at the last trick.

But suddenly a ray of light dawned. He played the ace of hearts from the table and led the queen of spades; on this he discarded the ace of diamonds! He played the king and queen of diamonds, discarding hearts; he played dummy's spade knave, discharging his last heart—and that was the end of the story.

A baby play to you, doubtless, O reader of infinite experience—especially when you know that the player had just been reading 'J for Jettison'! But seven (if not eight) out of any ten common-or-garden club players would not have *thought of* this discard to unblock.

8

Or consider this:

♠ 9 8 6 4 2	♠ Q J 7 5 3
♡ –	♡ 3
◇ A 9 7 6 5 4 2	◇ Q 10 3
♣ 4	♣ 8 7 5 3

Not, on sight, an attractive assortment with its combined count of 9. But W found himself in a contract of six spades!

E had dealt and passed; S had bid a heart and W had ventured a spade. N had got excited and found a forcing bid in clubs and E had heroically (and not vulnerable) bid four spades. Blackwood landed S in six hearts, against which W 'saved' in six spades. N's 'double' rocked the roofs a hundred yards away.

N led the knave of diamonds, covered by queen, king and ace. W led a trump, on which N jumped up with the king, catching partner's bare ace and a dirty look. S returned a heart 'before the rats got at it'—and W made his contract!

Had S read 'Play A—Z', she would surely have returned a diamond. Had N read it, she would *not* have led a diamond! Had either of them read it, they would have bid 6 NT and made it!

And had W been playing against people who *had* read it, he would probably not have been in six spades!

This is a *rara avis* among bridge books: it is a *practical* text-book. There is not a hand here but will illumine. The book will enable you to decide when a squeeze—that fascinating manœuvre—should be ignored and a simple 'bang-bang, poppa-momma' game has better chances of success; it will teach you to 'echelon' your tactics, so as to give yourself the maximum number of opportunities. It will, in fact, instruct you in the fundamental economy of bridge.

What is meant by the 'echeloning' of tactics is no more than the technical term for not putting all your eggs in one basket; giving yourself the additional chance: for instance:

♠ A 2	♠ Q 4 3
♡ 5	♡ K J 7 6 4
◇ 6 3	◇ K 9 8 2
♣ A K 10 9 6 5 4 3	♣ Q

On this horrible hand you are W playing 5 ♣. By the grace of heaven, N leads a spade and, by a further extension of grace, dummy wins with the queen. You play off the ♣ Q and come to hand with the ♠ A on which S plays the knave. You reel off a few trumps—

9

♠ A 2   ♠ Q 4 3
♡ 5   ♡ K J 7 6 4
◇ 6 3   ◇ K 9 8 2
♣ A K 10 9 6 5 4 3 ♣ Q

enough, you hope, to get the opponents reeling: say, six in all, for
you need two left when you embark on the red suits.

You opened 1 ♣—and N, marked in the play with K 10 9 x x x in
spades, did not overcall. Therefore (File I for Inference) he did *not*
hold a red ace as well. Therefore S holds them both. So?

The W who held this hand perceived he could not get to a good
heart in dummy even if he established it; so he led a diamond and,
with the ace offside (as he should have known) went one down. Now,
suppose he had led a heart and stuck in the knave: the worst that
could have happened was that S'would win with the queen and get
off play with the ace—an unattractive manœuvre at best. Now, W
must just pray the diamond is 'right' or—another chance—that the
ace is blank with S.

But if the heart queen lies N, S is end-played! Here, you have
nothing to lose by playing the heart first; instead, you have all to
gain. You see what the 'echelon' means: if you play diamonds first,
any chance of making a heart is 'out'. If you play the heart first, you
have two chances. Two are better than one. *Verb. sap.*

All the major writers on the game, Coffin among them, refer to
'strategy and tactics'. In a nutshell, strategy consists in recognition,
tactics in execution. For example, your strategical sense informs you
that a given hand must be played at a spade cross-ruff; your knowledge of technique leads you to cash the ace and king of a side-suit
before embarking on the main plan; but your tactical sense tells you
to win the king first and the ace of the side-suit second, in order to
have the lead in the right hand to start the cross-ruff. Or perhaps
tactics should dictate a high cross-ruff to avoid an over-ruff and a
subsequent trump lead.

It is, believe me, not only the palooka—the hopeless, out-and-out
dud who commits mayhem and murder and sacrilege against the
game every time he sits down at the table—who needs Mr. Coffin
and his 'A—Z'. It is also the average, the good, the near-master to
whom this book should be of very considerable value.

Even master-players will benefit from it—if I may be forgiven the
impertinent suggestion. For one thing, the hands will fascinate them,
and interest is always a positive value. For another, masters them-

INTRODUCTION

selves make mistakes: the 'chucks' of the masters are a traditional, perennial source of permanent delight—except to the master who makes them! It was Ely Culbertson, I think, who said that all bridge players were bad—and a master was merely one who was less bad than the others. A survey of match-records—a casual hour of looking on—will demonstrate that players of the highest class are not infallible: they get into ghastly contracts, they maul their dummies and manhandle the defence much more often than they should—though much less frequently than we do.

Coffin is famous for his ingenuity: in complex problems, in the construction of recondite hands, in the devising of technical terms and titles—but his 'A—Z' is both simple and, in my view, most readable. The example hands have been subjected to ruthless analysis; the bidding has been scrutinized and, where faulty, has been stigmatized as such. The situations, with one or two rare exceptions, are not artificial and, in almost 300 hands, fewer than half a dozen have been manufactured.

This is the bridge player's dictionary—*your* dictionary. It is not a piece of doctrine (as are most treatises on bidding) which is Authorized to-day, Revised to-morrow and placed, branded with Anathemas, on the *Index* the next day; this book is valid for so long as bridge is bridge.

Read, mark, learn and inwardly digest its teaching—then shall your partners (if not your opponents) rise up and call you blessèd.

AUTHOR'S PREFACE TO THE DOVER EDITION

The first three editions of this book were edited primarily for British bridge players. Naturally the Acol bidding system, an offshoot of the early Culbertson bidding system of 1930 and the "native" system of Britain, was favored. A fourth edition, amended and revised for use by American bridge players, was published, as part of *Bridge Play Four Classics*, a collection of four of my works on bridge. This was available in a limited edition of 1930 numbered and signed copies.

Dover Publications has decided to reprint *Bridge Play Four Classics*, issuing one of the four books at a time. *Bridge Play from A to Z* is the first in the series and the other three, *Bridge Perfect Plays and Match Point Ways*, *Double Dummy Bridge* and *Endplays* will follow in the near future.

11

PREFACE TO THE DOVER EDITION

Using the third edition of *Bridge Play from A to Z* (superior typographically to the fourth and thus better suited to the photo-offset process Dover uses) as the essential framework, Dover has added to it the most important improvements and additions of the fourth edition—those features that make the book more useful to the American player.

Most important for American players is that the auctions use standard American bidding (SAB). In 226 of the 273 deals in this book both Acol and SAB are the same. However, in 47 deals we have offered the alternate SAB in footnote form on each of the pages concerned. All in all, American bridge players and teachers now have a complete casebook of SAB play deals.

As a quick and handy reference for teachers or anyone looking for a specific hand, the Technical Card-Hand Index has been taken from the fourth edition and inserted here on page 6.

The Bibliography which originally appeared on pages 351–2 has been dropped from this volume to allow space for the new material; but a new and expanded Bibliography will be added in the other books of the series to come.

British spelling (such as *honour* instead of *honor*, and *no-trump* instead of *notrump*) has been left untouched. In addition, British terms, such as *No* (or *no bid*) instead of the American *Pass* (which should not be used in any case because it often sounds like *Heart*, thus creating euphonic confusion), and *knave* in place of *jack*, have also gone unchanged. These "Britishisms" should in no way detract from the general understanding of this book—in fact, it's nice to keep a "bit of Merrie Old England!"

8 September 1979 GEORGE S. COFFIN

AUTHOR'S PREFACE TO THE THIRD EDITION

I wish to thank the many readers of the previous editions of this book who have written me, mostly in praise. Several kindly took the trouble to point out errors, which this new printing has given me the opportunity to correct. For this helpful service I wish to thank Army Captain Wayne G. Barker; Richard L. Frey and Albert H. Morehead both of New York; P. H. Jones of Christchurch, New Zealand; Fred M. Odom of Shreveport, Louisiana; Alexander J. Oszy of Newtonville, Massachusetts; William G. Ringer of Chicago; W. Howard Woolworth of Hialeah, Florida; and many others.

GEORGE S. COFFIN

AUTHOR'S PREFACE TO THE FIRST EDITION

This work has three aims.

First, to offer the beginner basic concepts of play. The first deal of every lettered file illustrates its specimen type play in simple form, a *Matrix pura* or *Matrix typica.* Subsequent deals in each lettered file become progressively more complex and advanced.

Second, to present the student a valuable case-book of play.

Third, to introduce the new Coffin File arranged in twenty-six alphabetical chapters based on common nomenclature. Every file includes several deals, each illustrating a type-play. This Coffin File should furnish bridge teachers, collectors, writers, and especially students with a convenient reference system. In beginners' classes, a teacher may use the hands in the introductory sections and the simpler hands of each file.

I hope—I dare to believe—that this book outlines systematically all the strategies and tactics of play at bridge.

Strategy is defined as 'the science of military position and movement'. Bridge, like chess and similar war games, offers each of the four 'arm-chair generals' at the table excellent opportunities to deploy his card soldiers to what he considers the best advantage. Applied to bridge, we use the term strategy to imply general policies and master plans of declarer, or defenders, for the combined twenty-six cards held by the partnership.

Tactics are defined as 'the science and art of military and naval evolutions'. Tactics and strategy are analagous; but tactics imply the proper execution of the *details* of a plan rather than the entire plan itself. Stated another way, strategy wins rubbers and tournaments; tactics win tricks. Tactics cover one or more manœuvres in the play of a hand. Proper correlation and co-ordination of these manœuvres compose the master plan of strategy.

For example, the simple queen finesse with an A-Q is a tactical manœuvre, an attempt to win two tricks. General considerations, governing whether the finesse should be taken early or late in the play—or perhaps not at all—are governed by strategy. One may use proper strategy and still fail to fulfil a contract by overlooking a tactical detail: e.g. a declarer might decide, correctly, that he should establish the spade suit by finessing—but, in the heat of play, use up his entries outside spades so that the required number of finesses could not be taken.

PLAY, AS YOU READ!

Many deals in this book offer practical bridge problems for the reader to solve. In such deals you will find the bidding and opening lead followed by some such question as 'How do you plan the play?' 'How do you bag the game?', etc. At this point cover up with the palm of your hand the description under the deal. Don't peep, but decide how YOU would play it. This procedure will help you to help yourself to strengthen your game.

Good luck and plenty of tricks!

ACKNOWLEDGEMENTS

I wish to make acknowledgement to *Bridge Magazine, Contract Bridge Journal, European Bridge Review* and *The Bridge World* for kind permission to reproduce some of the deals which were originally published under my name in their columns. I also wish to make acknowledgement to Messrs. Alphonse P. Moyse, Jr., Frank K. Perkins, Alfred P. Sheinwold, Jerome Scheuer, W. Howard Woolworth and others whose published hands in daily newspaper bridge columns furnished much valuable source material.

SCHEMATIC STRUCTURE OF BRIDGE

The study of bridge is a fascinating science—playing the game well is what master players will tell you is an art.

In the natural sciences, a *kingdom* is progressively split into *divisions, classes, orders, families (tribes),* and *genera.*

A *genus* is sometimes sub-divided into *sections* of its *species.*

The *kingdom* of bridge consists of two natural *divisions,* the calling and the play. This book deals with the play.

Play occurs in three phases or *classes,* the opening lead (and defence), the middle-game, and the end-play. The middle-game encompasses most plays—in four *orders* and thirteen *families.*

CLASS I—OPENING LEADS (Opponents' Play)

CLASS II—THE MIDDLEGAME

Order 1, Positional Plays

Family   I. Avoidance, Hold.
Family II. Finesse.
Family III. Safety Plays.

Order 2, Suit Length Plays

Family   I. Blocking, Entry, Gambit, Jettison, Unblocking.
Family II. Knock, Long Suit, Loser on Loser.
Family III. Ruff.
Family IV. Tempo.

Order 3, Reconnaissance Plays

Family   I. Counting, Inference.
Family II. Deception.
Family III. Opponents' Play (also Class I).

SCHEMATIC STRUCTURE OF BRIDGE

Order 4, Plans and Strategy

Family   I. Percentage, Sure Tricks.
Family II. Melee, New Plan, Winning Line.
Family III. Quandary, Variety.

CLASS III—END-PLAYS

Here, each of the three *orders* contains one synonymous *family*. File X, Eliminations. File Y, Coups. File Z, Squeezes.

Section I

PLAYING SHAPES AND PLANNING
THE PLAY

There are in bridge three dominant Playing Shapes:
  I. No-trump Shape.
  II. Trump/No-trump Shape.
  III. Ruff Shape.

The Trump/No-trump Shape is a hybrid of a deal featuring no-trump strategy plus a trump suit. The deal is a true no-trumper, in which the trump suit acts purely to stop an established enemy suit.

The basic characteristic of a Ruff Shape is that one or more trumps can score tricks *only* by ruffing, for otherwise they would fall uselessly on high trumps. In fact, all Ruff Shapes are synonymous with, and comprise, the great family of trump plays grouped under File R for Ruff with its sub-families, trump end-plays, in Files X and Y.

I. *The No-trump Shape*

Every deal is played without a usable trump suit. This shape includes all no-trump contracts and, rarely, a trump contract which plays equally well at no-trumps or which features no-trump play after all trumps have been played. The basic strategy is to husband high cards in short suits as stoppers and to establish long suits in order to promote more tricks. Tempo (*vide* File T) is often the vital factor, as in the type deal on the following page:

17

Pinned Ace

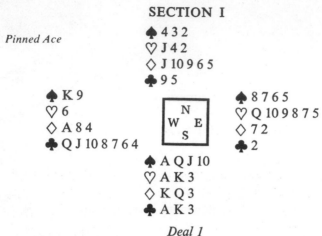

♠ 4 3 2
♡ J 4 2
♢ J 10 9 6 5
♣ 9 5

♠ K 9
♡ 6
♢ A 8 4
♣ Q J 10 8 7 6 4

♠ 8 7 6 5
♡ Q 10 9 8 7 5
♢ 7 2
♣ 2

♠ A Q J 10
♡ A K 3
♢ K Q 3
♣ A K 3

Deal 1

S, with 6½ quick tricks, or 26 points by the 4-3-2-1 point count, opened three no-trumps (or 2 ♣ with a 3 NT rebid). S has 'ideal no-trump distribution' according to bridge manuals, but we see nothing ideal about it—except possibly for the defence, whose chances are increased for winning tricks by reason of S's own utter lack of any five-card, or longer, suit to develop playing tricks. Generally, most no-trump play requires the backbone of a long suit to furnish enough tricks to get home, for no-trump games and slams are rarely made by the brute force of high cards alone.

W doubled 3 NT, and all passed. W realized that S might make it; but the powerful club suit with its two side entries, the ♠ K and ♢ A, to bring it in will at least give declarer a hard time. Moreover, the bid cannot be based on long minors, since W holds big clubs and ♢ A, and is not likely to be based on long hearts since they have not been bid, And if W happens to be lucky enough to find—improbably—♣ A-x or ♣ K-x (x represents any low card) with E, the chances of establishing clubs in one lead for a real slaughter are attractive.

Against three no-trumps W led the ♣ Q.

Declarer adopted the orthodox five-step method of planning his play at no-trumps first reduced to a formula by Ely Culbertson:

(1) He compared the number of tricks required by his contract (nine), with his tricks on top, ♠ A, ♡ A K and ♣ A K, or five. (The diamond suit has no trick on top, for the ace is missing.) Declarer is short of four tricks.

(2) He studied the card lead. Obviously the ♣ Q is the top of a

regular three-card sequence, ♣ Q J 10, probably heading a long suit.

(3) He studied the other three suits for sources of tricks to make up his four-trick deficiency. The diamond suit offers four secondary winners, if the ace can be driven out on the first or second diamond lead. The spade suit offers two additional tricks by straight leads, perhaps three if the ♠ K can be picked up.

(4) He compared his possible additional tricks with his four-trick shortage determined by Step (1). The four potential diamond winners will cover the shortage. If the defence holds up the ◇ A twice, the spade suit offers two promotional tricks in reserve.

(5) He looked for other sources of tricks, vital if Step 4 leaves him still short, such as deception plays, end-plays, safety-plays, etc. Result, negative.

So declarer won Trick 1 with the ♣ K and laid down the ◇ K, hoping to coax out the ace. W held off, and E played the ◇ 7, the higher of his two diamonds, to start an echo and give W the necessary information to enable him to judge precisely when to play his ◇ A.

To Trick 3 declarer led the ◇ Q. Again W held up his ace, because he noticed E's ◇ 7 play on the previous trick, the start of an echo if he held only two diamonds, marking declarer with three diamonds and making the hold-up vital to shut out dummy's long diamond suit. If E's ◇ 7 was a singleton, no play by W would make any difference, for S would hold four diamonds.

Declarer paused for a recount of tricks. W's ◇ A hold-up killed the diamonds in dummy. However, declarer now has two diamond tricks under his belt in addition to his five tricks on top, so he needs only two more tricks.

Normally W should be able to bring in his club suit in two leads with his two side entries, the ◇ A and ♠ K, but the threat of that long diamond suit effectively pinned his ace, so that he could not use it in time to get in and pump another club. The threat of the diamond suit in dummy robbed W of one time-unit—his otherwise normal play of the ◇ A—to let him get in and establish his clubs in time to score them.

To Trick 4 declarer, having milked the diamond suit dry, shifted to spades. He laid down the ♠ A which caught rags, then the ♠ Q which W won with his king. W shifted back to clubs, leading the ten, to drive out S's last club stopper, but S made his two secondary spade tricks to make up for his diamond deficiency. These, with two

19

diamond tricks already won, the ♠ A, ♡ A K, and ♣ A K totalled nine tricks for his well-planned, well-earned game.

II. The Trump/No-trump Shape

Every deal in this class has a trump suit whose sole function is to furnish additional stoppers for an unguarded suit. Declarer's strategic plan is to draw trumps immediately, and his remaining trumps serve as stoppers. The hand below shows typical play that occurs in every session of bridge.

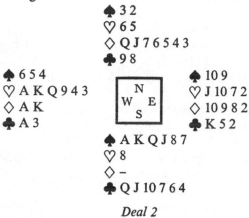

```
              ♠ 3 2
              ♡ 6 5
              ◇ Q J 7 6 5 4 3
              ♣ 9 8
♠ 6 5 4                        ♠ 10 9
♡ A K Q 9 4 3      N           ♡ J 10 7 2
◇ A K            W   E         ◇ 10 9 8 2
♣ A 3              S           ♣ K 5 2
              ♠ A K Q J 8 7
              ♡ 8
              ◇ –
              ♣ Q J 10 7 6 4
```

Deal 2

At game all W dealt and bid 2 ♡. N passed, and E made it 4 ♡. S bid 4 ♠ and W, quite insulted with his five quick tricks, promptly doubled. W led the ♡ K and continued with the ♡ Q.

Declarer adopted the five-stop method of planning his play of a trump contract.

(1) He compared his total number of immediate losers, three—the heart trick already lost and two club tricks—with losers permitted by his contract, also three.

(2) He studied the card led. The ♡ K and ♡ Q are tops of a solid suit.

(3) He studied the other three suits for top cards, for sluffs (discards) (none), finesses (none), gainful ruffs in dummy or in his own hand (none), and a long side-suit, clubs.

(4) He reviewed the time factor and decided on his strategy. Enemy trumps must split 3–2 so that only three trump leads are needed to draw trumps, leaving him with two trumps, representing two vital time units to lead clubs twice and establish them.

PLAYING SHAPES AND PLANNING THE PLAY

(5) He checked for other sources of tricks in case his plan should fail, such as end-play possibilities or deception plays if no other means offered a chance. He saw none.

So declarer ruffed the second heart lead, drew trumps in three swings, and led the ♣ Q which W won with the ace. W returned the ◇ A which S ruffed. Next S led a low club to dummy's nine which E grabbed with his king, and E returned a heart, taking S's last trump to win it. Now the clubs were all good for the balance of the tricks.

Note that S's two spades remaining after drawing trumps were just as good as aces and kings in the red suits to stop them while he worked on his long club suit.

At Trick 2 W chucked the game by leading another heart. In the auction E's jump raise to 4 ♡ showed four cards in the suit, so, despite only two hearts in dummy, declarer is now marked void of them. A forcing game is unlikely to succeed against a voluntary 4♠ bid. A switch to a diamond would have been equally futile, and unnecessary because, if declarer has any diamond losers in his own hand, he has no way to eat them. W's diamond tricks can wait.

To Trick 2 W should lay down the ♣ A. E would play the ♣ 5 as an encouraging card and W, failing to see the ♣ 2 appear, should not take long to catch on and lead another club to E's king. E would return a club, S must follow suit again, and W would ruff with the ♠ 4, the biggest little four in the British Empire, for it outranks dummy's ♠ 3.

At Trick 8 declarer gave the defence another chance to break the contract by a blunder that offered four tricks on a silver platter; but E was so busy wondering what he was going to use for money to pay the rent if he continued to hold such poor cards, that he handed the four tricks right back to S. This hand teaches a vital lesson most difficult to learn, viz, however hopeless a hand looks—however 'open and shut'—a player must acquire permanent vigilance, and remain unremittingly on the *qui vive* in case he may exploit an opponent's error. Despair is the foe of vigilance and must be ruthlessly combatted by every aspirant to 'class' play. (By the same token, 'invincible' hands breed a habit of over-confident manipulation—and this must similarly be shunned.)

When declarer led a low club to dummy's nine (he should have led a club *honour* to retain time-control), E should let the nine win! This simple hold-up of the ♣ K would have forced declarer to use his

21

last trump to get into his own hand and continue clubs, but it would have been too late. E would get in with the ♣ K and let W run the balance of four tricks in the red suits, with no trump left, to down the contract.

S, of course, should have led low to dummy's ♣ 8 on the first round, and lost an honour on the second as a simple measure of economy.

III. *The Ruffing Shape*

Low trumps must score tricks separately by ruffing lest they fall ineffectively on higher trumps. Usually these low trumps are in dummy where they ruff a short suit, but sometimes they lie in declarer's own hand when dummy has no ruffing trumps. Strangely enough, mediocre players overlook this line of play while rank beginners and master players win the maximum of ruffs. The reason is that the novice, oblivious of the traps of losing trump control, tends to play all trump hands as the simple ruffing game. Observe the deal below:

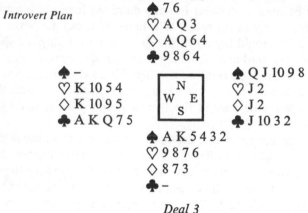

Introvert Plan

```
                    ♠ 7 6
                    ♡ A Q 3
                    ◇ A Q 6 4
                    ♣ 9 8 6 4
  ♠ -                              ♠ Q J 10 9 8
  ♡ K 10 5 4        N             ♡ J 2
  ◇ K 10 9 5     W     E          ◇ J 2
  ♣ A K Q 7 5       S             ♣ J 10 3 2
                    ♠ A K 5 4 3 2
                    ♡ 9 8 7 6
                    ◇ 8 7 3
                    ♣ -
```

Deal 3

S dealt and optimistically bid 1 ♠, W doubled for a take-out, and N redoubled to show his high cards. E bid 2 ♣, and competitive bidding finally pushed S into 4 ♠, a contract which E doubled with considerable pleasure.

W leads the ♣ K, which S ruffs. S lays down the ♠ A and confirms the bad news of three sure trump tricks for E, suspected from his double. Declarer also has two losing hearts and a losing diamond with perhaps another heart or diamond loser if E holds either red king. Despite these six sure losers, S can win ten tricks! How?

PLAYING SHAPES AND PLANNING THE PLAY

To Trick 3 S leads a heart and finesses the queen. Next S ruffs another club. The ♡ A scores to let S ruff a third club. N's ◇ Q is finessed successfully. N cashes the ◇ A, and S ruffs N's last club for the ninth successive trick, leaving S's king of trumps a positive tenth winner. This line of play leaves W 'holding the bag' with two heart tricks and a diamond trick which flop uselessly on E's three trump tricks, ♠ Q J 10 !

In the most common variety of Ruff shape, a declarer must score dummy's trumps separately by ruffing his own losers before drawing trumps. Take this deal :

Drawing Trumps

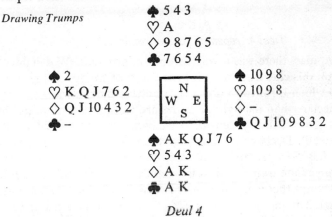

Deal 4

In a match point duplicate game in America, S dealt and bid 2 ♠, and W overcalled 3 ♡. N bid 4 ♡ to show the ♡ A, S bid 5 ♣ to show the ace, N bid 5 ♡ to show second round heart control (ace alone or ace king), so S jumped to 7 ♠, the final bid.

At one table W, who had wisely listened to the auction, realized that his heart suit offered no nourishment, so he opened the ◇ Q. E ruffed, W ruffed the ♣ Q return, and E ruffed another diamond to down the contract three tricks.

At other tables W made the mechanical opening lead of the ♡ K 'according to the book', which dummy's ace won.

If declarer immediately draws trumps, he ends with two heart losers in his own hand and no place to park them. He must trump two hearts in dummy before drawing trumps. To Trick 2 he led a club in order to recapture the lead, and led a heart for dummy to ruff. He was careful to select a club rather than a diamond because, with fewer clubs in the two hands, there was less danger of an adverse

23

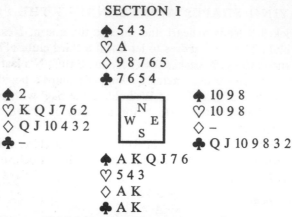

SECTION I

♠ 5 4 3
♡ A
◇ 9 8 7 6 5
♣ 7 6 5 4

♠ 2		♠ 10 9 8
♡ K Q J 7 6 2	N	♡ 10 9 8
◇ Q J 10 4 3 2	W E	◇ –
♣ –	S	♣ Q J 10 9 8 3 2

♠ A K Q J 7 6
♡ 5 4 3
◇ A K
♣ A K

Deal 4 (repeated for convenience)

void. But, alas, there was a void in both minor suits. W delightedly hopped on this club lead with his little deuce of trumps and returned the ◇ Q which E ruffed to break the contract by two tricks.

This declarer had the right idea, the proper strategic plan, but his technique, or tactical judgment, was bad. He overlooked a vital tactical detail. Declarer has only *two* heart losers in his hand while Dummy has *three* trumps; therefore, dummy can spare one trump for an immediate trump lead. It is one of the few exceptionless rules that *all* trumps that you can *afford to draw* should be drawn at once.

At Trick 2 at another table a successful declarer led a trump to his ace. This safety-play extracted two enemy trumps and protected declarer against the contingency that actually existed: a singleton trump and a club void in W. To Trick 3 declarer led a heart which dummy ruffed. S recaptured the lead with a club, for W's only trump was now gone, and declarer ruffed his last heart in dummy. S won another club, drew trumps, and spread his hand to claim the rest of the tricks for his grand slam.

An old whist adage says that hundreds of players pounded London's pavements, hungry and penniless, because they failed to lead trumps. To-day, their grandchildren are begging for a copper to get a cup of coffee—for the same reason. But there is another group, starving and homeless, who drew too many trumps too soon. Each deal is an entity to be considered individually. In this hand, *two* rounds of trumps would be fatal; *no* round disastrous. Precisely one round should, and must, be drawn.

Section II

THE 26 FILES

The 26 alphabetical files have been created to index the various tactical manœuvres and strategic devices of play.

Some typical manœuvres—such as the ducking play, for example—do not belong to any particular family or file, because they are aberrant tools serving a multiplicity of purposes. For example, D stands for Deception which includes false cards and stealing tricks by plays of ruse, but ducking is a tactical detail filed under whatever play or plan of play the particular duck happens to promote. If the duck aims to keep a dangerous opponent off lead, it comes under A for Avoidance; if it enables declarer to create a vital entry to bring in a long suit in dummy, it comes under E for entry.

The letters for Files X, Y and Z (Class III, End-plays) were selected to represent the three families of end-plays at the end of the alphabet, for these letters would not describe a file term such as F for Finesse, etc.

X, the most common letter in mathematics, was chosen for the commonest end-play family, eliminations,* also called strip and throwin plays.

Y stands for yoke, the trump tenace position, requiring end-play because partner has no trump to lead through, to neutralize the enemy trump tenace, so characteristic of the True Coups.

And the sonic Z fits the Squeezes.†

On the next page is a brief introductory glossary of all the Coffin Files. Look them over and get acquainted with them.

---

* An elimination precludes a defender from finding a safe eXit.—Editor.
† Sonic in Mr. Coffin's country, the U.S.A., where Z is pronounced, not zed, but zee.—Editor.

DEFINITIONS OF COFFIN FILES

Avoidance. Any trick development play based on keeping the dangerous opponent out of the lead, such as a duck or finesse up to the harmless opponent.

Blocking. Entry destroying play of a high card.

```
              ♠ A J
              ♡ 5 4 3
                 ┌───────┐
♠ Q 3            │   N   │         ♠ 8 7
♡ 8 7 6          │ W   E │         ♡ K 9 2
                 │   S   │
                 └───────┘
              ♠ K 2
              ♡ A Q J
```

S, on lead and needing all five tricks, leads the ♠ 2, intending to finesse dummy's knave to give dummy two leads through E's ♡ K; but W *blocks* by playing the queen.

Counting. Counting opponent's distribution and/or shape in order to discover the best play.

Deception. Concealment of strength or weakness by false-cards, swindle plays, or just plain hope, in order to win more tricks. Sometimes called 'the fourth dimension of bridge'.

Entry. Card which enables a player to take the lead. This file includes entry-creating plays and plays otherwise featuring entries.

Finesse. Third hand attempt to win a trick with a card inferior to another held.

Gambit. Deliberate sacrifice of a trick, or winner, for future gain.

Hold. To refuse a trick (hold-up), or to lead a loser from strength (holding play) in order to develop position.

Inference. Basis of play indicated by clues from bidding and/or previous play.

Jettison. To discard a top card or a winner for any purpose.

Knock. To drop a bare enemy high card, or to play so as to get two enemy high cards unnecessarily to fall together on the same trick.

Long Suit. Feature play to establish a long suit for discards.

Loser on Loser (sub-file LL). Play to discard a loser on a losing trick in order to improve position or to establish a winner in the suit led. Play to telescope the loss of two tricks into one.

Mêlée. Mixture of attack and defence plays in one deal.

THE 26 FILES

New Plan. Shift to a new line of attack in order to counter an un-expected development, such as a bad suit split, which invalidates the previously constructed strategical plan.

Opponents' Play. Opening leads, defensive suit shifts, and/or all types of defensive signals; any type of play peculiar only to the defence. Effective deception plays by the defence, however, are filed under D, and other declarer-type plays executed by defenders are filed under the play-type involved.

Percentage. Basis of play indicated by relative odds of suit splits, finesses, and/or other card positions.

Quandary. A choice of play involving pure guess. Dumping ground file for complex and/or unclassified deals.

Ruff. Any play featuring the scoring of a trump or trumps which cannot win in any other way.

Safety-Play. Basis of play to restrict the loss of tricks to a specified maximum, often at the expense of trying for extra tricks.

Sure Tricks (sub-file ST). Perfect percentage (100 per cent) plays and/or safety-plays, which restrict loss to a specified maximum of tricks regardless of defence and distribution.

Tempo. Time factor employed to establish and score tricks before the enemy does. No-trump play pre-eminently features tempo.

Unblocking. Playing a high card in order to let another player win a trick (or tricks) in the suit later.

Variety. File for any deal with two equally good winning lines of play, or for a 'cooked' hand.

Winning Line. The best plan of attack which requires study to select from other plausible lines of play.

X, Elimination. A type of end-play in which a player strips out enemy exit (or escape) cards and then throws the enemy into the lead to force a trick-losing return.

Y, Coup. End-play in which a trumpless player leads so as to let his partner finesse successfully in trumps by over-ruffing.

Z, Squeeze. End-play that forces the enemy to discard a potential winner or an essential guard to it.

27

Section III

CLASSIFYING A DEAL

The common run of deals is easy to classify and file, such as the one below:

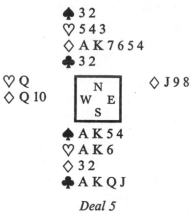

```
              ♠ 3 2
              ♡ 5 4 3
              ◇ A K 7 6 5 4
              ♣ 3 2
   ♡ Q                          ◇ J 9 8
   ◇ Q 10        N
             W       E
                 S
              ♠ A K 5 4
              ♡ A K 6
              ◇ 3 2
              ♣ A K Q J
```

Deal 5

S bid 2 ♣, N 3 ◇; S 3 ♠, N 4 ◇; and S 6 NT.
W leads the ♡ Q.

You have ten tricks on top in this 'baby' hand and need two more from diamonds to get home. You win the ♡ Q with the king and duck the first diamond lead in order to preserve the entry to dummy's long diamond suit *after* it is set up. This duck is called the *coup en blanc*. Clearly the purpose of the duck is to create an ENTRY to N, File E.

An occasional deal involves several plays, any one of which may furnish the main interest, but the final, or critical, play usually determines its primary file. Suppose you run across the deal below in your favourite bridge column. This deal is not easy to classify.

Hara Kiri Coup

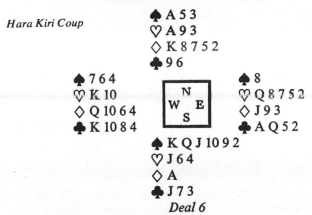

```
              ♠ A 5 3
              ♡ A 9 3
              ◇ K 8 7 5 2
              ♣ 9 6
♠ 7 6 4                      ♠ 8
♡ K 10          N           ♡ Q 8 7 5 2
◇ Q 10 6 4    W   E         ◇ J 9 3
♣ K 10 8 4       S          ♣ A Q 5 2
              ♠ K Q J 10 9 2
              ♡ J 6 4
              ◇ A
              ♣ J 7 3
```

Deal 6

S bid 1 ♠, N 2 ◇; S 2 ♠, N 3 ♠; and S 4 ♠.

W leads the ♣ 7 and E plays the ♣ 8. What plan of attack do you, S, adopt to win ten tricks?

Bear in mind that opponents will continue trumps if you try to promote a club ruff in dummy.

How many entries do you need in order to set up and cash a long diamond if the suit splits 4–3?

How do you think the enemy spades are divided?

Let us analyse the play factors for classification.

O for Opening Lead (OPPONENTS' PLAY). W's trump opening initiates an anti-ruff game.

R for RUFF. If you, S, win the trump opening and lead a club, W wins and returns a trump. If you lead another club, W wins and returns yet another trump, denuding dummy of trumps so that dummy cannot ruff your third club. The ruffing game cannot succeed unless trumps break 2–2—in which case the contract can scarcely be lost. It is, in fact, a 'pianola' hand which 'plays itself', requiring no executive technique from its declarer.

T for TEMPO. The defence used its vital tempo, the opening lead, to attack dummy's trumps and to rob you of one critical time-unit to set up a club ruff in dummy.

L for LONG SUIT. If diamonds split 4–3 (62% probable), you can ruff diamonds twice and set up a low diamond for your tenth trick and get two heart discards from your own hand.

E for ENTRY. This plan requires *three* entries to dummy, two to let you ruff diamonds and the third to cash the good low diamond. Dummy has two aces. Where is the third entry?

```
                    ♠ A 5 3
                    ♡ A 9 3
     ♠ 7 6 4        ◇ K 8 7 5 2      ♠8
     ♡ K 10         ♣ 9 6            ♡ Q 8 7 5 2
     ◇ Q 10 6 4                      ◇ J 9 3
     ♣ K 10 8 4     ♠ K Q J 10 9 2   ♣ A Q 5 2
                    ♡ J 6 4
                    ◇ A              Repeated for
Deal 6              ♣ J 7 3          convenience
```

F for FINESSE. W opened the 'top of nothing' in trumps, the ♠ 7, and E played the eight. E must have a singleton trump (or three trumps), for the play of the eight would be incorrect with any trump doubleton. If E held three trumps, this position is proved when S leads a trump, for if E holds three, W will show out.

U for UNBLOCK. So S wins Trick 2 with ◇ A to unblock diamonds, and leads his bottom trump. If W plays low, dummy finesses the five to win! S ruffs a low diamond, N re-enters with the ♠ A, S ruffs another diamond, and the ♡ A lets dummy in a third time to cash the ◇ K 8 for two discards. Note X plus 1 formula, two entries to N to ruff diamonds and a third entry (plus 1) to score them.

B for BLOCKING. But W blocks this strategy by putting up the ♠ 6 when S leads his bottom trump for the finesse, thereby killing declarer's crucial third entry to dummy.

Despite this (or any potential) defence, S can fulfil his contract!

After winning the trump opening with ♠ K and taking the ◇ A, *S should lead a club which W must win. The club-ruff threat in dummy compels W to return a trump.*

The ♠ 4 return lets dummy finesse the ♠ 5 immediately; so, instead, W returns the ♠ 6. But now dummy's ace wins while S unblocks by playing any high trump. This lets S lead the ♠ 2 later to the ♠ 5.

This is quite an assortment of plays, isn't it? Which one is the key play? Instructively, the deal illustrates any or all; but it belongs in File U for S's UNBLOCKING play in trumps.

If W happens to select the ♠ 4 for his opening lead, he can break the contract, and it is, in fact, better, when holding apparently insignificant trumps, to lead low than to follow the side-suit rule and lead 'top of nothing'.

File A

AVOIDANCE

A stands for Avoidance. The term means that you *avoid* letting in a dangerous opponent—you keep him off lead. The two characteristic elements of this great family of plays are: a shaky stopper, such as K x opposite x x, threatened by sudden death if the wrong opponent gets in to lead through it; and a suit which you can establish by ducking or finessing up to the opponent harmless on lead.

Avoidance is closely related to Hold-up, in which you hang on long enough to the top card of the suit the enemy is pushing in order to exhaust one opponent of it, and render him powerless to return the suit if he gets in.

Matrix pura

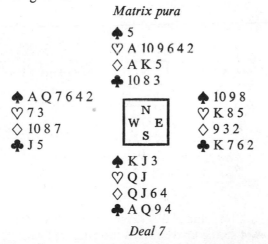

```
              ♠ 5
              ♡ A 10 9 6 4 2
              ◇ A K 5
              ♣ 10 8 3
♠ A Q 7 6 4 2        ┌───────┐        ♠ 10 9 8
♡ 7 3               │   N   │        ♡ K 8 5
◇ 10 8 7            │ W   E │        ◇ 9 3 2
♣ J 5               │   S   │        ♣ K 7 6 2
                    └───────┘
              ♠ K J 3
              ♡ Q J
              ◇ Q J 6 4
              ♣ A Q 9 4
```

Deal 7

At rubber game N dealt and bid 1 ♡, S 2 NT; N 3 ♡, and S 3 NT. The bidding is outrageous by any standard or on any system, and S is the culprit. He may bid 2 ♣ or 2 NT (if this is regarded as forcing) or 3 NT; or he may even on 16 points force with 3 ♣—but as soon as N rebids hearts, S must go to a heart game. Players like S

31

abound; and, like most of his type, he followed up his bad bidding by some worse play.

W opened the ♠ 6 and E's eight forced the knave. Playing S, 'Knucklehead Joe', the 'P.O. Prune' of bridge, promptly went after his nice long suit and finessed the ♡ Q. E won with the king and returned a spade to let W run five tricks in the suit, and down the contract by two. Joe didn't even think of the safety play of the ♡ A on the first heart lead to drop the possible lone king with E, but this (very slight) improvement in technique avails nothing in this case.*

Knucklehead needs only nine tricks for his contract: one spade, one heart, four diamonds, and three clubs. After winning the spade opening with the knave, cross to dummy's ◇ K and finesse the ♣ 8 (a vital entry-preserving card) to W's knave. W returns a heart, but dummy should pop on the ace, and lead the ♣ 10 for another finesse which wins. The third club finesse follows, and even Joe can now cash his top cards for game.

Playing for the hearts offers only an even chance, but the odds are 3 to 1 that *one* of the club finesses will win, which is all you need to make your (horrible) contract.

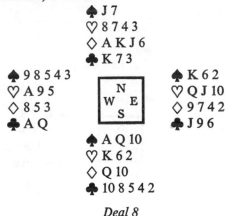

Deal 8

N bid 1 ◇, S 2 NT; and N 3 NT. N's rebid is a stretch.

W led the ♠ 4 so the knave forced the king and ace.

S led a low club, W played the queen, and dummy's king won

---

* The 'book' play, published many times, of 'ducking the first trick', obviously will not solve in this case, for E holds *three* spades; and will never solve if the adverse suit is 5–3. This is not to say that the play is not of value in certain circumstances. A duck in this hand would simply put the contract down for nothing .. and would be even worse than Knucklehead's usual form.

AVOIDANCE

and dummy lost a club to W's bared ace. W lost a spade to S who led a third club. E won and shifted to the ♡ Q.

Declarer needs luck to make the hand, but he overlooked the shut-out (Avoidance) play in clubs. S should let W win the first club lead with the queen; later, W scores the ♣ A; but the ♣ K wins the *third* round to clear the suit without letting E into the lead for the fatal heart switch. Declarer must lose *two* clubs however the suit splits, and must try to lose both to W.

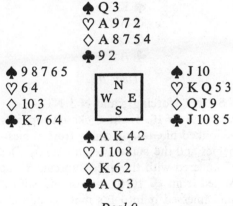

```
              ♠ Q 3
              ♡ A 9 7 2
              ◇ A 8 7 5 4
              ♣ 9 2
  ♠ 9 8 7 6 5           ♠ J 10
  ♡ 6 4         N       ♡ K Q 5 3
  ◇ 10 3      W   E     ◇ Q J 9
  ♣ K 7 6 4     S       ♣ J 10 8 5
              ♠ A K 4 2
              ♡ J 10 8
              ◇ K 6 2
              ♣ A Q 3
```

Deal 9

S bid 1 NT, N 3 NT. [This auction is horrible. See below *—G.C.]
W led the ♡ 6. How do you play to score nine tricks?

The natural-looking plan is to duck the ♡ 6, which E wins. E shifts to the ♣ J to set up three tricks in the suit for his side and later scores another heart trick to break the contract. S played the ♣ A and tried another heart finesse, which let E in again to lead another high club and W picked off the queen.

Analysis shows that the ♡ 6 lead is not a fourth best; for N and S hold *six* higher hearts and only *five* are possible by the Rule of Eleven, if it were the 'normal' lead. Declarer must hurry to clear diamonds before his ♣ A is driven out. This plan scores three spade tricks, the ♡ A, the ♣ A, and four diamond tricks for nine, i.e. game. When E wins the third diamond lead, he can score two heart tricks, but dummy's ♡ 9 is a fourth-round stopper.

*Playing no convention N should respond 3 ◇ forcing. N hopes that on four hearts S bids 2 ♡, then N 4 ♡, else 3 NT.

N's best is 2 ♣, the artificial forcing Kempson (Stayman) convention; S 2 ♠, then N 3 NT. By backing away from spades N guaranteed four hearts, so if S also has four hearts, he closes at 4 ♡. With no major S must rebid 2 ◇ artificially, *never* rebid 2 NT.

33

FILE A

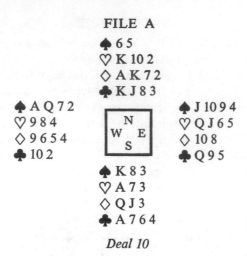

♠ 6 5
♥ K 10 2
◇ A K 7 2
♣ K J 8 3

♠ A Q 7 2
♥ 9 8 4
◇ 9 6 5 4
♣ 10 2

♠ J 10 9 4
♥ Q J 6 5
◇ 10 8
♣ Q 9 5

♠ K 8 3
♥ A 7 3
◇ Q J 3
♣ A 7 6 4

Deal 10

N bid 1 ◇, S 2 NT (forcing); and N 3 NT.

W opened with the ♣ 10. Eight tricks on top plus a ninth from the club finesse looked like taking candy from babies—but S wasn't playing with babies and the stakes weren't candy. Declarer finessed the ♣ J, and E covered with the queen, forcing S's ace.

S thought W led from ♣ 10–9, with or without four cards, so S led the ♣ 7 and finessed it into E's nine. E shifted to the ♠ J— curtains!

In his haste S overlooked the fact that players sometimes make waiting short-suits leads against no-trumpers, although we should have preferred the ♥ 9, which breaks the contract out of hand when S tries to develop the clubs himself.*

Dummy must duck the opening ♣ 10 lead and S must let it win! It is vital to keep E off lead. S gets in soon, lays down the ♣ A, and leads a third club.

On the opening club lead it is 'natural' play to cover with the knave immediately, and play W for ♣ 9 if E shows up with ♣ Q. But if W led from ♣ Q 10 9 x, declarer cannot get more than three club tricks however he plays, and he can delay the finesse to protect himself against the position that actually exists.

* A major rather than a minor; a 3-card suit rather than a doubleton for 'passive' leads against no-trumpers is a good rule-of-thumb when there is no better basis for selection.—Editor.

AVOIDANCE

♠ J 5 3
♡ A 7 4 3
◇ 10 9
♣ A J 10 8

♠ K Q 10 9   ♠ 8 7 6 4
♡ 8 6 2   ♡ 10
◇ A Q 8   ◇ J 6 3 2
♣ 7 6 4   ♣ K 5 3 2

♠ A 2
♡ K Q J 9 5
◇ K 7 5 4
♣ Q 9

Deal 11

S bid 1 ♡, N 3 ♡; and S 4 ♡.

The N hand is a bit skimpy for the jump raise, except playing Acol, where it is a limit, and not a forcing, bid.

W led the ♠ K. How do you play it?

S won the ♠ K with his ace, won the third trump lead taking care to keep his bottom trump (playing ♡ 9 under the ace), and led a low spade toward dummy's knave. W had to score his queen at once or lose her; so he won and switched to the ♣ 7, which dummy's ace won. Dummy scored the ♠ J for S's ♣ discard, then led the ♣ J which E covered (S discards if E ducks) and S ruffed. Later S got two diamond discards on N's good clubs, and S lost two diamond tricks, but with only a spade loser in addition, scored game.

If S tries the ♣ Q finesse through W, E scores his king, W two diamond tricks, which, with the ♠ Q, breaks the contract.

The Bidding: (Deal 12 overleaf)   *No score*

S	W	N	E
1 ♡	1 ♠	2 ◇	2 ♠
3 ◇	3 ♠	4 ♡	4 ♠
5 ♡	No	No	No

N and S have the balance of power, although E and W can win ten tricks at spades. They thought they could beat 5 ♡, which they did because declarer missed the point.

W led the ♠ K. How would you play it?

Dummy ruffed the ♠ K, the ♡ A won, dummy ruffed another spade, the ◇ Q won, and the ♡ K play discovered E's ♡ J too well chaperoned to be caught. So declarer cashed the ♡ Q also and lost

35

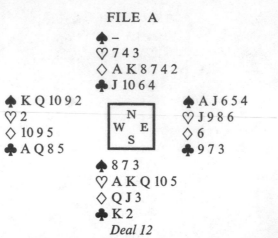

Deal 12

a low heart to E's knave. E cashed a spade and shifted to the ♣ 9 to set the declarer two tricks.

The hand can be made easily by avoidance play. Ruff the spade opening in dummy. Lead a trump and finesse the ten! It wins, so ruff another spade in dummy, re-enter via the ◊ Q, draw trumps, and run diamonds for thirteen tricks!

This play is not double dummy but is based on a sound reason. If the ♡ 10 finesse loses to the knave, even if it be a singleton, declarer later draws trumps and runs diamonds for eleven tricks. The key play is to keep E out of the lead. Safety play (like the ♡ 10 finesse) usually loses one trick to win more; here it actually gains!

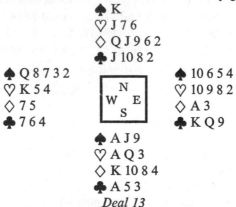

Deal 13

At game all, S bid 1 NT, N 2 NT; and S 3 NT.

W led the ♠ 3. Dummy won and pushed out the ◊ Q which E won and returned a spade which S finessed to W's queen, and W continued to knock out S's ♠ A. With only eight tricks on top now, S tried the ♡ Q finesse, which lost the game.

Declarer must set up his second heart trick *before* touching the alluring diamonds! If the ♡ Q finesse loses Trick 2, W is harmless on lead. W cannot return a spade without sacrifice, and any other lead gives S time to set up his diamonds. Declarer chucked the game because he preferred the wrong 'blonde' at Trick 2.

The next deal illustrates a different phase of time-control in avoidance play.

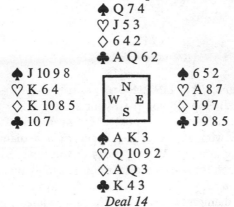

<pre>
                ♠ Q 7 4
                ♡ J 5 3
                ◇ 6 4 2
                ♣ A Q 6 2
    ♠ J 10 9 8   ♠ 6 5 2
    ♡ K 6 4   N   ♡ A 8 7
    ◇ K 10 8 5   W   E   ◇ J 9 7
    ♣ 10 7   S   ♣ J 9 8 5
                ♠ A K 3
                ♡ Q 10 9 2
                ◇ A Q 3
                ♣ K 4 3
</pre>

Deal 14

In the rubber game S bid 1 NT, N 2 NT; and S 3 NT.

W led the ♠ J. How do you plan the play?

With seven tricks on top declarer must promote two heart tricks. So dummy won the ♠ Q and led a heart which E grabbed fast with his ace, returning the ◇ J.

Now came the critical play. Declarer finessed the ◇ Q. W won and pushed diamonds to drive out S's ace. E and W got three diamond tricks and the ♡ A and ♡ K to break the contract.

If E had ducked dummy's heart lead at Trick 2, W would have won the trick with the ♡ K and declarer would have had no problem with W on lead, but E's fast ace play and diamond return put declarer squarely on the hot griddle.

Even so, S must play his ◇ A at once and resume hearts. W scores his ♡ K, well marked in his hand by E's play of ♡ A, but the defence has no way to get at S's ◇ Q before S scores the game.*

* If E has, deceptively, played ♡ A from both ace and king, the play of ◇ A loses nothing. The ◇ Q will win (if win she can), as well on the second or third round as on the first. As the cards lie, the play of ◇ A wins the game; and if E holds ♡ A K and W the ◇ K, nothing will win it. The play of ◇ A is a chance of gain against a certainty of loss.—Editor.

FILE A

Strategy at Trick One

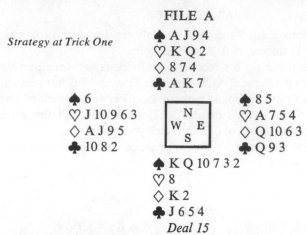

♠ A J 9 4
♡ K Q 2
◇ 8 7 4
♣ A K 7

♠ 6
♡ J 10 9 6 3
◇ A J 9 5
♣ 10 8 2

♠ 8 5
♡ A 7 5 4
◇ Q 10 6 3
♣ Q 9 3

♠ K Q 10 7 3 2
♡ 8
◇ K 2
♣ J 6 5 4

Deal 15

At rubber game N bid 1 NT, S 3 ♠; and N 4 ♠.
W led the ♡ J. How do you plan your strategy?

Declarer chucked the hand quickly. He covered the ♡ J with the queen which E won with the ace. E returned a diamond to cut through S's king and give W two tricks in the suit. Later E's ♣ Q broke the contract, for one club discard on N's ♡ K was not enough.

Dummy must duck the ♡ J opening! If E plays the ♡ A anyway, he can return a diamond for W's two tricks, but later S gets *two* club discards on N's unbroken 'marriage' in hearts. So E ducks the ♡ opening also, and W shifts to a club which dummy wins. Dummy wins the second trump lead and leads the ♡ K, E covers with the ace (if E ducks, S discards a diamond, for the ♡ A is marked with E) and S ruffs. Later S discards a diamond on N's ♡ Q. S loses only one heart, one diamond and one club (or two diamonds and no club) scoring game.

Half-Nelson Play

♠ 10 8 7 6 3
♡ 2
◇ 6 2
♣ 7 6 4 3 2

♠ Q 5
♡ J 9 8 4
◇ K 10 3
♣ A K Q 9

♠ K J 9 4 2
♡ 7 5
◇ J 9 8
♣ J 10 5

♠ A
♡ A K Q 10 6 3
◇ A Q 7 5 4
♣ 8

Deal 16

38

AVOIDANCE

At rubber game W bid 1 ♣, E 1 ♠, S 4 ♡; W doubled.
W led the ♣ K then ♣ Q. The auction indicates ♡ J x x x and
◇ K with W. How do you use these clues to land game?

S must establish diamonds, which must split 3 3 to give S a chance
Also S must avoid an enemy heart lead *from* E until dummy has
ruffed a diamond.

Ruff the second club, and push forward the ◇ Q! W must win—
and cannot return a trump lest he lose his ♡ J. Later dummy ruffs
the third diamond lead to establish the suit. All you lose is the ◇ K,
♡ J, and a club.

If you play diamonds ace then low, or low first, W ducks to let E
in to return a trump and kill dummy's vital ◇ ruff.

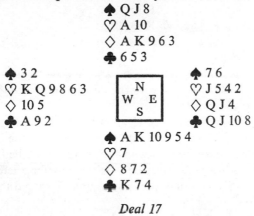

```
            ♠ Q J 8
            ♡ A 10
            ◇ A K 9 6 3
            ♣ 6 5 3
♠ 3 2                        ♠ 7 6
♡ K Q 9 8 6 3    N          ♡ J 5 4 2
◇ 10 5         W   E         ◇ Q J 4
♣ A 9 2          S          ♣ Q J 10 8
            ♠ A K 10 9 5 4
            ♡ 7
            ◇ 8 7 2
            ♣ K 7 4
```

Deal 17

At love all N bid 1 ◇, S 1 ♠, W 2 ♡; N 2 ♠, S 4 ♠.
W led the ♡ K. Should dummy play the ace?

Dummy won the ♡ A. S drew trumps, but soon discovered that
he had no way to establish diamonds without letting in E for the
fatal ♣ Q return.

Dummy must duck the opening lead—even with a singleton in one
hand and the ace in the other! This deal is one of those 'first-trickers'
in which if declarer thinks *after* he plays from dummy to the opening
lead, it may be too late. Superficially this heart duck appears foolish,
but you give the enemy nothing, for you merely exchange a heart
trick for that doleful diamond loser which you park on the ♡ A when
W leads another heart. Draw trumps, ruff high the third ◇ lead, and re-
enter dummy via a trump to cash 'stiff' diamonds for club discards.
You lose one trick each in hearts and clubs and score an overtrick.

Once more Avoidance—preventing E's entry with ◇ Q—is the key to the winning play.

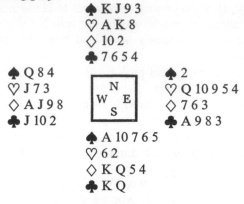

♠ K J 9 3
♡ A K 8
◇ 10 2
♣ 7 6 5 4

♠ Q 8 4
♡ J 7 3
◇ A J 9 8
♣ J 10 2

♠ 2
♡ Q 10 9 5 4
◇ 7 6 3
♣ A 9 8 3

♠ A 10 7 6 5
♡ 6 2
◇ K Q 5 4
♣ K Q

Deal 18

At rubber game S bid 1 ♠, N 3 ♠; and S 4 ♠.*†

W led the ♣ J which E won with the ace and returned ♣ 3. How do you develop the play?

At Trick 3 dummy won the ♠ K, then S the ♠ A when E failed. Dummy won the ♡ K and led toward S's ◇ K Q in hope E held the ace, but W killed off an honour with that card. W cashed the ♠ Q and exited with a heart. Dummy had only one trump left—insufficient to ruff *both* S's diamond losers, so E and W scored the penalty points.

At Trick 3 lay down the ♠ A, then lead a low ♠. Then:

(a) If W fails, dummy's ♠ K wins next and dummy leads a diamond. If E holds the ◇ A, he scores it and may draw a trump from dummy with the ♠ Q—but now you need only *one* diamond ruff in dummy. If W holds ◇ A, he has no trump to lead—and so cannot kill the second necessary ruff in dummy.

(b) If W follows suit on the second trump lead, dummy must finesse the ♠ J ! This is not a guess, because *the finesse cannot lose whoever holds the queen.* If W has the ♠ Q, dummy picks her up and can afford *two* diamond losers; if E wins the trump finesse, trumps split 2–2 so that dummy still has two trumps left for two diamond ruffs.

*N's 3 ♠ bid is a limit raise—a non-forcing game coax.
†*SAB:* S 1 ♠, N 2 ♣; S 2 ◇, and N 4 ♠.

AVOIDANCE

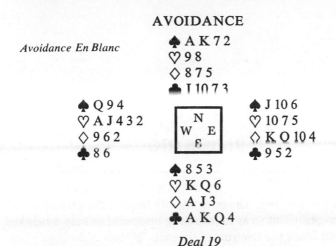

♠ A K 7 2
♡ 9 8
◇ 8 7 5
♣ J 10 7 3

♠ Q 9 4
♡ A J 4 3 2
◇ 9 6 2
♣ 8 6

N
W E
S

♠ J 10 6
♡ 10 7 5
◇ K Q 10 4
♣ 9 5 2

♠ 8 5 3
♡ K Q 6
◇ A J 3
♣ A K Q 4

Deal 19

At rubber game S bid 1 ♣, N 1 ♠; S 2 NT and N 3 NT.

W led the ♡ 3 and E played the ten. You have eight tricks on top. How do you promote a ninth?

Reject potential promotion of ◇ J, for if E holds both the king and queen, you have to let E into the lead for a fatal heart return. Spades offer the only real hope.

Win the ♡ 10 with the king and lead a low spade. Hope that W holds exactly ♠ Q x x . If W puts up the queen, let her win; but W ducks; so, score dummy's king. If dummy next lays down the ♠ A, W can unblock by ditching the queen; so, instead, win a club in S and lead another spade toward dummy. Again W plays low (*still* duck if W plays the queen) and score the ace; then lose a ♠ to W's queen. Spades split 3–3 which makes dummy's thirteener good for the game-scoring trick.

This play is called *Avoidance en blanc*, because there is no real finesse position to keep E off lead.

In the first edition Mr. Aksel J. Nielsen of Denmark and Captain Wayne G. Barker, U.S. Army, both found a cook in *Deal 18*.

At Trick 4 the ♠ K play has a slight edge to drop the queen. If not as occurs, S clinches game anyway by reverse dummy. S must ruff two clubs and the third heart in his own hand *before touching diamonds*. The immediate attack on diamonds at Trick 5 is fatal as shown. At Trick 4, the knave finesse or king play are both 'sure trick' plays for ten tricks. *Deal 18* should be reclassified into File V for Variety, q.v.

File B

BLOCKING

B stands for blocking. The term usually implies the play of a high card of an enemy suit so as to force one opponent to keep a blanked stopper and block the free run of the suit. Whenever declarer's purpose is to cut entry from one opponent to the other in order to avoid an enemy ruff or lead through a thinly-guarded honour, the play is a special type of Avoidance. In this case it is entry-destroying play, the antithesis of entry-creating play filed under U for Unblocking, q.v.

Matrix pura

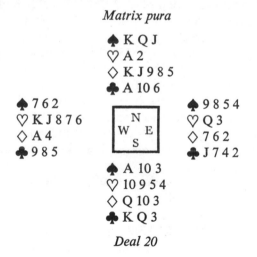

```
                  ♠ K Q J
                  ♡ A 2
                  ◇ K J 9 8 5
                  ♣ A 10 6
   ♠ 7 6 2                        ♠ 9 8 5 4
   ♡ K J 8 7 6      N             ♡ Q 3
   ◇ A 4          W   E           ◇ 7 6 2
   ♣ 9 8 5          S             ♣ J 7 4 2
                  ♠ A 10 3
                  ♡ 10 9 5 4
                  ◇ Q 10 3
                  ♣ K Q 3
```

Deal 20

After two passes N bids 1 ◇, S 2 NT; and N 3 NT.

W leads the ♡ 7. Playing S, our old friend, Knucklehead Joe, hastily ducked in dummy in order to exhaust E of hearts if he should hold only two. E won with the queen and returned a heart to dummy's ace. With seven top tricks Joe needed diamond tricks, but W quickly gobbled the first diamond lead with his ace and scored his hearts to break the contract.

BLOCKING

Declarer must play the ♡ A to Trick 1! Immediately he should push diamonds. Were W's hearts headed by K Q J, he would have led the king, not the seven; hence E must hold at least one heart honour.

If this honour be a singleton, it falls on the ace, and S's ♡ 10 9 5 becomes a second safe stopper.

If this honour be a doubleton, E is faced with a dilemma—to unload the queen on the ace—which promotes S's 10 9 x into a second stopper, or to keep the queen and block the suit, for W cannot afford to overtake. After W gets in via the ◇ A and returns a low heart, E scores his queen but has no heart left to let W run the suit. If E holds three hearts, neither opponent has dangerous length: they may make 3 hearts and a diamond and welcome—but that is the end of the story.

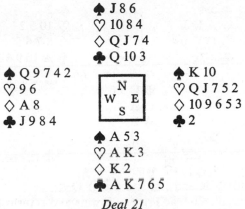

Deal 21

S bid 1 ♣, N 1 ◇; and S 3 NT. Alternative bidding: 2 NT—3 NT.

W leads the ♠ 4. Would you play dummy's knave?

S played ♠ J, hoping W had underled ♠ K Q x, E covered, and S held up the ace. E returned the ♠ 10 which S ducked and W overtook with the queen in order to clear the suit.

Even if S tries the improbable ♣ 10 finesse, he gets only eight tricks and must finally lose a diamond to W who scores his stiff spades.

We do not see eye to eye with declarer who, like the 'one-eyed knave',* took only one view: ♠ K Q x in W—the wrong view. The

---

* ♠ J, like ♡ J, are known—especially in freak poker pots—as 'one-eyed jacks'. These two cards, in profile, show only one eye. Note: the 'jack' is the correct name in poker, but in bridge it is 'knave'.—Editor.

odds are three to one that E holds the ♠ K or ♠ Q, so declarer should duck the spade opening in dummy and win with his ace. If E throws his king on the ace, he makes dummy's honour good, so: suppose E plays low, blocking the suit. Next S leads the ◊ K which W wins and returns a spade to E's king. E returns the ◊ 10 to dummy's knave, S wins a top heart and leads a low club for the ten finesse, which wins. This play is not double dummy, but an avoidance play to keep W out of the lead *in case* he holds ♣ J x x x; S doesn't care even if E scores the ♣ J, for game is safe without its capture.

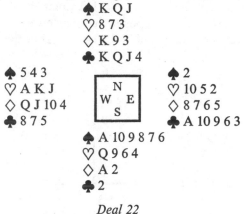

♠ K Q J
♡ 8 7 3
◊ K 9 3
♣ K Q J 4

♠ 5 4 3   ♠ 2
♡ A K J   ♡ 10 5 2
◊ Q J 10 4   ◊ 8 7 6 5
♣ 8 7 5   ♣ A 10 9 6 3

♠ A 10 9 8 7 6
♡ Q 9 6 4
◊ A 2
♣ 2

Deal 22

N bid 1 ♣, S 1 ♠; N 2 ♠ and S 4 ♠.

W leads the ♡ K and shifts to the ◊ Q.

(If W shifts to a club at Trick 2, E wins and returns a heart to let W break the contract before S gets started; but W had no reason to prefer a club shift and the ◊ Q shift will seem to any W more logical.)

S wins the ◊ Q with the ace, wins a trump and the ◊ K in dummy, and leads dummy's ◊ 9, which E cannot cover; S discards the ♣ 2, effectively blocking W's entry to E when W makes the ◊ 10. W loses a trump lead to dummy who leads the ♣ K, E covers with his ace (S discards if E ducks), and S ruffs. A low trump lead to dummy draws W's last trump and S parks two hearts on dummy's top clubs. The defence gets a diamond trick and two hearts—but declarer gets game.

A similar blocking play stops an adverse ruff in the next deal.

BLOCKING

Scissors Coup

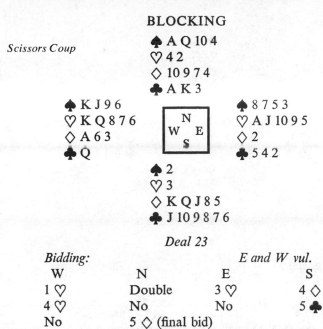

♠ A Q 10 4
♡ 4 2
◇ 10 9 7 4
♣ A K 3

♠ K J 9 6
♡ K Q 8 7 6
◇ A 6 3
♣ Q

♠ 8 7 5 3
♡ A J 10 9 5
◇ 2
♣ 5 4 2

♠ 2
♡ 3
◇ K Q J 8 5
♣ J 10 9 8 7 6

Deal 23

Bidding: *E and W vul.*

W	N	E	S
1 ♡	Double	3 ♡	4 ◇
4 ♡	No	No	5 ♣
No	5 ◇ (final bid)		

W led ♣ Q, which had all the earmarks of a singleton.

Clearly you are going to lose a diamond, a heart and a club ruff, i.e. one down, for W will surely underlead his ♡ A if he holds it. What can you do about it?

Win Trick 2 with the ♣ A and trot out the other black queen, the ♠ Q! On this, park your singleton heart. W wins with the ♠ K, but W has no way to put E in for a club return and ruff.

45

FILE B

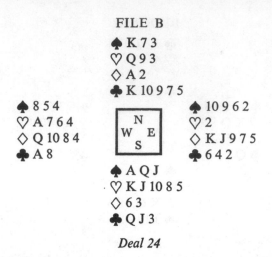

♠ K 7 3
♡ Q 9 3
◇ A 2
♣ K 10 9 7 5

♠ 8 5 4
♡ A 7 6 4
◇ Q 10 8 4
♣ A 8

♠ 10 9 6 2
♡ 2
◇ K J 9 7 5
♣ 6 4 2

♠ A Q J
♡ K J 10 8 5
◇ 6 3
♣ Q J 3

Deal 24

Bidding: *Rubber game*

S	W	N	E
1 ♡	No	2 ♣	No
2 ♡	No	4 ♡ (final bid)	

W leads the ◇ 4. Do you play dummy's ace?

Declarer played the ◇ A, and W ducked two trump leads, showing the bad split.

If S leads a third trump, W wins and forces S with a diamond. If S next draws trumps and pushes clubs, W wins and runs diamonds to break the contract.

So declarer must shift to a club at Trick 4 and W ducks, but wins the second club, E gets in with a diamond, and W ruffs a club; curtains.

To guard against the common 4–1 trump split, declarer, in order to block W's entry later to E for that fatal club ruff, must duck the diamond opening! E wins and can do little better than return a diamond to N's ace. W passes two trump leads, and S pushes clubs next. W wins the second club lead and *dummy can* ruff a third diamond lead, making game easy.

BLOCKING

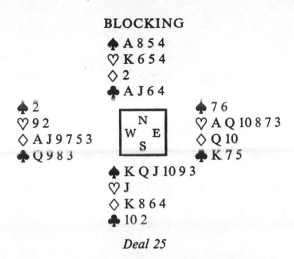

♠ A 8 5 4
♡ K 6 5 4
◇ 2
♣ A J 6 4

♠ 2
♡ 9 2
◇ A J 9 7 5 3
♣ Q 9 8 3

N
W E
S

♠ 7 6
♡ A Q 10 8 7 3
◇ Q 10
♣ K 7 5

♠ K Q J 10 9 3
♡ J
◇ K 8 6 4
♣ 10 2

Deal 25

With E and W vulnerable, S dealt and bid 3 ♠, N 4 ♠.

W leads the ♡ 9. How do you plan to get three diamond ruffs in dummy?

Declarer put up dummy's king, which fell to E's ace. The real purpose of the king play was to make a heart return appear attractive to E, but E would have none of it and returned a trump.

The trap is to let E's trump return run to dummy's eight; then E later over-ruffs a diamond to break the contract. Instead S must win the trump lead in his own hand.

S realizes the danger of another trump lead which will leave dummy one trump short, to ruff three diamonds; so he sets out to salvage that vital game-scoring ruff if possible.

If S leads a *low* diamond, he will let in whichever defender has the last trump to lead; so S makes the blocking play of the ◇ K. This play caters to the actual distribution—the fifty-fifty chance that the opponent with the ◇ A lacks the last trump.

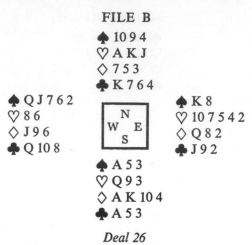

Deal 26

S bid 1 NT, N 3 NT.

W leads the ♠ 6 and E plays the ♠ K.

With eight tricks on top, how do you snare the ninth?

S held up his ♠ A until the third round, on which E made a brilliant play. He jettisoned the ◇ Q, establishing W's ◇ J as an entry, and declarer's game flew out of the window with her. This, though lucky, is not merely flashy. If S holds A K J of diamonds, the queen is useless anyway. Once again, it is a chance against a certainty.

S should win the *second* spade lead to block this defensive jettison. Besides, it is pointless to hold up the ♠ A *twice*, for if E has three spades, the suit is harmless.

To get a third club trick requires a 3–3 split plus a slim chance to duck a club into E through so many club intermediates.

Diamonds will do the trick if W holds any singleton or doubleton diamond honour, or if E holds exactly ◇ Q x x.

To Trick 3 lead a heart to dummy and return a diamond. If E plays the queen, duck; otherwise win with the ace. Go back to dummy with another heart and repeat the diamond play. Now, lose the third diamond lead to E's queen.*

In a different type of blocking play a defender deliberately blocks a suit in order to force a shift. Note the deal on the next page, which might be filed under O for Opponents' Play:

---

* Cf. deal 19 in File A.

BLOCKING

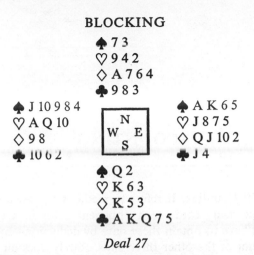

♠ 7 3
♡ 9 4 2
◇ A 7 6 4
♣ 9 8 3

♠ J 10 9 8 4
♡ A Q 10
◇ 9 8
♣ 10 6 2

♠ A K 6 5
♡ J 8 7 5
◇ Q J 10 2
♣ J 4

♠ Q 2
♡ K 6 3
◇ K 5 3
♣ A K Q 7 5

Deal 27

S bid 1 NT and all passed.

In this *defensive* problem you are West. How do you play to break the contract?

In an expert game declarer was defeated quickly. W led the ♠ J to E's king, and dropped the ♠ 10 under the ace. Next came the ♠ 5 which W took with the ♠ 9 and returned his ♠ 4 to E's six, effectively and deliberately blocking the suit.

This normally atrocious bridge crime had a legitimate purpose in this case. To Trick 5 E led the ♡ J in order to let W score three heart tricks instead of two in case he held the ♡ 10 with his ♡ A Q.

At Trick 5 E could have returned the ♣ J instead of ♡ J. His holding and dummy's were roughly equal, so the club looked equally logical, and let S score seven tricks: the club suit was never bid. So why did E return a heart?

Three Signals!

W signalled three times in spades! First was the routine knave lead to show the top of a sequence. Second, W played the ♠ 10, not the eight, a Nathan S. Kelly signal showing that W's remaining spades were solid and that S's queen was an honest drop, not a false card from ♠ Q 10 9, etc. And third, W won the third spade lead with the *nine*, not his equal-ranking eight. This was a Hy Lavinthal* suit-preference signal; the *higher* card to show E that W wanted E to shift to the *higher-ranking* suit; clearly hearts and not clubs.

---

*Sometimes incorrectly called the McKenney in Britain.

File C

COUNTING

C stands for Counting. It refers to methods of play aimed at discovering how many cards each opponent holds in a critical suit. Usually you have to obtain these data by deduction—by getting an accurate count of the other three suits. Rarely does an early manœuvre in the key suit itself reveal the winning way to play it, but we have included one case for the record.

The usual object of counting is to find out whether you should finesse against a specific enemy high card or fell it by straight leads of the top cards of its suit. Sometimes you can cash enough winners in other suits to force discards, as in a squeeze, and prove that one opponent holds no stopper.

Sometimes an accurate count ends in a clear-cut double dummy position as if all enemy cards were exposed; and if it proves to be an end-play, the deal is usually filed under X, Y or Z. Counting may lead to other files, for File C is usually reserved for placing an enemy high card in the grip of a tenace.

If an enemy bid indicates a suit length approximately as a clue to winning play, you may not be able to get an *exact* count; and play based on such a clue is usually filed under I for Inference.

In practice, counting is one of the most difficult phases of bridge, for you must keep accurate track not only of every card played but by whom. Forgetting one small (but not insignificant) card can throw your deduction awry and result in losing play. We have often been asked for special literature on Counting, usually step-motherly treated in most bridge textbooks. The subject is not easy to present, but we hope that the examples in File C will demonstrate the basic principles.

COUNTING

Matrix pura

♠ J 10 7 6 4
♡ K J
◊ J 10
♣ A 8 4 3

♠ A 3
♡ 10 7 3 2
◊ 9 6 5 4 3 2
♣ 6

♠ 2
♡ A Q 9 8 6 4
◊ A Q
♣ Q 10 7 5

♠ K Q 9 8 5
♡ 5
◊ K 8 7
♣ K J 9 2

Deal 28

The bidding:			Rubber game
W	N	E	S
—	—	1 ♡	1 ♠
2 ♡	3 ♠	4 ♡	4 ♠
Double	No	No	No

W led the ♡ 2 and the ♡ J lost to the ♡ Q. E returned the ♡ A which S ruffed. S led the ♠ K which W's ace won, and W exited with another trump to dummy's knave.

Dummy led the ◊ J which E won and E returned the ◊ Q to S's king. Dummy ruffed the third diamond lead and E discarded a heart.

Declarer stopped to count, for he must win four club tricks to score game.

W's ♡ 2 lead and heart raise showed (probably) four hearts. E's discard on the third diamond lead showed six diamonds with W, who also played two spades; *ergo* he can hold only ONE club.

Dummy cashed the ♣ A, S finessed the ♣ 9, dummy was re-entered via a trump, and S finessed the ♣ J.

If E shifts to a club at Trick 2, he can later give W a club ruff to break the contract. But how could E know?

Let S hold instead ♣ K Q 9 2 and E hold ♣ J 8 7 5 and you have the same sort of counting and final play.

You need a bit of luck on the next deal.

51

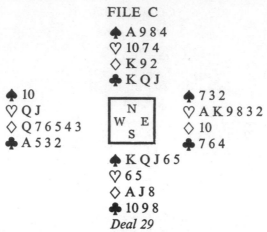

Deal 29

S bid 1 ♠, N 3 ♠; and S 4 ♠.

W led the ♡ Q, then ♡ J which E overtook with his king. And E returned the ♡ A which S ruffed high.

S drew trumps in three leads and led a club which W won. W returned a club and N won the third club lead.

So far, the play was good, but now declarer fumbled. He reasoned, 'The best chance is to finesse the ◇ J'—so he played the ◇ K then led a low diamond; but E's ten was a singleton and W scored his ◇ Q to break the contract.

Declarer should have stopped to *count*. E showed three spades, six hearts and three clubs; *ergo* his thirteenth card must be another club or a lone diamond, and declarer must be lucky enough to find that singleton an honour. Declarer should play the ◇ A, dropping the tell-tale ten, then finesse dummy's nine.

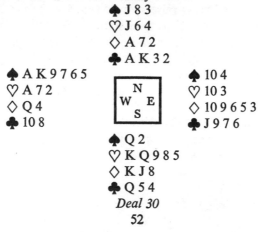

Deal 30

COUNTING

S	W	N	E
1 ♡	1 ♠	2 ♣	No
2 ♡	2 ♠	4 ♡ (final bid)	

W led the ♠ K, ♠ A, then ♠ 7 which E correctly, but unavailingly trumped high; S over-ruffed. S led a trump to dummy's knave and returned a trump on which E shed a diamond and W won with his ace. W returned a trump to S.

At this point declarer slipped. He tried the ♣ Q, ♣ K and ♣ A, but the clubs didn't drop 3 – 3. So he played the ◇ A and next finessed the ◇ J, which lost the game.

Before winning a club in dummy S should put his lazy nine of trumps to work and cash it, and park a diamond from dummy. Next dummy wins the third club lead, and S should stop to count in this position:

```
                        ◇ A 7
                        ♣ 3
        ♠ (?)          ┌─────┐        ◇ ? ?
        ◇ ? ? (?)      │  N  │        ♣ J
                       │W   E│
                       │  S  │
                       └─────┘
                        ◇ K J 8
```

E has three cards, the known ♣ J when clubs failed to split evenly, so not more than two diamonds. N cashes the ◇ A and leads the ◇ 7. When E's last diamond appears *not* to be the queen, S must play the king.

Leading that last trump lets S count E down to two diamonds, even if S didn't count W's hand; it is a type of squeeze manoeuvre that helps to get a perfect count on E. It is also certain that W can hold only two diamonds: he is marked with six spades, three hearts and two clubs!

FILE C

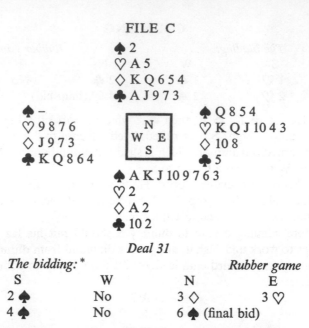

♠ 2
♡ A 5
◇ K Q 6 5 4
♣ A J 9 7 3

♠ –
♡ 9 8 7 6
◇ J 9 7 3
♣ K Q 8 6 4

♠ Q 8 5 4
♡ K Q J 10 4 3
◇ 10 8
♣ 5

♠ A K J 10 9 7 6 3
♡ 2
◇ A 2
♣ 10 2

Deal 31

The bidding: *			Rubber game
S	W	N	E
2 ♠	No	3 ◇	3 ♡
4 ♠	No	6 ♠ (final bid)	

W led the ♣ K which N's ♣ A won; E played the ♣ 5.

S won the ♠ A, and W discarded a heart, proving that E held the ♠ Q. How do you play for twelve tricks?

S saw two losers, a trump and a club, so he ran three top diamonds, but E trumped the third to spoil S's plan to sluff his losing club.

S should pause for a count. E showed four spades, and his vulnerable 3 ♡ bid showed a great heart suit of six or seven cards; hence he had a good chance to hold a singleton club.

To Trick 3, push trumps to drive out the queen. S gets in later to draw trumps, and *then* the dead club goes off on the third top diamond.

The point is that E cannot, with so many major suit cards advertised and/or shown in his hand *and* the club he has already played, hold *three* diamonds; therefore the scheme to shed the losing club on the third diamond before drawing trumps is surely a losing plan. S must hope that E holds a singleton club, a fair chance. If E holds two clubs, no plan works and the hand is doomed: S is down to playing E for a singleton club.

SAB: S 1 ♠, N 2 ◇, E 2 ♡; S 3 ♠, N 4 ♣; S 4 NT Blackwood, N 5 ♡; and S 6 ♠.

Deal 32

S bid 1 ♠, N 2 ♣; S 2 ♠ and N 4 ♠.
W led the ♡ Q.

Declarer saw three losers outside trumps, so he must pick up the king of spades. He won the ♡ Q with the ace, led the ♠ Q which W covered for obvious reasons and dummy won with the ace. Next declarer won the ♣ J, but W checked out, revealing that his trump king was bare and that E was bound to come to a natural trump trick to break the contract.

Declarer complained that he had no way of knowing that W's king was singleton, and N agreed; so the deal was chalked up as one down and promptly forgotten.

To Trick 2 S should lead the TEN of spades (intending to finesse), and not the queen. If W covers the ten with the king, the king is almost surely solus; for it would be poor play to cover the ten if the king is guarded lest E holds ♠ J x or J x x.

Dummy wins the ace and returns a trump, E plays low; and, as his best chance, S should finesse the seven!

FILE C

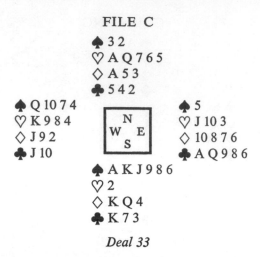

Deal 33

S bid 1 ♠, N 2 ♡; S 3 ♠ and N 4 ♠.

W led the ♣ J to E's ♣ A. E returned the ♣ 8, S won with the ♣ K, and W dropped the ♣ 10.

How should S play?

Declarer rapidly threw the game out of the window. He won Trick 3 with the ◇ A and returned a trump for the sour finesse of the knave. W returned the ♡ 9, which dummy's ace won and another trump lead revealed two trump losers and two club losers.

At Trick 3 declarer must first lay down the ♠ A before trying the finesse at all. This basic safety play caters for the queen singleton with W.

But a count of losers is the real point. The right play sequence, a top trump first, then the ◇ A and a trump return, finds E renouncing to show two trump losers. You must risk the heart finesse in order to get a club 'shake' on the ♡ A.

Declarer must get a count here, not on how many cards in a given suit an opponent holds, except indirectly, but on how many trump tricks he has to lose before deciding upon the heart finesse. With two trump losers, the heart finesse is the only chance for game; with no trump loser, he can finesse the ♡ Q for an extra trick without jeopardizing his game.

It is true he may go two down if the ♡ K is with E but, as he is not doubled, he should play to make his contract. The odds in his favour are 8 to 1 not vulnerable or 6 to 1 vulnerable.

File D

DECEPTION

D stands for Deception. In bridge the field for deceptive plays is so great that it would require a large book to cover all its ramifications. Plays of deception are referred to by various writers as bluff, embezzlement, forgery, knavery, razzle-dazzle, stealing, swindle, thievery, etc., but this transferred nomenclature boils down to one vital objective: to win tricks which simply are not in the cards by straightforward mechanical technique.

The two general types of deception plays are active and passive. By active deception you try to steal tricks either by offering opponents a plausible line of play or by a brazen bluff, plays which occupy most of File D. Passive deception refers to concealing your strength or weakness by routine false-cards or by not running a solid suit early so as to keep opponents in the dark and force them to guess.

Passive deception is too often overlooked by many dummy players. They fail to follow routine concealment technique. Take this common position:

LHO leads ◇ Q	◇ 8 7 6	Dummy
	◇ A K 3	Declarer

Suppose you as declarer decide to win the ◇ Q at once. Do you take it with the ace or king?

If you were on lead, you would normally lead the king to show your partner the ace (or queen) behind him; but as declarer you play so as to conceal information, not to give it.

At a trump contract, win with the ace. This conceals the location of the king from your left-hand opponent, who may think that his partner holds the king.

But at no-trumps play the king! This conceals the ace from East, for leader may well have held ◇ A Q J 10 x – from which the queen would not have been led against a trump contract. But let us get along to active deception.

FILE D

Matrix pura

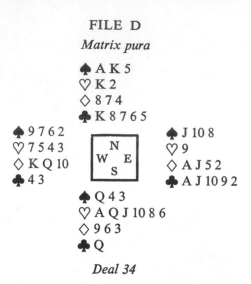

♠ A K 5
♡ K 2
◇ 8 7 4
♣ K 8 7 6 5

♠ 9 7 6 2
♡ 7 5 4 3
◇ K Q 10
♣ 4 3

♠ J 10 8
♡ 9
◇ A J 5 2
♣ A J 10 9 2

♠ Q 4 3
♡ A Q J 10 8 6
◇ 9 6 3
♣ Q

Deal 34

Playing the 'Weak Two', S bid 2 ♡ and N 4 ♡.

W led the ◇ K, and E won the third diamond lead, and shifted to the ♠ J at Trick 4, which dummy won.

To Trick 5 dummy led a low club, which threw E into a long squirm. If E plays the ace, S may be void of clubs and later get a critical discard on dummy's ♣ K; if E ducks the club lead, S may score his queen 'in the bathtub' (i.e. bare). Which view should E take?

E took the wrong view and ducked.*

If S makes the mistake of drawing trumps before leading a low club from dummy, he may give the defenders a chance to get a count on his shape. In fact, a sound rule for deception is 'the sooner the better'.

When you are a declarer, the manner of playing secondary honour sequences is vital. When you hold such combinations as ♡ K Q J, ♡ Q J 10, or ♡ J 10 9, etc., you have a choice of which equal to lead. The general principle is, *if you wish a defender to cover, lead high; otherwise lead low.*

---

* E was wrong, in theory as well as in practice, to duck. If S were void of clubs, he has nothing but spades to discard: no diamonds are left, and any trump winner W may hold he is bound to make. If S is void of clubs the only shape S can hold which will score if E wrongly goes up with ♣ A is 7 hearts and 3 worthless spades. With any other distribution, the play of ♣ A, even if S is void, will make no difference. *Defenders also should count.*—Editor.

58

DECEPTION

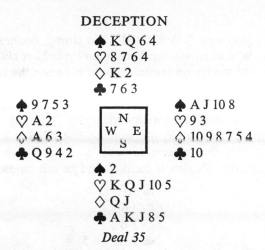

```
                  ♠ K Q 6 4
                  ♡ 8 7 6 4
                  ◇ K 2
                  ♣ 7 6 3
♠ 9 7 5 3                         ♠ A J 10 8
♡ A 2          ┌─────────┐       ♡ 9 3
◇ A 6 3        │    N    │       ◇ 10 9 8 7 5 4
♣ Q 9 4 2      │ W     E │       ♣ 10
               │    S    │
               └─────────┘
                  ♠ 2
                  ♡ K Q J 10 5
                  ◇ Q J
                  ♣ A K J 8 5
```

Deal 35

S bid 1 ♡, N 2 ♡; and S 4 ♡.

W led the ♣ 2 which S won with the knave.

S has to lose three aces, and clearly W can win the first trump lead to give his partner a club ruff. How can declarer stop it?

If S leads his trump king, W will clobber it at once with his ace and return a club.

Declarer's deception play is to lead a *lower* trump honour, the *queen*, to 'dope' W's ace and induce him to 'lay off'. This W probably should do, lest E hold the trump king bare. Next, a second trump lead drops all enemy trumps. But note what happened on the next deal:

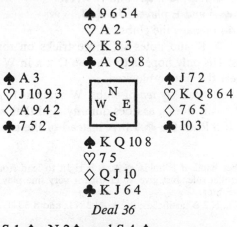

```
                  ♠ 9 6 5 4
                  ♡ A 2
                  ◇ K 8 3
                  ♣ A Q 9 8
♠ A 3                             ♠ J 7 2
♡ J 10 9 3     ┌─────────┐       ♡ K Q 8 6 4
◇ A 9 4 2      │    N    │       ◇ 7 6 5
♣ 7 5 2        │ W     E │       ♣ 10 3
               │    S    │
               └─────────┘
                  ♠ K Q 10 8
                  ♡ 7 5
                  ◇ Q J 10
                  ♣ K J 6 4
```

Deal 36

N bid 1 ♣, S 1 ♠; N 2♠, and S 4 ♠.

W led the ♡ J. How do you play trumps?

FILE D

Dummy won with ♡ A and led a low trump, declarer played the queen and W ducked without batting an eyelash. A club to dummy and E ducked the trump return. Should S finesse the ten or play E for the ace and go up with the king? It was a difficult guess and S viewed E for the lurking trump ace. S put up his king, losing *two* trump tricks, a heart and a diamond.

To eliminate guesswork, the winning line of play is to play the trump king first time in order to coax W to kill it with his ace if he has it. If he does, S's view is clarified and he can finesse the ♠ 10.*

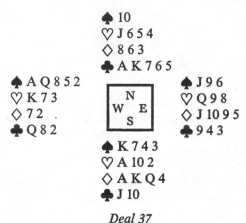

```
                      ♠ 10
                      ♡ J 6 5 4
                      ◇ 8 6 3
                      ♣ A K 7 6 5
      ♠ A Q 8 5 2                      ♠ J 9 6
      ♡ K 7 3           N              ♡ Q 9 8
      ◇ 7 2         W       E          ◇ J 10 9 5
      ♣ Q 8 2           S              ♣ 9 4 3
                      ♠ K 7 4 3
                      ♡ A 10 2
                      ◇ A K Q 4
                      ♣ J 10
```

Deal 37

S bid 1 ◇, W 1 ♠, N 2 ♣; and S 3 NT.†

W led the ♠ 5 and E played the ♠ J.

How do you manage the clubs?

S wins the ♠ K and notes six more tricks on top, so he must register clubs. His only hope is to find ♣ Q x x in W and to induce W to duck lest the suit be blocked.

To Trick 2 S leads a sly *ten* of clubs. W squirms long and uncomfortably and finally ducks, as does dummy, and that was the end for the defence. If S leads the ♣ J first instead of the tricky ten, W will cover.

---

* On the other hand, if E holds ♠ A, S is right to lead from dummy twice. There is no blanket rule. Just give W credit for very fine play. His first 'duck' was a decoy!—Editor.

†*SAB:* S 1 NT, N 2 ♣ (artificial); S 2 ♠, N 2 NT; and S 3 NT.

DECEPTION

♠ 8 7 3
♡ K Q J
◇ 7 4 3
♣ A 10 9 4

♠ K 9 6 5
♡ 9 6
◇ J 10 9 2
♣ J 8 2

N W E S

♠ A J 10 4
♡ 10 7 5 4 2
◇ 8
♣ Q 7 6

♠ Q 2
♡ A 8 3
◇ A K Q 6 5
♣ K 5 3

Deal 38

With all vulnerable S bid 1 NT, N 3NT.
W led the ◇ J. How do you snare nine tricks?

Declarer was in 3 NT with spades wide open, but such are the
hazards of bidding game at times. The diamond opening lead amused
S, but he realized that an enemy spade lead would not be so funny,
so he wiped off his grin. Also, the fall of E's ◇ 8 indicated four diamonds with W; but S noted also that this singleton would look like
an encouraging card to W. S solved his problem neatly and quickly.
He dropped ◇ 6, concealing ◇ 5.

W, encouraged by the fall of E's eight, thought he had found a
diamond mine; so he led another diamond which let S cash four
diamonds—Koh-i-noors—for game.

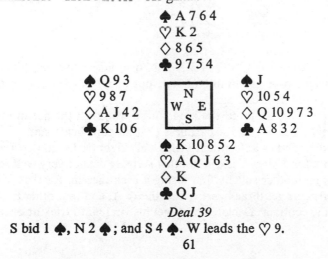

♠ A 7 6 4
♡ K 2
◇ 8 6 5
♣ 9 7 5 4

♠ Q 9 3
♡ 9 8 7
◇ A J 4 2
♣ K 10 6

N W E S

♠ J
♡ 10 5 4
◇ Q 10 9 7 3
♣ A 8 3 2

♠ K 10 8 5 2
♡ A Q J 6 3
◇ K
♣ Q J

Deal 39

S bid 1 ♠, N 2 ♠; and S 4 ♠. W leads the ♡ 9.

S bid 1 ♠, N 2 ♠; and S 4 ♠.

As in Deal 35, with a mere single raise opposite, there is no point in showing a second suit: the direct 4 ♠ bid is preferable.

W led the ♡ 9. You are declarer and win the heart opening with the king in dummy, cash the trump ace, then the trump king, only to find a natural trump loser plus three other losers on top. How do you plan to avoid a loser?

Since you never bid hearts, they are beautifully concealed from the defenders; so take advantage of this feature.

Cash the ♡ A and ♡ Q and park a club from dummy. Next make the key deception play of leading the *three* of hearts. W will most probably believe that E holds the master heart (♡ J) and hence will see no reason to ruff with his master trump and will discard. So you discard a second club from dummy. When E discards also, the swindle is exposed, but it is too late. Lead your last heart and ditch a third club from dummy. Later dummy ruffs the second club lead.

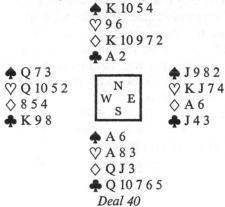

<pre>
                    ♠ K 10 5 4
                    ♡ 9 6
                    ◇ K 10 9 7 2
                    ♣ A 2
   ♠ Q 7 3   ♠ J 9 8 2
   ♡ Q 10 5 2   N   ♡ K J 7 4
   ◇ 8 5 4   W   E   ◇ A 6
   ♣ K 9 8   S   ♣ J 4 3
                    ♠ A 6
                    ♡ A 8 3
                    ◇ Q J 3
                    ♣ Q 10 7 6 5
</pre>

Deal 40

Playing Acol, S bid 1 NT, N 3 NT. N overbid on the length and dubious strength of the diamond suit, but many ticklish contracts stem from optimistic calling.

W led the ♡ 2, E played the king, and S won with the ace in the correct belief that W held a harmless (?) four-card heart suit.

Direct diamond establishment yields only eight tricks, so declarer looks about for a ninth trick in another suit. He cannot very well set up a trick in another suit by first losing a trick therein, for that will let the defenders get three heart tricks, the ◇ A, and that other trick to break the contract. Declarer must get his vital ninth trick at once, if at all.

DECEPTION

So to Trick 2 S leads the ♣ Q for a 'fool's finesse'. Now W has a 'timid' king—'sure' to score a third-round trick after dummy's doubleton ace, in view, is gone; so the ♣ Q is 'finessed' to win. It is another case of giving the enemy a chance to take a wrong view. Aces can be timid too, as in the next deal.

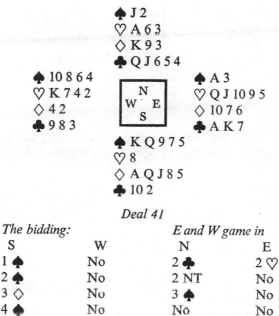

                     ♠ J 2
                     ♡ A 6 3
                     ◇ K 9 3
                     ♣ Q J 6 5 4
        ♠ 10 8 6 4   ♠ A 3
        ♡ K 7 4 2   N   ♡ Q J 10 9 5
        ◇ 4 2   W   E   ◇ 10 7 6
        ♣ 9 8 3   S   ♣ A K 7
                     ♠ K Q 9 7 5
                     ♡ 8
                     ◇ A Q J 8 5
                     ♣ 10 2

Deal 41

The bidding: E and W game in

S	W	N	E
1 ♠	No	2 ♣	2 ♡
2 ♠	No	2 NT	No
3 ◇	No	3 ♠	No
4 ♠	No	No	No

W led the ♡ 2. Two clubs and the trump ace are off the hand with strong chances that an opponent will hold ♠ 10 x x x to score another trump trick and break the contract.

Declarer infers the ♠ A with E from his heart overcall. So declarer won the ♡ 2 with dummy's ace.

What should declarer lead to Trick 2?

Declarer solves the problem neatly. He leads dummy's ♠ J. E ducks with the timid trump ace to let declarer take a 'losing finesse' into W; so dummy leads another trump to drop the 'timid' ace, letting it 'beat air'—cover only low cards: S later picks up W's ten.

E's duck, of course, was from excessive timidity. If W holds ♠ Q x x and E clobbers the ♠ J with the ace, W's trump queen will still not suffer loss. E is wrong even in theory. Only if S holds *seven spades*, missing the queen, can the duck gain—improbable after the diamond bid.

63

FILE D

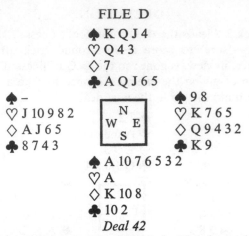

♠ K Q J 4
♡ Q 4 3
◇ 7
♣ A Q J 6 5

♠ -
♡ J 10 9 8 2
◇ A J 6 5
♣ 8 7 4 3

♠ 9 8
♡ K 7 6 5
◇ Q 9 4 3 2
♣ K 9

♠ A 10 7 6 5 3 2
♡ A
◇ K 10 8
♣ 10 2

Deal 42

Playing Acol, S bid 1 ♠, N 2 ♣, S 3 ♠, N 5 ♠; and S 6 ♠.

W led the ♡ J. How do you hope to score slam if the club finesse loses?

Declarer prepares for the possible losing club finesse at once by playing a deceitful ♡ Q from dummy, E covers, and S wins with his bare ace. (If dummy ducks, E plays the ♡ 7.) Declarer immediately leads the ♣ 2 and finesses dummy's knave, losing to E's king. E has a problem on what to return. It looks by the early heart play as if declarer holds another heart. As no one relishes leading to dummy's singleton, and as only if W holds *five* hearts does the play lose, E returns ♡ 5, and S wraps up the slam.

If declarer makes the error of drawing trumps before finessing clubs, W will discard ◇ J to scream for a lead to his ◇ A, and so get E off the guessing griddle when he gets in with the ♣ K.

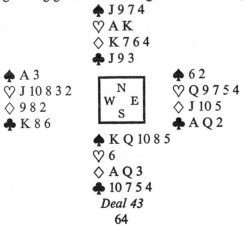

♠ J 9 7 4
♡ A K
◇ K 7 6 4
♣ J 9 3

♠ A 3
♡ J 10 8 3 2
◇ 9 8 2
♣ K 8 6

♠ 6 2
♡ Q 9 7 5 4
◇ J 10 5
♣ A Q 2

♠ K Q 10 8 5
♡ 6
◇ A Q 3
♣ 10 7 5 4

Deal 43

64

DECEPTION

S bid 1 ♠, N 3 ♠; and S 4 ♠.

W led the ♡ J. You are off three clubs and the trump ace, so how do you try to avoid a club loser?

Dummy wins two heart tricks and S discards a *diamond*. Next a trump lead lets in W with his ace.

If W leads a club, E and W can cash three clubs to break the contract. But S's phoney diamond discard induces W to think that S is in a hurry to shake off diamond losers, so W decides to 'lead a diamond through dummy's king'. S draws a trump and wins two diamond tricks, crosses to dummy with a trump; and his second prayer is answered when enemy diamonds fall 3–3, so he parks two clubs on ◇ K 7. Here, S has nothing to lose and all to gain by his discard.

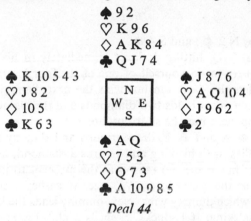

```
              ♠ 9 2
              ♡ K 9 6
              ◇ A K 8 4
              ♣ Q J 7 4
♠ K 10 5 4 3                 ♠ J 8 7 6
♡ J 8 2          N           ♡ A Q 10 4
◇ 10 5       W     E         ◇ J 9 6 2
♣ K 6 3          S           ♣ 2
              ♠ A Q
              ♡ 7 5 3
              ◇ Q 7 3
              ♣ A 10 9 8 5
```

Deal 44

S bid 1 ♣, N 1 ◇; S 1 NT and N 3 NT.

W led the ♠ 4 and E played the knave. How do you try to avoid a heart shift if the club finesse is sour?

S makes the startling play of winning the opening spade lead with his ace! This leaves the ♠ Q very bare, a brazen lady!

This play loses a trick if the club finesse wins, but then S needs only one spade trick to score game. In case W scores the ♣ K, the idea is to encourage W to return a low spade (instead of that deadly ♡ J) and let S steal the game. When W gets in with the ♣ K he confidently returns a *low* spade in order to let E score the 'marked' ♠ Q and rattle off four spade tricks to break the contract; but the brazen lady wins the trick for S instead of E, and lets declarer rattle off his required nine tricks.

65

FILE D

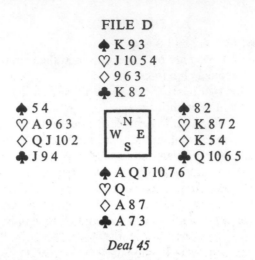

Deal 45

S bid 1 ♠, N 2 ♠; and S 4 ♠.

W led the ◇ Q, hitting declarer immediately in his weak spot. How do you try to rid yourself of one of the four losers?

Declarer lets the ◇ Q win but wins the next diamond lead, just in case one opponent holds two diamonds and the diamond trick of the other opponent may be shut out later.

Next the ♠ A and ♠ K draw trumps and dummy leads a low heart. If E 'flies' with his king and returns a diamond, he can break the contract; but E sees no reason at the moment to play his king and ducks; so the queen forces W's ace. W cashes a diamond and leads a club which dummy wins. Next dummy leads the ♡ J through E's 'soporific' king. If E ducks, S sheds a club loser; otherwise S ruffs the king, dummy re-enters in trumps, and the ♡ 10 lets S park his losing club.

This looks like sound and sure mechanical technique, but note what happens if S wins the second trump lead and returns the ♡ Q to Trick 4. W ducks and E scores the ♡ K. Later declarer has no way to pick up W's ace and the contract fails.

DECEPTION

Double False Card

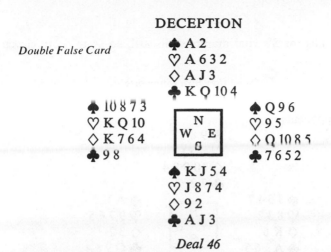

♠ A 2
♡ A 6 3 2
◇ A J 3
♣ K Q 10 4

♠ 10 8 7 3
♡ K Q 10
◇ K 7 6 4
♣ 9 8

♠ Q 9 6
♡ 9 5
◇ Q 10 8 5
♣ 7 6 5 2

♠ K J 5 4
♡ J 8 7 4
◇ 9 2
♣ A J 3

Deal 46

N bid 1 ♣, S 1 ♡; N 3 ♡, and S 4 ♡.

S's heart bid looks terrible, but S explained afterward that he was trying to coax N to bid a weak four-card spade suit if he held one. In good company 1 ♡ is the correct response, to explore the chance of a 4–4 trump suit.

W led the ♠ 3. This deal is from match point duplicate, in which it is vital to win an extra trick or two (if possible) for a top score.

If trumps split 3–2 normally, declarer can make game by simple straightforward play; so how does declarer give himself a chance for an extra trick?

Declarer has two natural trump losers and a diamond loser, but if the defence can be coerced into shunning diamonds until *after* declarer's *second* trump lead, S can park a diamond on the fourth club. So declarer at once plays a *double* false-card in spades, first by winning the spade opening in dummy with the ace and second by false-carding his own five. The deception is two-fold: first, by the ace play, to induce W to believe that S's spades are weak; and second, to conceal the four, in order to make whatever spade E plays look like the beginning of a high-low signal, 'peter' or echo, to show more spade strength than he really holds. Dummy leads a trump and S ducks to W's ten.

W, now completely sold on the idea that his side controls spades, returns the ♠ 7 right up to S's ♠ K J 4. S wins, lays down the trump ace, then pushes clubs. W can ruff the third or fourth club lead and shift to a diamond, but it is too late. Dummy plays the ace and

67

resumes clubs for S's vital diamond discard, so as to score eleven tricks.

Deception by Opponents

A special type of deceptive play, mostly false cards, are peculiar only to opponents.

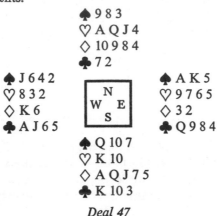

Deal 47

With sixty toward game S bid 1 ◇ and N 2 ◇.

W led the ♠ 2. You are E. How do you play to score three spade tricks?

E wins the ♠ 2 with the *ace* and returns the five! Declarer reasons that W must hold the king, so the best play seems to finesse the ten, but it proves to be wrong when W takes it with his knave (much to his surprise). W returns a spade 'for a ruff' but E wins and returns a club to let W get two club tricks. Later the ◇ K breaks the contract. This defensive gadget is worth remembering, as are several more shown below. We show only the key suit in each case.

♠ K 5   ♠ A J 8 2   ♠ 10 9 3
               ♠ Q 7 6 4

Spades are trumps and declarer needs all four trump tricks to go game. So he properly leads a low spade and finesses the knave. The 'standard' play is to bang down the ace next to drop W's king. But on the knave finesse, E plays the nine! Now it looks to declarer as if E held ♠ 10 9 doubleton. So declarer recaptures the lead in a side suit and leads the ♠ Q to 'scoop' E's supposedly now bare ten and promote dummy's eight. Too bad—we sympathize!

Here is another defensive razzle-dazzle.

DECEPTION

♠ K 6 3
♠ 10 9   ♠ A J 8 7 5   ♠ Q 4 2

Needing all five spade tricks declarer plays the ♠ K, intending (correctly) to finesse the knave next. But on the king W calmly drops the ten. This poses a problem and creates the impression that W holds ♠ Q 10 doubleton.

The swindle below is old but still good.

♠ A J 9 8
♠ 5 3 2   ♠ K 7 6 4   ♠ Q 10

Again declarer needs all four spade tricks, so he plays the king. E drops the queen! If declarer has no convenient or expendable side entry to his own hand, he may decide to finesse the nine next. If E knows S knows E is smart on false cards, E may play the ten on the king for the double double-cross! If S can afford an entry to his hand in this example, he should, of course, cash a winner in order to verify the adverse division.

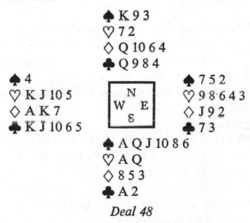

```
              ♠ K 9 3
              ♡ 7 2
              ◇ Q 10 6 4
              ♣ Q 9 8 4
♠ 4                              ♠ 7 5 2
♡ K J 10 5        N             ♡ 9 8 6 4 3
◇ A K 7       W       E         ◇ J 9 2
♣ K J 10 6 5      S             ♣ 7 3
              ♠ A Q J 10 8 6
              ♡ A Q
              ◇ 8 5 3
              ♣ A 2
```

Deal 48

At rubber game S bid 1 ♠, W doubled, E 2 ♡; S 3 ♠ and N 4 ♠.

W led the ◇ K. E holds a miserable hand with only one point in the form of the ◇ J, yet he foxed declarer out of a normally iron-clad game. On the ◇ K lead E played the nine! W continued with the ◇ A and E completed his discordant echo by playing the ◇ 2! It was the greatest bare-faced lie in all Great Britain. Implicitly trusting his partner, W pushed out the ◇ 7. Declarer was a good player who also took the deceptive echo in diamonds as showing a doubleton. Believing that E was going to ruff the third diamond lead, declarer correctly finessed dummy's ten—and the game flew out the window with it when E pounced on the trick with the only honour card in his miserable hand, the knave of diamonds. Later, W won a king for the setting trick.

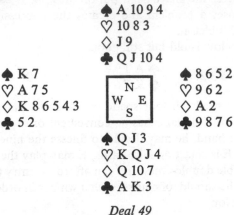

    ♠ A 10 9 4
    ♡ 10 8 3
    ◇ J 9
    ♣ Q J 10 4

♠ K 7   ♠ 8 6 5 2
♡ A 7 5   ♡ 9 6 2
◇ K 8 6 5 4 3   ◇ A 2
♣ 5 2   ♣ 9 8 7 6

    ♠ Q J 3
    ♡ K Q J 4
    ◇ Q 10 7
    ♣ A K 3

Deal 49

S bid 1 NT, N 2 NT; S 3 ♡, N 3 ♠; and S 3 NT.*

In the no-trump bidding, note how S and N checked up on their four-card majors so as not to overlook a superior major-suit game in case of a 4–4 fit with a side doubleton for ruffing.

W led the ◇ 5, his proper fourth best, E won with his ace and returned his deuce which W ducked by playing the six in order to create the impression of starting life with four diamonds. On the bidding, this false card can do no harm, for with W's high cards and E showing the ◇ A, it is clear that E will never get the lead again. Fooling E is, therefore, harmless.

Declarer has a problem in a choice of lines of play, to finesse spades or to promote hearts. A winning spade finesse brings home nine tricks, but a losing finesse spells ruin. If the enemy diamonds really split 4–4, as declarer cannot be blamed for viewing them, he can drive out the ♡ A and wrap up his nine tricks without risking the spade finesse. So declarer leads a heart which lets in W with his ace for a rattling good time with his deceitful diamonds.

SAB: S 1 NT, N 2 ♣ artificial; S 2 ♡, N 2 NT; and S 3 NT. The 2 ♣ bid asks for a major.

DECEPTION

♠ J 10 6 4
♡ A K 7 4
♢ 7 2
♣ K 10 9

♠ 9 8   ♠ 3 2
♡ Q 9 6 2   ♡ J 10 5 3
♢ J 10 9 8   ♢ K Q 6 4
♣ J 5 3   ♣ Q 8 2

♠ A K Q 7 5
♡ 8
♢ A 5 3
♣ A 7 6 4

Deal 50

S bid 1 ♠, N 3 ♠; and S 6 ♠.

W led the ♢ J. How do you plan to collect three club tricks without losing a club trick?

At first glance the ♡ K looks about as useless as a corpse in a solved murder mystery. S wins the ♢ K with the ace, and the ♠ A. Next the ♡ K wins and S ruffs a heart. Dummy re-enters in spades, drawing all enemy trumps, wins the ♡ A for a diamond discard, and S ruffs dummy's last heart to bail out that suit also.

Having stripped the hands for the throw-in play (the deal could be filed under X for Elimination), declarer makes a steadfast decision— to assume the enemy club honours are divided however the opponents may play. Declarer exits via his losing diamond which E wins. E is a strong player and knows what S is about, so E leads the ♣ Q! The idea is to make it appear that E holds the knave also (which would probably be the case if E were a rabbit and declarer would win with the ♣ K in dummy and finesse the ten on the return). But S knows E is a strong player so S sticks to his steadfast decision, wins with the ♣ A, and next finesses dummy's ten.

File E

ENTRY

E stands for Entry. Sufficient entries back and forth between dummy and closed hand are vital in many deals, and, despite the combination of entry management with plays of other families such as Finesse or Long Suit, they are filed under E whenever the problem of entries is of primary interest.

The subject of creating, destroying and preserving entries is so vast that it forms a natural sub-order, consisting of five families; B for Blocking (entry-destroying plays), E for Entry, G for Gambit, J for Jettison and U for Unblocking, q.v.

The basic family, Entry, is further divided into two natural tribes, plays to create entries by positive manœuvres and plays to conserve natural entries by avoiding the trap of cashing a winner prematurely without regard to its value as an entry-card.

This tribal-aspect, and the combination of entry as an accessory to develop a play of another unrelated family, preclude the possibility of any true *Matrix pura*, so we offer a

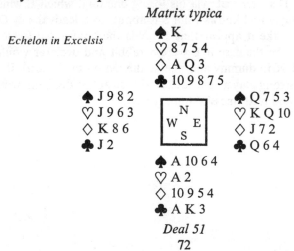

Matrix typica

Echelon in Excelsis

Deal 51

72

ENTRY

S bid 1 NT, N 2 NT; S 3 ♣, and N 3 NT.

W led the ♡ 3, E played the queen and S held up his ace, for any switch would relieve the attack on hearts. E continued with the ♡ K, dropping S's ace

How do you plan the play?

S chucked the game quickly. He played ace, king, and a small club. Soon he awoke to the lack of entry to his own hand to finesse diamonds and to separate the ♠ K and ♠ A.

The time for analysis is at Trick 3. Declarer counts two spade tricks, a heart, four clubs, and the ♢ A for eight tricks; hence the diamond finesse must win the game-scoring trick. Also, S must lose a club trick, so why not now? Lead the ♣ 3 and let opponents also take two heart tricks. Later, the ♣ A furnishes a valuable entry to finesse the ♢ Q, dummy cashes the ♠ K, the ♣ K lets S in again to score the ♠ A, and finally the ♢ A lets dummy in to score the stiff clubs. Here is echelon *in excelsis*.

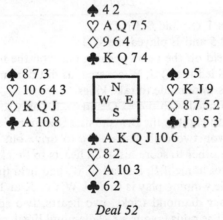

Deal 52

After two passes S bid 4 ♠. Such a pre-empt with three quick tricks is poor tactics first- or second-hand, but S was third-hand with practically no chance to miss a slam opposite a passing partner.

W led the ♢ K. S drew trumps over-hastily and led a club. W ducked and dummy's queen won. But dummy was stuck on lead with no way to get back to S for another club lead. Dummy exited with a diamond, W took two diamond tricks and shifted to the ♡ 3. The queen finesse was the only chance for game left and it failed.

Declarer needs *two* leads toward dummy's king-queen. S can afford the luxury of one trump lead. Next, he leads a club to dummy's

73

queen, S re-enters in trumps and draws them, then makes the second club lead to promote dummy's king, while the heart ace is there to cash it.

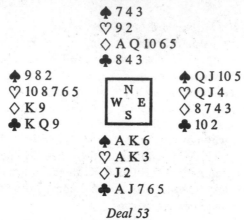

```
                    ♠ 7 4 3
                    ♡ 9 2
                    ◇ A Q 10 6 5
                    ♣ 8 4 3
  ♠ 9 8 2                              ♠ Q J 10 5
  ♡ 10 8 7 6 5        N                ♡ Q J 4
  ◇ K 9           W       E            ◇ 8 7 4 3
  ♣ K Q 9             S                ♣ 10 2
                    ♠ A K 6
                    ♡ A K 3
                    ◇ J 2
                    ♣ A J 7 6 5
```

Deal 53

S bid 1 ♣, N 1 ◇ ; and S 3 NT.

W led the ♡ 5 and E played the ♡ J.

S correctly held off the heart opening but won the next heart lead with the king. S led the ◇ J, W covered, as did dummy also, on the theory that aces were made to take kings.

Dummy continued with the ◇ Q and ◇ 10, only to discover that E held the biggest eight in the British Isles. Declarer tried to establish clubs, but W won two club leads—one to drive out S's last heart stopper and the other to score his good hearts to break the contract. S would have got home if E, instead of W, had held the three clubs.

But the simple winning play is to *duck* W's ◇ K at Trick 3 ! Then declarer gets four diamond tricks, two hearts, two spades and the ♣ A for game. The odds favour a 4–2 diamond break rather than the 3–3 split for which this S—a relative of Knucklehead Joe—played.

ENTRY

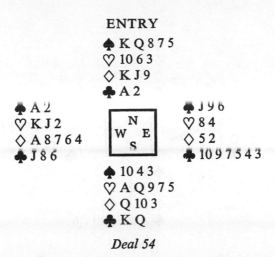

♠ K Q 8 7 5
♡ 10 6 3
◇ K J 9
♣ A 2

♠ A 2
♡ K J 2
◇ A 8 7 6 4
♣ J 8 6

♠ J 9 6
♡ 8 4
◇ 5 2
♣ 10 9 7 5 4 3

♠ 10 4 3
♡ A Q 9 7 5
◇ Q 10 3
♣ K Q

Deal 54

N bid 1 ♠, S 2 ♡; N 2 ♠, and S 3 NT. Theoretically, S would be better advised to call 4 ♠ rather than 3 NT; but as the cards lie, 4 ♠ cannot be made.

W led the ◇ 6. If W holds the ace of spades doubleton or tripleton, how do you play to collect nine tricks?

S won the diamond opening with his ten and returned a spade which dummy's queen won. S re-entered with a club and led another spade to force out W's ace and establish spades.

W divined that E held little in spades, nothing in hearts with S bidding them without W's ♡ K J 2, and nothing in diamonds; hence E must be long in clubs. So W returned the ♣ J which knocked together the ace and queen in a grand tumble. Dummy scored spades and S tried the heart finesse for his ninth trick, but W took care of the ♡ Q with his king and returned a club to let E win the balance.

Declarer fell into a trap at Trick 3 when he used the wrong suit, clubs, as the re-entry to lead a second spade. He should have used the ♡ A instead, still leaving him a play to establish hearts later should spades go wrong.

FILE E

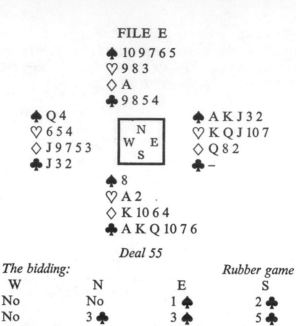

♠ 109765
♡ 983
◇ A
♣ 9854

♠ Q 4
♡ 6 5 4
◇ J 9 7 5 3
♣ J 3 2

♠ A K J 3 2
♡ K Q J 10 7
◇ Q 8 2
♣ —

♠ 8
♡ A 2
◇ K 10 6 4
♣ A K Q 10 7 6

Deal 55

The bidding:			Rubber game
W	N	E	S
No	No	1 ♠	2 ♣
No	3 ♣	3 ♠	5 ♣

W led the ♠ Q, then ♠ 4 which S ruffed.
What do you lead at Trick 3?

S laid down the ♣ A and found E chicane. The next cards were the ◇ A, ♣ K; diamond ruff in dummy, ♡ A, and another diamond ruff, leaving:

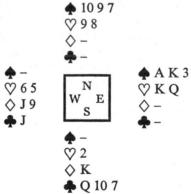

♠ 10 9 7
♡ 9 8
◇ —
♣ —

♠ —
♡ 6 5
◇ J 9
♣ J

♠ A K 3
♡ K Q
◇ —
♣ —

♠ —
♡ 2
◇ K
♣ Q 10 7

Four more tricks for game are easy if S can lead, but dummy is in. Dummy led a spade which E won as S ditched his heart. But E returned a spade to promote W's trump knave.

After ruffing the second spade lead at Trick 2, S wasted his trump

76

ace. Instead he should cash the ♢ A then use his otherwise wasted ♣ A as a valuable entry for a diamond ruff in dummy, the ♣ K for another diamond ruff, and the ♡ A lets S in a third time to draw trumps.

Another line, recently discovered by W. Howard Woolworth, is to cash ♣ A and ♣ K at Tricks 3 and 4, then to push high spades through E. E must cover lest S shed his heart loser, S trumps, and W overruffs with ♣ J for the last defensive trick.

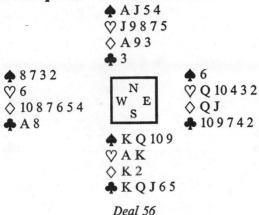

Deal 56

At rubber game S opened at 1 ♣ and against no adverse bidding S landed in 6 ♠.

W led the ♣ 2, which S won with the nine. S led the ♣ K which W's ace won, and W returned another trump to S's ten. S ruffed a low club in dummy, re-entered via the ♢ K and continued his plan to ruff out stray clubs lest the suit break badly. So S led his last low club, W ditched his singleton heart and dummy ruffed with his last trump. S tried to recapture the lead with the ♡ A, but W tagged this with a trump to break the contract.

S had a good plan but bungled his entries. The danger is an enemy discard on the third club lead. Declarer has more hearts than diamonds in his two hands, so hearts were more dangerous. S should use his dangerous entry, a heart, *before* the ♢ K in order to avert W's killing heart discard.

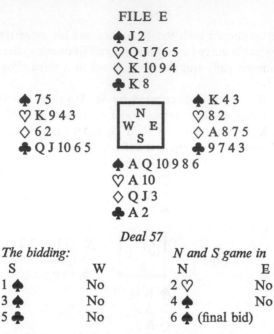

♠ J 2
♡ Q J 7 6 5
◇ K 10 9 4
♣ K 8

♠ 7 5
♡ K 9 4 3
◇ 6 2
♣ Q J 10 6 5

♠ K 4 3
♡ 8 2
◇ A 8 7 5
♣ 9 7 4 3

♠ A Q 10 9 8 6
♡ A 10
◇ Q J 3
♣ A 2

Deal 57

The bidding:		*N and S game in*	
S	W	N	E
1 ♠	No	2 ♡	No
3 ♠	No	4 ♠	No
5 ♣	No	6 ♠ (final bid)	

N's final jump to 6 ♠ was optimistic, but he felt that S must hold three aces for his slam-suggesting cue-bid of 5 ♣.

W led the ♣ Q.

Do you win the trick with the king or ace?

Declarer played dummy's king in order to finesse and draw trumps, which he did. Next S led the ◇ Q and W played his six to start his down-and-out signal, so E, given the count, held up his ace. S led the ◇ J and overtook with dummy's king, W played the deuce to show no more diamonds, so E clung to his ace again. Next, declarer quit the now hopeless diamonds and tried the heart finesse which lost the slam.

S should win the ♣ Q opening with the ace, and return the small diamond to dummy's nine. If E wins and returns a heart, S plays his ace, enters dummy via the ♣ K, and finesses trumps and draws them. Next, dummy overtakes the third diamond lead to score his fourth diamond for S's heart discard. If E holds up the ◇ A at Trick 2, next come trump pulling and diamond establishment. Then, if E holds up his ◇ A twice, the ♣ K stands ready as an entry to dummy to bring home the fourth diamond trick, on which S sheds his ♡ 10.

ENTRY

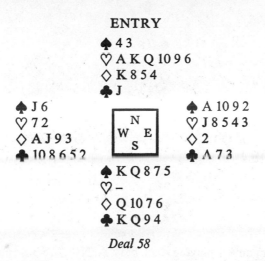

♠ 4 3
♡ A K Q 10 9 6
◇ K 8 5 4
♣ J

♠ J 6
♡ 7 2
◇ A J 9 3
♣ 10 8 6 5 2

♠ A 10 9 2
♡ J 8 5 4 3
◇ 2
♣ A 7 3

♠ K Q 8 7 5
♡ –
◇ Q 10 7 6
♣ K Q 9 4

Deal 58

The bidding:			No score
N	E.	S	W
1 ♡	No	1 ♠	No
2 ♡	No	3 ♣	No
3 ♡	No	3 NT (final bid)	

The bidding was queer, but so were the hands.

W led the ◇ 3. How do you play for nine tricks?

Dummy ducked the ◇ 3 and S won with his six. S lost the ♣ J to E's ace, and S won E's club return. A low diamond to dummy's king let dummy cash three top hearts, but the ♡ J failed to drop.

Dummy abandoned the hearts and led a spade which S's ♠ Q won. Now, however, S had to lead away from his high cards and lost the game.

On the ◇ 3 opening dummy must put his lazy ◇ 8 to work and play it at once. The Rule of Eleven shows that the eight will win the trick if W's lead was a legitimate fourth best: and there is no reason to suppose it is not, from the sight of the three.

In order to avoid the trap of a suicide squeeze by running hearts top down, dummy next leads the ♡ 10, which E wins. Later dummy re-enters via the ◇ K to score five heart tricks, and S still has time to develop a couple of black suit winners for game.

The deal came from Frederick B. Taylor of Lincoln, Mass.

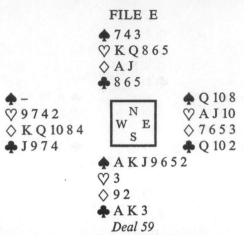

♠ 7 4 3
♡ K Q 8 6 5
◇ A J
♣ 8 6 5

♠ -
♡ 9 7 4 2
◇ K Q 10 8 4
♣ J 9 7 4

♠ Q 10 8
♡ A J 10
◇ 7 6 5 3
♣ Q 10 2

♠ A K J 9 6 5 2
♡ 3
◇ 9 2
♣ A K 3

Deal 59

At rubber game S, playing Acol, bid 2 ♠, N 3 ♡ ; S 3 ♠, and N 4 ♠.*
W led the ◇ K. How do you get ten tricks?

Dummy's ace won. S won the ♠ K and received a rude jolt when
W showed out. The ♡ Q lost to E's ace, and S finally lost a trick in
each suit for lack of entry to dummy to score that good ♡ K for a
club discard.

The opening ◇ K lead killed dummy's only natural entry immediately, before a heart trick could be set up; but despite this,
declarer has a neat play for game.

At Trick 2 he should finesse the ♠ J !

This is not a double dummy effort to win seven trump tricks, because S is willing to let W score the unguarded ♠ Q if he holds her.
In this event, dummy's ♠ 7 will be promoted to win the third trump
lead and serve as entry for the established heart and club sluff.

♠ K 4 3
♡ 8 6 2
◇ A 7
♣ A Q J 6 5

♠ Q 9 6
♡ 10 7 5 4
◇ Q 8 4 3
♣ 8 2

♠ J 2
♡ Q J 9
◇ K J 10 6 5
♣ K 9 4

♠ A 10 8 7 5
♡ A K 3
◇ 9 2
♣ 10 7 3

Deal 60

SAB: S 1 ♠, N 2 ♡; S 3 ♠ and N 4 ♠.

S bid 1 ♠ and N 4 ♠.

You won't like N's bid, nor do we. He should call 2 ♣ first and find out whether S has a five-card spade suit or prefers game in no-trumps.

W led the ◇ 3. How do you manage trumps?

Declarer won the ◇ A, ♠ K and ♠ A. The ♣ 10 finesse won, but next E gobbled the ♣ J finesse with the king and returned a club which W ruffed with the ♠ Q. Now those good clubs in dummy were very dead for lack of entry. Declarer also lost a diamond and heart and went down one.

Declarer let the defence block the club suit by leaving the master trump at large. After two trump leads declarer should lead trumps again immediately—on this hand he can afford two trumps to draw the outstanding queen—an anti-blocking play, in order to let dummy bring home clubs without interference.

Fine technique will both avert heart-breaking duplication and exploit a variant of standard practice on the next hand:

Deal 61

S, playing Acol, bid 2 ♠, N 3 ♡; and S 4 ♣ and N 4 ♠.
W led the ♠ 9.

How do you promote entry to dummy to score the ♡ A?

Declarer muffed the ball quickly. He won the trump lead and led a low club toward dummy's queen, hoping W held the king. But E gobbled the trick and returned a trump. After that, declarer couldn't get into dummy with a pick-axe to score the isolated ♡ A.

The better play at Trick 2 is to lead the ♣ J ! If E wins and returns a trump, S draws trumps and the ♣ Q in dummy brings home the ♡ A. If E lets the ♣ J win, next come the ♣ A and a club ruff in dummy to score the ♡ A for eleven tricks in all.

Instead of playing for the 50/50 chance of finding the ♣ K 'onside' with W, S should play for the 62/38 chance of finding clubs split 4–3.

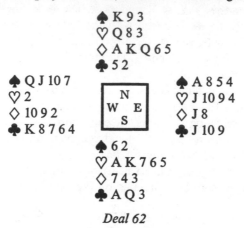

```
              ♠ K 9 3
              ♡ Q 8 3
              ◇ A K Q 6 5
              ♣ 5 2
♠ Q J 10 7                      ♠ A 8 5 4
♡ 2              N              ♡ J 10 9 4
◇ 10 9 2     W     E            ◇ J 8
♣ K 8 7 6 4        S            ♣ J 10 9
              ♠ 6 2
              ♡ A K 7 6 5
              ◇ 7 4 3
              ♣ A Q 3
```

Deal 62

S bid 1 ♡, N 2 ◇ ; S 2 ♡ and N 4 ♡.

W led the ♠ Q.

How do you plan to circumvent a 4–1 trump split?

Dummy ducked the ♠ Q, also the ♠ J next, in order to keep E out of the lead and avert a club attack. If E gets smart, he can overtake the ♠ J with his ace and push the ♣ J to break the contract, but this particular E didn't. S ruffed the third spade lead. So far, so good.

Next declarer led the ♡ Q and ♡ A, discovering the bad trump split. So he continued with the ♡ K then lost the heart to E, hoping E was out of spades; but E cashed a spade to break the contract.

To Tricks 4 and 5, S should lay down the ♡ A and ♡ K. If trumps split 3–2, the rest is easy; otherwise S shifts to diamonds and pushes them until E decides to trump. S ruffs the spade return and the commanding queen of trumps in dummy draws E's last, simultaneously acting as an entry to bring home the good diamonds.

ENTRY

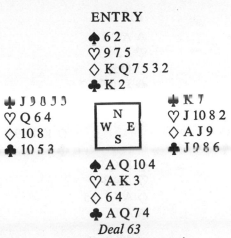

♠ 6 2
♡ 9 7 5
◇ K Q 7 5 3 2
♣ K 2

♣ J 9 8 5 5
♡ Q 6 4
◇ 10 8
♣ 10 5 3

♠ K 7
♡ J 10 8 2
◇ A J 9
♣ J 9 8 6

♠ A Q 10 4
♡ A K 3
◇ 6 4
♣ A Q 7 4

Deal 63

S bid 1 ♣, N 1 ◇; S 2 NT, and N 3 NT.*

W led the ♠ 5 and the king forced the ace. S made game look easy. To Trick 2 he led a diamond and on dummy's queen E (smugly regarding his second stopper) played his ace. E returned the spade which S's queen won. Next came the ◇ K then a low diamond went to E. E returned a club and declarer wrapped up eleven tricks.

Both E and S chucked. If E ducks the first diamond lead, the suit dies in dummy for lack of entries to establish *and* score it.

But S should never have given E a chance. When S leads a diamond to Trick 2, he should *duck* in dummy (!) and force the defence to burn a stopper *while declarer still holds a diamond.* Later, declarer can lead another diamond *from his own hand, without having to use the* ♣ K *entry in dummy to force out the* ◇ A. Now he can fetch home the rest of the suit.

* S, with 19 points, is worth 3 NT over 1 ◇.—Editor.

83

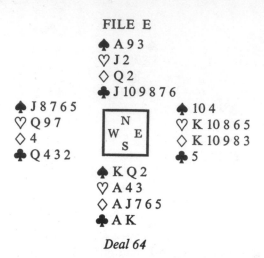

♠ A 9 3
♡ J 2
◇ Q 2
♣ J 10 9 8 7 6

♠ J 8 7 6 5   ♠ 10 4
♡ Q 9 7   ♡ K 10 8 6 5
◇ 4   ◇ K 10 9 8 3
♣ Q 4 3 2   ♣ 5

♠ K Q 2
♡ A 4 3
◇ A J 7 6 5
♣ A K

Deal 64

S bid 1 ◇, N 2 ♣; and S 3 NT.

W led the ♠ 6 and the ten forced the queen. Declarer played his clubs, only to find E show out; so he needed *two* entries to dummy; one to set up clubs and the other to score them.

W was heavy, in black cards, indicated by his spade opening and ♣ Q 4 3 2 proven, so E must be flush in red cards and probably held the ◇ K. So declarer selected dummy's nine of spades as the most likely candidate to furnish a second entry. If W's opening spade lead was a fourth best as was highly probable, there was little danger of E's being able to top the nine. So to Trick 4 declarer led the ♠ 2, W ducked, and that nine got the contract home.

W should have blocked the game by injecting his knave on the second spade lead to limit the table's entries to one. This obscure blocking play is rarely spotted even by experts in actual practice; but more opportunities occur for its employment than are realized.

ENTRY

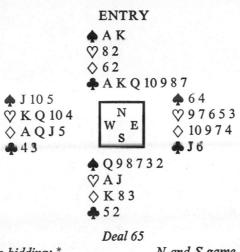

♠ A K
♡ 8 2
♢ 6 2
♣ A K Q 10 9 8 7

♠ J 10 5
♡ K Q 10 4
♢ A Q J 5
♣ 4 3

♠ 6 4
♡ 9 7 6 5 3
♢ 10 9 7 4
♣ J 6

♠ Q 9 8 7 3 2
♡ A J
♢ K 8 3
♣ 5 2

Deal 65

The bidding: *		*N and S game in*	
S	W	N	E
1 ♠	Double	3 ♣	No
3 ♠	No	4 ♠ (final bid)	

W led the ♡ K. How do you plan the play?

W's ♡ K gave S a severe case of entry-itis in his own hand if he plays off dummy's trumps immediately. Also, W's double showed the ♢ A over S's king, another danger spot in the hand.

Declarer won the ♡ K with the ace and played the ♣ A and ♣ K. Enemy clubs dropped fortunately, so next time the ♣ Q which E trumped (S discards the heart if E discards), S over trumped, and W obstinately discarded lest he make trump extraction easy for dummy in two leads.

Dummy won a trump, drawing E's last, led another club, and S parked the heart. W had to ruff. W could not very well get at the ♢ K, so he led the ♢ A then ♢ Q, hoping E held the ♢ K, but S scored this card. Now a lead to dummy's ♠ A drew W's last trump and let declarer romp home with the stiff clubs.

SAB: S is too weak to open 1 ♠, so if he passes, W opens 1 ♡, N doubles, E 2 ♡; S 3 ♠, N 4 ♣; and S 4 ♠. If playing weak two-bids, S can open 2 ♠, N says 3 ♣, S 3 ♢ to show a stopper in better than a minimum two-bid hand, then N says 4 ♠.

File F

FINESSE

F stands for Finesse. By definition a finesse is an attempt to win a trick with a card inferior to another card held.

The problem of a finesse may be simple or complex. If the aim is to gain a trick or two in the finessing suit without regard to other suits, the problem is simple and may be illustrated by a single-suit matrix. Complex tactical problems require full deals, which will appear later in this File.

Matrices purae

	(1)	(2)	(3)
	A Q	A 4 3	Q 4 3
K 9			
	3 2	Q J 10	A 5 2

The chances are 50–50 that the enemy king will be favourably located with W. In Matrix 1, S leads and inserts dummy's queen third hand, a simple envelopment movement round the king. In Matrix 2, S leads the queen and, if not covered, lets her ride. If she wins, S repeats the finesse. In Matrix 3, S under-leads his ace and hopes W has the king so that the queen will score.

In many cases it is better to defer a finesse for a strategic reason, or to try to drop the enemy high card first if you have equal tops as below:

	(4)		(5)
	5 4 3		7 6 5 4
	A K J 10		A K J 10

A careless player will lead low from N and finesse the knave immediately. The proper play (unless N is on lead for the last time) is to lay down a top card first in order to cater for the queen singleton in W, and to finesse later.

FINESSE

(6)	(7)
3 2	J 10 9
A K J 10 7 6	A K 7 6 5

In these matrices E may hold Q 8 x x which eludes capture if you first lay down a top card before finessing. If W holds a singleton, the odds are four to one against its being the queen. The finesse must be taken on the first round and repeated if successful.

(8)	(9)
K Q 10 8 7 6	K Q 10 9 5
2	3 2

If this is the trump suit, or the backbone of a no-trumper, finesse the ten at once. In Matrix 8, you must find A J x, J x x or J 9 in W. In Matrix 9, if you play the queen the first time and E wins the ace, J x x x in W cannot be captured.

(10)

J 9 8

Q 6 5 4

You need two tricks, so lead low and finesse dummy's eight. If, instead, you play the knave and E wins, later you can finesse the nine toward the queen, but 10 x x x in E or W will hold you to one trick.

Reaching for an honour in dummy to lead for a finesse is often tempting but unsound. Note this matrix:

(11)

J 6 3

9 7 4 2   K

A Q 10 8 5

To score five tricks from this suit dummy must lead a *low* card to cater for the blank king with E. Here is the antithesis which is equally often misplayed.

(12)		(13)	
A J 9 6 5		A J 9 8 7 6	
K 10 8 or		K 10 3	etc.
Q 7 4 3 2		Q 5 4 2	

You lead low and finesse dummy's knave, E fails, so W gives you the horse-laugh with his K 10. The proper technique is to lead the queen first.

A finesse against two enemy high cards is called a double finesse and against three high cards, a triple finesse.

(14)	(15)
A Q 10	A J 10
5 4 3	5 4 3

In both matrices finesse the ten. In Matrix 14 you hope W holds K J x to let you get three tricks. In Matrix 15 the odds are three to one that the enemy honours are divided or both with W to let you get two tricks. Finesse the ten, expecting to lose to E; then, later, finesse the knave against W's hoped-for remaining honour.

(16)	(17)
A Q 9	A J 9
5 4 3	5 4 3

These are triple finesse positions against three enemy honours. If you can afford to lose one trick in Matrix 16, you can improve your percentage by finessing the nine the first time to cater for J 10 x with W. In this case, the nine drives out the king, or (if W splits his equals), you cover the ten with dummy's queen which loses to the king, but next time round the finesse of the nine wins. If the nine finesse loses to the ten or knave first time, you still have the queen finesse to try next and you have lost nothing.

In Matrix 17, finesse the nine and hope W holds the ten with one picture or both.

A tenace heading a long suit is complicated by good chances to drop enemy high cards by straight leads from the top.

(18)	(19)
8 5 4 3	8 7 6 5 4
A J 10 7 6	A J 10 3 2

Odds slightly favour finessing twice, but much can be said for banging down the ace. If the enemy suit splits 2–2 in Matrix 18 or 2–1 in Matrix 19, or if an opponent holds a singleton honour in either matrix, first playing the ace simplifies matters. The finesse technique can prove embarrassing against K Q doubleton with W in Matrix 18.

When to cover an honour is an age-old problem.

(20)		(21)	
A J 9		A J 10 8	
K 4 3 10 6 5		K 4 3 9 7 6 5	
Q 7 2		Q 2	

When S leads the queen in either matrix, W should cover and promote E's ten or nine.

In a false compound finesse position, W should duck.

(22)			(23)	
	A 8 6			A 7 6
K 7 3		10 5 4	K 4 3	Q 9 8
	Q J 9			J 10 2

In Matrix 22, S leads the queen. If W covers, N wins with the ace and S finesses the nine on the return to get all three tricks. If W ducks, he can cover the knave next to promote E's ten. In Matrix 23, S leads the knave. If W covers, so does N who returns the suit to set up S's ten. Again W should duck.

Note this perfect compound finesse position.

	(24)	
	A 6 5	
Q 4 3		10 8 7
	K J 9 2	

The normal play for all four tricks is the ace (lest W hold the bare queen) and finesse the knave. But if the calling indicates the queen with W (he might have bid no-trumps) the presence of the nine in your hand offers a better method. Lead the knave, which wins if W ducks; otherwise N wins W's cover, and S finesses the nine on the return.

If dummy is on your right in Matrix 24, your only lead is the *knave*, your middle high card. This begets three tricks, or loses nothing if declarer on your left happens to hold A Q x.

The middle card lead is vital in similar positions, and it is especially clear whenever dummy is on your right.

(25)			(26)	
	K 4 3			4 2
A J 6		9 7 5	K 6 3	J 9 8
	Q 10 8			A Q 10 7 5

As S, lead the ten in Matrix 25 to set up two tricks. In Matrix 26 lead the queen. If declarer—West—wins with the king, partner may get in later and return the suit to let you pick up dummy's knave.

Psychology in Finessing

Certain finesse and pseudo-finesse positions lend themselves admirably to the art of thievery (cf. File D for Deception). They are, in

essence, plays of Deception; but they are filed here because they are
fundamentally types of finesse.

Here is an old chestnut that is still good.

(27)

J 10 6 4

Q 8 3 2   A 9 7 5

K

You lead the knave from dummy. E thinks you are going to finesse
the knave to his partner's queen and ducks, so you sneak home your
lone king.

Double Cross Plays

Each pair of matrices below shows how you, as declarer, can put
your opponents to the guillotine of the excruciating guess.

(28)		(29)	
7 6 5 4		7 6 5 4	
K 2	A	K 2	8 3
Q J 10 9 8 3		A Q J 10 9	

In a rubber bridge game declarer held the above trump suits.

In both matrices S led the queen. W, in Matrix 28, played his king
'before the rats get it'—only to have his irate partner's singleton ace
knock it off. A few deals later the calling marked the king with W,
so declarer again led the queen. W, still smarting from the biting
words of his partner in the first catastrophe, ducked. Next S laid
down his ace which gobbled W's king, and E tore up his cards!

(30)		(31)	
J 5 3		J 5 3	
Q 7 2	K 9 8	Q 7 2	10 9 8
A 10 6 4		A K 6 4	

In Matrix 30 declarer has no true finesse, for he lacks the nine. He
leads the four. If W 'flies' with the queen, he sets up a finesse against
his partner's king, so W should duck. But in Matrix 31 suppose
declarer leads the four, what should W do? He cannot be blamed
for ducking.

The Criss-Cross Double Cross

(32)		(33)	
K 8 7		K 8 7	
9 5 3	Q 6 2	Q 5 3	10 9 2
A J 10 4		A J 6 4	

Matrix 32 is the typical criss-cross finesse, for first you can 'criss' by leading the knave and hope W bites by covering. *If* W is a chronic 'cover-bug', *and* he unflinchingly ducks, you can place the queen with E, so you overtake the knave with dummy's king and 'cross' back and finesse the ten on the return.

But if W is a strong player he will play low without batting an eyelash when you lead the knave through his queen, and makes you sweat out the guess.

But suppose in Matrix 33 the bidding placed the queen with W. Clearly the usual play of the king then knave finesse won't work, so your only chance is the *double cross*, the technically unsound but psychologically sound lead of the knave from your own hand toward dummy, in the hope that W will duck without batting an eyelash! Of course, this should be done only when you are convinced W holds the queen.

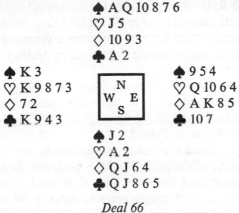

Deal 66

N bid 1 ♠, S 2 ◇; N 2 ♠, S 2 NT; and N 3 NT.

W led the ♡ 7, which drew the knave, queen and ace.

How do you play for nine prime tricks?

To Trick 2 S led the ♠ J which W covered, so declarer got six spade tricks, a heart and a club, one short of game.

Declarer must find both black kings with W in order to score his nine tricks, without losing the lead, so at Trick 2, he should lead the ♣ Q. The odds are three to one against finding both these cards in W, but it is S's only chance. The old dodge of putting in W in hearts to make a losing lead in clubs is out: E and W have diamonds to make as well.

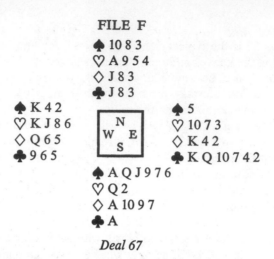

FILE F

```
              ♠ 10 8 3
              ♡ A 9 5 4
              ◇ J 8 3
              ♣ J 8 3
♠ K 4 2                        ♠ 5
♡ K J 8 6      N               ♡ 10 7 3
◇ Q 6 5      W   E             ◇ K 4 2
♣ 9 6 5        S               ♣ K Q 10 7 4 2
              ♠ A Q J 9 7 6
              ♡ Q 2
              ◇ A 10 9 7
              ♣ A
```

Deal 67

S bid 1 ♠, N 1 NT, E 2 ♣; S 3 ♠ and N 4 ♠.
W led the ♣ 9. How do you play for ten tricks?

S won the club, entered dummy via the ♡ A, and finessed the ♠ 10 which lost. Dummy had left one entry for a diamond finesse, but could not get in again for another vital one, so declarer lost a spade, a heart and two diamonds.

Declarer took the wrong finesse when he tried trumps, for he cannot finesse diamonds twice if the trump finesse loses. You have a 50–50 chance to win the trump finesse, but a 75% chance of finding enemy diamond honours divided.

To Trick 2 lay down the trump ace, adding to the recommended line a 10% chance of dropping the king singleton. It doesn't drop. Never mind: next lead the ♠ 9 and, if W ducks, overtake with dummy's ten to ensure a trump entry to dummy. W wins with the king (he might as well), and returns a club which you ruff. Next dummy wins a trump, drawing W's last, and finesses the ◇ 8, which W's queen wins. Later the ♡ A lets dummy lead the ◇ J for the second (and third) finesses.

FINESSE

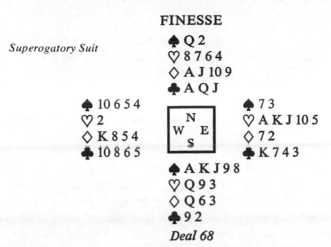

Superogatory Suit

♠ Q 2
♡ 8 7 6 4
◇ A J 10 9
♣ A Q J

♠ 10 6 5 4   ♠ 7 3
♡ 2   ♡ A K J 10 5
◇ K 8 5 4   ◇ 7 2
♣ 10 8 6 5   ♣ K 7 4 3

♠ A K J 9 8
♡ Q 9 3
◇ Q 6 3
♣ 9 2

Deal 68

E bid 1 ♡, S (vulnerable) 1 ♠, and N 4 ♠.

W led the ♡ 2, ruffed the third heart lead, and shifted to the eight
of diamonds. How do you win the balance?

Double dummy, the diamond finesse is obvious, but not to declarer,
to whom that ◇ 8 lead looked like the top of nothing, marking the
◇ K in E. So declarer played the ◇ A, drew trumps, and finessed
the ♣ J to go down two.

A count of winners shows that the repeating finesse in clubs is
utterly useless even if successful, for the third club trick gives S only
one diamond discard where he would need two. The diamond finesse
is essential for game and must be taken: the club is supererogatory.

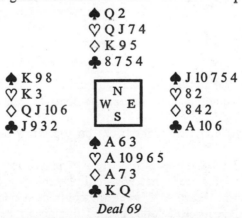

♠ Q 2
♡ Q J 7 4
◇ K 9 5
♣ 8 7 5 4

♠ K 9 8   ♠ J 10 7 5 4
♡ K 3   ♡ 8 2
◇ Q J 10 6   ◇ 8 4 2
♣ J 9 3 2   ♣ A 10 6

♠ A 6 3
♡ A 10 9 6 5
◇ A 7 3
♣ K Q

Deal 69

S bid 1 ♡, N 2 ♡; S 3 ◇, and N 4 ♡.
W led the ◇ Q. When do you finesse trumps?

Dummy won the ◇ Q with the king and took the trump finesse, which W won. W returned another diamond, driving out S's ace; so declarer eventually lost a trick in every suit.

S should win the diamond opening with the ace and lead a low spade. W wins with the king, and dummy wins the ◇ J return, cashes the ♠ Q, and leads the ♡ Q, but S must ignore that tempting trump finesse and clatter up with his ace in order to cash his ♠ A for a fast diamond discard in dummy.

If, at Trick 2, E kills dummy's ♠ Q with the king, a count of prospective winners shows that declarer *must* try the trump finesse as his last chance to score game. Finding the ♠ K in W makes the trump finesse unnecessary. The point is that declarer must delay his decision to finesse trumps until he has tested the spade position—a question of echeloning the plays.

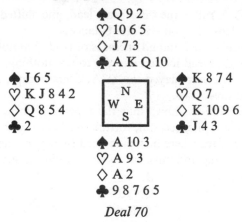

Deal 70

S bid 1 ♣, N 3 ♣; and S 3 NT.

W led the ♡ 4 and S held off E's queen, but S won E's heart continuation. (A diamond shift breaks the contract, but S has to take that chance.)

You are declarer with eight tricks on top. How do you get the ninth?

To Trick 2 S led the ♠ 3 and when W played low, S paused to consider. The inference is that W would play the ♠ K if he had it in order to cash his hearts and break the contract at once; so E must hold the ♠ K. Hence declarer inserted dummy's nine which drove out E's king, and the ball was over.

As the cards lie the deal is cooked, for declarer can run four club tricks first, re-enter via the ♠ A to cash his fifth routine club, and then take the ♠ 9 finesse. But the danger of unbuttoning spades is that E might hold so damaging a suit as ♠ K J x x x x and rook the game out of hand.

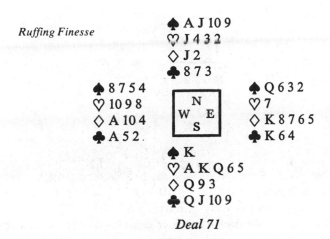

Ruffing Finesse

```
              ♠ A J 10 9
              ♡ J 4 3 2
              ◇ J 2
              ♣ 8 7 3
♠ 8 7 5 4          N          ♠ Q 6 3 2
♡ 10 9 8       W     E        ♡ 7
◇ A 10 4          S           ◇ K 8 7 6 5
♣ A 5 2                       ♣ K 6 4
              ♠ K
              ♡ A K Q 6 5
              ◇ Q 9 3
              ♣ Q J 10 9
```

Deal 71

S bid 1 ♡, N 2 ♡; and S 4 ♡. Despite his seven winners, S should bid only 3 ♡ on account of his lack of quick tricks in the minors. Alternatively and preferably he might make a Trial bid of 3 ♣ which, with no assistance for the second suit, N would 'correct' to a mere 3 ♡.

E and W have four quick tricks. However, W opened the ♡ 10 and gave S his chance. How do you plan the play?

S chucked the hand quickly. The plays were ♡ A, ♠ K, ♡ J and ♠ A on which S shed a diamond, and the ♠ Q failed to drop. Next dummy led the ♠ J which E covered and S ruffed. Now S had no way to get back to dummy to score the ♠ 10 for another vital diamond discard before the defence scored its four quick tricks.

To Trick 2 S wins another trump, and dummy must overtake the ♠ K and return the ♠ J for the ruffing finesse. This line lets S discard *two* diamonds, now or later, depending on when E covers; the trump knave still stands as re-entry if E covers early.*

* This is another case of balancing the *risk* of a two-trick defeat against the *certainty* of going one down. Since you are not doubled, the odds make the hazard acceptable.—Editor.

Scoop Finesse

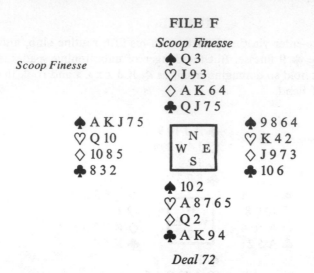

Scoop Finesse

```
                  ♠ Q 3
                  ♡ J 9 3
                  ◇ A K 6 4
                  ♣ Q J 7 5
♠ A K J 7 5                      ♠ 9 8 6 4
♡ Q 10           N              ♡ K 4 2
◇ 10 8 5      W     E           ◇ J 9 7 3
♣ 8 3 2          S              ♣ 10 6
                  ♠ 10 2
                  ♡ A 8 7 6 5
                  ◇ Q 2
                  ♣ A K 9 4
```

Deal 72

After three passes, S bid 1 ♡; W 1 ♠, N 3 ♡; and S 4 ♡.

W led the ♠ K, ♠ A, then the ◇ 10 which S's queen won.

How do you play to lose only one trump trick?

Having lost two spade tricks, declarer can afford only one trump loser. Without seeing the E and W trump holdings, S's trumps are nothing to write home about . . . except for more money! However, S made the best of his chances.

If W holds ♡ K Q doubleton, with ♠ A K, etc., shown by his opening play, he would have opened the bidding.

Other trump combinations S considered were ♡ 10 x x, ♡ 10 x, ♡ Q 10, or ♡ K 10 with W.

To Trick 4 S led a low trump, which W's queen won. N won the diamond return, and led the ♡ J for the 'scoop finesse'. This promoted the nine while trapping E's king and 'scooping', or shutting-out, W's 10.

If to Trick 4 W plays low from ♡ 10 x, dummy finesses the nine to drive the queen from E, and the scoop finesse of the knave later clears the suit. Of course, W may hold ♡ 10 x x instead, giving S a guess on his second trump play.

S bid 3 NT and N 6 NT in Deal 73 on the next page.

W led the ♠ J, drawing the queen, king and ace.

The ♠ J is apparently a short suit opening probably, a doubleton since S has the ten. Such a suit as J x x would be a lunatic choice from which to lead the knave.

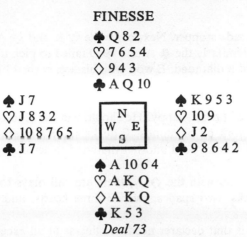

Deal 73

Declarer crossed to dummy in clubs and led the ♠ 8; E covered with the nine and S with the ten, 'scooping' W's seven.

Dummy won another club and led the ♠ 2, E played the three, and S finessed the four to get all thirteen tricks!

Declarer's play was correct, for the two spade leads from dummy always yield three spade tricks if W held ♠ J 9 (when ♠ 9 wins); J 5 or J 3.

Any opening except the ♠ J gives S a hard time! In theory, as in practice, W should lead a diamond.

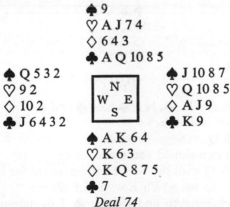

Deal 74

N bid 1 ♣, S 1 ◇; N 1 ♡, S 1 ♠; N 2 ◇, and S 3 NT.
W led the ♣ 3. How do you play for nine tricks?

One declarer took every finesse in sight. He finessed the ♣ 10 which drove out E's king. E shifted to the ♠ J which S won, and declarer finessed the ♡ J to E's queen. Another spade return drove out S's last spade stopper. Next came the ♡ K and ♡ A, but hearts didn't drop. Similarly the ♣ A and ♣ Q failed to pick up the knave, so dummy led a diamond. E won with his ace, cashed his heart, and a spade; and W overtook the next spade to score his ♣ J, downing declarer three tricks.

Declarer was finesse-happy. He should win the club opening with the ace and work on diamonds, E ducks and S's queen wins. Next, the ♡ A lets dummy lead another diamond to set up four diamond tricks.

If W shows up with the ◇ A, there are still plays to score three diamond tricks, two spades, two or three hearts, and one or two clubs.

The point is that declarer needs no finesse at all except to find E with ◇ A x x.

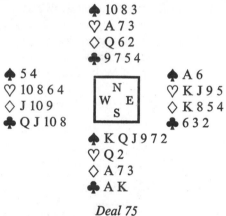

Deal 75

Playing Acol, S bid 2 ♠, N 3 ♠; S 4 ♣ and N—too weak to show ♡ A—signed off with 4 ♠.*

W led the ♣ Q.

Which red queen should you try to set up?

S won the ♣ Q with the ace. To promote entries to dummy, he led the ♠ 9 to the ten which E won with his ace.

S won the club return and led the ♠ 7 to dummy's eight and luckily trumps dropped, making that ♠ 3 another entry. Dummy returned a low heart toward S's queen, E stepped up with his king lest he lose it, and 'school was out'. E returned another club which S ruffed, cashed the ♡ Q, and the ♠ 2 to dummy's ♠ 3 let dummy score the ♡ A for a diamond 'shake'.

*SAB: S 1 ♠, N 1 NT; S 4 ♠.

FINESSE

Declarer echeloned his plans. If the ♡ Q loses to the king in W, S still has another try in reserve in the form of a lead toward dummy's ♢ Q. But if the diamond play is made first and fails, the defence can push diamonds and hold declarer to nine tricks.

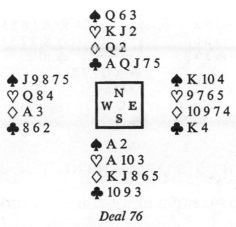

```
                    ♠ Q 6 3
                    ♡ K J 2
                    ♢ Q 2
                    ♣ A Q J 7 5
  ♠ J 9 8 7 5           N           ♠ K 10 4
  ♡ Q 8 4         W         E       ♡ 9 7 6 5
  ♢ A 3               S             ♢ 10 9 7 4
  ♣ 8 6 2                           ♣ K 4
                    ♠ A 2
                    ♡ A 10 3
                    ♢ K J 8 6 5
                    ♣ 10 9 3
```

Deal 76

S bid 1 ♢, N 2 ♣; S 2 NT, and N 3 NT.

S's 2 NT rebid was horrible on a minimum: he should rebid 2 ♢ and N will bid 3 NT.

However, S had to try to make nine tricks. W led the ♠ 7, dummy played low, E the ten and S the ace. S lost the club finesse to E who returned a diamond which S ducked and W won. W returned the ♠ J.

Seeing all four hands you know dummy should duck to block spades, but declarer has a vital clue for this correct duck play. What was this clue?

E's tell-tale shift to the ♢ 4 at Trick 3 indicated that E wanted W to lead spades through dummy's queen: hence, E must hold the ♠ K. Without this card, E would have returned spades instead of the diamond to help W clear them at once. So declarer's only chance to block spades was to duck and hope that E did not begin life with four (or more) of the suit.

FILE F

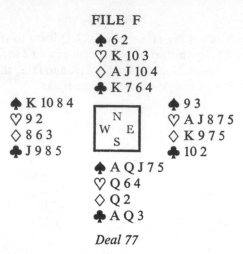

♠ 6 2
♡ K 10 3
◇ A J 10 4
♣ K 7 6 4

♠ K 10 8 4
♡ 9 2
◇ 8 6 3
♣ J 9 8 5

♠ 9 3
♡ A J 8 7 5
◇ K 9 7 5
♣ 10 2

♠ A Q J 7 5
♡ Q 6 4
◇ Q 2
♣ A Q 3

Deal 77

S bid 1 ♠, N 2 ◇ ; S 2 NT, and N 3 NT.

W led the ♡ 9.

Which heart do you play from dummy on this marked short-suit opening?

Declarer correctly put up dummy's ♡ K in order to create a doubled stopper against E, who won with the ace.

E switched to the ♠ 9. Declarer avoided the second finesse trap and played the ace. Next he finessed a diamond to E's king, and the defence was helpless.

The ♡ 9 opening was obviously the top of nothing in an effort to hit E's best suit, marking E with ♡ A J x x, etc., if declarer plays any heart except the king, he can stop hearts only once.

If declarer finesses spades at Trick 2, the ♠ K lets W in prematurely to clear the hearts before E loses his ◇ K.

File G

GAMBIT

G stands for Gambit. By dictionary definition the word is 'one of various openings in chess, in which a pawn or piece is risked to obtain an attack'. The term, with a synonymous meaning, I first extended to bridge in 1938: the risk or sacrifice of a master card, or a trick, to develop the attack. The purpose is to create, or use, a vital entry to partner's hand; or to destroy an enemy entry.

In the field of Entry play, gambits constitute a specialized tribe of entry-creating and entry-destroying manœuvres; and this tribe is further divided into two files: Jettison (*q.v.*) in which winners are discarded on another suit; and the gambits proper.

Gambit plays, filed under G, are again split into three sections: the trick-losing play of tail cards to create an entry; overtaking manœuvres; and destroying an enemy entry.

Gambit plays are rare and spectacular. At present the known types are narrowly limited.

Section I—Tail Card Gambits

Every book on play includes an example of creating an entry to dummy in the tail cards of declarer's long suit.

FILE G
Matrix pura

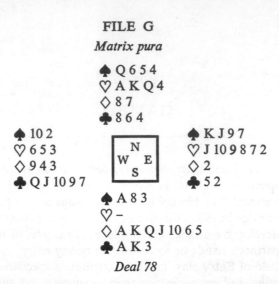

♠ Q 6 5 4
♡ A K Q 4
◇ 8 7
♣ 8 6 4

♠ 10 2
♡ 6 5 3
◇ 9 4 3
♣ Q J 10 9 7

♠ K J 9 7
♡ J 10 9 8 7 2
◇ 2
♣ 5 2

♠ A 8 3
♡ –
◇ A K Q J 10 6 5
♣ A K 3

Deal 78

S was playing Acol in a rubber game. He opened 2 ♣. N replied 2 ♡; and S jumped to 6 ◇. This last unscientific call was typical of the slap-happy bidding you meet in bridge clubs. Such speculative characters lose a few quid (*and* for their partners!) now and then, and the numbers of the species do not seem to be materially diminishing, despite the generally better standard of play.

W led the ♣ Q which S won with the ace. S drew trumps and led a low spade toward the queen; but E killed her off with his king and returned a club. S later lost a club and another spade, going down two, for dummy's heart tricks died of atrophy.

N suffered silently and said nothing until S bewailed his bad luck in finding the ♠ K in E. This was too much for N, who crimed S for not leading a *low* diamond at Trick 2. This play sacrifices a trick to the enemy's ◇ 9 (unless W happens to fall asleep at the switch), but dummy gets three heart tricks in return. That is a 200% return on the investment.

Incidentally, at 6 NT (with the same natural club opening) the deal is a Sure Trick problem; for 6 NT can be made against any defence and distribution.

GAMBIT

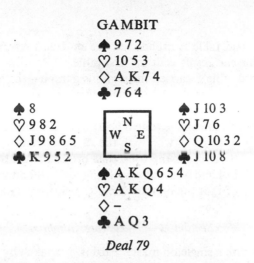

```
                ♠ 9 7 2
                ♡ 10 5 3
                ◇ A K 7 4
                ♣ 7 6 4
♠ 8                            ♠ J 10 3
♡ 9 8 2          N             ♡ J 7 6
◇ J 9 8 6 5   W     E          ◇ Q 10 3 2
♣ K 9 5 2        S             ♣ J 10 8
                ♠ A K Q 6 5 4
                ♡ A K Q 4
                ◇ –
                ♣ A Q 3
```

Deal 79

In U.S. card slang, a 'Greek' is a crooked player, a card-sharper, a mechanic who deals off the bottom of the pack, etc., and to 'Greek' means to cheat. Perhaps the card meaning stemmed from the old Virgilian adage, 'I dread the Greeks, especially when bearing gifts'.* However, the case at hand is strictly dinkum† without a trace of coffee-house.‡

The deal came from a pairs duplicate game, and the three S players discussed below all played the contract at 6 ♠.

In every instance W led the ♠ 8, which the nine, ten and ace covered in turn. Declarer, realizing his problem of entry to dummy's diamond tricks, led the ♠ 6 to Trick 2, planning to overtake with the seven if W played low. W failed, and declarer played the deuce from dummy.

At one table E grabbed the trick with the ♠ J and the battle was over. E returned the ♣ J on which S banged his ace immediately and led a low trump to let dummy in to cash two diamond tops for club discards.

At the other two tables E suspected that the eager and free offer of an unnecessary trump trick was a Greek gift, probably to create entry to score diamonds. So these players let the ♠ 6 win. Next S cashed three top hearts and led the heart thirteener on which dummy discarded a club.

* *Timeo Danaos et dona ferentes.*
† Australian—not Greek!
‡ Middle European slang for sharp practice.

103

At the second table E ruffed with his ♠ J and returned the ♣ J with the same end result as at the first table.

At the third table E carried through his gambit—the plan to sacrifice the easy, unnecessary and suspicious trump winner—to its logical conclusion. He refused declarer's second offer of the Greek gift and also discarded a club on the fourth heart lead. Declarer laid down the ♣ A then ♣ Q which W won with the ♣ K. W returned a club and E over-ruffed dummy for the trick that broke the contract.

At Table 3 the hand was really well played by S and well defended by E—a case of that tug-of-war when 'Greek joins Greek'.

Section II—Overtaking Gambits

In this section a singleton master card is overtaken by partner who vitally needs the lead at once in order to gain time or to lead through an enemy honour.

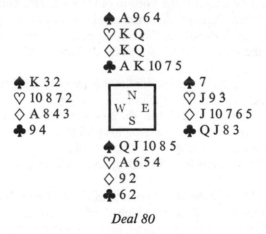

♠ A 9 6 4
♡ K Q
♢ K Q
♣ A K 10 7 5

♠ K 3 2
♡ 10 8 7 2
♢ A 8 4 3
♣ 9 4

♠ 7
♡ J 9 3
♢ J 10 7 6 5
♣ Q J 8 3

♠ Q J 10 8 5
♡ A 6 5 4
♢ 9 2
♣ 6 2

Deal 80

N bid 1 ♣, S 1 ♠; N 4 NT (Blackwood); S 5 ♢; and N 6 ♠.

W led the ♢ A and shifted to the ♡ 2 which dummy's queen won. Declarer went after clubs, ace, king, then a low one which he trumped and W over-ruffed to break the contract.

The danger of this over-ruff should be obvious. Against a 4–2 club split, dummy can set up a long club for a heart discard, and dummy has enough trumps to take care of another heart loser.

To Trick 2 declarer should break dummy's heart 'marriage' by overtaking the queen with the ace to finesse trumps.

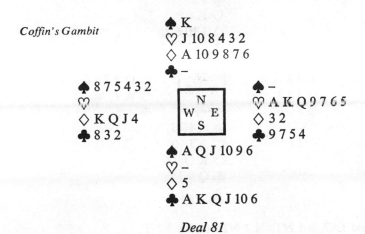

Coffin's Gambit

♠ K
♡ J 10 8 4 3 2
◇ A 10 9 8 7 6
♣ -

♠ 8 7 5 4 3 2
♡
◇ K Q J 4
♣ 8 3 2

♠ -
♡ A K Q 9 7 6 5
◇ 3 2
♣ 9 7 5 4

♠ A Q J 10 9 6
♡ -
◇ 5
♣ A K Q J 10 6

Deal 81

After two passes E bid 4 ♡, S 6 ♠ ; W doubled, and N redoubled. 'Lovely bidding'—but after E's correct pre-empt, what are N and S to do? W has a very promising double and N an equally promising redouble.

Perhaps over 4 ♡ S should go scientific and make a forcing bid of 4 NT or 5 ♡. However, as the shapes lie, N would respond in diamonds and S would land in 6 ♠ anyway. S's actual jump to 6 ♠ was a good shot, for the chances are slightly better than even that N holds the ♣ K or ◇ A.

W led the ◇ K which dummy's ace won. Declarer grunted about mucking the calling and missing the apparently lay-down grand slam 'with thirteen solid tricks'. He led the ♠ K and E failed, to reveal that the thirteen solid tricks were not so solid after all. S needed all his own master trumps to draw all W's, so he played the ♠ 6 on the king. Suddenly he awoke to his peril: no entry to his own hand without a catastrophic ruff.

Coffin's Gambit (also known as the Coffin Coup) solves the problem. Overtake the ♠ K with the ace and cash four more top trumps. This play sets up W's ♠ 8, but S simply 'rams' it by running clubs, retaining ♠ 6 to re-enter after W has ruffed.

Section III—Entry-Destroying Gambits

In an entry-destroying gambit, declarer hands the enemy a trick on a silver platter in order to shut out their long suit.

Deal 82

E bid 1 ♡, S 1 NT, N 2 NT; and S 3 NT.

W led the ♠ 6 and E played the king. How do you plan your attack?

The game is easy if W opens a heart.* W suspected S was weak in spades when he failed to make a take-out double.

Declarer won the ♠ K with the ace, entered dummy with the ♡ K, and led the ◇ J. If E ducks, S shifts to clubs and gets home with three club tricks, two spades, three hearts and a diamond. But E was on his toes (and off his partner's!) and stepped up with the ◇ A returning the ♠ 8, which W ducked to the knave in dummy. S needed club tricks for game and led one. E won with his last ace and a spade return let W break the contract.

The opening heart bid by E places him with both missing aces, so it is vital to suffocate the enemy spades. The only way is to lay off the ♠ K at Trick 1 ! E returns the ♠ 8 and S still ducks. He wins the third spade lead. Now S can set up the minor suits by driving out E's aces, and E, out of spades, has no way to put W in.

This is not an ordinary hold-up, for normally a declarer with A 10 x opposite J x will win to ensure two tricks in the suit. It is a true gambit: sacrificing one sure spade trick to shut out two for the defence.

---

* Although the spade opening gives any but an expert S a very tough time, W's spade lead is not recommended. A 5-card suit queen-high, with no re-entry is worse than dubious when E has bid another suit. Nine times out of ten, a bad hand should subordinate itself to partner.—Editor.

File H

HOLD

H stands for Hold. Declarer or, rarely, an opponent, deliberately loses a trick at a critical stage of the play in order to consolidate his forces and develop mastery or a firm *hold* on the position. Usually the loss of this trick enables the player to win the balance. A holding play is a strategic withdrawal from the battle for one trick or more in order to win the war for the contract.

Holding plays are classified in two sections: the standard *hold-up* of an honour card, usually at no-trumps in order to exhaust one opponent of the suit led; and *holding play* proper, which renders both opponents harmless.

Hold-ups are closely related to, or nearly synonymous with, Avoidance, Blocking, and Tempo (q.v.). In the true hold-up, a player holds on to the master card of the suit the enemy is pushing until the critical moment when playing it takes the last card of its suit from one opponent.

Holding plays are often compounded with plays of still other files such as end-plays, Finesse, Long Suit, etc. If the holding play is subservient to the play of another file, it properly belongs in that file. If the two play elements appear equally crucial or important, you may find yourself in a dichotomous position when you try to file it —unless you adopt the easy course of placing it in Q for Quandary.

A true holding play renders both opponents impotent. Letting an opponent win the pivotal trick at the critical stage, usually early in the hand, is like the throw-in lead of an elimination play—but with one major difference. In the holding play, the enemy's return lead does not cost opponents a trick as it does in an elimination play, but as a rule it leaves the opponents helpless to win any more tricks. Actually, elimination play (cf. File X) is a specialized type of holding play, as is also the deliberate loss of a trick incurred to 'rectify the count' of winners in setting up a squeeze position (cf. File Z).

Section I—The Hold-ups

Matrix typica

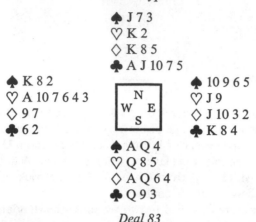

```
                    ♠ J 7 3
                    ♡ K 2
                    ◇ K 8 5
                    ♣ A J 10 7 5
    ♠ K 8 2                          ♠ 10 9 6 5
    ♡ A 10 7 6 4 3      N           ♡ J 9
    ◇ 9 7           W       E        ◇ J 10 3 2
    ♣ 6 2              S             ♣ K 8 4
                    ♠ A Q 4
                    ♡ Q 8 5
                    ◇ A Q 6 4
                    ♣ Q 9 3
```

Deal 83

With E and W vulnerable S bid 1 NT and N 3 NT.

W led the ♡ 6. Do you play dummy's king?

Dummy's ♡ K won the ♡ 6 opening and E took care to drop the knave to unblock. S won a diamond and remarking, 'Oh, well, either the club finesse wins or it doesn't', finessed the ♣ Q to E's king; and a heart return let W win five heart tricks to collect 100 points.

Declarer must duck the ♡ 6 lead in both hands in order to exhaust E of hearts before E makes the ♣ K. This line yields a heart trick, three diamonds, four clubs, and the ♠ A.

If W holds five hearts, the hold-up is futile,* but so is the ♡ K play to Trick 1 or any other play. Hence S should hold up in hearts for an extra chance against the actual distribution of six hearts with W and the ♣ K offside.

* If the hearts are 5 with W and 3 with E, W ducks the second round but wins the third.—Editor.

HOLD

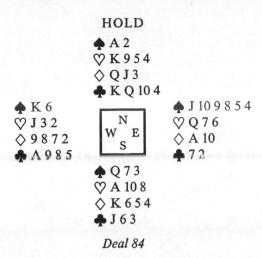

♠ A 2
♡ K 9 5 4
◇ Q J 3
♣ K Q 10 4

♠ K 6
♡ J 3 2
◇ 9 8 7 2
♣ A 9 8 5

♠ J 10 9 8 5 4
♡ Q 7 6
◇ A 10
♣ 7 2

♠ Q 7 3
♡ A 10 8
◇ K 6 5 4
♣ J 6 3

Deal 84

N bid 1 ♣, E 1 ♠, S 1 NT; N 2 NT, and S 3 NT.
W led the ♠ K. Do you win it?

Declarer chortled over that lucky ♠ K opening right into his ace and queen, and clobbered the king with the ace. He pushed clubs, W won with his ace, and returned another spade. S held up his queen but had to take the third spade lead. Declarer needed diamond tricks for game, but E grabbed the first diamond lead with his ace and smeared declarer for a loss of two down with good spades.

If declarer had started diamonds first instead of clubs, he would have got home; but it is pure guesswork which ace to try to knock out first.

If declarer had held the ace and king of spades, he might have recognized the proper hold-up on the first spade lead; but he was so busy gloating over that ♠ K opening that he let the game fly out the window.

Let the ♠ K win, and welcome; and no shift helps the defence. Next dummy wins the ♠ A and pushes clubs until W's ace wins. W has no spade left, so declarer wins a club return and drives out the ◇ A from E.

Of course, declarer needs some luck. Against a 2–6 spade split he must find the enemy aces divided or (most improbable) both in the short spade hand, W. The deal goes to show that 'easy aces'* at no-trumps are not always so easy to neutralize.

---

* 'Aces easy' was an auction bridge term to signify that each partnership held two: three aces scored as honours.—Editor.

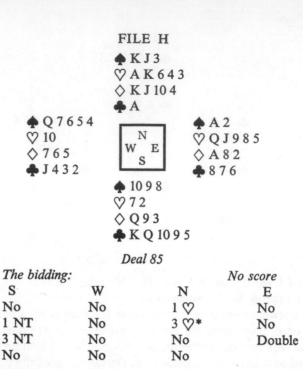

FILE H

            ♠ K J 3
            ♡ A K 6 4 3
            ◇ K J 10 4
            ♣ A

♠ Q 7 6 5 4   ♠ A 2
♡ 10   ♡ Q J 9 8 5
◇ 7 6 5   ◇ A 8 2
♣ J 4 3 2   ♣ 8 7 6

            ♠ 10 9 8
            ♡ 7 2
            ◇ Q 9 3
            ♣ K Q 10 9 5

Deal 85

E's double suggested that E was well heeled in hearts, despite N's jump rebid in the suit; so W led the ♡ 10.

Dummy won with the ♡ K, cashed the ♣ A; and the ◇ K drove out E's ◇ A. E returned his best heart, forcing dummy's ace. S won a diamond and tried to run clubs but the stubborn knave was well chaperoned and evaded capture; so E, re-entering with the ♠ A, eventually scored three heart tricks and two aces to break the contract.

That ♡ 10 opening was tainted, so S should not eat it but let it win. Now, W, out of hearts, has to switch which gives declarer time to set up and bring home a long club.

If E overtakes the ♡ 10 with his knave, dummy's six of hearts eventually becomes a surprisingly effective stopper.

Better defence is for E to overtake ♡ 10 and return ♡ Q which dummy wins. Dummy wins ♣ A and leads a low diamond to the nine as E ducks. S must not touch clubs now lest he squeeze dummy, instead should finesse ♠ J.

But hold-up play must be considered in the context of the whole hand. For instance:

* A better bid would be 3 ◇.

110

HOLD

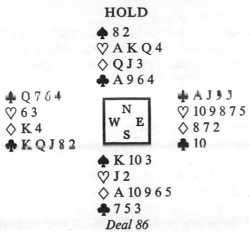

```
              ♠ 8 2
              ♡ A K Q 4
              ◇ Q J 3
              ♣ A 9 6 4
♠ Q 7 6 4                      ♠ A J 9 9
♡ 6 3          N              ♡ 10 9 8 7 5
◇ K 4      W      E           ◇ 8 7 2
♣ K Q J 8 2       S           ♣ 10
              ♠ K 10 3
              ♡ J 2
              ◇ A 10 9 6 5
              ♣ 7 5 3
```

Deal 86

N bid 1 ♣, S 1 ◇; N 1 ♡, S 1 NT; and N 3 NT, an overbid.
W led the ♣ K.

Declarer made the hold-up of the ♣ 4 from dummy, expecting another club lead; but W shifted to the ♠ 4 and E inserted his knave to let S's king win. S cashed the knave and queen of hearts, and tried the diamond finesse which lost; so opponents smeared the hand with a diamond trick, three spades, and a club.

That club hold-up was hollow. Declarer must finesse diamonds into the big club hand, W, who will always get four more club tricks unless the ♣ A play at Trick 1 happens to be lucky enough to drop a lone club honour with E to make dummy's nine a second stopper. An enemy 4–2 split is harmless also. The hold up, therefore, is 'out'.

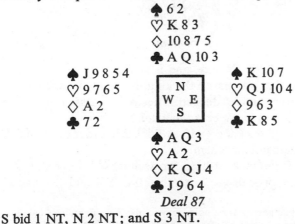

```
              ♠ 6 2
              ♡ K 8 3
              ◇ 10 8 7 5
              ♣ A Q 10 3
♠ J 9 8 5 4                    ♠ K 10 7
♡ 9 7 6 5      N              ♡ Q J 10 4
◇ A 2      W      E           ◇ 9 6 3
♣ 7 2           S            ♣ K 8 5
              ♠ A Q 3
              ♡ A 2
              ◇ K Q J 4
              ♣ J 9 6 4
```

Deal 87

S bid 1 NT, N 2 NT; and S 3 NT.
W led the ♠ 5 and E put up the king.

Declarer must develop both minor suits; and properly taking the pessimistic view on an offside club finesse, let the ♠ K win. He expected a spade return, but E shifted to the ♡ Q which declarer won with his ace. The ◇ K drove out W's ace and a heart return drove out dummy's king. Declarer won three diamond tricks and tried the club finesse, which lost the game; for the defence collected the ♣ K, ◇ A, two heart tricks and the ♠ K.

The hold-up is vital, but it is a phantom hold-up at Trick 1 on account of the threat of a shift to hearts.

Win Trick 1 with the ♠ A, drive out the ◇ A. Now a heart return is too late to do opponents any good, so W pushes another spade; and *now* is the time for declarer to hold up in order to exhaust E of spades. Next declarer wins the third spade lead and takes the club finesse, which goes into the non-spade hand.*

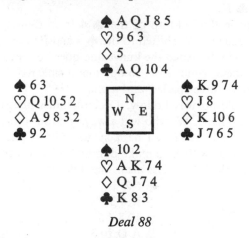

```
              ♠ A Q J 8 5
              ♡ 9 6 3
              ◇ 5
              ♣ A Q 10 4
  ♠ 6 3                        ♠ K 9 7 4
  ♡ Q 10 5 2      N            ♡ J 8
  ◇ A 9 8 3 2  W   E           ◇ K 10 6
  ♣ 9 2           S            ♣ J 7 6 5
              ♠ 10 2
              ♡ A K 7 4
              ◇ Q J 7 4
              ♣ K 8 3
```

Deal 88

N bid 1 ♠, S 2 NT; N 3 ♣, and S 3 NT.

W led the ◇ 3 and E played the king. E returned his ten, declarer put on the queen, and W ducked! The ♠ 10 finesse lost to E who returned the ◇ 6 to let W beat the hand.

Declarer should duck the ◇ 10 at Trick 2 in order to exhaust E of diamonds if he continues them!

At Trick 1 E can make it hard for declarer if E inserts the ◇ 10. If S wins it, the spade finesse loses, then the ◇ K and ◇ 6 undo S.

---

* There is no blanket rule for a hold-up; you may have to grab a single stopper at Trick 1; you may have to retain a double stopper till Tricks 2 and 3; you may have to hold-up, not on the first, but on the second, trick.—Editor.

HOLD

Although it does not seem so, since it is a 'finesse against partner' and there is nothing in dummy over which to keep the king or ace, the play of ◇ 10 is logical for E. The ◇ 3 opening shows by the Rule of Eleven that declarer has at least four diamonds; perhaps five, if he also holds the deuce; hence, S must come to at least one diamond trick. E should let S win it at once in case S holds ◇ Q J x x or ◇ J 9 x x x.*

However, S *can* make the very difficult play of ducking the ◇ 10 at Trick 1 and get home anyway.

Those diamonds are tricky.

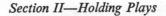

Section II—Holding Plays

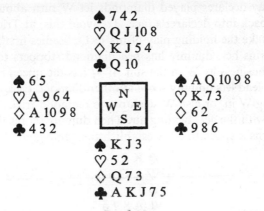

♠ 7 4 2
♡ Q J 10 8
◇ K J 5 4
♣ Q 10

♠ 6 5
♡ A 9 6 4
◇ A 10 9 8
♣ 4 3 2

♠ A Q 10 9 8
♡ K 7 3
◇ 6 2
♣ 9 8 6

♠ K J 3
♡ 5 2
◇ Q 7 3
♣ A K J 7 5

Deal 89

The bidding:			No score
S	W	N	E
—	—	—	No
1 ♣	No	1 ♡	1 ♠
1 NT	No	2 NT	No
3 NT	No	No	No

W led the ♠ 6 and E played the ♠ 9, going to S's knave. How do you play the diamonds?

S led a diamond to dummy's knave to Trick 2, and returned a low one to his queen which W won with the ace. W returned the ◇ 10 in order to set up a diamond trick for himself, and dummy's king won.

---

* This is on the same principle as the much-publicized *coup* of playing, as E, Q from A Q x on partner's lead against a no-trumper: the Q is won by S with the King, but E gets in and leads A and low to allow W to cash the balance. On the play of A, Q and low , S would hold-up his K until the third round.—Editor.

113

With only eight tricks secure now, declarer tried to smuggle through a spade trick by leading a spade from dummy, but E hopped up with his ace, and returned a low heart which let W get his ♡ A and ◇ 9; and W returned a heart to E's king, the setting trick.

If E had won Trick 1 with the ♠ A and returned a spade, S could have taken his second spade trick any time he wished which, with two diamonds and five clubs, scores game.

The auction and W's opening lead locate the red aces with W. The ♠ 6 opening, W's 'best' spade, *shows at most two spades in W*, for declarer has the 4, 3 and 2 in plain view; hence E is marked with five (possibly six) spades topped by A Q 10. With a side ace also, E would have opened the bidding.

The way declarer played diamonds let W turn about and throw the suit back into declarer's face. To avoid this, at Trick 2 declarer should make the holding play of his ◇ Q. 'Ladies first', you know!

If W wins her, dummy has *two* diamond stoppers to thwart any monkey business by W in the suit. If W lets the queen hold, another diamond lead lets dummy score another diamond trick at once without letting W in, or else W sets up two diamond tricks in dummy if he 'flies' with the ace, beating air. Then dummy scores the diamonds and returns a spade to let S establish the game-going trick.

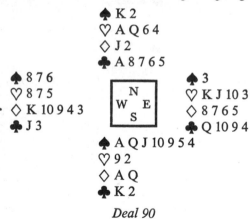

```
              ♠ K 2
              ♡ A Q 6 4
              ◇ J 2
              ♣ A 8 7 6 5
  ♠ 8 7 6                        ♠ 3
  ♡ 8 7 5          N            ♡ K J 10 3
· ◇ K 10 9 4 3  W    E         ◇ 8 7 6 5
  ♣ J 3            S            ♣ Q 10 9 4
              ♠ A Q J 10 9 5 4
              ♡ 9 2
              ◇ A Q
              ♣ K 2
```

Deal 90

S bid 2 ♠ (Acol) and N 6 ♠. *

N should have probed the bidding for a possible grand slam, but his direct jump depicts his hand accurately and it is typical of the non-scientific hoppety-skippety bidding one encounters in casual club play.

SAB: S 1 ♠, N 2 ♣; S 4 ♠, N 4 NT Blackwood; S 5 ♡ to show two aces, N 5 NT; S 6 ◇ to show one king, and N 6 ♠ or 6 NT.

W led the ♡ 8. How do you play to bag the slam?

Declarer reckons that one of the finesses would win so he put up ♡ Q which E won with the king. E took the view that diamonds were the only source of further nourishment for his side and led the ◇ 8. S finessed again, and the second red (or red hot!) king broke the contract. S wailed about his rotten luck.

Instead, S should 'fly' with the ◇ A at Trick 2, and make the hand. Next play the ♠ A, ♣ K, ♣ A, ruff a club high, ♣ K, ruff another club high, draw trumps, and re-enter dummy a third time via the ♡ A to score the fifth good club for the diamond discard.

However, S cannot make the hand if E returns the ♡ J to Trick 2. True, the diamond suit is the only source of further nourishment for opponents, W's king; but to protect it, E must return the ♡ J in order to drive a vital entry out of dummy, the ♡ A, and spoil the play on clubs.

In order to stop this line of defence, at Trick 1 declarer must make the holding play of a *low* heart from dummy!* E wins with the ten, but he cannot return a heart up to dummy's ace-queen without immediate suicide, so must shift to the ◇ 8 as the best shot. Now declarer can bang on the ◇ A and play on clubs unmolested.

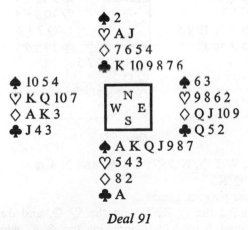

Deal 91

After two passes S bid 4 ♠.

W led the ◇ K and E played the ◇ Q to show diamonds solid,

* The low heart from dummy is the hold-up play plus that brings the slam home against any defence; and against any holding except a singleton heart with W or five or more clubs in one hand. This card is the only proper one to play to Trick 1.—Editor.

queen high. W, wisely ignoring the normal low-card continuation requested by this queen-play, next led the ◇ A and E played the ◇ 9, completing the circuit of his Q J 10 9 sequence and giving W an accurate count of the suit, marking S with only two diamonds.

To Trick 3 W shifted to the ♡ K.

How do you bag ten tricks?

Declarer won Trick 3 with the ♡ A in dummy, played the ♣ A and returned a heart to set up a heart ruff in dummy. But W won the heart lead and returned a trump, forever slamming the door on dummy.

Declarer must make the holding play of allowing the ♡ K to win Trick 3! This duck lets the defence spend its attack and become absolutely helpless. A trump shift leaves the ♡ A intact to bring home the ♣ K later, whereas a heart continuation leaves the low trump still in dummy to ruff the third round of hearts.

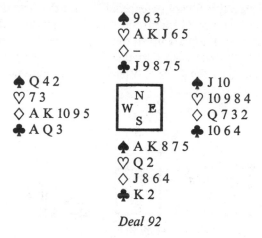

Deal 92

S bid 1 ♠, W 2 ◇, N 2 ♡; S 2 ♠, and N 4 ♠.
W led the ◇ K.

How do you play for game?

Dummy ruffed the ◇ K, S won the ♡ Q, and dummy ruffed another diamond. S tried to re-enter via the ♣ K, which W killed with the ace and W made the bright return of the ♠ 2!

S next won two trump leads, but could not afford a third one lest the enemy cash diamonds; so dummy played the ♡ K then ♡ A on which S parked one diamond, but W ruffed and scored a diamond and the ♣ Q to break the contract.

HOLD

Greed to save those little trumps in dummy were S's undoing—or possibly a failure in analysis coupled with 'automatic' play. The proper holding play is to lead a trump to Trick 2 and duck! This leaves one trump in dummy to stop diamonds while letting opponents score their natural trump trick at once. E wins the trump lead and shifts to clubs to let W pick off the king, but declarer loses only that one trump and the two clubs. When he gets in, he draws trumps and runs hearts uninterruptedly for plenty of discards.

Declarer needs only *one* diamond ruff in dummy against the normal 3–2 split in enemy trumps.

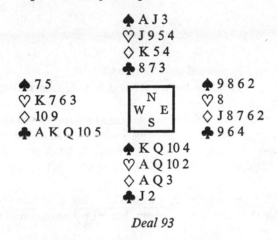

♠ A J 3
♡ J 9 5 4
◇ K 5 4
♣ 8 7 3

♠ 7 5
♡ K 7 6 3
◇ 10 9
♣ A K Q 10 5

♠ 9 8 6 2
♡ 8
◇ J 8 7 6 2
♣ 9 6 4

♠ K Q 10 4
♡ A Q 10 2
◇ A Q 3
♣ J 2

Deal 93

S bid 1 ♠, W 2 ♣, N 2 ♠; S 3 ♡, and N 4 ♡.*
W led the ♣ K, ♣ Q, then ♣ A.
How do you plan the play?

S ruffed the third club lead then led the ♡ A then ♡ Q which W let win. E discarded, revealing the bad trump split, and S found himself in boiling oil. He dared not lead another trump lest W win and push a club to force dummy's last trump. Declarer shifted to spades, but W ruffed the third spade lead and his ♡ K was the fourth and setting trick for his side.

The holding play is to lead the ♡ Q to Trick 4 in order to guard against the possible bad 4–1 trump split. W lets the ♡ Q win, so S pushes the ♡ 10 next. If W wins this and returns a club, S ruffs high to unblock and let *dummy* (entered by ◇ K) draw trumps. If W ducks the ♡ 10 also, S cashes the ♡ A and forces out W's now blank master trump with spade leads.

*SAB: S should open 1 ♡, W 2 ♣, N 2 ♡; S 2 ♠ and N 4 ♡, end.

117

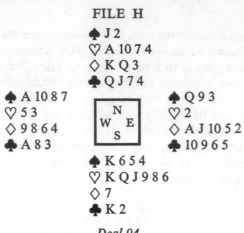

♠ J 2
♡ A 10 7 4
◇ K Q 3
♣ Q J 7 4

♠ A 10 8 7
♡ 5 3
◇ 9 8 6 4
♣ A 8 3

♠ Q 9 3
♡ 2
◇ A J 10 5 2
♣ 10 9 6 5

♠ K 6 5 4
♡ K Q J 9 8 6
◇ 7
♣ K 2

Deal 94

S bid 1 ♡ and N jumped to 4 ♡ (Acol).*

W led the ◇ 4, forcing the queen and ace. E returned the ◇ J. How do you plan the play?

S parked a club on the ◇ J and let it ride to dummy's king. S drew trumps and led the ♣ K, which W won with his ace and W returned a club. Dummy scored two club tricks which let S get rid of two spades, but S eventually lost two more spades, which cooked his goose.

If S discards a spade instead of a club at Trick 2, he later gets only one spade discard on dummy's promoted club honours and still has to lose two spade tricks.

The point at the crucial Trick 2 is that S *does not know what to discard*. Hence he should defer his discard and ruff the ◇ J ! Next he draws trumps and leads a *low* club from his own hand. This 'fixes' W.

If W 'flies' with his ace, later S gets two spade discards on dummy's top clubs and *another* spade discard on the ◇ K.

If W ducks the club lead, dummy wins. Next dummy cashes the ◇ K for the *club* discard! S can afford to lose two spade tricks later but W goes to bed with his ace of clubs. Whatever W does, S makes ten tricks if he ruffs the second diamond and leads the small club.

---

* N might well bid 2 ♣ and, over 2 ♡, bid 4 ♡—the 'delayed game raise'. —Editor.

HOLD

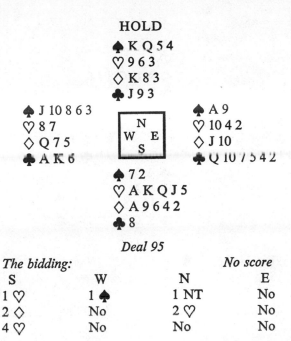

♠ K Q 5 4
♥ 9 6 3
◇ K 8 3
♣ J 9 3

♠ J 10 8 6 3
♥ 8 7
◇ Q 7 5
♣ A K 6

♠ A 9
♥ 10 4 2
◇ J 10
♣ Q 10 7 5 4 2

♠ 7 2
♥ A K Q J 5
◇ A 9 6 4 2
♣ 8

Deal 95

The bidding: No score

S	W	N	E
1 ♥	1 ♠	1 NT	No
2 ◇	No	2 ♥	No
4 ♥	No	No	No

W led the king, then ace of clubs, and S ruffed. S drew trumps in three leads and lost the third diamond lead to W who returned a club, punching out S's last trump. S scored two stiff diamonds, but when he led a spade to set up a spade trick in dummy, the royal couple there was lost, for the queen fell on the ace—inconsiderately and unexpectedly with E, who cashed his long club to break the contract.

At Trick 3 S may lead trumps once; then his plan is to establish a spade trick, ruff E's club return, then make the holding play of *losing* a diamond trick immediately by ducking!*

Now a fourth club lead from E lets *dummy* ruff and keeps S's trumps intact, and any other return lets declarer get in to draw trumps and run his spade and diamond tricks for game.

Note the trap in diamonds: If N wins the first diamond and S ducks the second round, W overtakes E's honour and returns a diamond for E to ruff. If declarer plays diamonds ace, king, then low, E discards his spade and W leads a spade for E to ruff. Declarer must duck the first round to preserve the hand from adverse ruffs in any suit.

* To play E for ♥ 10 is, admittedly, a risk; but it is the chance to take against the certainty of going down.—Editor.

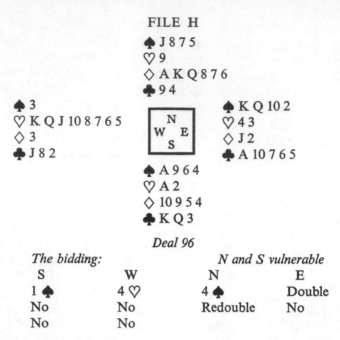

FILE H

```
                ♠ J 8 7 5
                ♡ 9
                ◇ A K Q 8 7 6
                ♣ 9 4
♠ 3                            ♠ K Q 10 2
♡ K Q J 10 8 7 6 5    N       ♡ 4 3
◇ 3               W       E   ◇ J 2
♣ J 8 2               S       ♣ A 10 7 6 5
                ♠ A 9 6 4
                ♡ A 2
                ◇ 10 9 5 4
                ♣ K Q 3
```

Deal 96

The bidding:			N and S vulnerable
S	W	N	E
1 ♠	4 ♡	4 ♠	Double
No	No	Redouble	No
No	No		

E was a fish to double 4 ♠, for his trumps were wrongly placed *under* declarer's, and W's 4 ♡ pre-empt showed nothing to offer E in the way of defensive tricks. E needed at least four defensive tricks, preferably five, in his own hand for a sound double; and the poor fish had only two.

But E knew S was a rabbit who would probably lose a trick or two in the play! Experience has proven that it is dangerous to play someone for a 'sucker', for you are apt to end up being the biggest fish of all! However, it didn't work out that way in this case.

Oblivious of pitfalls, S assumed two trump losers against a normal 3–2 enemy split and the ♣ A. S ignored the inference to be drawn from the double—four trumps with E—and wanted to get trumps out fast lest a diamond be ruffed.

S butchered the hand quickly. He won the ♡ K lead with the ace which was right, laid down the ace of trumps which was wrong, and led another trump, which was horrible. The hand collapsed completely.

S did not win any more tricks. Not one. E drew trumps, cashed the

♣ A, and led a heart to let W get seven heart tricks! E and W won eleven tricks for 4,600 points!

The correct holding play of leading a LOW trump at Trick 2 makes game and rubber for plus 1,230 points instead of minus 4,600, a net swing of 5,830 points!

S leads a low trump to Trick 2, inserts dummy's ♠ 8 and E wins with the ten. Dummy ruffs the heart return, leads the ♠ J which E covers and declarer . . . ducks! Another holding play. A heart return by E would make trouble but E is now out of the suit. Dummy gets in later with a diamond to let declarer lead dummy's ♠ 7 and overtake with the ♠ 9, clean out E's trumps, and run diamonds.

We have paid through the nose for partners who made similar blunders, and you can probably recall pet grouses of your own.

This deal and the next come from *End-plays in Bridge Taxonomy*, the author's article in the December 1952 issue of *The European Bridge Review*.

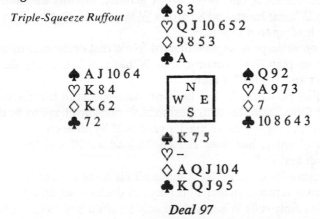

Triple-Squeeze Ruffout

Deal 97

This deal was reported by Eric Jannersten, Editor of that international magazine, in the October 1952 issue. It occurred in a team-of-four match between Germany and Sweden.

At both tables S played at 4 ◇. He made it easily at one table when W opened the ♠ A.

At the other table, W made things difficult by opening the ◇ 2 which dummy won with the nine. Next plays were the ♣ A, ◇ A, and three top club tricks on which both W and dummy shed spades.

Next dummy ruffed a spade and S a heart, leaving this bizarre ending:

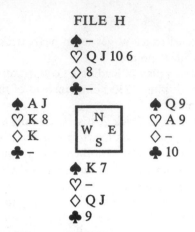

```
              ♠ —
              ♡ Q J 10 6
              ◇ 8
              ♣ —
  ♠ A J                    ♠ Q 9
  ♡ K 8        ┌───┐       ♡ A 9
  ◇ K        W │ N │ E     ◇ —
  ♣ —          │ S │       ♣ 10
               └───┘
              ♠ K 7
              ♡ —
              ◇ Q J
              ♣ 9
```

If N were on lead, two heart ruffs and a spade ruff bring home the three desired tricks. But *S* is on lead.

S leads the club, which triple squeezes W!

If W ruffs, school is out. If W drops a heart, N ruffs the club, S ruffs away W's last heart, and S throws W in with the ◇ K in order to force the lead up to S's ♠ K.

So—W's only escape is a spade discard. Note that declarer cannot decide what to play from dummy until W has acted. Dummy discards a heart and E wins his club.

This holding play fixes E, but he is not end-played in the classic sense of the three basic throw-in positions. E does not have to lead up to a tenace, nor a suit to its master card held by an enemy otherwise devoid of entry, nor does E have to lead a stiff suit to give declarer a ruff and sluff.

A heart return by E would let S make all his three trumps separately, so E must return a spade. This play lets declarer set up a good spade when dummy ruffs W's now bare ace. S ruffs a heart and leads his good ♠ K to force W.

The preparatory squeeze and throw-in plays simply culminate in a straightforward suit establishment play.

File I

INFERENCE

I stands for Inference. Plays filed here are based on drawing inferences from enemy bids and/or plays in order to locate specific cards. The complementary type consists of negative inferences drawn from the *failure* of an opponent to make a specific bid or play. These negative inferences are often overlooked in the heat of the game.

Suppose W opens 1 $\diamondsuit$, N and E pass, and S winds up at 4 $\spadesuit$; suppose, further, that during the early play E produces a king and a knave. E can hold nothing more in high cards, or he would have responded to W's opening bid. Hence W must hold all outstanding honours.

The degree of clarity in such inferences varies widely. An inference may be as obvious as a heavy chain, stout enough to moor a St. Bernard dog; or as obscure as the microscopic filament of the primary mycclium of a fungus. In the latter case the clue may be thin and open to technical challenge.

One feature of play too often stepmotherly treated in textbooks lies in the inferences you can draw from the normal fall of small cards. Note this position:

Dummy $\diamondsuit$ 9 7 6

You $\diamondsuit$ Q J 10   Partner $\diamondsuit$ 5 2

Declarer $\diamondsuit$ A K ?

Suppose declarer played the $\diamondsuit$ A and $\diamondsuit$ K while your partner played the $\diamondsuit$ 2 and $\diamondsuit$ 5.

Who holds the $\diamondsuit$ 4 and $\diamondsuit$ 3?

If E held either or both these cards, he would have played one on the second lead, NOT the five; and inference marks both four and three with declarer.

Furthermore, your partner played the deuce first. He did not peter to show a doubleton, so the *negative* inference is that he holds *more than two* diamond cards.

The only diamond not accounted for is the eight, which your partner must hold.

The information that declarer held ◊ A K 4 3 may be vital to you if declarer tries to pull off a pseudo-squeeze or other deceptive play in the end.

Watch the fall of those small cards like a hawk, for they will tell many stories. Often the information will have academic value only, but if you don't make a practice of following the spots, your cheque-book will have a spotty career.

The element of inference in play is adjunctive like Counting, Deception, Percentage and Safety-Play. By this we mean that there is no such thing as a pure inference play, for the inference is a sub-ordinate factor which guides the play, basically of another file, into winning channels. Plays are filed under I for Inference only when the element of inference is outstanding.

Inference and Counting are closely related. Inference furnishes a deduction that is not absolute or complete on account of the possi-bility of a wrong enemy bid or play. On the other hand, counting furnishes data that are usually more accurate and final. Inference and Counting sometimes appear synonymous. In such cases if the infer-ence is responsible for getting a tentative count on enemy holdings, the deal should be filed under Inference.

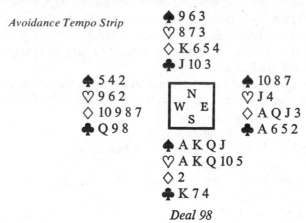

Avoidance Tempo Strip

```
                  ♠ 9 6 3
                  ♡ 8 7 3
                  ◊ K 6 5 4
                  ♣ J 10 3
  ♠ 5 4 2                      ♠ 10 8 7
  ♡ 9 6 2         N            ♡ J 4
  ◊ 10 9 8 7    W   E          ◊ A Q J 3
  ♣ Q 9 8         S            ♣ A 6 5 2
                  ♠ A K Q J
                  ♡ A K Q 10 5
                  ◊ 2
                  ♣ K 7 4
```

Deal 98

E bid 1 ◊, S 2 ♡, N 2 NT; and S 4 ♡.*
W led the ◊ 10.

With nine fast tricks in the majors, how do you promote your tenth trick?

SAB: E opens 1 ◊, S double, W 2 ◊; S 3 ♡, N 3 NT; and S passes or says 4 ♡.

Declarer let the ◇ 10 hold, W next led the ◇ 7, dummy ducked again and S ruffed. S drew trumps and took three spade tricks, leaving:

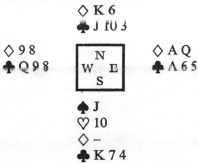

```
                    ◇ K 6
                    ♣ J 10 3
  ◇ 9 8                          ◇ A Q
  ♣ Q 9 8          N             ♣ A 6 5
                 W   E
                    S
                    ♠ J
                    ♡ 10
                    ◇ -
                    ♣ K 7 4
```

S then ruinously cashed his last winner, the spade knave, which squeezed dummy. Next S led a low club which W's queen won, and W returned a diamond which forced S's last trump. Declarer led another low club and E won the last two tricks to break the contract.

S played well until he reached the ending, but at Trick 9 he should withhold the fourth spade, which inflicts a suicidal squeeze on dummy.

Also, S must try to keep W out of the lead once while working on clubs in order to protect dummy's ◇ K from attack by W.

The inference is plain. E opened the bidding and must hold both missing aces and at least one queen. You know he holds ◇ Q.

To Trick 9 S should lead his ♣ K, which E wins. Now E cannot attack dummy's ◇ K. A club return sets up declarer's tenth trick at once, so E's better defence is to lay down the ◇ A which S ruffs. Again S must restrain any idea of cashing his damaging spade winner lest he squeeze dummy. S pushes another club. W scores his queen but N gets the ◇ K and a club.

If E holds the ♣ Q instead of a low club in the ending, it matters not whether S leads the ♣ K or a low club at Trick 9; but the ♣ K lead is vital in the actual case when the ♣ Q lies with W.

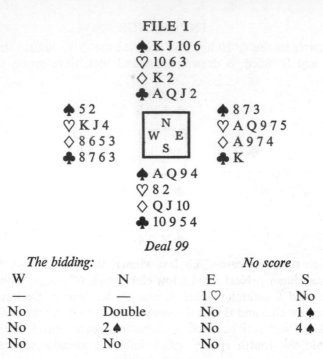

♠ K J 10 6
♡ 10 6 3
◇ K 2
♣ A Q J 2

♠ 5 2
♡ K J 4
◇ 8 6 5 3
♣ 8 7 6 3

♠ 8 7 3
♡ A Q 9 7 5
◇ A 9 7 4
♣ K

♠ A Q 9 4
♡ 8 2
◇ Q J 10
♣ 10 9 5 4

Deal 99

The bidding:			*No score*
W	N	E	S
—	—	1 ♡	No
No	Double	No	1 ♠
No	2 ♠	No	4 ♠
No	No	No	

W led the ♡ K, then ♡ J which E overtook with the ace, and E led the queen which S ruffed high. How do you plan the play?

To Trick 4 S led a diamond to the king which E won and returned a trump which S won, and S drew trumps.

Next declarer finessed the ♣ 10 which lost the fourth trick and game with it.

The negative inference of W's pass to E's opening 1 ♡ bid is the clue to playing the ♣ A to drop the bare king. W showed ♡ K J 4 in the play, and if he also had the ♣ K, he would have responded to E's opening bid. Hence E must hold the ♣ K and declarer's only chance to catch it is singleton by playing the ace at once.

INFERENCE

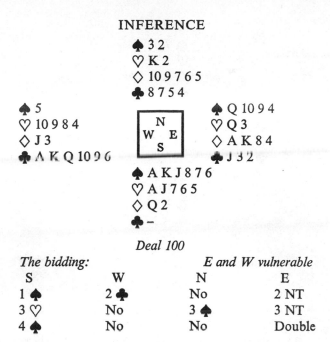

```
              ♠ 3 2
              ♡ K 2
              ◇ 10 9 7 6 5
              ♣ 8 7 5 4
♠ 5                              ♠ Q 10 9 4
♡ 10 9 8 4         N            ♡ Q 3
◇ J 3          W       E        ◇ A K 8 4
♣ A K Q 10 9 6     S            ♣ J 3 2
              ♠ A K J 8 7 6
              ♡ A J 7 6 5
              ◇ Q 2
              ♣ –
```

Deal 100

The bidding:		E and W vulnerable	
S	W	N	E
1 ♠	2 ♣	No	2 NT
3 ♡	No	3 ♠	3 NT
4 ♠	No	No	Double

W led the ♣ K. How do you play?

This deal might be called the case of two inferences, for S found himself sandwiched in the powerful jaws of strong enemy bidding on both sides. W bid clubs at the two level vulnerable, marking him with a powerful club suit; and the repeated no-trump bids by E marked the balance of missing high cards there.

S ruffed the club opening, entered dummy via the ♡ K, and S finessed the ♠ J to win. Next, the ♡ A dropped the queen and dummy trumped a low heart, which E over-ruffed. E took his two diamond tricks then forced S with a club. S drew trumps and scored the balance for game.

Declarer must plan a heart ruff in dummy, and E's over-ruff did no harm, for it used up E's natural trump trick.

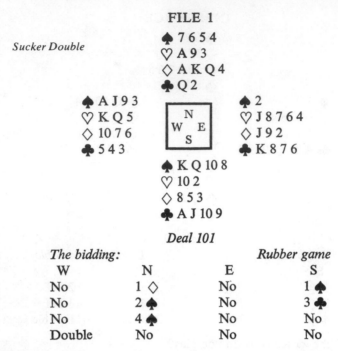

FILE 1

Sucker Double

♠ 7 6 5 4
♡ A 9 3
♢ A K Q 4
♣ Q 2

♠ A J 9 3   ♠ 2
♡ K Q 5   ♡ J 8 7 6 4
♢ 10 7 6   ♢ J 9 2
♣ 5 4 3   ♣ K 8 7 6

♠ K Q 10 8
♡ 10 2
♢ 8 5 3
♣ A J 10 9

Deal 101

The bidding:			*Rubber game*
W	N	E	S
No	1 ♢	No	1 ♠
No	2 ♠	No	3 ♣
No	4 ♠	No	No
Double	No	No	No

W was a fish to double, for he gave S the clue by which to fulfil a contract which would normally fail.

W led the ♡ K which the ace in dummy won.

How do you plan the play? This one is not easy.

To Trick 2 the ♣ Q finesse wins, and E must have the ♣ K to give S any chance. Next declarer must risk all on cashing three diamonds at once and the suit breaks 3–3 luckily. S finesses the ♣ J and lays down the ♣ A on which dummy sheds a heart, but the ♣ K fails to drop.

To Trick 8 S leads his last club, W ruffs with the ♠ 9 and dummy sheds a heart. Dummy ruffs the heart return, and S gets two more trump tricks.

If W sheds a heart at Trick 8, dummy ruffs and returns the stiff diamond, and S sheds the heart whether or not E trumps, in order to ensure two tricks on the trump end-play.

INFERENCE

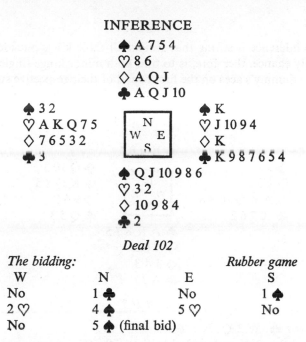

♠ A 7 5 4
♡ 8 6
◊ A Q J
♣ A Q J 10

♠ 3 2
♡ A K Q 7 5
◊ 7 6 5 3 2
♣ 3

♠ K
♡ J 10 9 4
◊ K
♣ K 9 8 7 6 5 4

♠ Q J 10 9 8 6
♡ 3 2
◊ 10 9 8 4
♣ 2

Deal 102

The bidding:			*Rubber game*
W	N	E	S
No	1 ♣	No	1 ♠
2 ♡	4 ♠	5 ♡	No
No	5 ♠ (final bid)		

N would be better advised to double 5 ♡ for a sure profit rather than to push on to 5 ♠; but he felt that the penalty at best would be small and that his side had a fair chance to win eleven tricks.

W led the ♡ A, ♡ K, and shifted to the ♣ 3.

It is easy when you see all four hands, but declarer did not have that advantage. He won Trick 3 with the ♣ A. He reckoned that he needed some lucky finessing, and returned the ♣ Q from dummy to Trick 4, E covered with the king, S ruffed and W discarded. S properly deduced that W's failure to over-ruff meant that E held the ♠ K, so S led a high trump to dummy's ♠ A, dropping it blank—the only hope. Next S won another trump in his own hand and returned the ♠ 6 to dummy's ♠ 7 and S parked two diamonds on the clubs, which were not enough discards. So S returned to his own hand via dummy's last trump and tried the diamond finesse, which lost to E's second bare king; and that was the end of the party for S.

S missed a simple inference. E can be counted with seven clubs and one spade. He had four hearts for he echoed on the opening leads. W passed originally, but came in on the second round vulnerable showing a fine heart suit, and produced the ace and king of hearts in the play. *If W had held any side suit king, he would have made an opening bid.*

The inference is strong that E held all three kings outside hearts. S's only chance, therefore, is to find both minor kings singleton and to play dummy's aces on the first round of their respective suits.

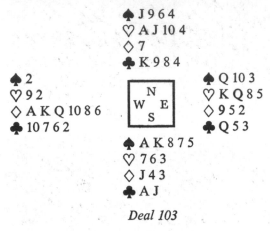

	♠ J 9 6 4	
	♡ A J 10 4	
	◇ 7	
	♣ K 9 8 4	
♠ 2		♠ Q 10 3
♡ 9 2		♡ K Q 8 5
◇ A K Q 10 8 6		◇ 9 5 2
♣ 10 7 6 2		♣ Q 5 3
	♠ A K 8 7 5	
	♡ 7 6 3	
	◇ J 4 3	
	♣ A J	

Deal 103

S bid 1 ♠, W 2 ◇, N 3 ♠; and S 4 ♠.

W led the ◇ K and shifted to the ♡ 9.

Declarer finessed the ♡ 10 which E won, and E shifted back to diamonds and dummy ruffed. S laid down the ♠ A and ♠ K, and the queen failed to fall.

Having lost a heart finesse and a diamond, and with a sure trump loser to come, declarer must win the balance. He can try a second heart finesse, or finesse the ♣ J and get a heart discard on the third club, but—which line is better?

If W had led another diamond at Trick 2, declarer would have finessed hearts twice and lost the game. The odds are 3 to 1 that the missing heart honours are divided or both with W whereas the ♣ J finesse offers only a 50% chance.

However, that ♡ 9 lead let declarer draw inferences which set him on the right track. The ♡ 9 lead looked like the top of nothing, offering the view that E held both heart honours. So to Trick 6 dummy ruffed the diamond, S finessed the ♣ J to win, cashed the ♣ A; and the ♡ A put dummy on lead to score the ♣ K for a heart discard.

Alternate play with less percentage is to refuse the ♣ J finesse at Trick 7. Win ♣ A, ♣ K, a club ruff; then lose a trump to E to force him to return a heart up to dummy's ace-knave.

INFERENCE

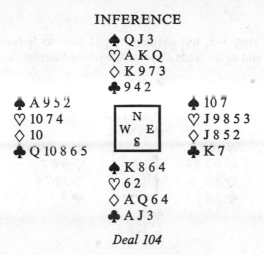

♠ Q J 3
♡ A K Q
◇ K 9 7 3
♣ 9 4 2

♠ A 9 5 2
♡ 10 7 4
◇ 10
♣ Q 10 8 6 5

♠ 10 7
♡ J 9 8 5 3
◇ J 8 5 2
♣ K 7

♠ K 8 6 4
♡ 6 2
◇ A Q 6 4
♣ A J 3

Deal 104

S bid 1 ◇, N 3 ◇; and S 3 NT. *

It is pointless for S to bid 3 ♠ over 3 ◇, for if N holds any kind of knave-high four-card or better spade suit, he should bid it before supporting diamonds.

W led the ♣ 6 and E put up his king.

Do you hold up the ♣ A?

Declarer notes seven tricks on top if diamonds are sour, otherwise eight; hence he needs a spade trick (or two) to get home.

Declarer is faced with a choice of combinations. Does W hold four, five or six clubs? Who has the ♠ A?

The ♣ A hold-up is immaterial against four or six clubs with W. If W has four clubs, his side gets only three club tricks and the ♠ A. If W has six clubs, E's king is a singleton. If S wins it, the ♣ J is a safe second stopper; or if S holds up, E must shift.

The problem boils down to five clubs with W. If W has the ♠ A, S must win the ♣ K in order to stop clubs again; but if E holds the ♠ A, S must hold up the ♣ A to exhaust E of clubs when he gets in later with the ♠ A.

Who holds the ♠ A?

A subtle clue indicates it is more likely to lie with W. If W held five straggly clubs with no side entry, he would prefer to open a short major suit against a no-trumper.

S wins Trick 1 with the ♣ A, returns a low spade which W ducks and dummy wins. Next plays are the ◇ K and ◇ A in order to cinch the game just in case E might have the ♠ A and held up with dia-

---

*SAB: S 1◇, N 1♡; S 1♠, N 3◇; and S 3 NT. N's delayed jump to 3◇ is a strong bid, asking S to bid 3 NT if he can stop clubs.

131

monds breaking 3–2, but diamonds split 4–1, so S needs **another** spade trick and again leads a low spade toward dummy's honour.

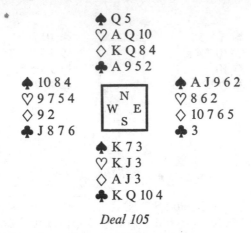

Deal 105

S bid 1 NT vulnerable, N 5 NT, and S 6 NT. N's jump to 5 NT was a small slam force, showing a combined partnership count of exactly thirty-three points, based on sixteen points for S's vulnerable opener.

W led the ♠ 4, dummy played the queen and E won with his ace. E returned the ♠ 2 which S won, and W played the eight.

Declarer counted eleven tricks on top plus a twelfth in clubs if they split 3–2, or if the knave, if well-guarded, could be located.

S ran four diamond tricks on which W shed a spade and a heart. Next S cashed three hearts, and all followed suit. So far, so good.

S counted four diamonds and three hearts with E. E had won the spade opening with the ace and returned the deuce, so S thought E might have started life with only two spades, hence four clubs. S won the ♣ K then ♣ A only to find the elusive knave in W for the setting trick.

The fault of S's inference lay in spades. If E held ♠ A 2, W started with ♠ J 10 9 8 6 4 and W would have opened the knave, not the six. Hence E must hold more than two spades, making four clubs impossible in his hand so the only danger was four clubs with W. This involved W in having led from a three-timer—but against a six bid, such leads are preferred to opening from J x x x.

Another inference was W's spade discard on the third diamond trick. Why should W discard a good spade unless he was protecting clubs—unless, which would be over-subtle of S to suppose, this was a double-cross. In fact, of course, E's being marked with spade length is the inescapable clue from which the winning inference is to be drawn.

Among the papers of my grandfather, William H. Coffin of Port-ledge, Clovelly, I unearthed a curious problem of deduction at whist which he collected in 1888. The opening play enabled South to place every card of a suit—quite a feat in those days when there was no dummy hand and the play was blind.

Modern bridge players should be able to solve this problem, offered for the beautiful manner in which *four* negative inferences fit together and yield an exact count of an entire suit.

One clue is given. In whist an encouraging card is used in the opening play only to ask partner to lead trumps. A condition of the problem is that N is weak in trumps, spades.

$$\heartsuit\ 8$$
$$\heartsuit\ 6 \qquad\qquad \heartsuit\ 9$$
$$\heartsuit\ J\ 7\ 3$$

W leads the $\heartsuit$ 6, N plays the eightspot, E the nine, and S wins with the knave. S started with $\heartsuit$ J 7 3.

S can place all the hearts. *Where are they?*

The Rule of Eleven enables S to mark W with three of the four missing honours, A, K, Q and 10.

W's only proper fourth best lead must be from A Q 10 6, for W would have led an honour from A K Q, A K 10, or K Q 10.

E would have played the king 'third hand high' if he held it, hence the nine is E's best heart and N holds the king.

N *failed* to play the deuce, four or five; therefore he holds none of these cards. N started with K 8 doubleton.

Finally, with five or more hearts W would have led the ace 'lest the mice get it' and not the six. Therefore E must hold the missing tail cards, the 5, 4 and 2. The full picture is:

$$\heartsuit\ K\ 8$$
$$\heartsuit\ A\ Q\ 10\ 6 \qquad\qquad \heartsuit\ 9\ 5\ 4\ 2$$
$$\heartsuit\ J\ 7\ 3$$

File J

JETTISON

J stands for Jettison. This nautical term means to throw cargo overboard to lighten an endangered ship. Also, jetsam is the non-floating part of the cargo so jettisoned, as opposed to flotsam. The late Norman J. Bonney, United States National Champion of 1930, formally introduced the term 'jettison' to the language of bridge in America, specifically to indicate the discard of a blocking winner, a *heavy* card such as an ace or a king as a rule, in order to save a hand from foundering.*

Unfortunately some non-academically minded bridge-writers have taken liberties with this precise term and incorrectly used 'jettison' as a simple synonym for any sort of discard.

Jettisons form a unique section in the tribe of gambit plays, and the character of discarding a winner separates them from the gambits proper. Jettisons are rare and spectacular, except in double-dummy problems; and they are regarded as curiosities whenever they occur during the rub of the green of actual play.

The tribe of jettisons has three *genera*, based on characteristic aims: pure jettisons, made to hold the lead and run the jettison suit; those to unblock and create a re-entry in the jettison suit; and those to avoid an enemy ruff.

* 'Jettison' was applied to (auction) bridge in 1921 by the late A. E. Whitelaw ('Pachabo').—Editor.

JETTISON

Genus I—Lead-holding Jettisons

Matrix pura

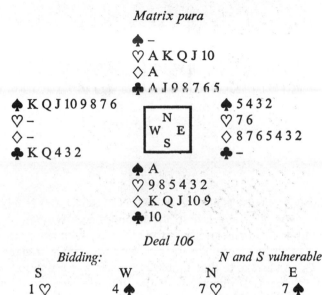

```
                    ♠ –
                    ♡ A K Q J 10
                    ◇ A
                    ♣ A J 9 8 7 6 5
♠ K Q J 10 9 8 7 6        ┌──────┐        ♠ 5 4 3 2
♡ –                      │  N   │        ♡ 7 6
◇ –                      │ W   E│        ◇ 8 7 6 5 4 3 2
♣ K Q 4 3 2              │  S   │        ♣ –
                         └──────┘
                    ♠ A
                    ♡ 9 8 5 4 3 2
                    ◇ K Q J 10 9
                    ♣ 10
```

Deal 106

Bidding: N and S vulnerable

S	W	N	E
1 ♡	4 ♠	7 ♡	7 ♠
7 NT	Double	Redouble	

S's bid of 7 NT is not so bad as it looks. Clearly on the 7 ♡ bid N must have the top hearts and a void in spades, for S himself holds the ♠ A.

W opened the ♠ K and dummy jettisoned the ◇ A. Next S won five diamond tricks while dummy made the quintuple jettison of his 150 honours in hearts. This let S score six heart tricks for his redoubled grand slam.

W can break the contract by opening a club honour, but W needed the services of a voodoo doctor or a crystal ball to envisage such a lead. This deal is illustrative rather than actual—but it may not be impossible.

FILE J

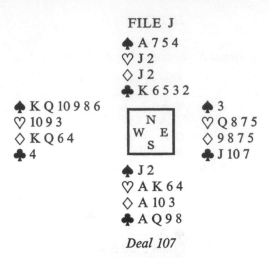

♠ A 7 5 4
♡ J 2
◇ J 2
♣ K 6 5 3 2

♠ K Q 10 9 8 6   ♠ 3
♡ 10 9 3   ♡ Q 8 7 5
◇ K Q 6 4   ◇ 9 8 7 5
♣ 4   ♣ J 10 7

♠ J 2
♡ A K 6 4
◇ A 10 3
♣ A Q 9 8

Deal 107

Vulnerable, S bid 1 NT, W 2 ♠, N 2 NT; S 3 ♡ and N 3 NT. W led the ♠ K. Do you hold up dummy's ace? Why?

S rapidly counted nine tricks on top and played dummy's ace without even bothering to consider a routine hold-up. Next he won the ♣ A and ♣ Q, and awoke to find something rotten in clubs despite their normal 3–1 break. If dummy wins the third club lead to draw E's last, the suit is hopelessly blocked.

S got a bright idea. Why not jettison a club on an enemy spade lead? So S led a spade to let W cash four spade tricks while S parked a club; but W started life with six spades and collected *five* spade tricks to beat the hand.

The bright idea came too late. Dummy must duck the spade opening, and duck another spade lead. Now dummy's 'double duty' ace not only scores a trick in its own right but also brings in that fifth club by letting S jettison his blocking card in the suit.

If W shifts at Trick 2, S wins and returns a spade for the enemy to win. Again, this lets dummy's ace win the third spade lead for the club jettison. A diamond lead sets up the ninth trick in that suit; and on a heart lead, S should hold off once to develop a possible squeeze against W for an extra trick. If W leads the ♥ 10 to Trick 2, the knave and queen cover and S holds up. Now E must return a diamond in order to break up a spade-diamond squeeze against W at the end.

JETTISON

Genus II—Entry-creating Jettisons

Hidden Entry

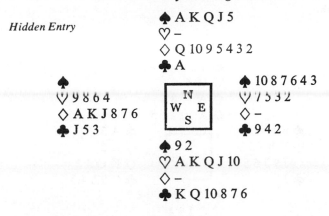

♠ A K Q J 5
♡ –
◇ Q 10 9 5 4 3 2
♣ A

♠
♡ 9 8 6 4
◇ A K J 8 7 6
♣ J 5 3

♠ 10 8 7 6 4 3
♡ 7 5 3 2
◇ –
♣ 9 4 2

♠ 9 2
♡ A K Q J 10
◇ –
♣ K Q 10 8 7 6

Deal 108

The bidding:		E and W game in	
S	W	N	E
1 ♣	1 ◇	Double	1 ♠
2 ♡	No	3 NT	No
6 ♡	No	No	No

S's bidding is very doubtful: he ought to fear two spade losers on top. But it is the play that matters.

W led the ◇ K and E put on his best trump, hoping to get the trick or at least to force a high trump from S and so promote a trump trick for W. S over-ruffed.

S drew trumps in four leads, on which dummy cast off diamonds and jettisoned the ♣ A. Next S played the ♣ K and ♣ Q, but the knave failed to drop, so S tried the court of last resort in spades, but E held the ten defended, as was to be expected by his spade bid, so the hand concluded with a spade loser and a diamond loser.

S neglected the *nine of spades* as the key card to score his slam. N must make the quadruple jettison of ♠ A K Q J on S's trump leads! Dummy enters via the ♣ A and returns a spade, and E can score his ten now or later as he pleases—the only trick for his side.

The ♠ 10 is marked with E by his spade call and the hand makes against any doubleton knave club holding as does the ♣ A jettison plan, and also against any ♣ J x x holding as above.

FILE J

This is an extremely unusual play which smacks rather of the midnight oil than a casual rubber—but it is none the less far and away the best shot.

Genus III—Ruff-avoiding Jettisons

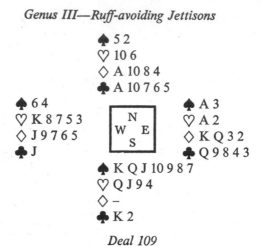

```
                    ♠ 5 2
                    ♡ 10 6
                    ◇ A 10 8 4
                    ♣ A 10 7 6 5
    ♠ 6 4                              ♠ A 3
    ♡ K 8 7 5 3         N             ♡ A 2
    ◇ J 9 7 6 5    W        E         ◇ K Q 3 2
    ♣ J                S             ♣ Q 9 8 4 3
                    ♠ K Q J 10 9 8 7
                    ♡ Q J 9 4
                    ◇ —
                    ♣ K 2
```

Deal 109

E bid 1 ♣ and S 4 ♠.

W led the ♣ J. How do you bag game?

S murdered the hand quickly. He won the club lead with the ace in dummy and led a trump which E grabbed with the ace. E returned a club and W ruffed the king of clubs.

Superficially the ♣ K appears alive enough, but declarer overlooked the fact that he was really very dead on account of the pending adverse ruff. Declarer couldn't eat the ace and king of hearts and went down one on a hand that is almost a pianola.

Even at bridge you cannot expect to get away with murder—unless you dispose of the *corpus delicti*. To Trick 2 declarer must jettison the corpse of the ♣ K on the ◇ A! So with no corpse, you have committed no murder! Note that S is lucky enough as it is: if E wins the first round of spades and leads ace and another heart, dummy's ♠ 5 shuts out E's ♠ 3 . . . unless S was foolish enough to lead it to Trick 3.

Elementary, isn't it, my dear Watson?*

---

* Referring, not to Sherlock's *fidus Achates* but to a bridge immortal, the late Louis H. Watson who, in 1934, wrote America's top bridge book, *Watson on Play*. It is now out of print and rare, and used copies currently bring five guineas each.—G. C.

JETTISON

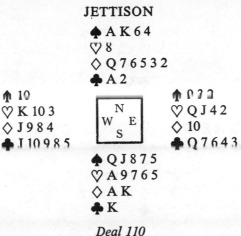

♠ A K 6 4
♥ 8
♦ Q 7 6 5 3 2
♣ A 2

♠ 10
♥ K 10 3
♦ J 9 8 4
♣ J 10 9 8 5

♠ 0 7 2
♥ Q J 4 2
♦ 10
♣ Q 7 6 4 3

♠ Q J 8 7 5
♥ A 9 7 6 5
♦ A K
♣ K

Deal 110

S bid 1 ♠, and after a lot of fancy bidding all round the mulberry bush, S landed in 7 ♠.

W led the ♣ J.

How do you plan to bring in dummy's diamonds?

S won the ♣ J, drew trumps in three leads, and played off the ♦ A and ♦ K only to find the bad 4–1 split with only one entry left in dummy. Diamonds could not be cleared *and* scored. Later dummy ruffed a low heart and the ♦ Q and ♣ A in dummy let S park two low hearts, but he was unable to eat his fourth heart loser.

To score his slam S wins the club opening, ♠ Q and ♦ A. Next dummy wins the ♠ A and ♣ A to let S jettison the ♦ K! S ruffs a diamond, N wins the third trump lead drawing trumps, and S ruffs another low diamond to make dummy high.

S's losing line catered only for a 3–2 diamond split, whereas the proper play caters also for the not unusual 4–1 division.

139

FILE J

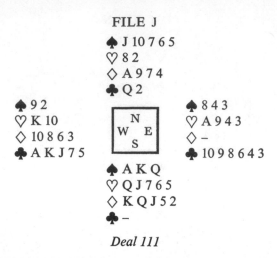

♠ J 10 7 6 5
♡ 8 2
◇ A 9 7 4
♣ Q 2

♠ 9 2
♡ K 10
◇ 10 8 6 3
♣ A K J 7 5

♠ 8 4 3
♡ A 9 4 3
◇ -
♣ 10 9 8 6 4 3

♠ A K Q
♡ Q J 7 6 5
◇ K Q J 5 2
♣ -

Deal 111

S bid 1 ♡, W 2 ♣, E 5 ♣; S 5 ◇, and W doubled.

W led the ♣ K. How do you plan the play?

E's tremendous jump raise in clubs suggested a void—probably in diamonds; so S managed trumps accordingly.

S ruffed high the ♣ K and laid down a diamond honour; E's failure confirmed S's suspicion.

Establishing hearts looked remote so S decided to play on spades, needing a 3–2 split to get home. So S won two spade tricks, and led a low trump. W inserted the eight topped by dummy's nine. Next S ruffed high dummy's club and returned his last carefully saved low trump and dummy finessed the seven. Next comes the ◇ A to draw W's last trump and let S jettison the blocking spade. Declarer loses two heart tricks at the end, but that is all.

If declarer uses a *low* trump to ruff a club, W can throw a monkey-wrench into the hand. This consists of the ten of trumps, injected when S leads his low trump. This hand is a combination of Reverse-dummy and Jettison.

File K

KNOCK

K stands for Knock. A knock is a drop play which takes advantage of a singleton or poorly guarded enemy winner. However, an ordinary play such as laying down an ace and king in such a suit as:

Dummy   10 8 6 4
Declarer   A K J 7 5

is not a 'knock' in the special sense of the term, but an ordinary play for a drop. The odds are almost equal for the drop or a second-round finesse against the queen. According to the modern theory of pattern symmetry, master players go for the drop if they see no singleton or void in another suit, otherwise they finesse.*

The family of knock plays is divided into two distinct tribes, the Knocks proper and the Scoop plays.

Matrix pura

K 6 3

A 9   J 10 8

Q 7 5 4 2

S leads the four, W must duck, and dummy's king wins. S ducks the return lead to knock W's now bare ace and promote S's queen and, incidentally, the entire suit. The old manuals labelled this duck the 'finesse obligatory', a term we never approved because the second-round duck is not even remotely related to a finesse.

Here is another knock position:

♠ 2

♠ A   ♠ K Q 7 6 5 4 3   ♠ J 10 9 8

Spades are trumps and S must play low at Trick 1 in order to cater for the possible singleton ace. Declarer must always lose two tricks

* Some masters 'play for evens' when there is a void about; all who believe in symmetry finesse with a singleton.—Editor.

141

however enemy spades fall, and an honour lead on the second round holds the enemy to two tricks against all 3–2 splits.

Suppose you need four trump tricks from:

Dummy $\heartsuit$ J

Declarer $\heartsuit$ A K 9 6 5

How do you play?

Lead low to the knave to drive out the queen. This line yields four tricks against $\heartsuit$ 10 x x on either side, for the third lead drops the ten and leaves the nine master. Laying down the ace and king first caters only for Q 10 x in one hand—against which the recommended line also wins.

The Scoop

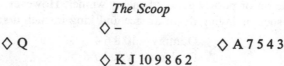

$\diamondsuit$ –

$\diamondsuit$ Q $\diamondsuit$ A 7 5 4 3

$\diamondsuit$ K J 10 9 8 6 2

Diamonds are trumps. The only chance for six tricks is to lead the king and 'scoop' W's bare queen.

The Futile Knock

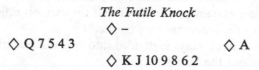

$\diamondsuit$ –

$\diamondsuit$ Q 7 5 4 3 $\diamondsuit$ A

$\diamondsuit$ K J 10 9 8 6 2

Note that leading a low card to knock the singleton ace is futile, for the queen always comes to a second trick for the defence. In other words, against unknown E and W distribution the king lead can lose nothing and *may* scoop the queen.

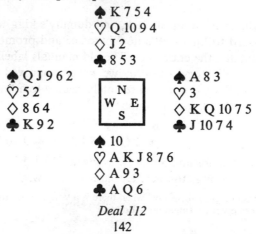

♠ K 7 5 4
♡ Q 10 9 4
◇ J 2
♣ 8 5 3

♠ Q J 9 6 2   ♠ A 8 3
♡ 5 2   ♡ 3
◇ 8 6 4   ◇ K Q 10 7 5
♣ K 9 2   ♣ J 10 7 4

♠ 10
♡ A K J 8 7 6
◇ A 9 3
♣ A Q 6

Deal 112
142

KNOCK

S bid 1 ♡, N 2 ♡; and S 4 ♡.

W led the ♠ Q. Should dummy cover?

Declarer covered in dummy, as did E, so declarer eventually lost a spade, a diamond and two clubs to go down one.

The knock play is to duck the opening lead. Play ♠ 4 on ♠ Q. Sound players do not lead a queen from A Q J against trump contracts, so the ♠ Q opening marks the ace with E. W switches to the ◇ 8 and E plays high enough to drive out the ace. Dummy wins a trump. S ruffs a low spade; N wins a trump and ruffs another low spade which knocks down E's ace. Later, S loses the club finesse, but parks a club loser on dummy's set-up spade king to score game.

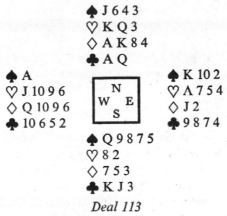

```
                    ♠ J 6 4 3
                    ♡ K Q 3
                    ◇ A K 8 4
                    ♣ A Q
  ♠ A                              ♠ K 10 2
  ♡ J 10 9 6        N              ♡ A 7 5 4
  ◇ Q 10 9 6      W   E            ◇ J 2
  ♣ 10 6 5 2        S              ♣ 9 8 7 4
                    ♠ Q 9 8 7 5
                    ♡ 8 2
                    ◇ 7 5 3
                    ♣ K J 3
```

Deal 113

N bid 1 ◇, S 1 ♣; and N 4 ♣.

W led the ♡ J, forcing the queen and ace. E returned a heart which dummy won.

Declarer must lose a diamond trick also, so his only chance for game is a trump swindle, holding his loss to a single trump. S hopes E holds precisely ♠ K 10 2. If so, there is more than a chance.

To Trick 3 dummy leads the knave of spades and E grabs the bait with his king only to see his partner's bare ace knock it. There are plenty of entries for the marked second-round finesse against the ten.

The deal could be filed under D for Deception, but the basis of the theft is to get enemy trump honours to knock heads on one trick. E should not be in such a hurry to make the standard cover here. The cover ruins the defence if W holds a lone trump honour. If W holds one low trump, the cover will enable an astute declarer to locate the ten with E and to finesse through it.

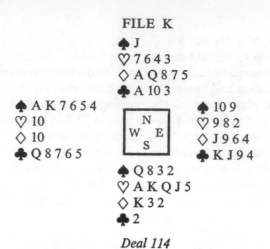

FILE K

♠ J
♡ 7 6 4 3
◇ A Q 8 7 5
♣ A 10 3

♠ A K 7 6 5 4   ♠ 10 9
♡ 10   ♡ 9 8 2
◇ 10   ◇ J 9 6 4
♣ Q 8 7 6 5   ♣ K J 9 4

♠ Q 8 3 2
♡ A K Q J 5
◇ K 3 2
♣ 2

Deal 114

S bid 1 ♡, W 1 ♠, N 2 ♡; S 3 ♡, N 4 ♡; S 5 ◇ and N 6 ♡.
N and S dragged themselves to this slam by their boot-straps.

W led the ♠ K on which E dropped his ten to start an echo, but
W shifted to the ♡ 10 which S won.

How do you plan the play?

The auction and the carding indicate that E might well have left
the now lone ♠ 9. Also, more than one spade ruff in dummy is
futile, for dummy's trumps are babies which E can almost certainly
over-ruff. Hence S drew three rounds of trumps, then ruffed the
fourth diamond lead when that suit failed to split three to two. Next
S led the ♠ Q, knowing W held the ace, so W covered and dummy
ruffed, scooping the nine from E. This made S's' eight the biggest
card in all London,* and S parked his low spade on dummy's fifth
good diamond.

* Or at least the biggest spade left in this deal!—Editor.

KNOCK

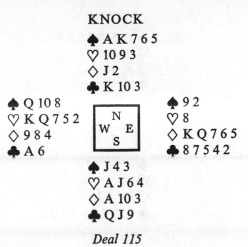

♠ A K 7 6 5
♡ 10 9 3
◇ J 2
♣ K 10 3

♠ Q 10 8   ♠ 9 2
♡ K Q 7 5 2   ♡ 8
◇ 9 8 4   ◇ K Q 7 6 5
♣ A 6   ♣ 8 7 5 4 2

♠ J 4 3
♡ A J 6 4
◇ A 10 3
♣ Q J 9

Deal 115

N bid 1 ♠, S 3 NT.*

W led the ♡ 5 which S let ride round to his knave. Next came the
♠ K and ♠ A; and the ♠ Q for W. W returned the ♡ K, E showed
out, and S won. S led a club and would have got home if E held the
ace, but W won and laid down the ♡ Q, scooping dummy's last high
heart, and W's seven drew S's baby six. The last heart broke the
contract.

On the opening ♡ 5 lead S scuttled the heart suit when he failed
to split equals in dummy. If dummy wins the heart opening, this play
preserves the knave of hearts as a third stopper.

*SAB: N 1 ♠, S 2 ♡; N 2 ♠, S 3 NT. Or N 1 ♠, S 2 NT on his well dispersed 13
points; N 3 ♠ and S 3 NT or 4 ♠. S's direct jump to 3 NT is Acol.

FILE K

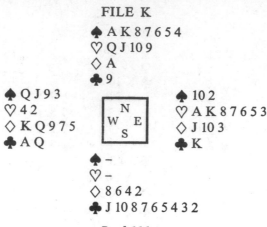

♠ A K 8 7 6 5 4
♡ Q J 10 9
◇ A
♣ 9

♠ Q J 9 3   ♠ 10 2
♡ 4 2   ♡ A K 8 7 6 5 3
◇ K Q 9 7 5   ◇ J 10 3
♣ A Q   ♣ K

♠ –
♡ –
◇ 8 6 4 2
♣ J 10 8 7 6 5 4 3 2

Deal 116

The bidding:			*E and W vulnerable*
S	W	N	E
—	—	1 ♠	2 ♡
No	2 NT	No	4 ♡
5 ♣	Double (final bid)		

W led the ♡ 4, forcing the king, and S ruffed.

How do you plan the play?

The deal was shown us by Frank K. Perkins.

The ◇ A won Trick 2 to let S park two diamonds on N's top spades. Next S ruffed a heart, and dummy ruffed S's last diamond. N led a spade which E ruffed with his singleton king to break the contract, foundering S's wild freak hand.

Improper attention to detail let the enemy escape S's plan to knock the enemy trump honours.

After the ◇ A wins Trick 2, dummy should lead a heart, E covers (S discards if E ducks), and S ruffs. Next ruff a diamond in dummy, cash one top spade for a diamond discard and lead a top heart to let S park his last diamond, and W ruffs. S ruffs whatever W returns, for E still has a spade, and S leads a trump to make enemy trump honours knock heads.

The heart rebid by E shows long hearts and therefore probably short spades, and W's penalty double suggests two trump honours there. The key is to play to compel E to keep a spade lest he score his trump king separately by a ruff.

KNOCK

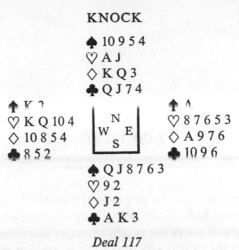

♠ 10 9 5 4
♡ A J
♢ K Q 3
♣ Q J 7 4

♠ K 2
♡ K Q 10 4
♢ 10 8 5 4
♣ 8 5 2

♠ A
♡ 8 7 6 5 3
♢ A 9 7 6
♣ 10 9 6

♠ Q J 8 7 6 3
♡ 9 2
♢ J 2
♣ A K 3

Deal 117

S bid 1 ♠ and N 4 ♠.*

W led the ♡ K. How do you plan the play?

Dummy won the ♡ K. S won a club and led the queen of trumps, hoping to steal the hand if W plays high with a doubleton trump honour. But W knew his way about the bridge table and refused to be taken in by the swindle. W played low. The defence collected a heart, the ♢ A, and two top trumps to break the contract.

The deal came from a duplicate game where another declarer bagged the game by play against which there is no defence. Declarer let dummy win the third club lead and dummy led his last club, E and S each shed a heart, and W ruffed low. S got in again quickly and led a trump to make the enemy trump honours knock heads.

If E ruffs the fourth club lead, S still discards a heart, and later drives out the other enemy trump honour.

The deal might well be placed in Subfile LL, for that fourth club lead lets S discard a *Loser on a Loser*, that dead heart, while the defence was wasting a natural trump trick.

*SAB: S 1 ♠, N 3 ♠; and S 4 ♠. N should really hold at least ♠ J x x x but ♠ 10 9 5 4 will do. An indirect route is S 1 ♠, N 2 ♣; S 2 ♠, and N 4 ♠.

File L

LONG SUIT

L stands for Long Suit. In all games of the whist family, and especially in whist and in its direct descendants—bridge, auction and contract—a long suit offers the richest source of extra tricks. Setting up a long suit is the primal key to consistent winning play.

A large proportion of contracts depend on bringing home a long suit under the protection of a trump fortress or of ample stoppers in other suits at no-trumps.

Long suit play is so common that it is taken for granted in deals appearing in all the files. It appears incidental but it is often the vital foundation to the special play of the file involved. File L, therefore, is limited to deals requiring special focus on long suit play.

Time, and the time factor, are vital in the race to establish low cards of your long suit before the enemy does the same, hence Long Suit play is often closely integrated with the Tempo plays in File T.

Many deals offer ruffs in dummy as well as long suit play. Declarer should usually abstain from early ruffs in dummy in order to use the table's trump tricks as entries to promote dummy's long suit.

Actually such deals belong to File R for Ruff; but again, simple trump management is taken for granted when used to promote suit lengths. Complex ruffing plays are another matter.

The long suit may contain vital intermediate cards or remainder (tail) cards or both.

File L is divided in three sections: Developing the Long Suit; Choosing the Better Suit; and Developing Two Long Suits.

Section I—Developing the Long Suit

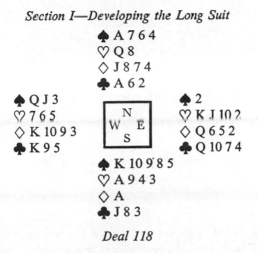

♠ A 7 6 4
♡ Q 8
◇ J 8 7 4
♣ A 6 2

♠ Q J 3
♡ 7 6 5
◇ K 10 9 3
♣ K 9 5

♠ 2
♡ K J 10 2
◇ Q 6 5 2
♣ Q 10 7 4

♠ K 10 9 8 5
♡ A 9 4 3
◇ A
♣ J 8 3

Deal 118

S bid 1 ♠, N 3 ♠; and S 4 ♠.*

W led the ◇ 10. Dummy and E ducked, and S won.

S has two club losers, a heart and probably a trump. S leads the ♡ 4 in hopes W has the king. This play scores the ♡ Q at once or lets dummy get a club discard on the ♡ A later. But E kills this plan by taking the ♡ Q with the king and returning a diamond luckily for S (a club return is fatal) which S ruffs. Next the ♠ K and ♠ A plays reveal a trump loser, so an extra heart trick is vital. Dummy leads the ♡ 8, intending to let it ride with the idea that it would cost nothing and might turn up something good. E covers the eight with the ten and S wins with the ace.

Declarer notes that W dropped the ♡ 5 and ♡ 6, placing the deuce with E. Hence S next lays down the ♡ 9, scooping W's seven while dummy parks a club and E wins. E returns a club which dummy's ace wins. S ruffs a diamond to get in and scores his infant prodigy, his master ♡ 3 which is high against E's deuce, and lets dummy park his last club.

This long suit deal, with its unusual scoop play, is a hang-over from File K for Knock, and it also embodies the principle of loser on loser, the discard of a losing club from dummy on the losing ♡ 9.

*SAB: S 1 ♠, N 2 ◇; S 2 ♡, then N 4 ♠; end.

FILE L

Matrix pura

♠ K Q 10 4
♡ A 2
♢ 10 2
♣ 6 5 4 3 2

♠ 7 2
♡ K 10 8 4
♢ Q 8 7 2
♣ K J 9

♠ 6 3
♡ J 7 6 5
♢ K J 9
♣ A Q 10 8

♠ A J 9 8 5
♡ Q 9 3
♢ A 6 5 4
♣ 7

Deal 119

S bid 1 ♠, N 3 ♠; and S 4 ♠. The 3 ♠ bid is a limit raise.*
W led the ♠ 7. How do you play if trumps split evenly?

S wins the trump opening and leads the club which E wins. E returns another trump, reducing dummy to two trumps.

Superficially declarer has only three losers but he realizes that the attack on trumps leaves only two trumps in dummy—too few to ruff his own three losers: a heart and two diamonds. The preferred play is to set up that 'worthless' six-high club suit.

Dummy wins the second trump lead, S ruffs a club, and S plays the ace, then low in diamonds. E wins and returns a diamond. Dummy ruffs two diamonds and S two more clubs alternately to establish dummy's fifth club for the vital game-scoring trick.

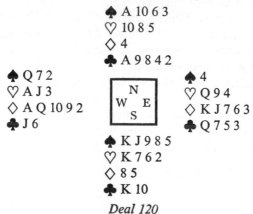

♠ A 10 6 3
♡ 10 8 5
♢ 4
♣ A 9 8 4 2

♠ Q 7 2
♡ A J 3
♢ A Q 10 9 2
♣ J 6

♠ 4
♡ Q 9 4
♢ K J 7 6 3
♣ Q 7 5 3

♠ K J 9 8 5
♡ K 7 6 2
♢ 8 5
♣ K 10

Deal 120

SAB: S 1 ♠, N 2 ♣; S 2 ♢, N 3 ♠; and S 4 ♠, end of auction bids.

S bid 1 ♠, W 2 ◇, N 4 ♠.*

W led the ◇ A and shifted to the ♣ J.

How do you play for ten tricks?

In the actual event, S won Trick 2 with the ♣ K and played the ♠ A then ♠ K, without dropping the queen. S ruffed the diamond in dummy, playing the ♣ A, continued with the ♣ 9 which E covered and S ruffed. This long suit play set up two good clubs in dummy, but alas! N had no entry to score them. S lost a trump to W's queen. W opened the heart suit which let S make his king, but S lost two heart tricks for defeat by one trick.

There are two good lines of play: neither of which declarer selected.

Win Trick 2 with the ♣ K, lay down the ♠ K, finesse the ♠ 10, and play the ♠ A. As the cards lie, this line of play wins the hand. Next play the ♣ A and lead high clubs through the ♣ Q, marked in E by W's ♣ J lead at Trick 2. This promotes dummy's two club tricks with the diamond ruff as entry to score them to let you park two hearts. Finally, dummy leads a heart to let you play the ♡ K for an extra trick, but you can afford to lose two heart tricks and still get home.

If at Trick 4 the ♠ 10 finesse loses, you can still play on clubs for heart discards and make the hand if you find the ♡ A with E.

Another line, based on a pseudo-elimination play, was suggested by Ely Culbertson on page 39 of *The Encyclopaedia of Bridge*, published by *The Bridge World*, 1935.

Ruff the diamond at Trick 3, take the ♠ K, lead the club to the ace in dummy and return the ♣ 9, E covers, S trumps and W over-ruffs. Any red card return by W lets S get home but a trump return breaks the contract.

This deal is the historic 'Bennett Murder Hand'. We were tempted to style it The Three Kings Murder Case, because in 1931 John S. Bennett, a prosperous perfume salesman of Kansas City, U.S.A., was shot dead by his wife because he opened 1 ♠ on three kings and failed to make game.

S has a dubious opener even by original Acol standards (closely similar to the original Culbertson System of 1931). We wonder how many Acol players would open on it to-day. Compare the hand with Mr. M. Harrison-Gray's opening bid of 1 ♡ on:

    ♠ Q J x   ♡ K J 9 x x   ◇ x   ♣ K 10 x x

quoted at page 223 of *Bridge is an Easy Game* by Iain Macleod, M.P. (Falcon Press).

*SAB: S pass, W 1 ◇, N pass, E 3 ◇; S double for takeout, N 3 ♠, E 4 ◇; and S 4 ♠.

Mrs. Bennett's jump raise to 4 ♠ on the N hand was also a slight stretch, and had she only jumped to 3 ♠, she might have saved herself a trial for murder and a perfectly good husband.

Despite the calling, Mr. Bennett had two chances to save his life which, literally for once, hung upon the play of a card.

According to Culbertson's report, the game continued after the fateful hand, amid repeated caustic remarks by Mrs. Bennett about lousy bridge-players, aimed at her husband, and his acrid retorts, which increased in crescendo and broke up the game.

While the opponents (another married couple) were donning their wraps to depart, Mrs. Bennett dashed into her mother's bedroom, snatched a revolver from the bureau drawer, and darted out. Seeing her thus armed, Mr. Bennett rushed into the bathroom and slammed the door behind him, and allegedly stopped two bullets which crashed through the door panel. Bennett staggered out and into a chair moaning, 'She got me', and died. The police found Mrs. Bennett bent over him, sobbing wildly.

According to Alexander Woollcott in his book, *While Rome Burns*, Viking, Press, New York, 1934, the fatal shooting occurred on 29th September 1929.

Mrs. Bennett's hand bears a strange resemblance to the Dead Man's Hand of Wild Bill Hickok, who was plugged in the back on 2nd August 1876 by a cowardly, tinhorn gambler, one Jack McCall, in Deadwood, South Dakota, U.S.A. (See page 234 of my *The Poker Game Complete* (Faber & Faber).) Wild Bill's poker hand contained two aces, two eights and a fifth card whose rank and suit is lost in the haze of the past. 'Aces and eights' are still known as 'Dead Man's Hand'. Mrs. Bennett also held two aces and two eights! *

Jack McCall was hanged, but Mrs. Bennett was acquitted.

In parenthesis, since 4 ◇ is ice-cold against N and S, one down at 4 ♠ was not a bad result. If N jumps to 3 ♠, E probably bids 4 ◇ and S goes to 4 ♠—unless E and W are love. The final result is the same, unless W bids 5 ◇, as he might well after E supports him, and goes down one to give N and S a plus score on the deal.

*Today any bridge hand three kings high is called a dead man's hand.

LONG SUIT

Hasty Ruff

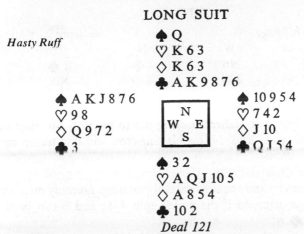

Deal 121

S bid 1 ♡, W 1 ♠, N 2.♣; S 2 ◇ and N 6 ♡.

N was a bit brash to jump directly to slam without first either calling a Blackwood four no-trumps to test for aces, or otherwise testing the quality of S's hand, especially the heart suit.

W leads the ♠ K and shifts to the ♡ 9.

S won the trump shift, ruffed the spade in dummy, and drew trumps. Next he tried to set up clubs but the bad 4–1 split made it impossible to bring home the suit.

Dummy's spade ruff must be saved as an entry to promote clubs. (If W leads another spade to Trick 2, he breaks the contract.) S wins two trumps and two clubs. The trumps are lucky for S, because W cannot ruff the second club lead after two rounds of trumps. S ruffs a club, N ruffs the spade, and S ruffs the fourth club. S draws E's last trump and the ◇ K puts dummy in to score the good clubs.

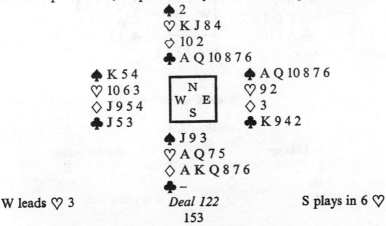

W leads ♡ 3   *Deal 122*   S plays in 6 ♡

S	W	N	E
1 ♦	No	2 ♣	2 ♠
3 ♡	No	4 ♡	No
5 ♡	No	6 ♡ (final bid)	

S's call of 5 ♡ is an indirect asking bid to see if N can stop the first or second spade lead. N, on his singleton and fine trump support, bids the slam.

W leads the ♡ 3.

The deal is tricky and requires careful planning. Dummy must ruff a spade AND a diamond if diamonds split 4–1; and S can park a spade on the ♣ A.

So dummy wins the trump opening and shifts to a spade immediately which E wins. E returns a trump which S wins in his own hand. Next dummy ruffs a spade and dummy scores the ♣ A to let S park his last spade.

If declarer draws trumps now, the bad diamond split breaks the contract. So declarer must instead lay down two top diamonds. If all follow suit, the rest is easy; but E fails, showing the bad break and luckily has no trump left. Dummy ruffs a low diamond, S ruffs a club and draws trumps.

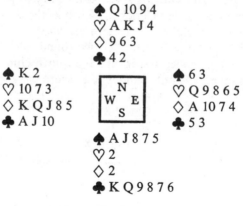

Deal 123

The bidding: *Rubber game*

S	W	N	E
1 ♣	1 ♦	1 ♡	2 ♦
2 ♠	3 ♦	4 ♠ (final bid)	

W leads the ◇ K then ◇ J which S ruffs.

What do you lead to Tricks 3 and 4?

Declarer led the heart to dummy's king at Trick 3, which was right; and he led the ♠ Q and finessed which was wrong—the lead, not the finesse. W won and returned a diamond which S ruffed. S led a spade to dummy's nine, leaving this ending:

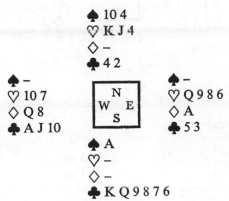

Dummy led a club and the king forced the ace. W returned a heart to dummy's king and the rest was easy. S won a club, dummy ruffed a club to clean out enemy clubs and S ruffed a heart.

W should let the ♣ K win in the diagram in order to give S entry trouble. This defence was overlooked in the heat of play, but S can avoid the trap at Trick 4 by starting clubs at that point instead of too late.

With a two-suiter, the preferred policy is to set up your side suit first. Trumps can *usually* wait—unless, of course, you have so many you can afford to draw them and still have sufficient ruffs.

Section II—Choosing the Better Suit

When you have a choice of two suits to develop, seriously consider selecting the right one. Many factors such as entries, the time factor, or the texture of the suits should be weighed carefully before you decide to launch an attack in either suit. If you pick the wrong suit, you may not have time later to swop horses in mid-stream.

Right Finesse First

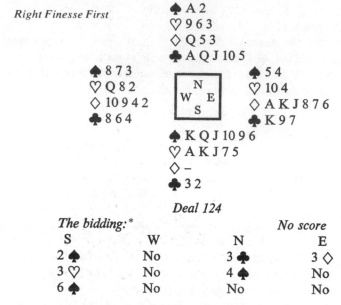

♠ A 2
♡ 9 6 3
◇ Q 5 3
♣ A Q J 10 5

♠ 8 7 3   ♠ 5 4
♡ Q 8 2   ♡ 10 4
◇ 10 9 4 2   ◇ A K J 8 7 6
♣ 8 6 4   ♣ K 9 7

♠ K Q J 10 9 6
♡ A K J 7 5
◇ –
♣ 3 2

Deal 124

The bidding: *   *No score*

S	W	N	E
2 ♠	No	3 ♣	3 ◇
3 ♡	No	4 ♠	No
6 ♠	No	No	No

S has a typical Acol two-bid which led to the logical spade slam, although declarer messed up the play and went down.

W led the ◇ 2, dummy ducked, and the knave forced S to ruff. Which suit do you develop, hearts or clubs?

S scored the ♠ K, ♡ K, then ♠ A in dummy and lost the ♡ J finesse. Later the club finesse lost also and broke the contract.

In this deal declarer should go for dummy's clubs, not his own hearts. Declarer took the selfish view of his own two-suiter without considering dummy's assets in clubs.

Draw trumps in three leads—no need to work on the side suit first in this hand—and finesse a club, which loses. The rest is easy, for dummy's good clubs allow declarer to park three hearts. If E refuses to win the first club finesse, quit clubs instantly and work on hearts.

SAB would go:

S	W	N	E
1 ♠	No	2 ♣	2 ◇
3 ♡	No	3 NT	No
4 ◇	No	4 ♡	No
6 ♠	No	No	No

LONG SUIT

Right Echelon

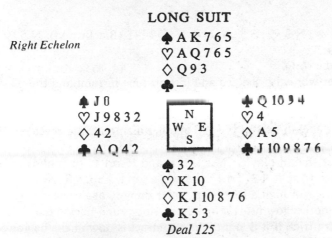

```
        ♠ A K 7 6 5
        ♡ A Q 7 6 5
        ◇ Q 9 3
        ♣ —
♠ J 0                    ♣ Q 10 9 4
♡ J 9 8 3 2             ♡ 4
◇ 4 2                   ◇ A 5
♣ A Q 4 2              ♣ J 10 9 8 7 6
        ♠ 3 2
        ♡ K 10
        ◇ K J 10 8 7 6
        ♣ K 5 3
```

Deal 125

S bid 1 ◇, N 2 ♠; S 3 ◇, N 3 ♡; S 4 ♡ and N 6 ◇.

W led a diamond to E's ace and E returned a diamond which S won. Dummy had one trump left and S had three club losers to worry about.

Do you play on spades or hearts?

Declarer made the wrong choice. He played the ♡ K and ♡ A only to find the heart-breaking (and contract-breaking) 5–1 split. Next declarer played dummy's top spades and ruffed a spade, praying for a 3–3 split. The more normal 4–2 split prevailed and broke the contract.

Declarer should play on spades first which score the slam if they split no worse than 4–2. If they split worse, declarer can try hearts next which also yield the slam if they split 4–2 or 3–3.

If hearts are attacked first and prove sour, declarer needs the very lucky salvation of a 3–3 spade split (odds 2–1 against) to get home.

```
        ♠ 9 2
        ♡ A K 7 6 5
        ◇ A Q 7 6 5
        ♣ 2
♠ 8 7 5 4               ♠ 3
♡ Q 10 9 4             ♡ J 8 3
◇ 2                    ◇ K J 3
♣ Q J 10 9            ♣ 8 7 6 5 4 3
        ♠ A K Q J 10 6
        ♡ 2
        ◇ 10 9 8 4
        ♣ A K
```

Deal 126

W leads ♣ Q   S plays in 6 ♠

S bid 2 ♠, N 3 ♡; S 3 ♠, N 4 ◇; S 4 NT (Blackwood), N 5 ♡ and S 6 ♠.* †

W led the ♣ Q.

Declarer won with the ace and lost no time in fumbling the play. S was lured to his fate by that glittering siren diamond suit of nine cards. S drew trumps in four leads and finessed the ◇ 10 to E's knave. E returned a club to S's king and another diamond lead revealed W out. . . .

Declarer should play on hearts first and resort to diamonds only if hearts fail to split 4–3. To Trick 2 win a top trump in S. Next, cash a top heart, ruff high a low heart, enter dummy again via the ♠ 9, and ruff another low heart. Next draw trumps and finesse the ◇ Q‡ for an extra trick if it is right. Your contract is now in the bag anyway, for the ♡ A and good low heart in dummy give S two diamond discards.

Section III—Developing Two Suits

Sometimes you have to set up TWO suits in order to get home. Deals requiring such treatment are usually complex. They require careful planning and deep insight for the best results.

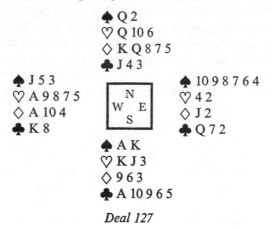

Deal 127

Not vulnerable, S bid 1 NT, N 2 NT; and S 3 NT.
W led the ♡ 7.

S took care to win the heart opening with his king in order to unblock for later developments, and led a low diamond. W ducked, and the queen won.

N led a low spade, E played the ten as a signal to show that he controlled spades from the ten down, and S's ♠ A let S lead another diamond toward dummy. W 'drew' with his ace. Instead of returning hearts W made the enlightened shift to the ♠ J, causing the king and queen to knock heads. Now declarer found only eight tricks on top.

Opening the spade suit was dangerous, and a simple count of winners points the way to game. When the ♢ Q wins Trick 2, declarer now has a diamond trick under his belt and he should shift to the ♣ J and finesse. This loses, and later dummy gets in again with a heart for another club finesse to let S score four club tricks. These, with the diamond, two hearts and two spades, spell game.

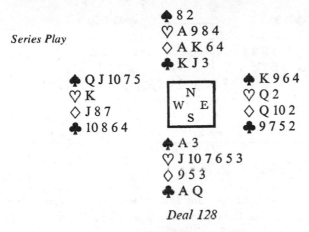

Series Play

    ♠ 8 2
    ♡ A 9 8 4
    ♢ A K 6 4
    ♣ K J 3

♠ Q J 10 7 5   ♠ K 9 6 4
♡ K   ♡ Q 2
♢ J 8 7   ♢ Q 10 2
♣ 10 8 6 4   ♣ 9 7 5 2

    ♠ A 3
    ♡ J 10 7 6 5 3
    ♢ 9 5 3
    ♣ A Q

Deal 128

S bid 1 ♡, N 4 ♡; and S 6 ♡.*†

S won the ♠ Q opening with the ace. He realized that he must lose a trump trick, so he played the ♡ A; then he cashed three club tricks for a quick spade discard, and ruffed the spade.

Declarer still had a diamond loser to worry about, so he played dummy's top diamonds and threw E on lead with a trump, hoping

* A 4 ♡ bid on 15 points is, on any but a direct system, lunacy. N, with big heart support, should force with 3 ♢; S bids 3 ♡; N may now bid 4 NT (either Culbertson or Blackwood) and S, 5 ♡ (B) or 5 NT (C). The slam is now reasonable. If N bids only 4 ♡, S might well pass but, after the force and heart support, his two black controls might induce a cue-bid. Any S who, on the sequence as given, bid 6 ♡ over 4 ♡, even if this is reasonably strong such as 12 or 13 points, is heading straight for the 'bin'.—Editor.

†SAB: S 1 ♡, N 2 ♢; S 2 ♡, N 4 NT Blackwood; S 5 ♡ to show two aces and N 6 ♡.

E would have no diamond left. But E scored the ◇ Q also to break the contract.

A neat sequence of discards makes the hand. Before touching trumps, discard a DIAMOND on the third club trick; ruff the third diamond lead which finds the lucky 3–3 split. Then re-enter dummy with the trump ace to lead the good diamond and park the spade. E can get his only trick, the top trump, now or later.

The 3–3 diamond split occurs only 36% of the time whereas the chances of finding two or fewer diamonds in the same hand with the enemy trump winner is 32% or less. The long suit play in this case has the slight edge of 4%.

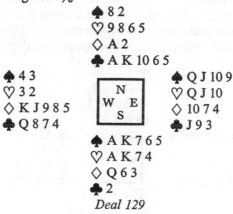

```
              ♠ 8 2
              ♡ 9 8 6 5
              ◇ A 2
              ♣ A K 10 6 5
  ♠ 4 3                        ♠ Q J 10 9
  ♡ 3 2          N             ♡ Q J 10
  ◇ K J 9 8 5  W   E           ◇ 10 7 4
  ♣ Q 8 7 4       S            ♣ J 9 3
              ♠ A K 7 6 5
              ♡ A K 7 4
              ◇ Q 6 3
              ♣ 2
```

Deal 129

S bid 1 ♠, N 2 ♣; S 2 ♡, N 4 ♡; and S 6 ♡. *
W led the ♡ 3.

S won the trump opening and laid down another top trump. Trumps must split 3–2 or the contract fails, and S must guard against a cheap over-ruff in the hand holding only a doubleton.

Dummy ruffed the third spade lead, S ruffed the third club lead, and dummy ruffed another spade, leaving:

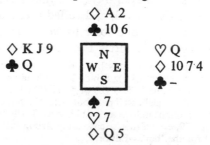

```
              ◇ A 2
              ♣ 10 6
  ◇ K J 9        N            ♡ Q
  ♣ Q         W     E         ◇ 10 7 4
                 S            ♣ –
              ♠ 7
              ♡ 7
              ◇ Q 5
```

*SAB: S 1 ♠, N 2 ♣; S 2 ♡, N 4 ♡; S 4 NT, N 5 ♡; then S 6 ♡.

Dummy led a club, E discarded, and S ruffed. This play set up a good club in dummy. S led his stiff spade to let dummy shed the low diamond and E ruffed. The ◇ A and the good club won the last two tricks.

In this deal declarer had to set up BOTH side suits in order to eke out enough tricks for the slam.

Blocking That Block!

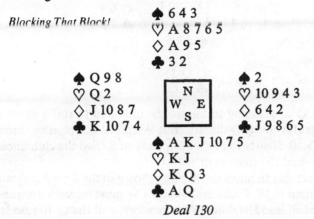

♠ 6 4 3
♡ A 8 7 6 5
◇ A 9 5
♣ 3 2

♠ Q 9 8
♡ Q 2
◇ J 10 8 7
♣ K 10 7 4

♠ 2
♡ 10 9 4 3
◇ 6 4 2
♣ J 9 8 6 5

♠ A K J 10 7 5
♡ K J
◇ K Q 3
♣ A Q

Deal 130

S bid 2 ♠, N 3 ♡; S 3 ♠, N 4 ♠; S 4 NT (Blackwood), N 5 ♡; and S 6 ♠. S has plenty of high cards to open 2 ♣, but he preferred to suggest a strong trump suit by starting with 2 ♠ (forcing for one round).

W led the ◇ J which ran to S's king.

How do you play to score the slam?

S tried to drop the trump queen on the ace and king. Despite W's guarded queen, S can score slam if the club finesse wins or hearts split no worse than 4–2. S properly decided to go for hearts first with the club finesse in reserve if hearts split badly.

Next S played the king then ace of hearts and ruffed a heart. W refused to help by over-ruffing, leaving the position shown on the next page.

FILE L

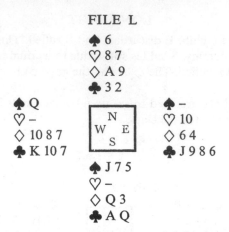

```
                    ♠ 6
                    ♡ 8 7
                    ◇ A 9
                    ♣ 3 2
      ♠ Q                          ♠ –
      ♡ –          ┌─────────┐     ♡ 10
      ◇ 10 8 7     │   N     │     ◇ 6 4
      ♣ K 10 7     │ W   E   │     ♣ J 9 8 6
                   │   S     │
                   └─────────┘
                    ♠ J 7 5
                    ♡ –
                    ◇ Q 3
                    ♣ A Q
```

S led the ◇ 3, planning to finesse the nine and to ruff a heart to set up a heart for the ♣ Q discard. But W spiked this plan by throwing in the ◇ 10. Hearts were now hopeless so S tried the club finesse which lost—and the slam went with it.

S has a neat way to make the hand as shown in the 7-card diagram.

Lose a trump to W. Clubs are taboo so W must return a diamond. A low diamond lead lets dummy's nine score, and the ◇ 10 lead lets dummy win with the ace on which S throws the queen to unblock and make the nine the last diamond winner.

SUBFILE LL
LOSER ON LOSER

Loser on loser is a relatively new bridge term for any sort of play in which one partner leads a losing card on which the other discards a loser. This play telescopes the loss of 'two tricks into one'. The gadget is a sort of Houdini act in which declarer (usually) makes a losing trick apparently vanish into thin air.

The loser on loser device is generally used to promote high cards or a long suit under trump protection. Hence, loser on loser plays are a part of long suit play, yet they are sufficiently distinctive to be set apart in a special subfile. When the trump position is complex, the play is filed under R for Ruff.

162

LONG SUIT

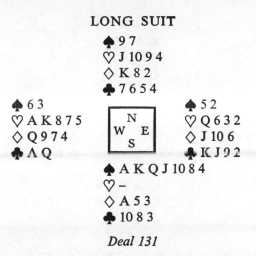

♠ 9 7
♡ J 10 9 4
◇ K 8 2
♣ 7 6 5 4

♠ 6 3
♡ A K 8 7 5
◇ Q 9 7 4
♣ A Q

♠ 5 2
♡ Q 6 3 2
◇ J 10 6
♣ K J 9 2

♠ A K Q J 10 8 4
♡ –
◇ A 5 3
♣ 10 8 3

Deal 131

After two passes S bid 4 ♠, W doubled, and all passed.

Opposite a passing partner S saw almost no chance for slam and decided to pre-empt rather than to fool around and let E and W organize their calling cheaply.

W led the ♡ K.

How do you develop a heart trick in dummy?

S ruffs high the ♡ K and leads the ♠ 8 to the ♠ 9 in dummy. Dummy returns a heart, E ducks, S parks a club which is the loser on loser play, and W wins with the ace. W's play denies the ♡ Q, locating this card with E. W shifts to the ♣ A then ♣ Q which E overtakes and E returns the ♣ J which S ruffs high. Dummy's ♠ 7 wins the next trick and dummy leads another heart.

If E ducks, S discards a diamond. But E covers and S ruffs. S draws trumps if any are still out then uses the ◇ K to re-enter dummy, who has the good heart for a diamond discard.

Hidden Ruff

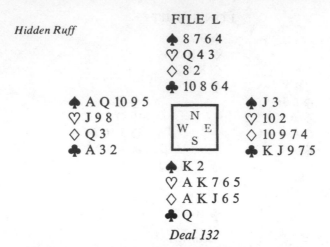

♠ 8 7 6 4
♡ Q 4 3
◇ 8 2
♣ 10 8 6 4

♠ A Q 10 9 5
♡ J 9 8
◇ Q 3
♣ A 3 2

♠ J 3
♡ 10 2
◇ 10 9 7 4
♣ K J 9 7 5

♠ K 2
♡ A K 7 6 5
◇ A K J 6 5
♣ Q

Deal 132

S bid 2 ♡, N 2 NT, S 3 ◇, N 3 ♡; and S 4 ♡.*
W led the ♣ A then ♣ 3 which S ruffed.

If someone told you that the key play to this deal is to ruff a spade *in dummy*, you would probably say 'Nuts!'

S scored the king and queen of trumps, then laid down the ace and king of diamonds, dropping the queen. Next S led a low diamond, W ruffed, and dummy parked a spade, the peculiar loser on loser manœuvre of the deal.

Back came a club which S ruffed, and S scored two more diamond tricks and dummy shed more spades. Later the defence got a spade trick but dummy ruffed the second spade lead. This ruff was perfectly concealed at the beginning.

If W discards on the diamond at Trick 7, dummy ruffs. S ruffs a club and draws trumps. Against the defence which allows N to ruff the diamond on the third round—forfeiting W's ♡ J—S can afford *two* spade losers.

SAB: S 1 ♡, W 1 ♠, S 3 ◇, N 3 ♡; and S 4 ♡.

LONG SUIT

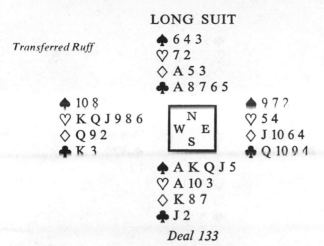

Transferred Ruff

```
              ♠ 6 4 3
              ♡ 7 2
              ◇ A 5 3
              ♣ A 8 7 6 5
♠ 10 8                        ♠ 9 7 ?
♡ K Q J 9 8 6      N          ♡ 5 4
◇ Q 9 2         W     E       ◇ J 10 6 4
♣ K 3             S           ♣ Q 10 9 4
              ♠ A K Q J 5
              ♡ A 10 3
              ◇ K 8 7
              ♣ J 2
```

Deal 133

S bid 1 ♠, W 2 ♡, N 2 ♠; and S 4 ♠.

W led the ♡ K, E played the five and S won with the ace. S returned the ♡ 10 which W won and E completed his echo by dropping the four.

To Trick 3 W led the ♡ Q.

Your natural losers are a club, a diamond and a heart. Also a heart over-ruff by E threatens to break the contract.

How do you bag the game?

Declarer used a form of the loser on loser play to solve his problem. On the third heart lead he simply discarded from dummy . . . a diamond! W shifted to a diamond, and declarer ruffed the third diamond lead in dummy unmolested.

The diamond discard on the third heart lead simply transferred dummy's essential ruff to a suit that could not be over-ruffed. E was helpless.

For the last deal under Files L and LL we offer one of Frank K. Perkins's rare creations, a loser on loser play to set up one long suit followed by ruffing out and establishing another suit.

165

FILE L

```
              ♠ A Q 9
              ♡ 7 2
              ◇ A J 10 4
              ♣ 8 6 5 3
♠ -                            ♠ 8 7 3
♡ K J 10 8 5      N            ♡ 9 6 4 3
◇ K Q 9 7 5    W   E           ◇ 8 6 3 2
♣ K J 9           S            ♣ 10 2
              ♠ K J 10 6 5 4 2
              ♡ A Q
              ◇ -
              ♣ A Q 7 4
```

Deal 134

The bidding:			*No score*
S	W	N	E
2 ♠	3 ♡	3 ♠	No
4 ♡	No	5 ♠	No
6 ♠	Double	No	No
Redouble	No	No	No

N's jump to 5 ♠ showed real slam help and, indirectly, two aces. W's penalty double looked good enough, but it proved to be a costly indiscretion.

W led the ◇ K.

How do you plan the play, assuming all finesses wrong?

Declarer dug up a neat line of play. Dummy won the ◇ K with the ace and S took care to discard a low *club*. Dummy returned the ◇ J and S shed another club, the loser on loser play; W won with the queen. This line of play did not fool W into a heart or club shift, so W passively returned a diamond which dummy's ten won and S parked the ♣ Q.

S scored the ♣ A, won a trump in dummy and ruffed a club; won another trump in dummy and ruffed a third club, making dummy's last club good. Dummy won the third trump trick which drew E's last trump and dummy scored the club for the ♡ Q discard.

No finesse was necessary, just straightforward play.

If declarer discards the ♡ Q on the ◇ A and plays on clubs, he will land in hot water—or, perhaps, in the soup.

166

File M

MÊLÉE

M stands for Mêlée. It means hand-to-hand fight. The type deal features a sequence of different types of plays, often in hotly contested skirmishes between declarer and opponents.

Mêlée is one of a natural group or *order* of five closely related files. A common characteristic of this order is involved and/or heterogeneous strategy in a deal, arising from two (or more) different types of play. No particular type is featured.

The order of five files divides naturally into two families based on the arrangement of the plays in a deal as follows:

Vertical Arrangement. One type, or plan, of play is made early in the hand and another type occurs later.

Parallel Arrangement. Two play plans or types appear simultaneously and declarer must select one to the exclusion of the other.

Below is a simple key of the entire order:

Order 2—Involved Strategy

Family 1—Vertical Arrangement

Mêlée. A sequence of skirmishes involves more than one type of play.

New Plan. A bad suit break requires declarer to formulate and adopt a new plan of attack.

Quandary. A compound type of play fits no other file, or two play types of equal importance have no special relationship to each other. Deals filed here may contain plays in vertical or parallel arrangement or in a combination of both.

Family 2—Parallel Arrangement

Winning Line. Declarer has an obscure choice of different yet apparently equally good lines of play.

Variety. Two or more equally good lines of play offer no superior choice. Variety deals are usually bridge curiosities. Such deals have academic or historic interest, but little practical value. Double-dummy problems in this file are called 'cooked', and they are worth-less.

Matrix typica

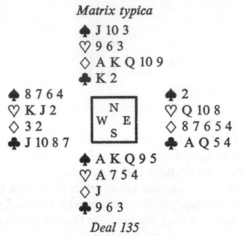

♠ J 10 3
♡ 9 6 3
◇ A K Q 10 9
♣ K 2

♠ 8 7 6 4
♡ K J 2
◇ 3 2
♣ J 10 8 7

♠ 2
♡ Q 10 8
◇ 8 7 6 5 4
♣ A Q 5 4

♠ A K Q 9 5
♡ A 7 5 4
◇ J
♣ 9 6 3

Deal 135

S bid 1 ♠, N 2 ◇; S 2 ♠, and N 4 ♠.

W led the ♣ J and E scored two club tricks when dummy covered. For Trick 3, E shifted to the ◇ 8.

How do you play it?

The hand looks easy. Let dummy win the third trump lead and score diamonds, but the 4–1 trump split spoils this plan.

S wins the ◇ J at Trick 3 and the ♠ A. Next he wins another trump in dummy, only to find W grinning at him, having started life with four trumps.

Declarer parks his last club on a diamond from dummy. Dummy leads another diamond, S sheds a low heart and W ruffs. W returns a club, hoping to shorten dummy's trumps but declarer ruffs high. A trump to dummy draws W's last and the diamonds let S shake off his own heart losers.

Here we have a brilliant blocking play by E's diamond lead at Trick 3, declarer's counter-attack, in the form of a gambit, to let W score a diamond ruff, and W's final attempt to shorten dummy's trumps, another blocking play which proved futile.

MÊLÉE

Merrimac Coup

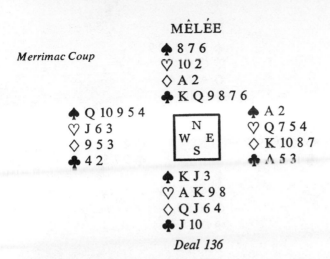

Deal 136

S bid 1 NT, N 2 NT; and S 3 NT.

W led the ♠ 10 to E's ace, and E returned the ◇ K!

How do you plan the play?

E's gambit return of the ◇ K is the Merrimac Coup, aimed at sinking dummy's great club suit. Dummy's ace wins and declarer decides to play on hearts. He leads the ten from dummy and lets it ride to W's knave. A spade return is hopeless, so W leads the ◇ 9, forcing S's queen. S leads a club, W plays the four and dummy overtakes. E must duck to shut out the suit. S finesses the ♡ 9 and cashes two more heart tricks. S leads another club which dummy overtakes and E wins with his ace. E returns a spade to S's king, and S pauses for a count which reveals:

S has won seven tricks. The play marks W with five spades and three hearts. W echoed in clubs to show two clubs, so W started with three diamonds. E is now marked with two diamonds and a club as in the diagram.

S cashes the ◇ J and loses his last diamond to E who has a club left for dummy to win and score declarer's ninth trick.

169

FILE M

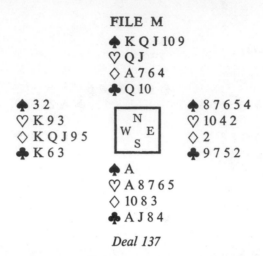

♠ K Q J 10 9
♡ Q J
◇ A 7 6 4
♣ Q 10

♠ 3 2
♡ K 9 3
◇ K Q J 9 5
♣ K 6 3

♠ 8 7 6 5 4
♡ 10 4 2
◇ 2
♣ 9 7 5 2

♠ A
♡ A 8 7 6 5
◇ 10 8 3
♣ A J 8 4

Deal 137

In rubber game N bid 1 ♠, S 2 ♡; N 2 ♠, and S 3 NT.
W led the ◇ K.

How do you play the play?

The immediate attack on dummy's only quick entry and the blocked spades faced declarer with a puzzle which he solved neatly.

He ducked the ◇ K as routine hold-up play, as he did also the ◇ J which followed and E let go a club. W had no good shift without making game easy for declarer, so W had to stick to the straight and narrow path in diamonds and led his queen to Trick 3. Again declarer ducked, but dummy won the fourth diamond lead on which S jettisoned the ace of spades.

However, declarer had only eight tricks on top and he was not yet out of the wood. Dummy cashed four spades, leaving:

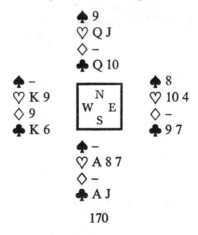

♠ 9
♡ Q J
◇ –
♣ Q 10

♠ –
♡ K 9
◇ 9
♣ K 6

♠ 8
♡ 10 4
◇ –
♣ 9 7

♠ –
♡ A 8 7
◇ –
♣ A J

170

MÊLÉE

On dummy's last spade lead S shed a heart, and W went into a long squirm and finally parted with his good diamond.

'Why?' thought declarer. He read the situation correctly and played ace then low in hearts to force a club return from W.

W's best defence on the last spade lead is to discard a low club quickly and quietly. This will make it almost impossible for declarer to take the right view.

File N

NEW PLAN

N stands for New Plan. In deals of this file a bad suit break or an unexpected twist in the defence forces a player to abandon his original plan of play and to form a new one.

Theoretically, type deals should be common, but as a practical matter they are scarce.

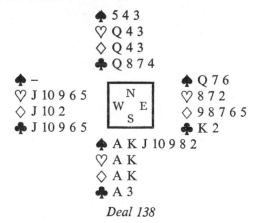

```
                    ♠ 5 4 3
                    ♡ Q 4 3
                    ◇ Q 4 3
                    ♣ Q 8 7 4
        ♠ -                         ♠ Q 7 6
        ♡ J 10 9 6 5        N       ♡ 8 7 2
        ◇ J 10 2        W       E   ◇ 9 8 7 6 5
        ♣ J 10 9 6 5        S       ♣ K 2
                    ♠ A K J 10 9 8 2
                    ♡ A K
                    ◇ A K
                    ♣ A 3
```

Deal 138

The bidding:		Rubber game	
S	W	N	E
2 ♠ (forcing)	No	2 NT	No
3 ♣	No	4 ♣	No
4 NT	No	5 ♣	No
5 NT	No	6 ♣	No
6 ♠	No	No	No

S used Blackwood and quickly found the ♣ K off the hand, so he conservatively and wisely stopped at 6 ♠.

W led the ♡ J and S won. S wished he had bid the grand slam. His plan is to cash two top trumps to draw trumps, cash his top hearts

172

and diamonds, and enter dummy with his spade deuce to get a club discard on a red queen.

So to Trick 2 S laid down a top trump, finding Q x x in E, and making S's deuce useless.

The original plan is *kaput* and S has to form a New Plan.

Although the odds are slightly more than even that W holds the ♣ K (showing out of spades hence more clubs), there is no hope if he does; therefore the New Plan is to exit with a spade and compel E to lead either a red suit to dummy or away from his ♣ K.

Declarer must play off his three ace-kings before throwing E on lead; otherwise E can get off lead comfortably.

Often it is an opponent who must formulate a new plan, as in the next deal.

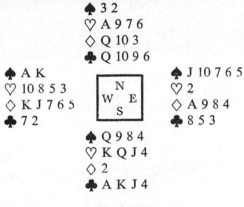

Deal 139

S bid 1 ♣, W 1 ◇, N 2 ♣, E 2 ◇; S 2 ♡, N 3 ♡; S 4 ♡ and W doubled. N should bid 1 ♡, not 2 ♣, then raise in clubs later if convenient.

W led the ♠ A, intending to continue with the ♠ K to show ace-king blank, then to put E in with a diamond and to get a spade ruff to break the contract.

When dummy went down and revealed only two spades, this plan proved futile. However, W played the ♠ K next anyway and led a low diamond to E's ace, and E returned a diamond which S ruffed. Declarer easily wrapped up the game. He drew three trumps, went to dummy with a club and drew W's last trump, and the good clubs and ♠ Q won the rest.

To Trick 2, W must formulate a new plan, keep the ♠ K and lead a diamond to E's ace. E returns a diamond and S ruffs. Now S is in hot water, for if he sets up his spade trick, W returns the $\Diamond$ K to force S to trump again and promote W's ten of trumps for the fourth trick to break the contract.

File O

OPPONENTS' PLAY

O stands for Opponents' Play. The subject is so tremendous that four complete books have been published exclusively on the defensive play of declarer's adversaries.

These are *Defensive Bridge* by E. M. Lagron of Chicago, Illinois, in 1934 and out of print. He covered both defensive bidding and play. Two others are *Defence at Contract Bridge* by 'Goulash' (Thorsons), an elementary text; and *Modspillet* by Aksel J. Nielsen, in Danish. The latest is an exhaustive masterpiece, *Winning Defence* by John Brown (Duckworth) which has attracted wide attention on both sides of the Atlantic.

File O is confined mostly to plays *inherently peculiar to the defence*, defensive communication signals such as standard leads, discards and echoes, and some special peters.

Some clarification of terms is in order. An adversary is either player against you, regardless of who is declarer. However, the term opponent implies an adversary of declarer, since the *Official Laws of Contract Bridge* refer to declarer's adversaries as LHO (Left Hand Opponent) and RHO.

We omit standard tables of leads and discards, for they appear in a plethora of pertinent basic literature. We aim to present special signals and the new Kelly Leads and Echoes, first published in *The Bridge Book Collector* of December 1952.

Special Signals

Special signals, including honour signals, fall into the seven categories below:

1. Peter for a special purpose.
2. Discarding an honour to show solidity.
3. Following suit with an honour on partner's winner.
4. Honour signal to show a doubleton.

5. Kelly solid suit signals.
6. Suit preference signal.*
7. Suit continuation length signals.

Let us examine these in detail. Everyone believes that a high-low signal, also called an echo or peter, is made to show a desire to ruff or to show support in the suit led, or to show a worthless doubleton when merely following suit to declarer's leads. In the latter case, it is made to give partner a count; elsewhere, for whatever reason, it is made to request a continuation.

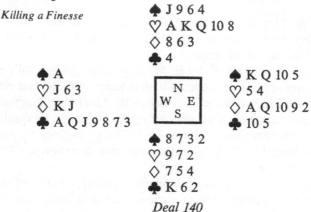

Killing a Finesse

          ♠ J 9 6 4
          ♡ A K Q 10 8
          ♢ 8 6 3
          ♣ 4

♠ A   ♠ K Q 10 5
♡ J 6 3   ♡ 5 4
♢ K J   ♢ A Q 10 9 2
♣ A Q J 9 8 7 3   ♣ 10 5

          ♠ 8 7 3 2
          ♡ 9 7 2
          ♢ 7 5 4
          ♣ K 6 2

Deal 140

At rubber game W bid 1 ♣, N 1 ♡, E 1 ♠; W 3 ♣, E 3 ♢; W 4 ♣ and E 5 ♣.

N led the ♡ K then ♡ Q, S failed to peter, so N shifted to a diamond which dummy won. The trump finesse succeeded, so W wrapped up his club game.

A highly intelligent kibitzer asked S why he didn't peter (deceptively) in hearts to ask for a third heart lead to force dummy, so that declarer could get only *one* lead through the trump king. S replied that he had thought of this protective echo but feared a Bath Coup by W with ♡ A J x.

S failed to draw inferences from the calling. Why did E and W shy away from three no-trumps and bid a minor suit game? They found they had no heart stopper. S, in fact, chucked.

---

* Some doubt exists in Britain whether William E. McKenney or Hy Lavinthal was primarily responsible for the suit-preference signal. Here it is universally styled—with whatever correctitude—a 'McKenney'.—Editor.
Lavinthal published his signal in *The Bridge World* of June 1934.—G.C.

Trump Echo

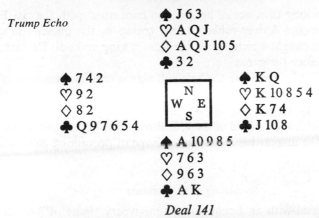

Deal 141

S bid 1 ♠, N 2 ♢; S 2 ♠, and N 4 ♠.

W led the ♡ 9 which the ace in dummy won. Next came a trump to the ace and a trump return to E's king.

E counted on his ♢ K for his third trick and, having noticed W play the deuce then four on trump leads, thought W was out of trumps, so E led the knave of clubs, hoping for a club trick to break the contract. S won, drew trumps, and lost the diamond finesse but scored game.

W should use the trump echo and play the four then deuce to show E a third trump plus the desire to ruff. Now E has no problem. At Trick 4 he cashes the ♡ K and gives his partner a heart ruff.

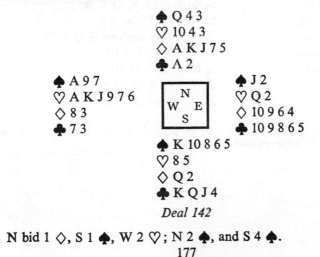

Deal 142

N bid 1 ♢, S 1 ♠, W 2 ♡; N 2 ♠, and S 4 ♠.

177

W led the king then ace of hearts, and continued with the six, E trumped low and S over-ruffed. A low trump to the queen and a trump return caught a rich dish of the knave, king and ace. Declarer won the balance for game.

At Trick 3 W should use Coffin's ruff signal and lead the *nine* of hearts, *his best heart under dummy's ten*, asking partner to put on his best trump. This play sets up W's nine of trumps for the setting trick. Even without the lead of the 9, E should ruff high with a value-less trump (the unguarded knave) in the hope of promoting partner's holding.*

Signalling with Honours

'Never signal with an honour' is a time-weary cliché of Auction Bridge days, strictly for the birds. This defunct axiom refers chiefly to showing a doubleton of partner's led suit. This, and honour discards, are admittedly spectacular; yet they form a technically sound part of Opponents' communications system. Signalling with honours is stepmotherly treated in most basic texts.

Throwing away an honour card with apparent abandon usually shows a wealth of top cards in the suit, and selecting the proper honour shows partner exact suit texture.

1. Discarding an Honour to show Solidity

HONOUR DISCARD	WHAT IT SHOWS
Ace	Solid suit (A K Q J, etc.)
King	Solid king high
Queen	Solid queen high or A Q J 10
Knave	A J 10 9 or K J 10 9
Ten	A K 10 9, A Q 10 9,
	A 10 9 8, K Q 10 9,
	K 10 9 8 or Q 10 9 8

---

* Trump promotion for partner by ruffing high is aptly styled the 'upper-cut' by Charles H. Goren.—Editor.

2. Following Suit with an Honour

PARTNER LEADS	YOU PLAY	SHOWING
Ace	King	K Q J
	Queen	Q J 10*
	Knave	K J 10†
	Ten	K Q 10 9
		K 10 9 or
		Q 10 9
King	Queen	Q J 10 9
		Q J blank
	Knave	A J 10†
	Ten	A Q 10 9,
		A 10 9 or
		Q 10 9

After playing the queen to partner's king lead, partner continues *low* to your knave (or to your void for you to ruff). This may let you in for a vital lead through one of declarer's tenaces.

3. Honour Signal to show a Doubleton

When partner opens his suit, rarely signal with an honour to show a doubleton such as Q x, J x or 10 x, for the nature of your holding is revealed on the second lead. The only valid exception is to play the knave from J x when partner leads the king at no trumps. This cannot possibly show A J 10, for partner must hold at least A K 10 or K Q 10 heading his suit. If your partner opened the king from A K 10 x x, the knave play suggests a shift to put you in and let you return his suit through declarer's queen. But it is more probable that your partner led from K Q 10 x x and the knave play assures partner that declarer is not playing a Bath Coup with A J x.

4. Kelly Solid Suit Signals

Mr. Nathan S. Kelly of Boston, Mass., world whist champion, has devised a neat system of signals which enables the opening leader to show the exact strength of his suit when partner returns it. Kelly's signals require close attention to small cards in order to draw correct deductions. Here is a basic position:

* And suggests a shift, for it shows the king with declarer.
† Suggests that partner continue the suit, especially if the queen appears to be trapped.

♡ K 5

Declarer ♡ A Q   ♡ 8 4   Dummy

♡ J 10 2

Partner (North) leads the five and your ten forces the queen. Later you get in via another suit and you lead the knave, declarer plays the ace and partner drops the king!

Who controls the hearts?

The king play shows that N controls hearts and declarer has no further stopper. With the A, K, Q, J, 10 and 8 played, N holds the nine and seven. Furthermore, Kelly makes a second stipulation, at no-trump play only that *N held at least five hearts.*

The complete picture is:

♡ K 9 7 5 3

♡ A Q 6   ♡ 8 4

♡ J 10 2

N may hold the six also in a six-card suit, but you learn the vital fact that he has three good hearts.

If Kelly opens fourth best from a knave- or ten-high suit, he disregards the five-card restriction and signals with a four-card suit also. This play warns that the suit is poor and it may give the clue for a killing shift by partner. For example:

♡ 10 5

Declarer ♡ A Q   ♡ 8 4   Dummy

♡ J 9 2

N led the five and your knave forced the queen. You get in via another suit later, and return the nine to declarer's ace and N drops the ten! What hearts does N hold?

With K 10 7 5 3 N would have signalled with the king and with K 10 7 5 he would have played the seven. N is showing you *secondary* heart solidity, having led from 10 7 6 5 (3).

If a defender cannot spare his best card to show a sequence, he may follow suit with his *second best*.

♡ 9 5

Declarer ♡ K Q   ♡ 8 4   Dummy

♡ J 7 2

N led the five and your knave drove out the king. You later get in and return the seven which W's queen wins and N drops the nine! From what did N lead?

The hidden cards are A, 10, 6 and 3. N's fourth best opening shows *two* of the three cards higher than the five, that is, A 10, A 6, or 10 6.

If N holds 10, 6, his suit was 10 9 6 5 and he would have played the ten instead of the nine on the second round. This indicates the ace with N, supported by further evidence that W would have played it if he had held it.

If N had A 10 9 5, his proper opening lead is the ten, not the five; and even if he had opened the five incorrectly, his suit is solid when W plays the queen and N would have won with the ace. Here is the complete picture:

$$\heartsuit \text{A 9 6 5 3}$$

$$\heartsuit \text{K Q 10} \qquad\qquad \heartsuit \text{8 4}$$

$$\heartsuit \text{J 7 2}$$

A similar position follows below:

$$\heartsuit \text{7 5}$$

$$\text{Declarer } \heartsuit \text{A Q} \qquad\qquad \heartsuit \text{8 4 Dummy}$$

$$\heartsuit \text{J 9 2}$$

N leads the five and your knave forces the queen. You get in later and push the nine, W plays the ace and N drops the seven!

With what hearts did N start life?

Again N gives you an exact reading. N would have played the ten from 10 7 6, for these cards are equals when the nine and eight have fallen; or the king from K 10 7 5 3. So W must hold the ten and N the king for one of his three cards higher than his fourth-best opening, the five. The full picture is:

$$\heartsuit \text{K 7 6 5 3}$$

$$\heartsuit \text{A Q 10} \qquad\qquad \heartsuit \text{8 4}$$

$$\heartsuit \text{J 9 2}$$

These second-best-card solid-suit signals also show a five-card or longer suit as a rule.

5. The Suit Preference Signal

The lead directing suit preference signal was invented by Hy Lavinthal of Trenton, New Jersey. It enables an opponent to show his partner which suit to lead. A high-card signal indicates a higher-ranking suit, a low card requests a lower-ranking suit; while an intermediate card suggests no clear choice.

A restriction is that the signal must never be made if it can be misinterpreted as an ordinary encouragement or discouragement card. The suit of the signal card may have been supported by one defender in the calling, confirming solidity. Dummy may be void of the suit and have ample trumps, or the suit may be otherwise neutral with no trick-winning interest.

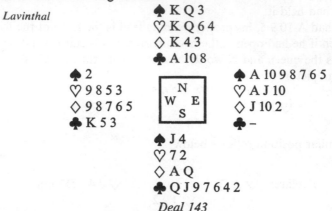

Lavinthal

♠ K Q 3
♡ K Q 6 4
◇ K 4 3
♣ A 10 8

♠ 2
♡ 9 8 5 3
◇ 9 8 7 6 5
♣ K 5 3

♠ A 10 9 8 7 6 5
♡ A J 10
◇ J 10 2
♣ -

♠ J 4
♡ 7 2
◇ A Q
♣ Q J 9 7 6 4 2

Deal 143

N bid 1 NT, E 3 ♠, S 4 ♣; N 4 ♡, and S 5 ♣.

E won the ♠ 2 opening with the ace and returned the ♠ 5 which W ruffed. W huddled long and painfully over his next lead and decided that a diamond was safer than attacking dummy's strong hearts. S won the diamond, finessed trumps, and rattled off his game by parking his heart losers on the third diamond and spade tricks.

Some players in W's position might return a heart on the slender clue that S backed away from the heart suit in the calling; but S could hold the ♡ A instead of the ◇ A and call the same way.

At Trick 2 E should return his best spade, the ten, to W for a heart return. Here there is no ambiguity in the signal.

6. Suit Continuation Length Signals

Kelly borrowed from whist a valuable set of honour signals to show partner the length of your suit.

Suppose you lead the king and it wins. Which card do you lead to Trick 2 from these suits:

K Q J 4   K Q J 7 5

Continue with the queen to show a four-card suit, but lead the knave to show five cards.

K Q J 10 9   K Q J 10 9 8

Lead the knave to show five cards, but the ten to show six cards.

K Q J 8 7 6   K Q J 8 7 6 5

In these cases the best you can do is to lead the knave, for you lack the ten to show six cards or the nine to show seven.

The basic principle of these length showing leads is: *the longer the suit, the lower the second card led.* These niceties will help your partner get a count on your hand and, *ergo*, a count on declarer.

If you are lucky enough to be on lead against no-trumps with such a suit as A K Q 4 3 or A K Q 4 3 2, *open with the queen* in both cases, then continue with the ace to show five cards or the king to show six cards. These leads cannot be confused with A K Q 2, for with only four cards you would open naturally with the king.

These special signals help partner to count so that he can unblock if necessary. Suppose the position is:

◇ 7 6 5 4

Dummy   ◇ J 8   ◇ 10 9   Declarer

◇ A K Q 3 2

You open the queen and partner starts a Foster echo to show four (or more) cards in your suit by playing his *second best*, the six. Next he drops the four on your ace, so you lead the three next, your original fourth best, for him to win and you win the fourth and fifth leads.

Without knowing that N holds four cards, you would bang down all three honours first and partner must block the suit on the fourth lead.

Alternately N can show 7 6 5 4 by dropping the five then the six and hope that you see the four fail to drop (in case you happened to fail to show A K Q x x by opening with the king).

If N holds J 6 5 4, he should play the six first as the beginning of a Foster echo, then drop the *five* instead of the four next in order to show an honour card.

Look over the defensive deals below. They cover opening leads, the middle game, and a couple of endings. They show aspects of defence unknown in ordinary parlour bridge.

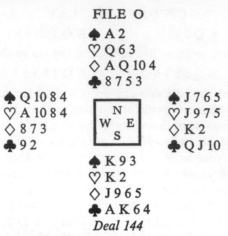

♠ A 2
♡ Q 6 3
◇ A Q 10 4
♣ 8 7 5 3

♠ Q 10 8 4
♡ A 10 8 4
◇ 8 7 3
♣ 9 2

♠ J 7 6 5
♡ J 9 7 5
◇ K 2
♣ Q J 10

♠ K 9 3
♡ K 2
◇ J 9 6 5
♣ A K 6 4

Deal 144

S bid 1 NT and N 3 NT.*

If you are W, do you open spades or hearts? Why?

The old axiom of opening your longest and strongest suit at no-trumps is much overworked. If declarer or dummy bid your longest suit or suits, often the best opening is an *unbid* suit even if short, preferably a major. And as with the case in hand, the *weaker* of two equally long suits should be opened. The proper opening is the ♠ 4, not the ♡ 4. The idea is to use the ♡ A as an entry to bring in the spades, for the ♠ Q may be too remote an entry to bring in hearts.

If W opens a heart to S's king, the diamond finesse loses. E returns a heart to clear the suit and dummy scores the queen; and S gets home with two spade tricks, two hearts, three diamonds and two clubs.

If W opens a spade, declarer is left to his own devices and gets only one heart trick, falling one trick short of game.

Contra Ruff?

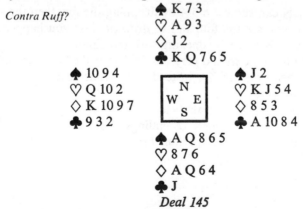

♠ K 7 3
♡ A 9 3
◇ J 2
♣ K Q 7 6 5

♠ 10 9 4
♡ Q 10 2
◇ K 10 9 7
♣ 9 3 2

♠ J 2
♡ K J 5 4
◇ 8 5 3
♣ A 10 8 4

♠ A Q 8 6 5
♡ 8 7 6
◇ A Q 6 4
♣ J

Deal 145

SAB: S 1 ♣, N 1 ◇; S 1 NT, and N 3 NT.

S bid 1 ♠, N 2 ♣; S 2 ◇, N 3 ♠; and S 4 ♠.

What should W lead?

W took the view that dummy will ruff his diamonds held with S and opened a trump. S won, cleared clubs, and got two heart discards on dummy's top clubs.

A trump opening is often good against declarer's known two-suiter, but in this case *dummy bid a third suit* which threatened to furnish discards. W must abandon the anti-ruff plan and open the unbid heart suit, the deuce, for early heart tricks before declarer can get discards.

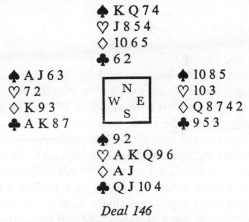

♠ K Q 7 4
♡ J 8 5 4
◇ 10 6 5
♣ 6 2

♠ A J 6 3   ♠ 10 8 5
♡ 7 2   ♡ 10 3
◇ K 9 3   ◇ Q 8 7 4 2
♣ A K 8 7   ♣ 9 5 3

♠ 9 2
♡ A K Q 9 6
◇ A J
♣ Q J 10 4

Deal 146

S bid 1 ♡, W doubled, N 2 ♡; and S 4 ♡.

W opened the ♣ K.

What should W lead to Trick 2?

Mr. Arthur Bell of Boston, Mass., was W. After some thought he made an atrocious-looking lead away from his king of diamonds. He shifted to the ◇ 3, drawing the queen and ace. S drew trumps and led the ♣ 10, hoping to catch W napping, but W scored his aces and the ◇ K to break the contract.

If W leads any suit but diamonds to Trick 2, declarer has time to draw trumps and set up clubs for diamond discards from dummy.

W found 'a shift in time to hold to nine'!

FILE O

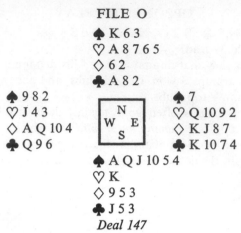

♠ K 6 3
♡ A 8 7 6 5
◇ 6 2
♣ A 8 2

♠ 9 8 2   ♠ 7
♡ J 4 3   ♡ Q 10 9 2
◇ A Q 10 4   ◇ K J 8 7
♣ Q 9 6   ♣ K 10 7 4

♠ A Q J 10 5 4
♡ K
◇ 9 5 3
♣ J 5 3

Deal 147

S bid 3 ♠ and N 4 ♠.

W opened the ♠ 9, the conventional top of nothing, and a trump to avoid opening a tenace suit, and S won with the ace.

S cashed the ♡ K and led a diamond to W's ten. W returned the deuce of trumps which the six in dummy held. *This windfall gave declarer an extra entry to dummy to promote hearts.* S ruffed a heart, scored the trump king, and ruffed another heart. The ♣ A put dummy in to cash the ♡ A and ♡ 8 for two discards and game.

In America a small group of experts now leads the *bottom* card from 9 x x, and these experts relish the deal above to prove their point. If W opens the *deuce of trumps*, he can break the contract!

The underlead from 9 x x is good in trumps, but we question its value in a plain suit, where the standard 'top of nothing' practice is still preferable.

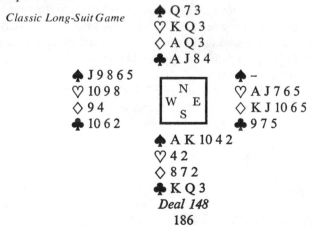

Classic Long-Suit Game

♠ Q 7 3
♡ K Q 3
◇ A Q 3
♣ A J 8 4

♠ J 9 8 6 5   ♠ –
♡ 10 9 8   ♡ A J 7 6 5
◇ 9 4   ◇ K J 10 6 5
♣ 10 6 2   ♣ 9 7 5

♠ A K 10 4 2
♡ 4 2
◇ 8 7 2
♣ K Q 3

Deal 148

With game-in, N bid 1 NT, E 2 ♡, S 4 ♠, and W doubled.

W led the ♡ 10 to the queen and ace. Dummy won the heart return, and laid down the trump queen to discover the horrible 5–0 split.

S won a club, lost the ◇ Q finesse, and dummy won a diamond return. Next S made the critical play. He ruffed the heart.

S won a club, then dummy won another, and S shed the diamond on dummy's last club, boxing W's trumps. W was down to ♠ J 9 8 5, had to ruff the club for his only trump trick and lead up to ♠ A K 10.

W opened hearts, hoping to shorten declarer's trumps to give W trump control and E several heart tricks, the classic long suit game. However, W's trump holding is not the right type for this long suit plan, for the trump ending which occurred is imminent.

W must try for a ruff from the start and open the ◇ 9. However S plays, W gets a diamond ruff *and* a natural trump trick, and E gets a heart and a diamond to break the contract.

E told W that he was a sucker to double 4 ♠, but W would have escaped the ire had he defended properly.

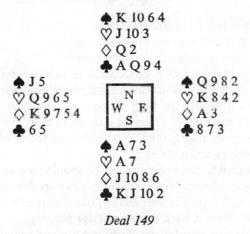

Deal 149

S bid 1 ♣, N 1 ♠; S 2 ♠, N 3 ♣; and S 3 NT.

W led the ◇ 5 to E's ace. E returned the ◇ 3 like a good parrot who always plays on his partner's suit regardless, and W won with his king. W realized that diamonds were hopeless and shifted to the ♡ 5, drawing the ten, king and ace. S now has nine tricks on top, with a play in hearts for a tenth trick at match points.

E should do a little counting *at Trick 1* and break the contract.

Clearly W has five diamonds at most* which place four diamonds with S. S probably holds four clubs for his club bid and three spades for his spade raise, hence only TWO hearts.

If S holds ♡ A Q, a heart return at Trick 2 is harmless; but if S holds ♡ A x, as is the case, a low heart shift ruins him.

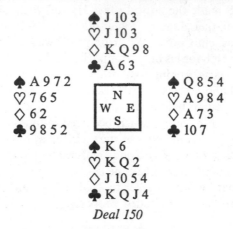

Deal 150

At no score S bid 1 NT and N 3 NT.

W led the ♠ 2 and dummy played the knave.

As E, how do you defend? Do you cover?

Like a good trained seal E conformed to two axioms: 'cover an honour with an honour' and 'third hand plays high'. He played his queen which S won with the king. S drove out the ◇ A, E returned a spade to W's ace and W returned a spade to clear the suit. But S collected two spade tricks, three diamonds, and four clubs, without touching hearts, to wrap up game.

Before E played to the opening lead, he should stop to count. W's spade deuce was a fourth best, placing only two spades with declarer. If they are A x, E's play is immaterial; but if they are A K or K x, the queen play gives a trick to declarer for nothing.

E has nothing to lose by the duck and a good chance to gain a trick: the contract-breaker in this case. E should, of course, encourage by playing ♠ 8.

* E can count the diamonds easily: W led ◇ 5; ◇ 3 and ◇ 2 are both visible, so W can have at best a five-card suit, holding ◇ 4. If he held K J 10, he would have opened ◇ J; even if he holds K 10 9 5 4, he would have led ◇ 10. The only holding he can have when an immediate diamond return would work is K J 9 5 4. Against the chance of that one holding, a heart holding damaging to declarer is odds on.—Editor.

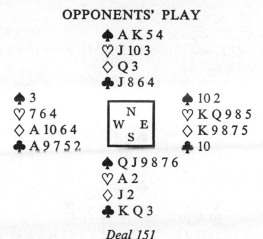

Deal 151

In rubber game S bid 1 ♠, N 3 ♠ a limit raise, and S 4 ♠.*
W led the ♣ A then the ♣ 2 which E ruffed.

E returned the ♡ K to S's ace, and S scored game. S drew trumps, cashed his club, and entered dummy with a trump. Off went S's heart on the ♣ J, and dummy led the ♡ J which E covered and S ruffed. Another trump to dummy let S park a diamond loser on the good ♡ 10.

E wailed about his rotten luck, for he was a big loser for the night. W pointed out that his ♣ 2 lead to Trick 2 was a suit preference signal, requesting a *diamond* lead to Trick 3. If E returns a diamond instead of a heart at Trick 3, W wins and gives E another club ruff, and E scores the ♢ K to set the contract two tricks.

Japanese Seki Position

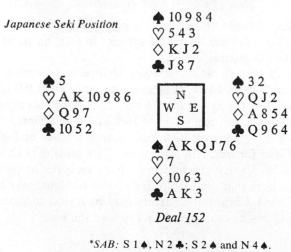

Deal 152

SAB: S 1 ♠, N 2 ♣; S 2 ♠ and N 4 ♠.
189

W bid 1 ♡, E 2 ♡; and S 4 ♠.

W led the ♡ K and E played the ♡ Q. Next W led the ♡ 10 to E's knave and S ruffed.

S decided to try for an ending in diamonds, so he cashed the ♠ A then ♠ 10 and ruffed the table's last heart. Next S played clubs top down to throw E on lead in this ending:

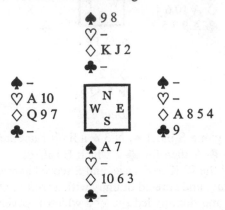

A club return by E is suicide by ruff-discard, so E exited gracefully with the ◇ 4, S ducked, W spoiled the opponents' holding play by putting up his queen and the ball game was over.

W missed the point of E's lead.

W must duck! This holding play lets the knave win, but creates a *seki* position. Declarer loses *two* diamond tricks however he plays.

Remarks on Special Signals

On concluding this file on opponent's play, we wish to caution readers on the excessive use of special signals: in fact, on standard echoes and peters in general.

The echo-fiend tries to signal at every chance and watches his partner's low cards like a hawk. If he sees a seven or eight fall from his partner's hand on the first lead of a suit, Mr. Fiend gets right in there and pushes that suit regardless of Hell and high water.

Remember that partner may be forced to drop a seven or higher card on a first lead for lack of a lower card. This possibility should always be considered, and if you try to get a tentative count on unseen hands, you may learn that what looks like a come-on signal may be a forced natural card. Conversely, partner may be forced to throw a deuce from K Q 2—for example when you lead the ace.

Beware of the Lavinthal. Selectively used on urgent occasions, it is a beautiful defensive tool. But, like all tools, it was designed for a specific purpose. It has cost defenders more chucked games and slams than it has salvaged through constant abuse. An ordinary echo may be made on the majority of deals, but the need for a Lavinthal appears about twice in one hundred deals, or nearly once in an average session of bridge.

Kelly solid suit signals (and suit continuation length signals) should not be used unless both you and your partner have studied and analysed them carefully. They are difficult and tricky. Their value appears chiefly in no-trump play, and great care should be taken to avoid confusing them with Lavinthal and/or other signals.*

PERCENTAGE FREQUENCIES OF SUIT SPLITS

Enemy cards				
7	4–3 .. 62%	5–2 .. 31%	6–1 .. 7%	7–0 .. ½%
6	4–2 .. 48%	3–3 .. 36%	5–1 .. 15%	6–0 .. 1%
5	3–2 .. 68%		4–1 .. 28%	5–0 .. 5%
4	3–1 .. 50%		2–2 .. 40%	4–0 .. 10%
3	2–1 .. 78%			3–0 .. 22%
2	1–1 .. 52%			2–0 .. 48%

When opponents hold an odd number of cards, they are more often than not as evenly divided as possible; whereas an even number of cards is more often unevenly divided.

As soon as any enemy short suit is revealed, these percentages change.

DECLARER'S PERCENTAGE FREQUENCIES OF DROPPING A SINGLETON KING BY PLAYING THE ACE

11 cards .. 52%   10 cards .. 26%   9 cards .. 12%
8 cards .. 6%   7 cards .. 2%   6 cards .. 1%

DECLARER'S PERCENTAGE FREQUENCIES OF DROPPING A DOUBLETON QUEEN BY PLAYING THE ACE AND KING

10 cards .. 78%   9 cards .. 40%   8 cards .. 27%
7 cards .. 16%   6 cards .. 9%   5 cards .. 5%

* The Kelly signals are virtually unknown in Britain.—Editor.

File P

PERCENTAGE

P stands for Percentage. Every deal has some percentage aspect, usually so basic or incidental that it is taken for granted. File P contains only those deals where percentage values dominate the strategy.

Two special books have been published on bridge percentages, *Mathematical Odds in Contract* by Eugene Northrup and Arthur Stein in 1933, a basic primer now out of print; and *Theorie Mathematique du Bridge,* par Emile Borel et Andre Cheron (Gauthier-Villars, Paris, 1940). The latter is an exhaustive scientific tome of 412 pages in French. We can do little more than hit the high spots in a general work like this.

Percentage Plays, Safety Plays and Sure Trick Plays all form a natural part of the Winning Line Tribe and have one characteristic in common. Declarer always has a choice of plays from which to select the winning line. Plays under these four files are separated by their individual characteristics as follows :

Percentage Play. The key to winning is to select from parallel possibilities the line of play offering the best odds and to exclude other lines; or to echelon a vertical series of plays in the best order for top percentage. *Vide* opening paragraphs under M for Mêlée.

Safety Play. The popular book-definition is a method of play which limits the loss of tricks if distribution is unfavourable. Gambit is usually involved, because play for a *maximum* number of tricks is abandoned in order to insure a specified *minimum.* Single suit safety plays belong in this file, but when a combination of suits is involved, a border-line deal straddles the Percentage and Safety Files.

Sure Trick Play. For convenience in alphabetical filing, this is considered a sub-file of Safety Play. As a practical matter, it is a percentage play with favourable odds of unity, or 100%.

Winning Line. Plays belonging under the three foregoing files are excluded. Usually declarer relies on deductions from enemy bids

and/or plays in order to select the winning line of play from attractive-looking choices.

THE THREE LAWS OF PROBABILITY

All percentages are based on the Three Laws of Probability. The student should understand these three laws and how they apply to computing odds at bridge.

LAW OF SINGLE EVENT

The probability of a favourable event equals one divided by the number of possible events, provided that every possible event has an equal chance to occur.

For example, take the simple ace-queen finesse. The number of possible events is finding the king on or off side. Each outcome equals one-half and their sum is unity. The favourable outcome is winning the finesse, which is one-half or 50%.

Note the basic premise: *every possible event has an equal chance to occur.* In the early play of a hand this condition exists if shapes are balanced and enemy calling and/or plays do not indicate that one opponent is more likely to hold the king than the other.

Conventional percentage tables in textbooks are based on this assumption. However, as the play of a hand progresses *the odds constantly shift as certain cards and distributions are revealed.*

Textbooks ignore, or at best casually mention, this factor, analysed in great detail in only one work, *Theorie Mathematique du Bridge.*

With deals under File P, space permits only a brief percentage analysis to approximately the nearest 1%, usually without minor adjustments for shifting odds. A perfect analysis in each case would require countless formulae and would run from two to fifty pages.

For an example of shifting odds, note the simple finesse matrix below:

$$\diamondsuit \text{A Q 7 4} \qquad \text{Dummy, North}$$
$$\diamondsuit \text{6 5 3} \qquad \text{Declarer}$$

Suppose at Trick 2 you have no inkling of the enemy shapes and you decide to finesse. Your odds for success are 50%.

Now suppose that you avoid this suit until late in the play of the hand and you get an exact count of four diamonds with W and two with E. What chance has the queen finesse now?

The solution is based on the Law of Either/Or.

FILE P

If a favourable event may occur in two or more mutually independent ways, the probability of the favourable event equals the SUM *of the probabilities of the necessary single events.*

E's known doubleton may occur in the fifteen mutually independent ways below:

K J	K 10	K 9	K 8	K 2
	J 10	J 9	J 8	J 2
		10 9	10 8	10 2
			9 8	9 2
				8 2

Each doubleton will occur once in fifteen times, and the sum of the probabilities of each of the ten favourable kingless doubletons is 10/15ths or 2/3rds or 66 2/3%.

Section I—Parallel Arrangement of Plays

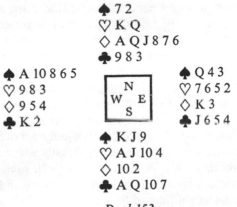

```
                    ♠ 7 2
                    ♡ K Q
                    ◇ A Q J 8 7 6
                    ♣ 9 8 3
♠ A 10 8 6 5                        ♠ Q 4 3
♡ 9 8 3          ┌─────────┐        ♡ 7 6 5 2
◇ 9 5 4          │   N     │        ◇ K 3
♣ K 2            │ W   E   │        ♣ J 6 5 4
                 │   S     │
                 └─────────┘
                    ♠ K J 9
                    ♡ A J 10 4
                    ◇ 10 2
                    ♣ A Q 10 7
```

Deal 153

S bid 1 NT, N 3 ◇; S 3 ♡, and N 3 NT.

W led the ♠ 6 to E's queen.

What plan do you adopt?

S took the ♠ Q with the king and, dazzled by the glitter of the diamonds, he finessed the ◇ 10. This play, with its 50% odds, lost to E's king and E returned a spade through S's knave to let W get four spade tricks and rook the game.

In his haste declarer overlooked the fertility of the club suit, offering three potent elements. First, by avoidance play, finessing clubs

into W, S can keep E off lead and protect the ♠ J. Second, declarer needs only *three club tricks* for game. With a spade trick, four hearts and the ◇ A they total nine tricks. Third, the diamond finesse offers only 50% odds whereas the clubs offer much more. How much more? This brings us to the

LAW OF COMPOUND EVENT

If a favourable event depends mutually upon two or more single events, the probability of the favourable event equals the PRODUCT *of the probabilities of the necessary single events.*

Win Trick 2 with the ♡ K and finesse the ♣ 9.

What are the odds of winning four club tricks?

You have one chance in two or 50% of finding the knave with E; and the same for the king. Now only *half the time* while E holds the knave will he also hold the king, so he will hold both honours only a QUARTER of the time. This compound event is the PRODUCT, 50% of 50% equals 25%.

If E holds ♣ K J x, you get four club tricks, a spade, and four hearts which you cash for game. After you have these nine tricks securely tucked away in your satchel, you can afford the luxury of a gamble on the diamond finesse for extra tricks.

But W takes the ♣ 9 with the king, marking the knave with E W returns a diamond, but with only three club tricks now available, you must play the ◇ A and finesse clubs again to pick up the knave.

By the same Law of Compound Event, W will hold ♣ K J (x) 25% of the time, unfavourable odds. Hence your remaining odds for game by playing on clubs are 75% favourable; on diamonds only 50%.

And in this 25% zone (♣ K J x in W) the ◇ A play has a little percentage to drop the lone king from E. Of the 28% odds for a 4–1 diamond split, E will hold the singleton half the 28% of the time —or 14%. When this occurs E's singleton may be any one of five cards, so 1/5th of 14% equals nearly 3%. This raises your 75% to 78%.

GLOSSARY OF TERMS

In order to shorten percentage analyses, we use several terms in a rather specialized way.

Chances. A general term not specifying any particular odds.

Combined. Of two frequencies whose percentages are added in order to obtain the frequency of the desired outcome by the Law of Either-Or.

Complex. Combined and compound.

Compound. Of two frequencies whose percentages are multiplied in order to obtain the frequency of the desired outcome by the Law of Compound Event.

Event. Any one of several ways in which opponent's cards may fall, each of which has an equal chance of occurring.

Frequency. The mathematical probability of the occurrence of any event, expressed in this book in %.

Odds. Odds are usually expressed in small fractions or ratios such as once in four times or 1/4th which equals 3–1 odds against, and NOT 4–1 odds against (which would be 1/5th). In this book we express odds in percentages and use the word 'odds' to imply favourable odds.

Outcome. The percentage result of a computation in probabilities.

Percentage. The number of favourable outcomes in 100 cases and expressed in percentage, to wit, 40%, 78%, etc.

Produce or *Product.* Implies multiplication of two percentages in accordance with the Law of Compound Event.

Sum (or *Added* or *Total*). Implies addition of two percentages in accordance with the Law of Either-Or.

Zone. The remaining number of unfavourable outcomes expressed in percentage after the percentage of favourable outcomes has been computed or estimated. For example, if a favourable outcome depends upon the 2–2 split of opponent's cards of a suit with 40% odds, the zone would be 60%.

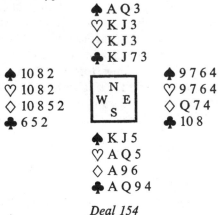

Deal 154

Playing Acol S bid 2 NT on his 20 points and N made it 7 NT on his 18 points, seeing 38 points combined. *

*SAB: S 1 ♣, N 1 ◇; S 3 NT to show 19 to 21 points, and N 7 NT on a total of 37 partnership points guaranteed.

PERCENTAGE

W leads the ◇ 2. Do you finesse the knave at once ?

A thoughtless player finessed the knave at once. It had a 50% chance of winning. E covered with the queen and declarer couldn't eat the ◇ 10 at the end and lost a trick.

The proper technique is to *echelon your plays and pyramid the odds in your favour*. The ◇ 9 is worth an extra 25% in odds if you duck the ◇ 2 opening in dummy.

Compare the two plays: the immediate knave finesse and the duck. If W holds ◇ Q 10 x, either play wins; if E holds ◇ Q 10 x, neither play wins; and if W holds the queen and E the ten, either play wins (by finessing knave on first or second round respectively).

But if W holds the ten and E the Queen, the immediate knave finesse loses with almost no chance of recovery; *but the duck forces out the queen at once.*

Exchange the ◇ 9 for the ◇ 7. You should still duck in dummy to enjoy the 1% improvement in odds that E holds the blank queen plus an undeterminable percentage, based on human error, that E will blunder and put up the queen instead of finessing the nine.

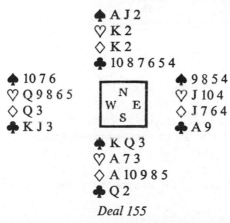

```
              ♠ A J 2
              ♡ K 2
              ◇ K 2
              ♣ 10 8 7 6 5 4
♠ 10 7 6                        ♠ 9 8 5 4
♡ Q 9 8 6 5      N              ♡ J 10 4
◇ Q 3        W       E          ◇ J 7 6 4
♣ K J 3          S              ♣ A 9
              ♠ K Q 3
              ♡ A 7 3
              ◇ A 10 9 8 5
              ♣ Q 2
```

Deal 155

Playing Acol, S bid 1 NT*, N 3 NT.

W led the ♡ 6. With seven tricks on top, how do you play for two more in diamonds?

Declarer won the ♡ 6 with the king in dummy. He avoided the error of a hold-up, which might let opponents get a heart trick, a diamond and three clubs to break the contract.

* A super-maximum, with 15½ points and a five-card suit, for an Acol (13–15 non-vulnerable) no-trumper.—Editor.

197

Declarer cashed the ◇ K which was correct, and finessed the ◇ 10 to W's queen, which lost the game.

When E follows low to the second diamond lead, S must pop on the ace in an attempt to drop W's honour. S continues diamonds to drive out the knave and score four diamond tricks.

If W holds ◇ Q J x x, the suit is hopeless; and if diamonds split 3–3, either line of play wins. The diamond doubletons in W are the only critical holdings, of which eight include an honour and six no honour; so the percentage play on the second diamond lead is the *ace* for a drop of Q or J.

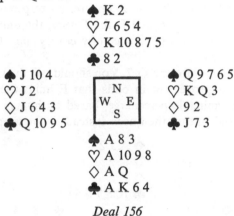

Deal 156

Playing Acol, S bid 2 NT and N 3 NT.

W led the ♠ J. How do you score game?

S won the ♠ J with the ace, cashed the ◇ A Q, and led a low heart, hoping for a club shift to gain time to set up a heart trick. However, W won with the knave and returned a spade to the king in dummy. The ◇ K failed to drop the knave, so the skids were under S and he skidded to defeat.

S bet either on a 3–3 diamond split for 36% odds, or a doubleton knave for 16% totalling 52%. (Of 15 possible doubletons, only five include the ◇ J. And 5/15ths of 48% for a 4–2 split equals 16%.)

Win the spade opening with the ace, cash the ◇ A and *overtake* the queen with the king. If the knave or the 'neglected' nine drops, continue diamonds to establish them. This line yields game with the same 52% odds *plus four doubleton nine possibilities* for 13% more, or 65% in all. And 65% is a better bet than 52%.

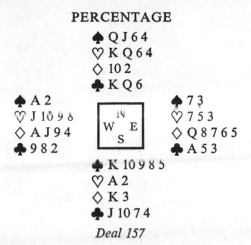

♠ Q J 6 4
♡ K Q 6 4
◇ 10 2
♣ K Q 6

♠ A 2   ♠ 7 3
♡ J 10 9 8   ♡ 7 5 3
◇ A J 9 4   ◇ Q 8 7 6 5
♣ 9 8 2   ♣ A 5 3

♣ K 10 9 8 5
♡ A 2
◇ K 3
♣ J 10 7 4

Deal 157

S opened 1 ♠, N jumped to 3 ♠; and S said 4 ♠.*
W led the ♡ J.

S chucked this one quickly. He won the ♡ A and led the ♠ 8 which W grabbed with his ace. W shifted to a club to E's ace and E dug out a diamond to let W pick off S's ◇ K for two diamond tricks to break the contract.

The bugaboo of a heart ruff by W scared S off the winning path. S should cash dummy's top hearts at once for a diamond discard. If E trumps a heart, S over-ruffs and still has a chance to score the ◇ K.

Starting trumps at once risks defeat if W holds the ◇ A and E *either* black ace as entry for a diamond lead through the king.

50%

E will hold the ◇ A 50% of the time, favouring declarer.

12½%

W will hold the ◇ A 50% of the time, of which he will also hold both black aces 25% of the time, producing 12½%.
S has a sum of 62½% odds to favour starting trumps at once.

Better Odds, Hearts Break 62%

Odds of 62% favour a 4–3 split, leaving a 31% zone when an opponent trumps the third heart lead in a 5–2 heart split.

8%

Of this 31%, half or 16% of the time E will trump to let S over-ruff; then half again or nearly 8% if the ◇ K play scores.
The sum of 62% and 8% is 70%, favouring play on hearts at once.

*SAB: S 1 ♠, N 3 ♠; and S 4 ♠.

Penetrating the Percentages

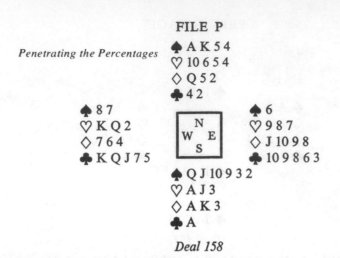

Deal 158

S bid 2 ♠ (Acol), N 5 ♠; and S made it 6 ♠.*†

W led the ♣ K which declarer won. Next came the ♠ Q, ♠ A, and a club ruff, followed by the ◇ A, ◇ K, then ◇ Q.

Thus declarer drew trumps and properly bailed out the minor suits in order to set the stage for an end-play, the *cross-ruff fork strip*, so called because you try to force an enemy lead that lets you ruff in one hand while you sluff in the other, or to lead up to your fork, or tenace.

To Trick 8 declarer led a low heart to his ace and returned a low heart, hoping to find ♡ K Q, K x or Q x doubleton. But W's royal couple scored two heart tricks to break the contract.

To Trick 8 declarer should insert the knave third hand and stick to a decision to play enemy heart honours *married in one hand*. In other words, if W held ♡ K x or Q x, this plan fails; but the odds are 35% for the ace play and 53% for the knave play.

Remember the combination, for you lack the nine of hearts for a sure trick play of 100% odds. Here is the comparative analysis.

Ace 29%, Knave 19%

The 4–2 heart split of 48% frequency occurs fifteen different ways including nine ways with a doubleton honour, so 9/15ths of 48% equals 29% for the ace play and 19% for the knave play.

* Preferable bidding would be 2 ♠–3 ♠; 4 NT–5 NT (the too-often-overlooked response to the Culbertson 4 NT: 5 NT is the reply on (a) two aces or (b) one ace and *all* the bid kings (for now the 4 NT bidder is sure to have 3 aces). In this case, 'all' the bid kings means only one. But at least S knows his trumps are solid. —Editor.

†*SAB:* S 1 ♠, W 2 ♣, N 2 ♠, E 3 ♣, S 4 ♣, N 5 ♠; and S 6 ♠. N's jump to 5 ♠ shows an original fat raise including the ace or ace-king of trumps.

If you can get a count on enemy shapes that proves a 4–2 heart split, the ace play has a 10% edge (actually a 19% edge for the 48% odds of the 4–2 heart split becomes unity or 100%).

But this is not the whole story.

Ace 0%, Knave 18%

The 3–3 split of 36% frequency finds the honours married half the 36% time producing 18% when the knave play wins. The ace play always loses, so the knave gains 18% here.

Ace 5%, Knave 15%

The 5–1 split of 15% frequency finds the king or queen bare twice in six ways, so 1/3rd of 15% produces 5% for the ace play. But the knave play wins all 15% of the time, gaining 10%. (The knave play includes those cases when second hand plays an honour which the ace wins.)

Ace 1%, Knave 1%

In the 6–0 split of 1% frequency, the knave play always wins, and the ace usually wins, for E with ♡ K Q 9 8 7 2 usually splits his equals in honours. Credit both plays 1% each.

Total Odds are 35 % for the Ace and 53% for the Knave

We conclude that the ace play has about one chance in three to win while the knave play has better than an even chance.

Section II—Plays in Vertical Arrangement

In this section, declarer may have to make more than one play in order to bring home his contract; and his problem is to co-ordinate his plays in the best possible sequence to obtain top percentage. Declarer should make a comprehensive plan, offering a second try for the contract if the first play fails, and better still, having a third play in reserve if the first two fail. Stated another way, keep as many strings to your bow as possible.

FILE P

Two Plays in Echelon

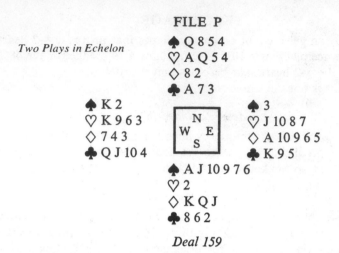

♠ Q 8 5 4
♡ A Q 5 4
◇ 8 2
♣ A 7 3

♠ K 2
♡ K 9 6 3
◇ 7 4 3
♣ Q J 10 4

♠ 3
♡ J 10 8 7
◇ A 10 9 6 5
♣ K 9 5

♠ A J 10 9 7 6
♡ 2
◇ K Q J
♣ 8 6 2

Deal 159

Playing Acol, S bid 1 ♠, and N 4 ♠.*†

W led the ♣ Q, attacking declarer in his weak spot, and E played the nine to indicate the king. How do you play?

Declarer won with the ace in dummy and reached for the ♠ Q on which E played the three. S reasoned that E lacked the ♠ 2 and probably held ♠ K 3. S finessed, and W scored the ♠ K, two clubs, and E the ◇ A to break the contract.

Declarer has two finesses to consider. The immediate trump finesse is tempting but unsound, for it puts all S's eggs into one basket. S can improve these 50% odds by making *two* plays in echelon.

Lead the ♠ Q to coax a cover; E plays low, so play the ace. After E shows a trump, the odds are 52% that the two remaining spades will split 1–1, and about half of this time or 26% the king will be bare.

The king fails to drop, so the heart finesse must be risked to win and let S park a club on the ♡ A for game.

The echelon of the two plays, the ♠ A first followed by the heart finesse, favour declarer by 63% odds. This is 26% odds for the ♠ K to drop bare plus 50% (heart finesse) of the remaining 74% zone when the ♠ K fails to drop, or 37%. The two percentages total 63%.

---

* This is a maximum direct 4 ♠ raise (strong) at Acol. Cf. Deal No. 128.
—Editor.

†*SAB:* S 1 ♠, N 3 ♠; then S 4 ♠.

202

PERCENTAGE

Augmenting Percentage

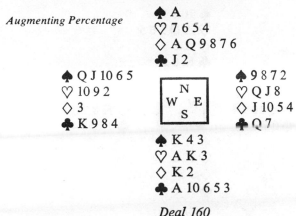

♠ A
♡ 7 6 5 4
◇ A Q 9 8 7 6
♣ J 2

♠ Q J 10 6 5
♡ 10 9 2
◇ 3
♣ K 9 8 4

♠ 9 8 7 2
♡ Q J 8
◇ J 10 5 4
♣ Q 7

♠ K 4 3
♡ A K 3
◇ K 2
♣ A 10 6 5 3

Deal 160

At rubber game S bid 1 NT, N 3 ◇ ; and S 3 NT.

W led the ♠ Q. How do you play?

Declarer gloated over his eight tricks on top with a nice big diamond suit for plenty more tricks. He won the ♠ A, ◇ K then ◇ Q; but his elation vanished like a debtor when a creditor appears. Those dim-dam-diamonds split 4–1 and dropped deader than a kippered herring along with any possible third heart trick, for lack of further entry to dummy.

Declarer cashed the ◇ A and tried to make something of clubs by leading the knave, but E quickly squashed this plan by covering with the queen.

Declarer has 68% odds to split diamonds 3–2; but in his haste to knock off what looked like a sitting duck he had banged away at a decoy while the real game took wing.

In this is another case of augmenting percentage by echelon. To Trick 2 declarer should play the ♡ A, then ♡ 3. The enemy wins and returns a spade to the king, the ♡ K drops hearts 3–3, clinching the game-going trick in case diamonds turn sour (as they did), with three extra tricks if they don't.

S has 36% odds for hearts to split 3–3, leaving a 64% zone when they don't. In this 64% zone, odds to split diamonds 3–2 are 68% or a product of 44%. The sum of 36% and 44% give S 80% odds instead of the 68% upon which he relied solely. Moreover, it cost nothing: you do not *release* the heart suit even if it breaks badly. The heart duck is a play for twelve tricks instead of eleven even if the diamonds are kind—and should therefore be made anyway.

FILE P

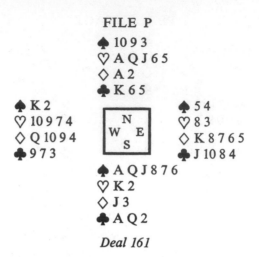

Deal 161

S bid 1 ♠, N 2 ♡; S 3 ♠, and N 6 ♠.
W led the ◇ 10. How do you play it?

Declarer won the diamond opening with the ace. He sighed and remarked: 'The finesse wins or it doesn't' as he reached for the ♠ 10 which he finessed to W's king. W returned a diamond and E's king broke the contract.

The trump finesse offers simple odds of 50%, but a combination of other events offers more percentage.

6%

At Trick 2 declarer should refuse the trump finesse and clatter up with the ace. This play offers a preliminary 6% shot to drop the singleton king which would score the slam with an over-trick.

34%

The trump king fails to drop, leaving a zone of 94%. Next come the king, knave, then ace of hearts with 34% odds (36% of the 94% zone) for a 3–3 split to clinch the slam. But E trumps, S over-ruffs, and the ♣ K lets dummy in to play another top heart for the diamond discard. Opponents may score their only trump, the king, now (if E has it and plays it), or later.

34% More

The 4–2 heart split carries 45% odds (48% of the 94% zone) reduced by one adverse combination of two hearts and the ♠ 5 with W. Half this 45% of the time or 22½% will W hold the two hearts, and

204

half again of this 22½% or 11% will he also hold the ♠ 5 to break the contract. This cuts down our favourable odds to 34% to score slam,

Total Favourable Odds, 74%

The ♠ K drops on the ace	6%
Hearts split 3–3	34%
Hearts split 4–2 with ♠ 5 in E	
whenever W holds two hearts	34%

Trumps will split 4–0 about 10% of the time. If E is void, the trump finesse is automatically abandoned. If W proves void on the ace play (third heart lead) declarer has an equal chance, so the two events balance each other out.

Percentages in Depth

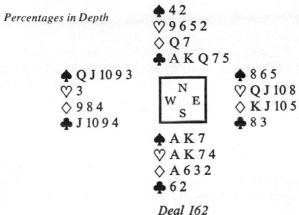

           ♠ 4 2
           ♡ 9 6 5 2
           ◇ Q 7
           ♣ A K Q 7 5

♠ Q J 10 9 3   ♠ 8 6 5
♡ 3   ♡ Q J 10 8
◇ 9 8 4   ◇ K J 10 5
♣ J 10 9 4   ♣ 8 3

           ♠ A K 7
           ♡ A K 7 4
           ◇ A 6 3 2
           ♣ 6 2

Deal 162

S bid 1 ♡, N 2 ♣; and S 3 NT. With four cards in partner's trump suit and two doubletons, N should unquestionably make it 4 ♡, but that is another story. Frederick B. Taylor of Lincoln, Mass., showed us this deal.

Against 3 NT W led the ♠ Q. How do you play it at:
1. Rubber bridge or total points?
2. Match point duplicate?

Declarer has eight tricks on top with chances for more:
    3–3 club split 36% odds (playing ♣ A K Q);
    3–3 *or* 4–2 club split 84% odds (first round duck);
    3–2 heart split 68% odds;
    ◇ Q play 50% odds (lead to her, or an end-play).

S won the ♠ Q with the king and cashed ♣ A K Q, but clubs split 4–2. He tried hearts, 4–1! Finally, he led low to the ◇ Q, which the king gobbled. Declarer won only his eight tricks on top and grumbled about all the bad breaks.

Let us examine the combined odds favouring S's echelon, the sequence of plays which he actually made.

36%

S will split clubs 3–3 36% of the time, fail in a 64% zone.

44%

The 3–2 heart split yields 68% of this 64% zone producing compound odds of 44%.

10%

The sum is 80%, leaving a 20% zone when both splits fail. Of this the ♢ Q play has a 50% chance, producing 10% more.

The sum of 36%, 44% and 10% is 90%. Not at all bad.

The bridge columnist who wrote up the deal recommended an immediate club duck, which scores game without further ado. His plan is to try hearts if clubs prove really sour, then play on the ♢ Q if both suits prove sour. Let's add up his odds.

84%

The 3–3 or 4–2 club splits offer 84% odds, leaving a 16% zone. The enemy wins the club duck (a gambit, losing a trick to 3–3 splits) and returns a spade which S passes, and S wins the next spade lead.

5%

In the 16% zone S has 68% odds to split hearts 3–2, but half the time W will hold three hearts with his good spades, halving this 68% to 34%. And 34% of 16% produces 5%, the favourable occasion when W holds two hearts only with his spades.

This leaves two zones, 5% when W holds three hearts with his good spades and 6% when hearts split 4–1 or 5–0 with a 5–1 or 6–0 club split.

2%

In the 5% zone S has 40% odds to find the ♢ K with W (not 50% for indicated spade and heart lengths shorten W's diamonds) which declarer can neutralize by a squeeze strip. He gets W down to ♢ K x and only two established cards in the four-card ending and throws W in with a heart, so the 40% of 5% produces 2%.

3%

In the remaining 6% zone S has a 50% chance by a similar end-play, producing 3%.

These odds, 84%, 5%, 2% and 3%, total 94%.

The immediate club duck adds only 4% to declarer's odds while sacrificing the extra tricks of the 90% method. Assuming game is worth 500 points, note the comparative total scores in 100 cases.

Playing Clubs to Drop, 90%

	Points
90 games at 500 points each	45,000
36 times clubs drop 3–3 and yield 30 points for an extra trick	1,080
68% (hearts 3–2) by 36% (clubs 3–3) produces 24%, so 24 times 30 points for a second extra trick	720
	46,800

Immediate Club Duck, 94%

	Points
94 games at 500 points each	47,000
4 less defeats at 50 points each	200
	47,200

In 100 cases the immediate club duck yields only 400 points more, or four points per deal. On a total point basis this gives the immediate club duck an advantage of only 0·8% instead of 4%.

Match-point play places artificial premiums on extra tricks, and so most declarers will play clubs to drop 3–3.

The declarer who went down and the bridge columnist both overlooked the best way to echelon the plays.

Test Hearts first, by laying down the ace and king. Game is sure if they prove 3–2, and you can then afford the luxury of trying for five club tricks.

If hearts prove sour, crawl into your shell and duck a club!

68%

The 68% odds of the 3–2 heart split leaves a 32% zone.

27%

The club duck wins 84% of the time in this 32% zone, producing 27%; and raising the overall odds to 95%. This leaves a 5% zone.

2½%

In this 5% zone you have 50% play on the ◇ Q producing 2½% more, raising the grand total to 97½%.

Therefore playing on hearts before clubs offers the best odds, 97½%. These top 94% and 90%, and approach the Sure Trick realm of 100% or unity. Also this sequence of plays gives you a free play for five club tricks without risking the contract *after* hearts have been found to split 3–2, which will happen 68% of the time. Duplicate players will relish this feature.

Conclusion

From the analyses of the foregoing deals, do not jump to the conclusion that you can increase over-all odds simply by making a play with low odds before one with higher odds. Let us clarify this mathematical fallacy.

COFFIN'S LAW OF EQUAL ODDS

If declarer can make two mutually independent plays in one sequence or another, provided that failure of the first play does not jeopardize the contract, the combined odds favouring each sequence are equal.

In several illustrative deals the second play has higher odds, but these odds were changed by the outcome of the first play. The two plays were NOT mutually independent. For example, playing trumps first reduced the danger of an enemy ruff on the second play. In another deal, the outcome of the heart split altered the method of playing the club suit. Note the difference in this deal:

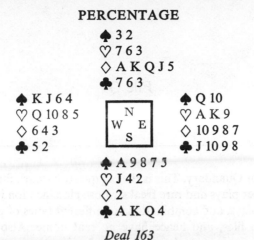

♠ 3 2
♡ 7 6 3
◇ A K Q J 5
♣ 7 6 3

♠ K J 6 4
♡ Q 10 8 5
◇ 6 4 3
♣ 5 2

♠ Q 10
♡ A K 9
◇ 10 9 8 7
♣ J 10 9 8

♠ A 9 8 7 3
♡ J 4 2
◇ 2
♣ A K Q 4

Deal 163

S bid 1 ♠, N 2 ◇; S 2 NT and N 3 NT.
W leads the ♠ 4 to the queen, and your ace wins.
Should you attack diamonds or clubs first?
Mathematically, there is no difference.

4–3 Diamond Split, 62%

The play on diamonds first leaves a zone of 38% in which clubs
will split 3–3 36% of the time, producing 13·68% odds; and total
odds of 75·68%.

3–3 Club Split, 36%

The play on clubs first leaves a zone of 64% in which diamonds
will split 62% of the time, producing 39·68% odds; and total odds
of 75·68%.

The play on diamonds first offers a slight psychological advantage,
because a defender holding four clubs might err and discard one.
But no defender in his right mind who holds five diamonds with
those he sees in dummy would be foolish enough to discard a diamond on a club lead.

File Q

QUANDARY

Q stands for Quandary. This is the big question-mark file. Here you will find queer plays and rare freaks whose classification is in doubt; compound plays, and combinations of different types of plays which straddle two files, and hence have no real home. Also here were hundreds of vagrant deals awaiting reclassification until they got caught in the spring cleaning. A few good deals were salvaged and re-filed properly, but most got the old heave-ho.

In File Q are the quandaries of several bizarre characters among bridge authorities; a bit of gossip and bridge surrealism; and a little comedy to lighten the strain of your studies in other files—notably in percentage!

If you read bridge newspaper columns daily, as I have for years, you will see the same old chestnuts appear again and again and again. One American columnist has her own pet system for repetition of other experts' choice deals. She names the expert as the hero, making the brilliant play. A year or two later, she publishes the hand again in slightly different window-dressing and casually mentions the expert. On subsequent re-hashes, she claims the hand as her own original masterpiece!

There should be a law against the asinine tripe published in a couple of American syndicated bridge columns. One column averages three serious blunders a week! Its writer is a glib newspaper feature salesman but a poor analyst and a worse player. Once he sold an article of a dozen 'choice' deals to a big-circulation magazine. For a week the delighted editors received a truckload of mail daily.

'This bridge writer is quite the drawing card, isn't he?' mused the editors—until they read some of the letters. All complained caustically of gross blunders in the hands.

Did you know that J. B. Ellwell, bridge expert and author of *Practical Bridge** in 1908 and other books on cards, was murdered

* Pre-auction!—Editor.

in his New York City flat? Whodunit? That is a quandary which still remains unsolved.

Have you heard the chestnut about the lady who mailed a bridge question to an expert? He sent the answer with a bill for five guineas 'for professional services rendered'. Enraged, she consulted her lawyer, who said she must pay. Next month she received another bill for five guineas—from her lawyer!

Every bridge 'great' has been named the goat in this yarn, despite standard practice to answer free of charge any question on bridge if accompanied by a properly stamped and self-addressed envelope. Who started this story and when? Was it true? This is a quandary in comics.

Did you know that a world-renowned bridge expert, author of over 100 books on bridge and other games, was caught cheating and barred from clubs? Despite his phenomenally successful career, he spent his last days as a pauper on a special charity pension kindly set up for him by an American playing-card manufacturer. His identity must (and so far as this book goes, will) remain a reader's quandary!

Do you know the strange legal battle of the curious copyrights? A sued B for writing and selling a book on A's bidding system. A lost his case. Immediately A wrote a similar book *on his own system*. B turned about and sued A for infringement of copyright, and the New York courts awarded B huge damages! Who were A and B? You would not believe me if I told you!

Let us return to the main business in hand.

In File V for Variety (see opening paragraphs under M for Mêlée), declarer has two different winning plays to choose from, both equally good. In Quandary the two plays are equally good technically, but by a queer twist of fate one play is a loser. Declarer has no clue to the winning play and he is put to a pure guess. He ends in a Quandary. For example:

FILE Q

♠ K J 10
♡ 3 2
◇ Q J 10 9 7 6
♣ 3 2

♡ Q led
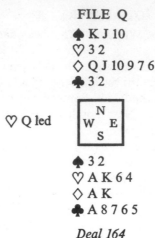

♠ 3 2
♡ A K 6 4
◇ A K
♣ A 8 7 6 5

Deal 164

S bid 1 ♣, N 1 ◇; S 2 ♡, N 2 ♠; S 2 NT, and N 3 NT.

N's semi-psychic bid of 2 ♠ is made primarily to show stoppers for no-trumps, and it is fairly safe after S has bid two suits; for it is very remote that S will hold four spades and raise.

W led the ♡ Q which S won. S cashed the ◇ A K to unblock and led a low spade to get into dummy to score the diamonds. W played a low spade. Should dummy finesse the ten or hop up with the king?

'Play the king!' advised one well-known authority. 'The king play is a finesse against one card, the ace; whereas the ten is a finesse against TWO cards, the ace and queen.'

Bunk. Utter bunk.

The ace and queen of spades will be divided one of four ways, each with equal frequency as follows:

W	E	W	E
Ace-Queen	—	Ace	Queen
—	Ace-Queen	Queen	Ace

In the first two cases you will, or will not, get into dummy, regardless of how you play, so disregard them.

The king play wins in the third case and the ten in the fourth. The ten is a finesse NOT against two cards but against ONE the queen; for if W holds the queen, you don't care who holds the ace.

Which, then, is the correct play? King? Or Ten?

Don't ask me. Go and consult a voodoo doctor!

If you want to be really up-to-date, get one of the new electronic wonders called Coffin's Queen Locator. The shop where you bought this book sells it for ten guineas . . .

212

QUANDARY

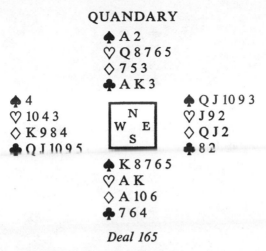

♠ A 2
♡ Q 8 7 6 5
◇ 7 5 3
♣ A K 3

♠ 4
♡ 10 4 3
◇ K 9 8 4
♣ Q J 10 9 5

♠ Q J 10 9 3
♡ J 9 2
◇ Q J 2
♣ 8 2

♠ K 8 7 6 5
♡ A K
◇ A 10 6
♣ 7 6 4

Deal 165

S bid 1 ♠, N 2 ♡; S 2 ♠, and N 4 ♠.

The deal was played by John O'Donnell of Boston, Mass.

W led the ♣ Q. How do you play the hand?

Dummy won the ♣ Q, and S cashed two hearts. S played the ♠ K, then ♠ A, and discovered the horrible 5–1 trump split.

With a club loser, two diamond losers, and *three* trump losers, the contract looks impossible. Next dummy cashed the ♡ Q for a club discard, and S got a break: the 3–3 heart split. Dummy led a fourth heart which E ruffed and S shed a diamond. E returned a diamond to the ace in S, dummy won another top club; and the last good heart let S park his last diamond loser.

The defenders won only three natural trump tricks and Mr. O'Donnell chalked up game.

A queer feature is that S can stand a bad trump split better than a poor heart split. Even if trumps split 3–3 the contract is wellnigh impossible against wrong hearts and the club opening, which attacks dummy's scarce entries at once.

Incidentally N can make 4 ♡; but if hearts fail to split 3–3, N will have real trouble. The 3–3 heart split is vital with *either* major suit as trumps.

FILE Q

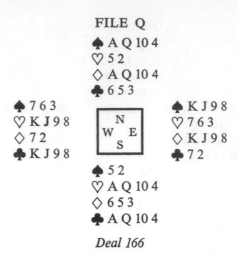

♠ A Q 10 4
♡ 5 2
◊ A Q 10 4
♣ 6 5 3

♠ 7 6 3   ♠ K J 9 8
♡ K J 9 8   ♡ 7 6 3
◊ 7 2   ◊ K J 9 8
♣ K J 9 8   ♣ 7 2

♠ 5 2
♡ A Q 10 4
◊ 6 5 3
♣ A Q 10 4

Deal 166

A practical joker slipped this deal into a duplicate game in Hong Kong, China. He heard how expressionless the Chinese were regardless of the intensity of their feelings.

As expected, the calling went S 1 ♣, N 1 ◊; S 1 ♡, N 1 ♠; S 1 NT, and N 3 NT.

The prankster did not play; and a local rule barring kibitzers forced him to keep a respectful distance of forty feet. He reckoned that going down five tricks would startle even the unsuspecting Chinese declarers into an expression of disgust, but they were deadpan as usual.

The prankster was in for a rude shock when he sneaked a peek at the travelling score slip when the tourney ended.

Every declarer had won thirteen tricks!

A quaint Chinese custom is to play cards counter-clockwise!*†

* At least that is how they play Mah Jong!—Editor.

† I was introduced to real Chinese bridge in March 1945 at the Pueblo Army Air Base in Colorado by flying officers of the Chinese Air Force stationed there for training at the time. In this game was a 'blind widow' of four cards. When the calling ended (on 12 cards in each hand), declarer looked at these four cards and distributed one to each hand as he pleased.

Chinese bridge has two other peculiarities. In the calling there is no limit to the number of times players may double and re-redouble, and the turn to bid and play always went *counter*-clockwise. I described the game in detail in *The Bridge World*.—Author.

QUANDARY

Compound Play

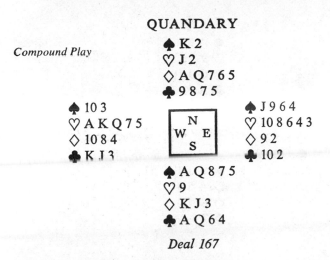

♠ K 2
♡ J 2
◇ A Q 7 6 5
♣ 9 8 7 5

♠ 10 3
♡ A K Q 7 5
◇ 10 8 4
♣ K J 3

♠ J 9 6 4
♡ 10 8 6 4 3
◇ 9 2
♣ 10 2

♠ A Q 8 7 5
♡ 9
◇ K J 3
♣ A Q 6 4

Deal 167

S bid 1 ♠, W 2 ♡, N 2 ♠; and S 4 ♠.
W led the ♡ K then ♡ Q.
How do you map your campaign?

S ruffed the second heart lead and played off three top trumps. But the spades failed to split 3–3, so S shifted to diamonds, hoping E held four of them, but E ruffed the third diamond lead. E returned the ♣ 10 to the queen and king, and W's heart shift took S's last trump. S had no entry to dummy's diamonds, so he cashed the ♣ A, and the hand collapsed two down.

Two to one odds favour a 4–2 trump division, and S should make the classic 'protective' discard, a club on the second heart lead, so that *dummy* can ruff the third heart lead to protect S's trump length from a damaging force. This compound Holding Play and Ruff compromises these files H and R; hence the deal appears here under Q for Quandary.

Dummy ruffs the third heart lead (if made), cashes the ♠ K, S wins a diamond and the ♠ A Q. Now S makes a fourth trump lead to drive out the master knave, lest it cut off dummy's diamonds; and S has a fifth trump to stop hearts. This line gives S four trump tricks, five diamonds and the ♣ A for game. Any continuation but a heart at Trick 3 by W simplifies the play. Obviously, if E plays a club after the ♠ J, S crashes on the ace.

Usually you can leave an enemy master trump at large and force it with a solid plain suit, but in the classic position above, entry trouble thwarts this plan.

FILE Q

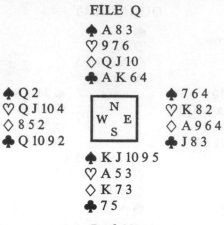

♠ A 8 3
♡ 9 7 6
◊ Q J 10
♣ A K 6 4

♠ Q 2
♡ Q J 10 4
◊ 8 5 2
♣ Q 10 9 2

♠ 7 6 4
♡ K 8 2
◊ A 9 6 4
♣ J 8 3

♠ K J 10 9 5
♡ A 5 3
◊ K 7 3
♣ 7 5

Deal 168

In the New England championships before the war, at one table
S bid 1 ♠, N 2 ♣; S 2 ♠ and N 4 ♠.

W led the ♡ Q to the ace. Dummy won the ♠ A and E threw the
four. Dummy returned the ♠ 8, E HESITATED A FEW MOMENTS AND
PLAYED THE SIX. If you are S, do you finesse?

S finessed to the bare ♠ Q, and the ♡ J, ♡ K and ◊ A broke the
contract.

S was furious and he beckoned to the tourney director to register a
protest. The official laws provided no redress. On questioning, E
explained that he had hesitated over playing the ♠ 6 or ♠ 7 on the
second trump lead. E had a point, for the seven play is a good false
card to induce declarer to place the six with W and possibly the
queen with E. However, this alibi failed to make sense because *E
failed to play the seven*, so the tourney director suspected E of a
'coffee-house'* and warned him.

However, S had missed the point. If E had held ♠ Q 6 4, E would
have had no reason to hesitate. S should have marked E's balk as a
crude deception and gone right up with the king of trumps!

Of course, E might have been one of those smart birds, a master
of the 'double-cross coffee-house' who hesitates *with* ♠ Q 6 4!

* A 'coffee-house' is a piece of chicanery difficult to bring home to the offender
as a piece of demonstrable cheating. The term derives from Vienna where the
coffee-house—analagous to the cafés of France—is a social centre where cards are
played. The clientèle was apt to be 'mixed'; and if a piece of malpractice was
perpetrated in a gentleman's club, or private house, it was condemned as 'the sort
of thing one might expect in a coffee-house'. Now the word has become an
abstract noun and even a verb.—Editor.

QUANDARY

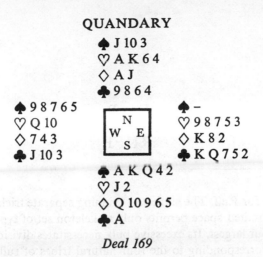

♠ J 10 3
♡ A K 6 4
◇ A J
♣ 9 8 6 4

♠ 9 8 7 6 5
♡ Q 10
◇ 7 4 3
♣ J 10 3

♠ –
♡ 9 8 7 5 3
◇ K 8 2
♣ K Q 7 5 2

♠ A K Q 4 2
♡ J 2
◇ Q 10 9 6 5
♣ A

Deal 169

S opened 1 ♠ and arrived at 6 ♠ against no enemy bid. W kept quiet lest he spill the beans about his five trumps.

W led the ♣ J to S's lone ace, and dummy won a trump, discovering the 5–0 split.

How do you plan your play?

The right play is tricky—almost double dummy. S cannot stand a club ruff except in one vital matrix which he must set up. Also he must hope for no enemy plain suit void or singleton.

To Trick 3 declarer cashed the ♡ K in dummy, the key play.

Next comes the ◇ A, then ◇ J to E's king. S ruffs the expected club return, and pushes top diamonds. W's goose is cooked in the weird trump ending.

If W ruffs, it shortens his trumps and lets dummy over-ruff. Now, S draws trumps.

If W always discards, off go dummy's hearts, dummy's ♠ J finally ruffs S's ♡ J and S ends with ♠ A K Q for his last three cards.

Early in the hand dummy cannot cash both top hearts lest E lead a heart later to promote the setting trick from W's trumps. Try playing the deal without cashing any heart trick at all and see what happens!

Another line is to finesse ◇ J at Trick 2. E wins with king. S ruffs club return and wins ♠ A, which discovers bad trump split. N wins ◇ A, ♡ K and ♡ A. S ruffs low another club and wins ◇ Q; finally cross-ruffs the last four tricks with top trumps.

File R

RUFF

R stands for Ruff. The subject of winning separate tricks by ruffs is vast and limited space permits only a skeleton set of type deals; yet File R is our largest. Its excessive bulk necessitates division into four sections, corresponding to the four natural tribes of ruff plays, Declarer's Ruffs, Dummy's Ruffs, Inverted Ruffs (Dummy Reversal) and Cross-Ruffs. Trump end-plays are excluded here, for they are filed under X, Y and Z.

In some parts of the United States, as in Scotland, the word 'cut' is used instead of 'ruff', derived from the French *couper*, meaning to strike or *cut* and, at cards, to 'cut in' by trumping.*

Basic Trump Structures

Examine the prosaic shape of the trump suit below:

$$\begin{array}{ccc} & 9\,8\,3 & \\ 10\,2 & & Q\,J\,4 \\ & A\,K\,7\,6\,5 & \end{array}$$

At no-trumps, declarer's problem is simple—to lose one lead and score four tricks.

As trumps, however, his suit may expand to a plethora of powers, depending upon plain suit shapes. Maxima are a merry cross-ruff by opponents for five tricks or by declarer for eight tricks!

Every trump deal contains three kinds of trumps: high, short and long. Note S's suit in the diagram:

A	K	7	6	5
high	high	short	long	long

If S leads his high trumps and loses his short trump, he comes to two long trumps as automatic winners. Likewise E holds one high trump with two busy shorts, N three shorts and W two shorts.

---

* The close Franco-Scottish liaison of the fifteenth and eighteenth centuries is recalled linguistically in a 'gigot' of mutton—the Scottish term for leg—and in other phrases.—Editor.

RUFF

Why do we call them shorts? These low trumps are too *short* of rank to win straight trump leads, and they score only by ruffing *short* suits. Shorts have two other values: to guard high trumps, or to be led and destroy a ruffing trick, usually in dummy.

The battle of trumps is usually to score as many shorts as possible. Opponents try to cross-ruff before their shorts are drawn, or opponents may adopt the anti-ruff tactics of leading trumps to prevent declarer from ruffing his own plain suit losers with dummy's short trumps.

The family of true ruffing plays under File R is divided into four natural tribes, based on the distributions of short trumps and how they score tricks.

Tribe 1. Declarer's Ruffs

Dummy may have a few trumps utterly worthless for ruffing purposes or no trumps at all, and declarer holds one or more short trumps which may score only by ruffing. Former authorities have confused this type of deal with the 'Trump No-Trump' Shape, which looks superficially the same with no ruffers in dummy but declarer holds no short trumps. The two types are basically different. File R for Ruff includes only those trump plays in which *short trumps are used to score ruffing tricks*. 'Trump No-trump' Shapes are excluded, because only *long trumps* have any ruffing play, purely to stop an enemy suit.

Tribe 2. Dummy's Ruffs

This tribe is the commonest, and most trump contracts are played to exploit dummy's short trumps by ruffing declarer's own losers.

Tribe 3. Inverted Ruffs (Reverse Dummy)

Here declarer scores ruffs with his own trumps and later uses dummy's high trumps to draw enemy trumps. Stated another way, declarer uses his own hand for 'dummy ruffs' and the dummy hand as the 'declarer' or master-trump hand, later, to draw trumps.

Tribe 4. Cross Ruffs

Declarer and dummy alternately trump in order to score most of, or all, their trumps separately.

Let us examine some typical deals of Tribe 1.

219

Matrix pura

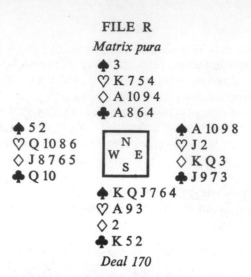

♠ 3
♡ K 7 5 4
◇ A 10 9 4
♣ A 8 6 4

♠ 5 2
♡ Q 10 8 6
◇ J 8 7 6 5
♣ Q 10

♠ A 10 9 8
♡ J 2
◇ K Q 3
♣ J 9 7 3

♠ K Q J 7 6 4
♡ A 9 3
◇ 2
♣ K 5 2

Deal 170

S bid 1 ♠, N 2 ♣; S 2 ♠, N 2 NT; and S 4 ♠.
W led the ♡ 6 to the knave and ace.
How do you manage trumps?

To Trick 2 S led the ♠ K to the ace, and dummy won E's heart
return. S won a club to cash two top trumps, but they split 4–2, so
S lost two trump tricks, a heart and a club for defeat.

The 4–2 trump split was 68% probable, and the actual split gave S
two long trumps and a short instead of the three longs hoped for
with a 3–3 break. S must get home both his long trumps *and his short*
by ruffs to score game, thus:

Dummy wins Trick 2 with the ◇ A, S ruffs a diamond, and loses
a high trump to E's ace. Dummy wins the heart return, S ruffs
another diamond and lays down two top trumps in case they split
3–3 but they don't. Next come the ♣ K, ♣ A, and the third diamond
ruff to fetch home S's short trump.

RUFF

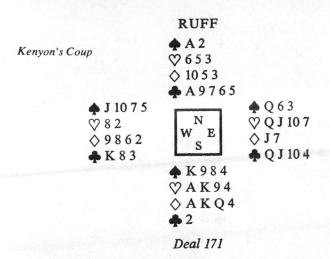

Kenyon's Coup

♠ A 2
♡ 6 5 3
♢ 10 5 3
♣ A 9 7 6 5

♠ J 10 7 5   ♠ Q 6 3
♡ 8 2   ♡ Q J 10 7
♢ 9 8 6 2   ♢ J 7
♣ K 8 3   ♣ Q J 10 4

♠ K 9 8 4
♡ A K 9 4
♢ A K Q 4
♣ 2

Deal 171

S bid 1 ♠, N 2 ♠; and S 4 ♠.

N's spade raise is a bad bid—he should instead respond 1 NT; but S's problem is to win ten tricks from his trump-shy rock-crusher.

W led the ♡ 8 to the ten and ace.

What plan do you formulate?

The deal came from the late Otis A. Kenyon of Braintree, Mass. S sees eight top card tricks (unless one is ruffed adversely); and S needs two short trump tricks by club ruffs without an over-ruff in order to get home.

S wins the ♡ A and two diamonds, dropping the knave from E which is disheartening. Dummy wins the ♣ A and S ruffs a club, and returns a low diamond to the ten which E ruffs. E returns a heart to the king in S. Dummy wins the ♣ A and S ruffs another club. The ♠ K draws E's last trump and the ♢ Q brings home Trick No. 10 for game.

Contra Contra Ruff

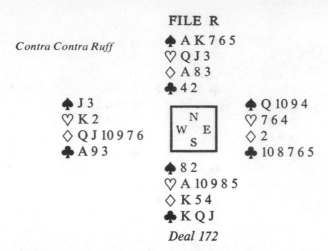

♠ A K 7 6 5
♡ Q J 3
◇ A 8 3
♣ 4 2

♠ J 3
♡ K 2
◇ Q J 10 9 7 6
♣ A 9 3

♠ Q 10 9 4
♡ 7 6 4
◇ 2
♣ 10 8 7 6 5

♠ 8 2
♡ A 10 9 8 5
◇ K 5 4
♣ K Q J

Deal 172

N bid 1 ♠, S 2 ♡, W 3 ◇; N 3 ♡, and S 4 ♡.

W led the ◇ Q. How do you manage the red suits?

W's overcall of 3 ◇ on only Q J 10 to so many suggested a six-card suit, and declarer took the precaution of winning the first diamond in dummy lest the ace be led through later and ruffed by E. Dummy led the ♡ Q but declarer tripped over the second hurdle when he finessed to W's king. E ruffed the diamond return. E returned a club to W's ace, and E ruffed another diamond to break the contract.

At Trick 2 S should play the ♡ A and return another trump at once. This safety-play holds E to one diamond ruff.

An alternative line is to set up clubs immediately for a diamond discard in dummy.

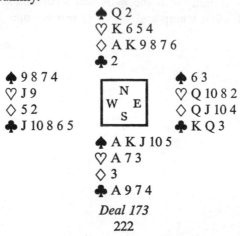

♠ Q 2
♡ K 6 5 4
◇ A K 9 8 7 6
♣ 2

♠ 9 8 7 4
♡ J 9
◇ 5 2
♣ J 10 8 6 5

♠ 6 3
♡ Q 10 8 2
◇ Q J 10 4
♣ K Q 3

♠ A K J 10 5
♡ A 7 3
◇ 3
♣ A 9 7 4

Deal 173

RUFF

N bid 1 ♢, S 2 ♠; N 3 ♢, S 3 ♠; N 4 ♠, and S 6 ♠.
W led the ♠ 9. How do you play?

Dummy won the spade opening with the queen, and declarer went after a club ruff in dummy like a cat after cream. The ♣ A, a club ruff, ♡ A, and four trump leads drew all W's. Next declarer won two diamonds for a heart discard and ruffed a diamond, but the suit split 4–2 and the contract was defeated.

If W had opened a diamond or a club, club ruffs in dummy yield slam; but after W's opening attack on trumps, declarer should shun club ruffs and play the long suit game.

Declarer should win the trump opening himself to preserve an entry to dummy, win a diamond and *lose a* LOW *diamond while S sheds a heart.* E wins and returns a trump to the bare ♠ Q. S ruffs high a low diamond, draws trumps, and the ♡ K gets dummy in to score three diamond tricks for discards. A heart opening sets S.*

Deal 174

N bid 2 ♡, S 2 ♠; N 4 ♡, and S 4 ♠.
W led the ♣ 2.
How do you bring home the game?

Dummy lacked trumps to lead, so declarer had to use the great heart suit as a substitute for trump leads and massage the enemy trumps. Dummy won the ♣ A, two top hearts while S shed the club, and dummy continued with the ♡ Q, on which S shed a diamond and W ruffed.

W returned a diamond to the ace and dummy led a stiff heart.

If E ruffs, S sheds a diamond, a loser-on-loser-play; and later S can play ace then low in spades to make the enemy trump honours knock heads.

* Elmer Luehr of Florida found that a ♡ opening lead breaks the contract.

But E discarded as did S, and W ruffed again. S ruffed the club return and laid down the ♠ A, picking up W's now bare king of trumps and holding E–W to only one more trump trick, the queen.

Note that N has no play for 4 ♡ unless an opponent is kind enough to lead a spade. The deal illustrates the principle that the *weaker* hand usually makes a better declarer's hand than a dummy —except, sometimes, in no-trumps.*

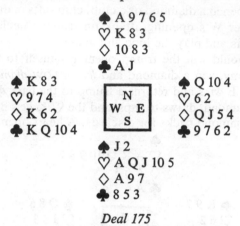

$$\begin{array}{c}
\spadesuit \text{ A 9 7 6 5} \\
\heartsuit \text{ K 8 3} \\
\diamondsuit \text{ 10 8 3} \\
\clubsuit \text{ A J}
\end{array}$$

♠ K 8 3   N   ♠ Q 10 4
♡ 9 7 4   W E   ♡ 6 2
♢ K 6 2   S   ♢ Q J 5 4
♣ K Q 10 4   ♣ 9 7 6 2

♠ J 2
♡ A Q J 10 5
♢ A 9 7
♣ 8 5 3

Deal 175

S bid 1 ♡, N 1 ♠; S 2 ♡, and N 4 ♡.

W led the ♣ K to dummy's ace. How do you play it?

With four prospective losers S saw his only chance was to split enemy spades 3–3 and score dummy's long spades.

To Trick 2 dummy led a low spade to the knave and king. So far declarer was right.

W cashed the ♣ Q and came along with the ♣ 10 as ruff bait. Declarer was the poor fish who swallowed it hook, line and sinker, with dummy's low trump. Next came the ♠ A and a spade ruff to set up spades, but dummy had one trump fewer than W, who could stop the run of spades.

The key play is to let W win that ♣ 10 and welcome, the last defensive trick. Dummy discards a diamond.

If W leads another club, S ruffs; and dummy wins the third trump lead to draw W's last, and score the good (and fortunately 'breaking') spades.

* Granted equal length, it is better, almost always, to have the weaker suit as trumps.

Tribe 2. Dummy Ruffs

The vast majority of trump declarations fall into Tribe 2, because declarer's commonest play is to ruff his own losers in dummy. Beginners are prone to lead too many trumps too early, and awaken too late to discover that dummy is denuded of trumps to take care of declarer's own losers. When to lead trumps is the ancient, vexing problem left over from whist, and it is even more vital in modern bridge.

Trump-leading policies in whist were determined largely by rote and blind instinct, because all four hands were played closed; whereas exposure of a dummy hand in bridge at once reveals the best policy to pursue . . . as a rule.

This reminds me of the story of Terence Reese who saw two tattered beggars squatting pitifully in Carlton House Terrace, hungry, penniless and pleading for a crust of bread. He recognized them as former members of a famous London bridge club.

'What brings you two to this?' asked Mr. Reese.

'I *never* led trumps,' replied one beggar.

'I *always* led trumps,' replied the other.

The story is fiction, but the spectre of the two beggars rears its ugly head time and time again in every bridge session. The basic rule for declarer is, *always draw as many trumps as possible without eopardizing your plan of play*. Your plan of play is the critical part of the deal. Perhaps you must score dummy's trumps separately by ruffs first, or perhaps get some fast discards on dummy's winners before touching trumps. The first question to ask yourself is, 'How many losers must I ruff in dummy?'

If you need all dummy's trumps to ruff your own losers, you cannot lead trumps until all ruffing in dummy is finished. If dummy has an established (or establishable) side suit, you may draw down to one trump in dummy as a guard to stop an enemy suit until you can bring home dummy's long suit.

However, beware of one trap. If you have to lose the lead to develop the play, *dummy may need an extra trump lest opponents lead trumps*. Illustrative type deals to follow will clarify these principles.

FILE R

Matrix pura

♠ J 4 3
♡ 9 2
◊ A 7 5 4
♣ K Q J 4

♠ Q 8 7
♡ K 10 6 4
◊ Q J 10
♣ 8 5 3

♠ 6 2
♡ J 8 7 5
◊ 9 8 2
♣ A 10 9 6

♠ A K 10 9 5
♡ A Q 3
◊ K 6 3
♣ 7 2

Deal 176

S bid 1 ♠, N 2 ♣; S 2 NT, N 3 ♠;* and S 4 ♠.
W led the ◊ Q. How many trumps do you draw?

S won the ◊ K, the ♠ A, and lost the ♣ J to E's ace. E returned a ♠ to S's king, N won two clubs while S shed a diamond, and the heart finesse lost to W's king. W lost no time in grabbing the ♠ Q to wipe that last trump off the table and break the contract. S lost a trump, the ♣ J, and *two* heart tricks.

Dummy's short trumps for ruffing the third heart lead must be protected, and declarer cannot afford even one trump lead, for he has to lose the lead *twice* to opponents, which represents *two* chances for them to lead trumps.

S should win the diamond and start clubs at once. When E shows up with the ace, the heart finesse must be tried.

If W plays the ace on the first or second club lead from S, declarer can afford one trump lead immediately.

---

* N's 3 ♠ bid—far from being a sign-off—is 100 per cent forcing on this sequence. If N were poor with spade support he would bid 2 ♠ at once—for, if a hand is worth only one bid and can support partner's major, that is the best bid to make. So N is worth two bids, and can indicate willingness to play in spades *or* no-trumps at the game level.—Editor.

226

RUFF

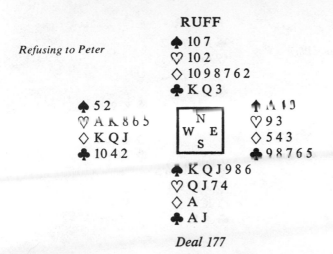

♠ 10 7
♥ 10 2
♦ 10 9 8 7 6 2
♣ K Q 3

♠ 5 2   ♠ A 10
♥ A K 8 6 5   ♥ 9 3
♦ K Q J   ♦ 5 4 3
♣ 10 4 2   ♣ 9 8 7 6 5

♠ K Q J 9 8 6
♥ Q J 7 4
♦ A
♣ A J

Deal 177

S bid 1 ♠, W 2 ♥; S 3 ♠, and N 4 ♠.

W led the ♥ K on which E played the three, refusing to peter, and W shifted to the ♦ K.

How do you manage trumps?

S won the diamond shift, the ♠ 10 won, but E grabbed the next trump lead with his ace. E led a heart to W's ace, and E ruffed a heart return to break the contract.

S was lulled into a false sense of security by E's failure to echo in hearts, but S failed to reckon on (as he should) five hearts with W for his over-call at the two-level. E wisely did not echo because it would take his ace of trumps to over-ruff dummy. S's trumps are solid from the king to the six!

At Trick 3 S should lead a heart, and get a heart ruff in dummy before dummy's trumps are gone, and park another heart on the third club trick so that it will not be ruffed by E.

If W shifts to spades at Trick 2, E must duck. S still leads a heart and W wins. Now W can *either* lead a spade to void N of trumps—but cannot regain the lead to give E his ruff; *or* he can lead a heart—in which case N will ruff with ♠ 10. In either event, E is held to only one trump trick.

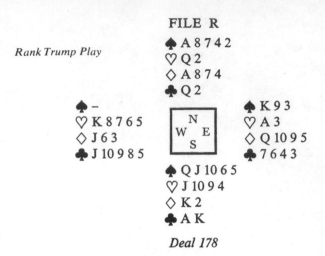

Rank Trump Play

♠ A 8 7 4 2
♡ Q 2
◇ A 8 7 4
♣ Q 2

♠ —
♡ K 8 7 6 5
◇ J 6 3
♣ J 10 9 8 5

♠ K 9 3
♡ A 3
◇ Q 10 9 5
♣ 7 6 4 3

♠ Q J 10 6 5
♡ J 10 9 4
◇ K 2
♣ A K

Deal 178

S bid 1 ♠ and N 4 ♠.*

W led the ♣ J to S's ace. S returned the ♠ Q and W discarded the
♡ 5. Do you overtake with the ace in dummy?

Dummy did overtake with the ace and continued trumps to E's
king. Before returning partner's club suit, E laid down the ♡ A 'to
have a look-see' at the heart position, and W's encouraging eight
dropped, revealing gold. Another heart to W's king let W return a
heart for E's deadly over-ruff of dummy, breaking the contract.

The key play is to let the ♠ Q ride at Trick 2 in order to keep the
♠ A in dummy to ruff the third heart lead high enough to shut out
E's lethal over-ruff.

If E ducks the ♠ Q, declarer can play the ♠ A next and lead a
third round of trumps to exhaust E—or even leave ♠ K at large:
that card is sure to win, whether as a ruff or a natural trump trick.

SAB: S 1 ♠, N 3 ♠; then S 4 ♠. N's jump to 4 ♠ as shown above is the Acol
System bid.

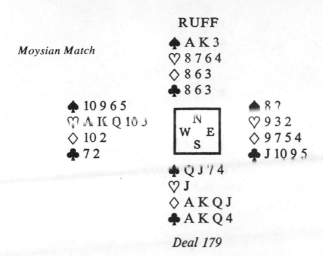

RUFF

Moysian Match

♠ A K 3
♡ 8 7 6 4
♢ 8 6 3
♣ 8 6 3

♠ 10 9 6 5
♡ A K Q 10 5
♢ 10 2
♣ 7 2

♠ 8 ?
♡ 9 3 2
♢ 9 7 5 4
♣ J 10 9 5

♠ Q J 7 4
♡ J
♢ A K Q J
♣ A K Q 4

Deal 179

S bid 1 ♢, W 1 ♡; S 1 ♠, N 2 ♠; and S 4 ♠.

Over W's 1 ♡ overcall N could find no logical bid despite his two quick tricks, so he felt obliged to raise, on the second round, S's 'reversed' spade suit on only three trumps for lack of any better action. W's hearts will break 3 NT at once and 4 ♠ is the only possible game.

W led the ♡ K then ♡ Q which S ruffed. S cashed the ♠ A then ♠ Q but quit trumps lest they fail to split 3–3, and S adopted the counter-forcing tactics of pushing diamonds. W discarded clubs and dummy a heart on the last diamond leads. Next W ruffed a top club, forced dummy's last trump with a heart, and S counter-forced W again with a top club. Declarer ruffed W's heart return and the last top club scored the game-going trick.

It is curious that, if W pursues the alternative line of discarding on S's top club at Trick 9, ruffing the second club, S will still make his contract! If W returns a heart at Trick 11, it looks as if S will be left with ♣ 4, which E's knave will win; but this is illusory.

If S draws three trumps from W early, the hand collapses.

229

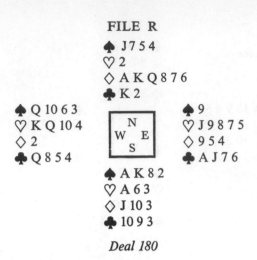

FILE R

```
              ♠ J 7 5 4
              ♡ 2
              ◇ A K Q 8 7 6
              ♣ K 2
♠ Q 10 6 3                      ♠ 9
♡ K Q 10 4      N              ♡ J 9 8 7 5
◇ 2          W     E           ◇ 9 5 4
♣ Q 8 5 4       S              ♣ A J 7 6
              ♠ A K 8 2
              ♡ A 6 3
              ◇ J 10 3
              ♣ 10 9 3
```

Deal 180

N bid 1 ◇, S 1 ♠; N 3 ♠, S 3 NT; and N 4 ♠.

E–W can win nine tricks at hearts if they get into the act and go flag flying, but neither opponent alone has enough strength to make any move. W is not strong enough to hazard a take-out double to obtain a heart or club answer from E, even by the most shaded— or shady!—modern standards.

W led the ♡ K. How do you plan the play?

S won the ♡ K with the ace, and went after a heart ruff in dummy like a cat after cream—which proved to be poison in this case.

Next S won the ♠ A and led a low spade toward dummy's ♠ J 7, W stepped up with the queen, and returned a heart to force dummy's knave and make W's ♠ 10 a winner. E and W got two trump tricks and, later, two club tricks to break the contract.

Declarer must shun that ruinous heart ruff in dummy and make the safety-play—ace, then low—in trumps at once, in order to retain trump control. W can make his ♠ Q now or later, but gets only one trump trick. On the immediate ♠ Q play and heart return, dummy ruffs, cashes his trump knave, S wins a diamond and draws trumps. . . . Alternatively, E and W can cash their two clubs before leading a second heart.

That early heart ruff in dummy was a snare and a delusion that led declarer to his downfall. The heart ruff is pointless with the perfect diamond suit ready to run for discards as soon as trumps are drawn.

RUFF

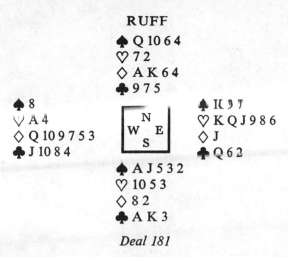

♠ Q 10 6 4
♡ 7 2
◇ A K 6 4
♣ 9 7 5

♠ 8
♡ A 4
◇ Q 10 9 7 5 3
♣ J 10 8 4

♠ K 9 7
♡ K Q J 9 8 6
◇ J
♣ Q 6 2

♠ A J 5 3 2
♡ 10 5 3
◇ 8 2
♣ A K 3

Deal 181

S bid 1 ♠, N 3 ♠, E 4 ♡; and S 4 ♠.*
W led the ♡ A, then ♡ 4 to E's ♡ J.

To Trick 3 E returned the ♡ Q and W had the perspicacity to put on his 'worthless' eight of trumps. Should dummy over-ruff?

Dummy did over-ruff, but it took an honour. Dummy led the ♠ Q which E and S covered, and the ♠ J play discovered a trump winner with E. This with two heart tricks already lost and an inescapable club loser broke the contract.

The winning gadget is a club discard from dummy on E's third heart lead. Now declarer can pick up all E's trumps via finesse, and *dummy* ruffs the third club lead.

The club discard transfers dummy's ruffing trick to a harmless suit and avoids demoting declarer's high-card trump strength. You cannot place the cards in such a position that the over-ruff by the dummy will gain—except, possibly, for an over-trick at match points if E holds K x of trumps.

*SAB: S 1 ♠, N 2 ◇, E 3 ♡; N 3 ♠, and S 4 ♠.

FILE R

Ruff Strategy in Depth

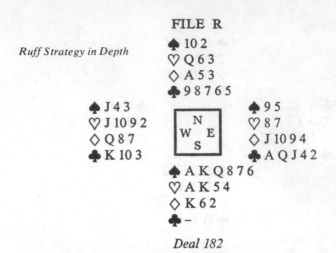

♠ 10 2
♡ Q 6 3
◇ A 5 3
♣ 9 8 7 6 5

♠ J 4 3　　　　　　　　　　**♠** 9 5
♡ J 10 9 2　　　　　　　　**♡** 8 7
◇ Q 8 7　　　　　　　　　　**◇** J 10 9 4
♣ K 10 3　　　　　　　　　　**♣** A Q J 4 2

♠ A K Q 8 7 6
♡ A K 5 4
◇ K 6 2
♣ –

Deal 182

S bid 2 **♠**, N 3 **◇** (to show ace); S 3 **♡**, N 4 **♡**; and S 6 **♠**.

N's heart raise suggested a picture card to fill out hearts and possibly his diamond suit might have been an 'honest' five-carder.*

W led the **♡** J. How do you plan the play?

Before drawing trumps dummy wins the **♡** Q and S the **♡** A. Declarer must find a 3–3 or 4–2 heart split to have any chance, and he had to risk an enemy heart ruff.

Next dummy wins the **◇** A and returns a heart which E delightedly ruffs, letting S get away a *low* heart: E, therefore, ruffs a loser, not a winner. E tries to make his **♣** A at once but S ruffs it. S lays down the **♠** A, drawing E's last trump and cashes the **♡** K for a diamond discard from dummy. S wins the **◇** K and ruffs his last diamond in dummy. S ruffs a club, draws trumps, and claims his slam.

If E refuses to ruff the third heart lead, S wins it and dummy scores the fourth round ruff of hearts with the **♠** 10, S now conceding a diamond at the end.

S needs luck to make his slam, and this line is the only way. A 3–3 heart split (obviously) simplifies matters.

* The showing of aces immediately in response to a game-, or one round-forcing bid is not recommended; only the **CAB** system in Britain, and one or two variants of Culbertson's forcing-two in America sanction this technique. Normally, a suit-bid over an opening force means a biddable alternative trump suit: aces can be shown later.—Editor.

RUFF

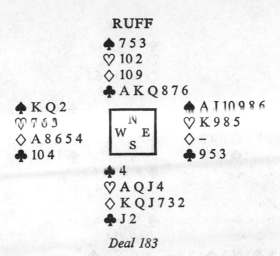

♠ 7 5 3
♡ 10 2
◇ 10 9
♣ A K Q 8 7 6

♠ K Q 2
♡ 7 6 3
◇ A 8 6 5 4
♣ 10 4

♠ A J 10 9 8 6
♡ K 9 8 5
◇ -
♣ 9 5 3

♠ 4
♡ A Q J 4
◇ K Q J 7 3 2
♣ J 2

Deal 183

S bid 1 ◇, N 2 ♣, E 2 ♠; S 3 ♡, N 4 ♣; S 4 ◇, and N 5 ◇.
W led the ♠ K, then ♠ Q. How do you play for eleven tricks?

S ruffed the ♠ Q at Trick 2 and led a low trump to dummy's nine,
which won, but E checked out to show the bad 5–0 split. This discovery stopped S's long suit plan to draw trumps and run clubs.
Clubs won't run for heart discards, so S had to risk heart finesses.

Dummy finessed the ♡ 10, then S the ♡ J and S played the ♡ A.
Dummy won two top clubs and S ruffed the third spade with his
short trump leaving:

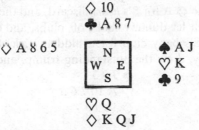

◇ 10
♣ A 8 7

◇ A 8 6 5

♠ A J
♡ K
♣ 9

♡ Q
◇ K Q J

S led the ♡ Q for dummy to trump and the ◇ A was W's only
remaining trick.

If W plays his ace to the first trump lead and forces S with a spade,
the same plan wins game. If, instead, W returns a trump, declarer
can resume his long suit plan—draw trumps and run clubs without
bothering with the heart finesse.

FILE R

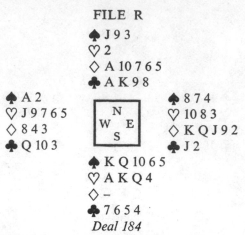

♠ J 9 3
♡ 2
◇ A 10 7 6 5
♣ A K 9 8

♠ A 2
♡ J 9 7 6 5
◇ 8 4 3
♣ Q 10 3

♠ 8 7 4
♡ 10 8 3
◇ K Q J 9 2
♣ J 2

♠ K Q 10 6 5
♡ A K Q 4
◇ –
♣ 7 6 5 4

Deal 184

S bid 1 ♠, N 4 ♠; S 6 ♡, and N 6 ♠.*

N's trumps were a bit short and weak for the jump to game until S had shown a fair five-card spade suit (instead, N should bid 2 ◇); but he reckoned his trumps would make valuable heart ruffers and he intended to bid 4 ♠ eventually anyway.†

W led the ace then low in trumps, which reduced dummy to one trump. Another worry for declarer was a low club loser.

One line is to ruff out diamonds to get two club discards, but odds are against a 4–4 diamond split.

S solved his problem neatly by a better line. Dummy won the second trump lead, led the ◇ A for S's *heart* discard, and the ♣ A K. S won three hearts which let dummy shake off clubs, and dummy ruffed a club, setting up S's baby club for a hidden trick. Now S ruffed a diamond for entry, drew the outstanding trump, and made ♣ 7.

♠ J 9 3
♡ A 10 7 6 5
◇ 10 9 3
♣ K 2

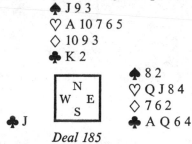

♠ 8 2
♡ Q J 8 4
◇ 7 6 2
♣ A Q 6 4

♣ J

Deal 185

SAB: S 1 ♠, N 2 ◇; S 2 ♡, N 3 ♣; S 4 ♣, N 4 ♠; and S 6 ♠.

†N, with three suits playable—both minors in his own hand and S's spades—should take no such unilateral decision as to bid 4 ♠. There might be 6 (or even 7) in either minor available—and if S has a shaded four-card spade suit 3 NT might be better. However 'direct' you like to make your bidding, here is an occasion for slow and exploratory approach.—Editor.

S bid 1 ♠, N 2 ♠; and S 4 ♠.

W led the ♣ J which dummy ducked, and you are E.

How do you defend?

E overtook the ♣ J with the queen and returned a trump which S won with the king and W played the six. S returned a club to your ace. Now, what do you return?

E returned another trump to W's ace and W led a third trump, denuding dummy of ruffers. Here is the full deal:

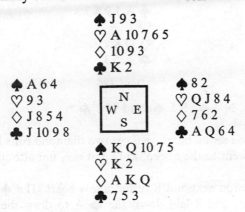

```
                    ♠ J 9 3
                    ♡ A 10 7 6 5
                    ◇ 10 9 3
                    ♣ K 2
  ♠ A 6 4                        ♠ 8 2
  ♡ 9 3           N              ♡ Q J 8 4
  ◇ J 8 5 4    W     E           ◇ 7 6 2
  ♣ J 10 9 8       S             ♣ A Q 6 4
                    ♠ K Q 10 7 5
                    ♡ K 2
                    ◇ A K Q
                    ♣ 7 5 3
```

Declarer lost the ♠ A and *three* club tricks, due to W's astute duck on the first trump lead by E.

In the actual game E was right but W wasn't so astute. W won the first trump lead with the ace and returned a trump. When E won the Second club lead, he was out of trumps and had no defence to break the contract. He tried a diamond which S won, and dummy got his club ruff for game.

W must duck the first trump lead, for he has no entry except the ♠ A to get in and lead that killing third trump.

FILE R

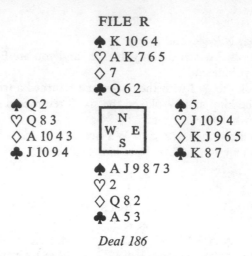

♠ K 10 6 4
♡ A K 7 6 5
◇ 7
♣ Q 6 2

♠ Q 2
♡ Q 8 3
◇ A 10 4 3
♣ J 10 9 4

♠ 5
♡ J 10 9 4
◇ K J 9 6 5
♣ K 8 7

♠ A J 9 8 7 3
♡ 2
◇ Q 8 2
♣ A 5 3

Deal 186

S bid 1 ♠, N 4 ♠; S 5 ♠, and N 6 ♠.*
W led the ♣ J.

How do you set up hearts *and* get two diamond ruffs in dummy?

The ♣ J went to the queen, king and ace, unbuttoning declarer's weak suit.

The ♡ K won next and S ruffed a low heart. The ♠ K let S ruff another heart, and S laid down the ♠ A to draw the outstanding trump. S had no entry to dummy except by a *third* trump lead, which let S park two dead clubs. Declarer lost a diamond, dummy ruffed a diamond with his last spade, but S lost another diamond trick for defeat, due to trump shortage in dummy.

Dummy must win two trump leads for entries, yet keep two trumps to ruff diamonds. The critical play—and the sole solution—is to finesse dummy's ten of trumps!

---

* The hazard of the play only goes to show that the slam is a bad proposition and should not be bid. S has no 5 ♠ (or 5 ♣) trial, even if N's 4 ♠ is regarded as a strong bid. If S finds an 11-count (admittedly with a six-card suit and an unbalanced hand) provocative of slam aspirations, he should bid 5 ♣ rather than 5 ♠. When N co-operates by bidding 5 ♡, S, however sanguine a player, should view his diamond holding with alarm and despondency and—sign off rapidly in 5 ♠. N, viewing his club queen and single diamond with favour, might shoot the slam—in which case S must adopt the author's plan (if he is so good a player!) and carry his bidding courage into his play.—Editor.

RUFF

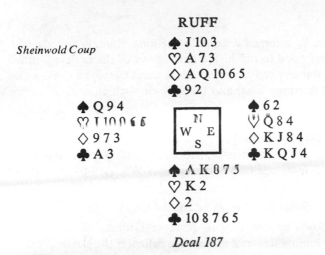

Sheinwold Coup

♠ J 10 3
♡ A 7 3
◇ A Q 10 6 5
♣ 9 2

♠ Q 9 4
♡ T 10 0 6 6
◇ 9 7 3
♣ A 3

♠ 6 2
♡ Q 8 4
◇ K J 8 4
♣ K Q J 4

♠ A K 8 7 5
♡ K 2
◇ 2
♣ 10 8 7 6 5

Deal 187

S bid 1 ♠, N 2 ◇; S 2 ♠, and N 4 ♠.

The first four tricks were the ♡ J to the ace, a club to the knave, a trump to the ace, and a club to the ace, leaving:

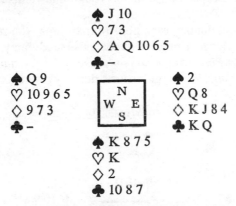

♠ J 10
♡ 7 3
◇ A Q 10 6 5
♣ –

♠ Q 9
♡ 10 9 6 5
◇ 9 7 3
♣ –

♠ 2
♡ Q 8
◇ K J 8 4
♣ K Q

♠ K 8 7 5
♡ K
◇ 2
♣ 10 8 7

What is W's million quid lead to break the contract?

This deal comes from Mr. Alfred P. Sheinwold, of New York City; a quiet, lovable bridge expert of British origin known as 'Freddy'. He had 'ghost-written'* more bridge books than you can count on your two hands, plus a daily bridge column in several hundred American newspapers.

Have you found W's killing lead in the diagram?

* A literary 'ghost' is a temporarily anonymous professional whose work appears under the signature of a person well known in the subject to which the book or article is devoted.—Editor.

237

In practice, W returned a heart to the king, dummy ruffed a club (it does W no good to ruff high a club ahead of the table); S ruffed a heart, and dummy ruffed another club. Next came the ♢ A, a diamond ruff, the trump king, and the stiff club which held W to one trick, the ♠ Q.

In the diagram The Sheinwold Coup is to lead . . . the spade queen! This play looks idiotic, but it begets two tricks! S wins with the king. Now if S draws trumps, he loses two club tricks; if dummy ruffs a club, S loses one club and promotes W's ♠ 9 to the rank of master trump.

Tribes 3 and 4. Inverted and Cross Ruffs

Inverted Ruffs appear only in Reverse Dummy deals. Reverse dummy, or Dummy Reversal as it is also called, is the classic position in which declarer uses his own hand as 'dummy' to score ruffs and later uses dummy as the master trump hand to draw trumps. The position is not so rare as is usually thought, for it is often well-concealed and escapes notice in the rough-and-tumble of ordinary play.

If declarer and dummy each hold four trumps, you may have the typical upside-down arrangement of reverse dummy without inverted ruffs. *True inversion occurs only when declarer starts with more trumps than dummy.* When this occurs, dummy reversal is not so easy to recognize.

Matrix typica

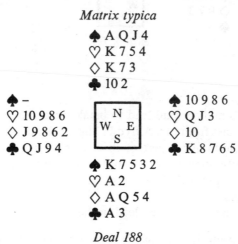

```
              ♠ A Q J 4
              ♡ K 7 5 4
              ♢ K 7 3
              ♣ 10 2
  ♠ –                        ♠ 10 9 8 6
  ♡ 10 9 8 6     N           ♡ Q J 3
  ♢ J 9 8 6 2  W   E         ♢ 10
  ♣ Q J 9 4      S           ♣ K 8 7 6 5
              ♠ K 7 5 3 2
              ♡ A 2
              ♢ A Q 5 4
              ♣ A 3
```

Deal 188

S bid 1 ♠, N 4 ♠; and S 6 ♠.*

*SAB: S 1 ♠, N 3 ♠; S 4 NT Blackwood, N 5 ♢ to show one ace; S 5 NT, N 6 ♡ to show 2 kings; and S 6 ♠.

W led the ♣ Q to the ace. S won and led a low trump, and W failed. How do you plan the play?

Declarer has eleven tricks on top, and the play for No. 12 is by reverse dummy, i.e. by two heart ruffs in S.

Dummy wins the trump lead, S the ♡ A dummy the ♡ K, ᴏ ruffs a heart, and dummy wins the ◇ K.

Dummy leads the last heart, E sheds a club, and S ruffs to score that vital extra trick. S cashes his ♠ K and leads his last trump to draw E's trumps. Eventually, S on dummy's last spade, throws his dead club. S loses a diamond trick but scores slam.

If E ruffs the fourth heart lead, S over-ruffs or, if he prefers, still sheds the dead club, casting the fourth (losing) diamond on the fourth trump in dummy.

In this reverse dummy deal dummy leads hearts through E's known trumps, not caring whether E trumps or discards. The slam can also be made by a complex squeeze. (*Vide* File Z for Squeezes.)

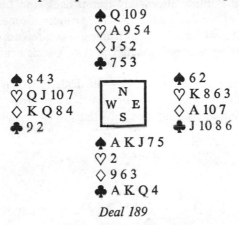

```
              ♠ Q 10 9
              ♡ A 9 5 4
              ◇ J 5 2
              ♣ 7 5 3
♠ 8 4 3                          ♠ 6 2
♡ Q J 10 7        N             ♡ K 8 6 3
◇ K Q 8 4      W     E          ◇ A 10 7
♣ 9 2             S             ♣ J 10 8 6
              ♠ A K J 7 5
              ♡ 2
              ◇ 9 6 3
              ♣ A K Q 4
```

Deal 189

S bid 1 ♠, N 2 ♠; and S 4 ♠.

W led the ♡ Q. Where is the tenth trick?

Declarer played this one *mit verstandt*. He has five trump tricks, three clubs and the ♡ A for nine tricks. The odds are against a 3–3 club split or that the opponent short of clubs lacks three trumps (to let declarer draw only two trumps and ruff the fourth club lead in dummy). So declarer kept these ideas in reserve and adopted a better plan.

He won the heart opening with the ace and immediately ruffed a heart. Dummy reversal begets the tenth trick if S ruffs *three* hearts in his own hand, bringing his holding down to *two trumps* against dummy's three; these three top trumps are used later to draw the enemy spades.

The difficulty is that there are only two entries to dummy to do this, the ♡ A and one trump lead (lest the drawing process be blocked in the end). Declarer needs co-operation by an opponent.

To Trick 3 S led a diamond to W's queen, hoping to seduce a heart return. W co-operated and S ruffed. A trump to dummy let S ruff high a third (the last) low heart, and S's last trump to dummy—a low one—let N draw trumps. The three top clubs made the game. The effect of dummy reversal is to 'lengthen' declarer's trump suit: three ruffs plus dummy's three trump leads give S six tricks out of a five-card suit. A cross-ruff, or ruffs in dummy, similarly 'lengthen' the trump suit.

Tribe 4. Cross-Ruffs

Declarer and dummy alternately trump back and forth in order to score most of, or all, their trumps separately. Sometimes a true cross-ruff occurs with a paucity of trumps, just a few top ones which must be scored separately by ruffs lest they knock heads if trumps are led.

A fundamental principle of cross-ruff deals is to cash plain suit winners as early as possible—before starting the cross-ruff—lest an opponent, during the ruffing, discard from the plain suit and, later, ruff its top cards.

Matrix pura

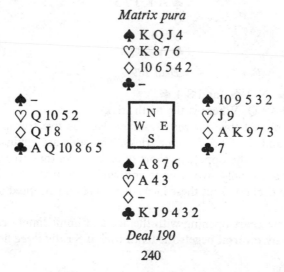

♠ K Q J 4
♡ K 8 7 6
◇ 10 6 5 4 2
♣ -

♠ -
♡ Q 10 5 2
◇ Q J 8
♣ A Q 10 8 6 5

♠ 10 9 5 3 2
♡ J 9
◇ A K 9 7 3
♣ 7

♠ A 8 7 6
♡ A 4 3
◇ -
♣ K J 9 4 3 2

Deal 190

240

RUFF

S dealt and bid 1 ♣, pleasing W who passed; and N replied 1◇, pleasing E who passed. S bid 1 ♠, and N 4 ♠.

W led the ◇ Q. How do you play it?

S ruffed the ◇ Q and at once embarked on a merry cross-ruff to score all his eight trumps separately, while E discarded hearts. When declarer tried to cash a top heart, E unkindly ruffed and scored five trump tricks to break the contract by two.

Declarer *must* cash his ace and king of hearts first, before cross ruffing. This prevents E from discarding hearts under the high ruffs.

The next deal illustrates the bizarre power of a few trumps favourably placed, and the fundamental principle of cashing side tricks first is equally vital. Thirteen years ago Mr. John Campbell of Boston, Mass., scored a small slam against *nine* enemy trumps!

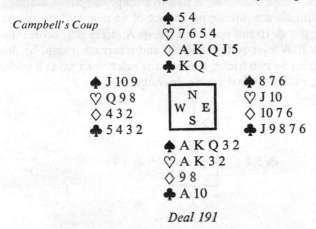

Campbell's Coup

```
              ♠ 5 4
              ♡ 7 6 5 4
              ◇ A K Q J 5
              ♣ K Q
♠ J 10 9                    ♠ 8 7 6
♡ Q 9 8         N          ♡ J 10
◇ 4 3 2       W   E        ◇ 10 7 6
♣ 5 4 3 2       S          ♣ J 9 8 7 6
              ♠ A K Q 3 2
              ♡ A K 3 2
              ◇ 9 8
              ♣ A 10
```

Deal 191

Mr. Campbell was S and bid 1 ♠, N 3 ◇; S 3 ♡ and N 5 ♡. Next Mr. Campbell bid 6 ♣, purely to show his ♣ A, but N misinterpreted this 6 ♣ call and passed! E felt smug about his two apparent trump tricks to break the slam. He figured that N and S had got their wires crossed and dared not double lest he let the cat out of the bag. Any other six is arctic, as are 7 ♠, 7 ◇ or 7 NT: *not* a good pass by N!

W opened the ♠ J. Twelve tricks with two trumps apiece in N and S looked impossible, but Mr. Campbell won them! He cashed three spade tricks, three diamond tricks, and two heart tricks, leaving the position shown on the next page.

241

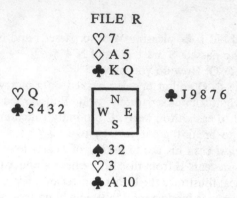

Dummy ruffed a spade, and E found himself in the silly position of having to discard a trump!

Dummy returned a diamond, E had to trump, and Mr. Campbell over-ruffed with his ace, taking no chance of an over-ruff by W. As the cards lay, the ♣ 10 ruff wins, but the ♣ A safety play scores the slam anyway. If W over-ruffs the ♣ 10 and returns a trump, he defeats the contract by two tricks, whereas the safety play saves a trick. Next dummy ruffed the last spade, leaving:

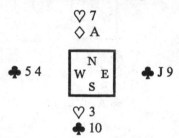

Mr. Campbell had won eleven tricks. When dummy leads the ♢ A to Trick 12, E can score the ♣ J now or later. Either way, the ♣ 10 scores the twelfth trick for slam. This play is called *en passant*, a term I borrowed from Chess in 1938 which has now been adopted by all leading bridge writers.

RUFF

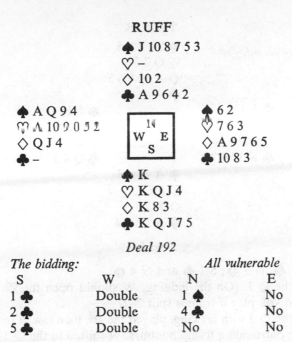

♠ J 10 8 7 5 3
♡ –
◇ 10 2
♣ A 9 6 4 2

♠ A Q 9 4
♡ A 10 9 0 5 2
◇ Q J 4
♣ –

♠ 6 2
♡ 7 6 3
◇ A 9 7 6 5
♣ 10 8 3

♠ K
♡ K Q J 4
◇ K 8 3
♣ K Q J 7 5

Deal 192

The bidding: All vulnerable

S	W	N	E
1 ♣	Double	1 ♠	No
2 ♣	Double	4 ♣	No
5 ♣	Double	No	No

The calling has several points. First W preferred a take-out double
to calling hearts, offering E a grand fit in both majors. S is strong
enough to make a reverse bid of 2 ♡ instead of bidding 2 ♣, but the
singleton spade weakened his hand, and he also felt that W must be
rich in hearts. N preferred the jump raise to 4 ♣ rather than to rebid
his spades on the same theory, and also realizing that S would strain
to prefer a 4 ♠ contract if S held a couple of spades including an
honour.

W led the ◇ Q to E's ace, and S won the diamond return. Next,
S drew E's three trumps. S was subsequently to regret this drawing
dummy down to two trumps when *three* were vital; one to ruff out
the ♡ A on S's ♡ K lead, another for S's low heart, and a *third* for
S's diamond loser. S overdrew his trump account, lost two aces, and
a low red card when dummy ran out of trumps at the end.

After finding the bad trump split, S must plan to use three trumps
in dummy for ruffs before drawing E's clubs. The best line is to lead
♡ K immediately after cashing one trump and learning of the 3–0
split. W covers, now or later, and dummy ruffs. A spade return is
safe, for W is almost sure to have the ace, and has no trump to lead.

Decisive Discard

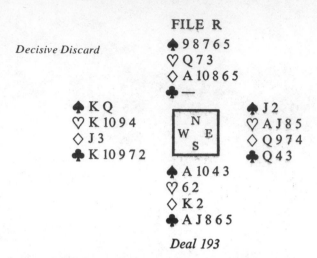

Deal 193

S bid 1 ♣, N 1 ◇; S 1 ♠ and N 4 ♠.

W led the ◇ J. (On the bidding, W should open the ♡ 10.)
How do you play if trumps split 2–2?

S won the ◇ J with his king, played the ace then low in trumps to
knock the outstanding trump honours. W shifted to the ♡ 10 and S
ruffed the third heart lead, reducing his hand to one trump in this
position:

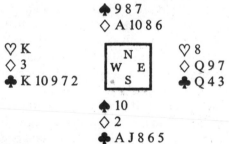

Dummy won the ◇ A and S ruffed a diamond with his last trump,
but diamonds refused to split 3–3 and the contract was broken.

If S has one more trump and dummy one fewer in the diagram,
declarer can ruff out diamonds and get home.

The key play to win the hand is to cash the ♣ A for a heart discard
from dummy *before* the second trump lead. Now *dummy* can ruff the
third heart lead and preserve two trumps in S to ruff out, and bring
in, the diamonds.

SAFETY PLAY

S stands for Safety Play. The definition is 'play to limit the loss of tricks if the distribution is unfavourable'. The basic safety principle occurs in many files, such as Avoidance, Percentage, drawing enemy trumps to avoid enemy ruffs, etc.

The safety play proper, however, involves only one suit. It is usually a protective finesse; or a duck in a long suit—the backbone of a no-trump contract; or the side suit of a trump contract; or the trump suit itself. A safety play caters for a bad suit-split—one in which all enemy strength is massed in one hand. A few plays of this type also appear under Finesse and Knock (q.v.).

The family of safety play requires careful study. The serious student of bridge should familiarize himself with each matrix which follows in order to recognize it instantly in the heat of play. This will give declarer more time for strategic analysis of his combined forces. Observe this deal:

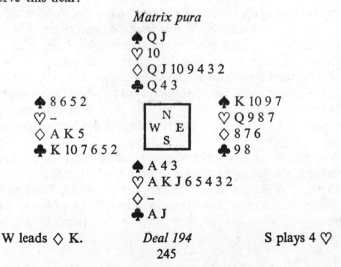

Matrix pura

♠ Q J
♡ 10
♢ Q J 10 9 4 3 2
♣ Q 4 3

♠ 8 6 5 2   ♠ K 10 9 7
♡ –   ♡ Q 9 8 7
♢ A K 5   ♢ 8 7 6
♣ K 10 7 6 5 2   ♣ 9 8

♠ A 4 3
♡ A K J 6 5 4 3 2
♢ –
♣ A J

W leads ♢ K.   *Deal 194*   S plays 4 ♡

At rubber game S bid 1 ♡, N 2 ◇ ; and S 4 ♡, end.

W led the ◇ K. How do you play trumps?

Declarer took a quick look at dummy, ruffed the ◇ K, and laid down the ace of trumps. This uncovered two trump tricks for E, who also scored the ♠ K because S could not get to dummy to finesse spades. Later E got in and led a club, S finessed, and the ♣ K from W broke the contract.

If trumps had split no worse than 3–1, or if the club finesse had won, declarer would have got home. But he was lulled into a false sense of security by his eight-card trump suit topped by three honours. Declarer was a typical 'fair-weather player' who failed to take adequate precautions against a possible distributional storm; the 4–0 heart split in this case.

Declarer has only two black losers and he can afford to lose one trump trick—a small premium to pay to avoid TWO trump losers, and ensure game. To Trick 2 he should lead a *low* trump to dummy's ten.

Of course, this safety play gives up a trick to the queen singleton or doubleton, but there happens to be some salvage value in the fact that W might hold Q x x and duck, fearing that E held the king.

Strangely enough, declarer's actual play is correct at match point duplicate, because the match point premiums for extra tricks are relatively high. In this type of game, most declarers would properly bang down the ace of trumps first, be set one trick, and . . . earn an average score on the board! The danger of the safety play is that declarer would win just ten tricks for his contract against a 2–2 trump split or queen alone, and earn a zero score because all other declarers won eleven tricks by first laying down the ace of trumps.

The deal above illustrates a typical single-suit safety play. Such plays are too numerous to illustrate in complete deals. Also, they are easier and quicker to learn as one-suit matrices. They occur in a profusion of shapes and types, and many bear structural relationships to each other. In order to clarify and simplify these relationships in discussions, we refer to prototypes and their derivatives defined below.

Prototype. A basic matrix whose structure and play are used as criteria for similar types. (*Proto* = primitive, original.)

Altertype. A matrix of one low card fewer in one hand and one card more in the other hand than in its prototype. (*Alter* = other.)

Brevitype. A matrix of one card shorter than its prototype. (*Brevi* = short.)

Contratype. A matrix simulating a prototype but requiring an opposite kind of play. (*Contra* = against.)

Cotype. A derivative of two types. (*Co-* = together.)

Subtype. A matrix in which the high cards rank lower than in its prototype, but otherwise is the same. (*Sub* = under.)

Synotype. A matrix closely related to its prototype by identical basic structure and play. (*Syno-* = identical.)

These terms are used only for the ensuing study of comparative morphology and are not to be construed as bona fide names for the matrices. Later, we offer a simple table of taxonomy in which safety play matrices are classified in natural groups.

Some matrices occur in pairs of polymorphous forms; an imperfect safety play and a perfect safety play. The former improves your chances and the latter raises them to the perfection of 100% play to win the specified number of tricks against any defence and distribution of the suit. Below is the basic pair of polymers.

The prototypes below are identical except for the nine and four in dummy. An enemy split of 2–2 or 3–1 makes five tricks solid, and the problem is to guard against a 4–0 split and trap the knave. In both matrices play the ace first—the standard rule of 'win the first trick in the hand with two honours'. This discovers any 4–0 split immediately and lets you pick up J 9 8 7 with E in Matrix 1. You can do nothing about it if W holds these cards. But in Matrix 2 you can win five sure tricks by trapping J 8 7 4 regardless of whether W or E holds these cards, a perfect safety play.

1	2
Q 4 3 2	Q 9 3 2
A K 10 6 5	A K 10 6 5

For this reason perfect safety plays are often called Sure Tricks.

In Matrix 1 the safety play is *single* because it protects against one opponent whilst in Matrix 2 it is *double*, pinioning both opponents simultaneously. These do not always coincide with imperfect and perfect safety plays respectively, for some sure trick subtypes are single, yet perfect. Cotype 3 and its subtypes below form an interesting series.

Perfect Single Safety Plays

3	4	5
J 8 3 2	10 7 3 2	9 6 3 2
K Q 9 6 5	Q J 8 6 5	J 10 7 5

In every case S should lead an honour first from his own hand (or low from dummy to the double honour) to guard against four cards of the suit in W. A low lead from S first is harmless if E happens to hold four cards. The next matrix and its subtypes form another series.

Imperfect Safety Plays

6	7	8
Q 4 3 2	Q 4 3 2	Q 4 3 2
A K 9 6 5	K J 8 6 5	J 10 7 6 5

Matrix 6 is the contratype of Matrix 1, with the ten replaced by the nine. Here the ace play is useless, for J 10 8 7 massed with either opponent will come to a trick if the first trick is won by South. The safety play is the queen first. If this discovers J 10 8 7 in E, declarer can lead through E twice to neutralize his potential stopper (providing, of course that N has a side-suit entry). Matrices 7 and 8 are similar; requiring the play of the single honour first.

9	10
Q 9 3 2	Q 8 3 2
A K 10 6	A K 9 6

Matrix 9 is a brevitype of Matrix 2. Discovery of a 5–0 split or singleton knave by the ace play clarifies matters at once, but usually you catch only low cards. If the eight drops, you can next lead *through* its holder to discover if it is J 8 doubleton, or a singleton, which reveals how to pick up the knave.

Matrix 10 is a cotype of Matrices 1 and 2. Its best play requires a comparison of odds. Playing the queen first is effective against five cards in E or a singleton honour in W. The 5–0 split (with 5% odds) occurs half this time or $2\frac{1}{2}\%$ with E only long in the suit.

A 4–1 split is 28% probable, but as the queen play wins only if E holds four cards, the odds are 14%. And only in 2/5ths of this 14% or a net of 5·6% will W hold a lone honour. Added to $2\frac{1}{2}\%$ gives us 8·1% for the queen play.

The ace play first is effective if W or E holds a lone honour, which is 2/5ths of 28% or 11·2%. Thus the ace play has a 3·1 % advantage over the queen play.

11	12	13
Q 8 3	Q 8 3	Q 8 3
A K 9 5 2	A K 9 5	A K 9 5 4 3

Matrices 11 and 12 are brevitypes of Matrix 6, and Matrix 13 is an altertype. The only play is the queen first to cater for a void or blank honour in W. Dummy is too short of low cards for the ace first play; for if E drops an honour, declarer cannot next make a discovery play but would have to guess whether E held a singleton or doubleton.

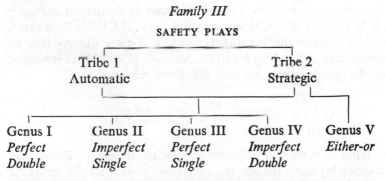

14	15
A J 8 6 5	K 10 7 6 5
Q 4 3 2	Q 8 4 3 2

In both matrices automatically lead *toward* the queen first. This restrains the balance of missing cards in W to one trick.

16	17	18
A K Q 8 5	K Q 10 7 5	Q 10 9 6 5
J 3 2	J 3 2	J 3 2

In Matrix 16, playing a top card first from dummy loses a trick to 10 9 7 6 4 in W because S can get only one low card lead through W. In Matrix 16 and its sub-types, play the knave first.

Let us pause and take a bird's-eye view of safety plays. We have arranged them in natural groups in the chart below.

Family III

SAFETY PLAYS

| | Tribe 1 Automatic | | | Tribe 2 Strategic | |

Genus I	Genus II	Genus III	Genus IV	Genus V
Perfect	*Imperfect*	*Perfect*	*Imperfect*	*Either-or*
Double	*Single*	*Single*	*Double*	

This chart is confluent like some other charts of plays, because both tribes converge upon four genera in common. Genus V, however, is strictly strategic.

Automatic means that the safety play is made automatically to ensure the maximum number of tricks as in Matrices 1 and 2.

Strategic implies variation in play to meet declarer's aims. A strategic safety play usually involves gambit, giving up some chances for the maximum number of tricks in order to ensure the lesser, but essential, number. In other words, if you need all the tricks possible for your contract, play boldly; but if you can afford to lose a trick, play safely.

The Either-or Safety Play is a complex rarity to be explained later with examples.

Perfect Double Safety Plays

19	20	21
J 2	10 2	9 2
A K 9 6 5 4 3	K Q 8 6 5 4 3	Q J 7 6 5 4 3

22	23	24
10 2	9 2	8 2
A K Q 8 5 4	K Q J 7 4 3	Q J 10 6 4 3

These matrices are purely strategic, because their proper play depends upon the number of tricks needed. If you need all seven tricks from Matrix 19 for your contract (or for a good score at match point duplicate which places a premium on winning the maximum number of tricks), your only play is to bang down the ace and king, poppa-momma fashion, and hope for a 2–2 split. But if strategic considerations show that you can afford to lose one trick BUT NOT TWO, the safety play is to lead low toward the knave in dummy at once.

If W holds Q 10 8 7, he gets one trick only; if E holds these cards, the knave drives out the queen, and you re-enter dummy later to lead through and pick up E's 10 8 7. Matrices 19 and 22 are synotypes and the other matrices are their respective subtypes.

25	26
Q 4 3 2	J 7 6
A 10 9 8 7 6	A 9 5 4 3 2

Matrix 25 is another synotype of Matrices 19 and 22. If you need six tricks, lay down the ace. It scores a bull's-eye if E or W holds the bare king. The other choice, to lead the queen for a scoop finesse, wins only if W holds the lone knave with chances only half as good. For five sure tricks lead low toward the queen to cater to K J x in W; or better, lead low, to 10 if E ducks, for six tricks if E has lone K.

Matrix 26 loses *three tricks* if you plank down the ace and an opponent fails. First lead low toward the knave to hold K Q 10 8 in one enemy hand to two tricks. If both opponents follow suit, you can later play the ace to clean out the suit should it split 2–2.

27. *Discovered Safety Play*	28. *Two Way Safety Play*
10 4 3	K 9 5 4
A K 8 6 5	A 10 6 3 2

You want four tricks from Matrix 27. You have no immediate safety play, for a 5–0 split is hopeless, so you play the ace to see what it fetches down. If an honour drops, it looks mighty tempting to lay down the king next to pick up Q J doubleton, correct if you need five tricks. In this case the ace play discovers a brevitype of Matrix 19 for four sure tricks if you next lead low toward the ten.

Matrix 28 will yield four tricks if you lead low from either hand (two way), and finesse the nine or ten if second hand plays low.

29	30
A 9 5 4 3 2	K 8 5 4 3 2
10 7 6	10 7 6

These are imperfect subtypes of Matrix 26. In Matrix 29, a low lead toward the ten limits the loss to two tricks if W holds K Q J 8. In Matrix 30 a low lead toward the ten restrains A Q J 9 in E to three tricks whereas any other play loses four.

Imperfect Double Safety Plays

31	32	33
K J 3	K 9 3	K 10 3
A 9 6 5 4	A J 6 5 4	A 9 5 4

In Matrix 31 lay down the king. If all follow low, you discover a brevitype of Matrix 19, so re-enter your own hand in a side suit and lead low toward J x.

Matrix 32 is a contratype of Matrix 31 with the knave and nine switched. Lay down the ace first then lead low. If W plays low a second time, insert the nine. This guards against Q 10 x x in W.

Matrix 33 is a *seki* suit which you should try to get an opponent to open for you. But if you must attack it yourself, the choice is close with odds favouring your cashing both tops in the hope of dropping a doubleton honour and still scoring on any 3–3 split.

34	35
K 6 3	K 10
A 10 4 3 2	A 9 7 6 5

In Matrix 34 the optimistic, and only, play for five tricks is to plank down the ace and king and hope for Q J to drop doubleton. The safety play is to cash the king first then finesse the ten to guard against Q J x x in E. In brevitype 35 the best way to develop the suit is to lead low and finesse the ten. This play yields four tricks against Q J x x or a doubleton honour in W or any 3–3 split.

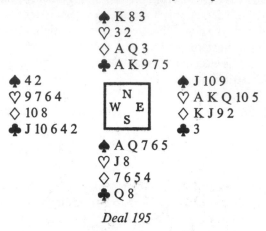

♠ K 8 3
♡ 3 2
♢ A Q 3
♣ A K 9 7 5

♠ 4 2
♡ 9 7 6 4
♢ 10 8
♣ J 10 6 4 2

♠ J 10 9
♡ A K Q 10 5
♢ K J 9 2
♣ 3

♠ A Q 7 6 5
♡ J 8
♢ 7 6 5 4
♣ Q 8

Deal 195

At rubber game N bid 1 ♣, E 1 ♡ (or double), S 1 ♠; N 3 ♠ and S 4 ♠, end.

W led the ♡ 4 to E's queen. E won another heart and shifted to the ♠ J. S won three trump tricks and the ♣ Q. Next S led the ♣ 8, W played low, and dummy made the safety play of the nine! This let S park two diamond losers on dummy's top clubs. S later lost the diamond finesse but scored game.

That ♣ 9 'finesse' was made in case W held five clubs. The play is a sure trick that cannot lose. If E wins the ♣ 9, the enemy club split proves no worse than 4–2, and dummy's clubs are all good for S's three diamond discards.

If W covers the ♣ 8, dummy wins with the king. Next dummy returns the nine to let W win a club trick while S sheds a diamond; and dummy has two top clubs left for two more diamond sluffs.

Declarer never had to risk his contract on the diamond finesse. The deal illustrates the strategic aspects of safety play and Avoidance to keep W off a diamond lead until clubs were established. If E doubles the opening bid, S should avoid the diamond finesse at all costs.

SAFETY PLAY

Often Misplayed

36	37
A J 5 4	A J 6 5 4 3
K 7 3	Q 2

The invariable popular method in Matrix 36 is to play the king then finesse the knave. This is correct if you need four tricks, or three quick winners if you cannot afford to lose the lead. But the safety play for three tricks when you can afford to give up a trick is to cash the ace and king at once, lest E hold the doubleton queen, then to lead low toward the knave. This technique begets three tricks if W holds the queen or in a 3–3 split. If E holds Q 10 x x , neither method wins.

In Matrix 37 the only play for all six tricks is a swindle by leading the queen and hoping that W has K x x and fails to cover. To develop five tricks, many players first lead low toward the queen. This loses TWO tricks if W holds the lone king, and the safety play is to lay down the ace first. If E holds K 10 9 x, you cannot prevent him from getting two tricks however you play the suit.

Versus King Solus

38	39
A Q 7 6 5	A Q 7 6
8 4 3 2	8 4 3 2

If you need all five tricks from Matrix 38, the queen finesse is the best shot. If you can spare a trick, play the ace first, then return to your own hand in another suit and lead toward the queen to neutralize W, if he started with K J x.

Brevitype 39 contains a sure loser *regardless of distribution*, and a first round finesse loses three tricks if E holds the lone king. The safety play is to start with the ace or, if you must retain quick control, to duck the *first* lead from either hand.

40	41	42
A Q 3	10 6 3	A 10 3
10 6 5 4 2	A Q 5 4 2	Q 6 5 4 2

In these altertypes of Matrix 39 first lay down the ace to avoid losing three tricks. If opponents play low cards the second play in Matrix 40 is to lead low toward the queen, in others toward the ten.

Certain finessing positions with an unapparent paucity of high cards demand respect if you wish to develop a suit to its maximum.

FILE S

43	44
A J 10 4	A J 10 5 4 3
Q 5 3	9 2

In both cases S should lead his *bottom* card in case W holds a singleton honour.

Versus The Ace

45	46	47
K J 5 4	6 5 4 3	–
Q 6 5	K 9 8 7 5	K Q 6 5 4 3 2

In Matrix 45 the automatic play is to lead low toward the knave. If it wins, re-enter your own hand and lead low toward the king. This keeps your picture cards out of the way of the ace if W holds it doubleton or singleton.

If you must have four tricks from Matrix 46, lead low to the king and hope that E holds A x. If you can spare two tricks but not three, the safety play is a first round duck to cater for the chance of the lone ace in W.

Matrix 47 is typical of a trump suit you may hold in misfit hands. You must lose two tricks however you play. The routine safety play is to lead low first to cater for the ace alone. This restricts loss to three tricks.

If both opponents follow suit, next time you get in, push an honour to cater to a 2—2 split of the remaining four enemy cards to win five tricks. This has 40% chances to win, a marked edge over leading low again to drop the now bare ace with only 13% chances to win.

Either-or Safety Plays

48	49	50
Q 10 3 2	J 9 3 2	10 8 3 2
A K 8 6 5	K Q 7 5 4	Q J 6 5 4

Matrix 48 is a cotype of Matrices 1 and 6. You can EITHER lay down the ace to guard against J 9 7 4 in W, OR lead low to the queen to guard against J 9 7 4 in E. But, unlike Matrix 2, YOU CANNOT GUARD AGAINST BOTH CONTINGENCIES SIMULTANEOUSLY.

Before committing yourself to a choice, first snoop around in other suits in order to get a count of enemy shapes—if this be not too hazardous.

The position is NOT a double safety play, but a combination of two single ones. Subtypes 49 and 50 resolve to similar analyses.

Defensive Safety Plays

51	52	53
K 2	K 2	Q 2
5	5	5
J 4 3	10 7 6 4	A 10 3

In all these matrices W leads the five against your no-trump contract. In Matrices 51 and 52, the sure way to stop the suit is to duck in dummy. Similarly, in Matrix 53, duck to ensure TWO stoppers, unless you *must* gamble on the queen's winning immediately for strategic reasons.

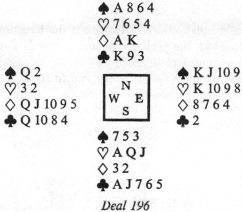

                    ♠ A 8 6 4
                    ♡ 7 6 5 4
                    ◇ A K
                    ♣ K 9 3

    ♠ Q 2   ♠ K J 10 9
    ♡ 3 2   N   ♡ K 10 9 8
    ◇ Q J 10 9 5   W   E   ◇ 8 7 6 4
    ♣ Q 10 8 4   S   ♣ 2

                    ♠ 7 5 3
                    ♡ A Q J
                    ◇ 3 2
                    ♣ A J 7 6 5

Deal 196

S bid 1 ♣, N 1 ♠; S 1 NT, and N 3 NT; cnd.
W led the ◇ Q.
S took the typical hacker's* view that clubs might easily yield five tricks for game with a heart finesse in reserve if the club finesse failed.

He won the ◇ Q opening in dummy then the ♣ K. He led another club only to see E discard. Later he finessed hearts twice, but three heart tricks, two diamonds, two clubs, and a spade totalled one trick short of game.

If S makes the Matrix 32 safety play in clubs and later takes a heart finesse, he scores game as the cards lie. But this is not the whole story. Declarer cannot see opponents' hands as you can in your easy chair reading this book.

Should declarer play clubs wide open for five tricks, or safely for four?

* 'Hacker'—the latest U.S. slang for inferior player—*ci-devant* palooka. —Editor.

How can he tell?

At Trick 2 declarer has no way of knowing, but he can employ correct strategy to find out.

At Trick 2, finesse a heart at once! If this loses and W knocks out your last diamond stopper, you must play on clubs for five tricks as the only chance. But if the heart finesse wins as it does, you will need only FOUR club tricks so you should consolidate your position immediately and make the safety play in clubs. Don't fall into the trap of another early heart finesse if the first finesse wins, for W might hold up the king once and spoil your plans. Echelon your plays.

Subfile ST

A perfect safety play matrix often forms the backbone of a Sure Trick deal. However, the presence of such a matrix does not necessarily produce sure trick play.

In this subfile we offer problems for you to solve. These are new problems, amending the book, SURE TRICKS.

WIN 13/13

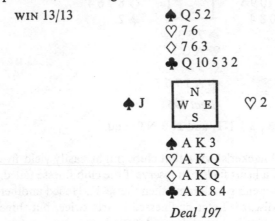

♠ Q 5 2
♡ 7 6
◇ 7 6 3
♣ Q 10 5 3 2

♠ J
♡ 2

♠ A K 3
♡ A K Q
◇ A K Q
♣ A K 8 4

Deal 197

In a rubber game S bid 4 NT, N 6 NT; and S 7 NT, end.

With ten tricks on top and flat shape S did not want to mess about with a forcing bid which would obviously elicit a negative response and no information.

The best opening on this once-in-a-lifetime hand is 4 NT.* This bid is not forcing but asks partner for one raise for each honour card higher than a knave. With two queens N properly gave a double

* Unless this bid be played as a direct inquiry for aces, on Culbertson or Blackwood lines.—Editor.

raise to 6 NT. The located black queens filled S's hand except for the fourth club. S properly figured that the odds of finding a stray knave or promotional suit length in N warranted his 7 NT call.

W led the ♠ J and E discarded the ♡ 2.

N–S win ALL THIRTEEN tricks against any defence and distribution.

Solution on page 261.

WIN 9/13

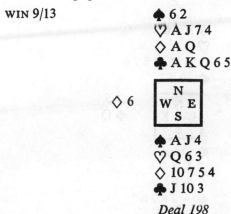

```
              ♠ 6 2
              ♡ A J 7 4
              ◇ A Q
              ♣ A K Q 6 5

                   N
◇ 6            W       E
                   S

              ♠ A J 4
              ♡ Q 6 3
              ◇ 10 7 5 4
              ♣ J 10 3
```

Deal 198

N bid 1 ♣, S 1 NT; and N 3 NT, end.

It would be pointless for N to bid hearts on the second round, for S would have bid 1 ♡ instead of 1 NT on ♡ Q x x x or better.

W led the ◇ 6.

N–S win NINE tricks against any defence and distribution.

Solution on page 261.

WIN 9/13

```
              ♠ Q J 6 4
              ♡ Q 2
              ◇ 10 7 3
              ♣ 7 6 5 4

                   N
♡ 10           W       E
                   S

              ♠ A 10 3
              ♡ A K J 4
              ◇ A K J 5
              ♣ K 2
```

Deal 199

FILE S

S bid 2 ♣, N 2 ◇; S 2 NT, and N 3 NT, end.

W led the ♡ 10.

If you finesse the ♠ Q, it wins.

How do you continue after the spade finesse wins in order to make nine tricks a lead-pipe cinch?

What is the additional safety play for an extra trick?

N–S win NINE tricks against any defence and distribution.

Solution on page 261.

WIN 11/13

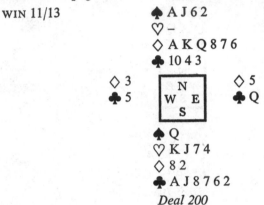

Deal 200

S bid 1 ♣, N 2 ◇; S 2 ♡, N 2 ♠; S 3 ♣, and N 5 ♣; end.

W led the ◇ 3 to dummy's queen. Dummy returned the ♣ 3, E played the queen, S the ace and W the five.

N–S win ELEVEN tricks against any defence and distribution.

Solution on page 261.

WIN 12/13

En Passant Blanc

Deal 201

SAFETY PLAY

Bidding:			
S	W	N	E
1 ◇	No	2 ♣	2 ♡
2 ♠	No	4 ♠	5 ♡
6 ♠	No	No	No

N bid 2 ♣ instead of 1 ♠, for he intended to bid spades later as a reverse to show extra strength. S dared not cue-bid hearts later lest he tip off W what to lead in case N held no quick club stopper and a quick heart trick for S's vital club discard.

W led the ♡ K.

N–S win TWELVE tricks against any defence and distribution. Solution on page 262.

Macleod's Sure Trick

WIN 12/13

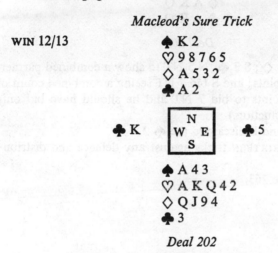

♠ K 2
♡ 9 8 7 6 5
◇ A 5 3 2
♣ A 2

♣ K   ♣ 5

♠ A 4 3
♡ A K Q 4 2
◇ Q J 9 4
♣ 3

Deal 202

S bid 1 ♡, N 3 ♡; S 4 NT, N 5 ♡; and S 6 ♡, end.
W led the ♣ K to the ace in dummy and E played the ♣ 5.
N–S win TWELVE tricks against any defence and distribution.
Solution on page 262.

The Queen Trap

WIN 13/13

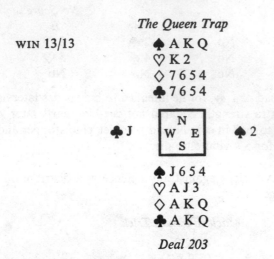

Deal 203

S bid 2 NT, N 3 ◇; S 3 ♠, N 5 NT to show a combined partnership count of 34 points; and S bid 7 NT seeing a combined count of 36. (S needs 37 points to bid 7 NT and he should have bid only 6 NT, closing the auction.)

W led the ♣ J and E discarded the ♠ 2.

N–S win ALL THIRTEEN tricks against any defence and distribution.

Solution on page 263.

SAFETY PLAY

Deal 197. S plays to get a count on enemy shapes in order to determine which way to play clubs, representing Matrix 48

S wins the ♣ J with the ace and cashes all his red winners. Knowing that W started with seven spades, S can count W's other six cards. If W shows only two red cards, he is marked with four clubs; otherwise only E can possibly hold four clubs and S plays clubs accordingly, the queen first.

Deal 198. Declarer finessed the ◊ Q which E won with the king, E shifted to a spade and S was in trouble. He held up the ♠ A twice but he was forced to win the third spade lead. He tried a heart finesse which lost, and the defence gathered enough spade tricks to break the contract.

The sure trick play is the ◊ A to Trick 1. S wins a club and loses the heart finesse, but diamonds are secure.

If E scores the ◊ K and returns a low diamond, S plays the ten, which wins or else W started with only four diamonds. If E returns a low diamond to the king in W, the ten becomes an automatic stopper if W continues diamonds.

Deal 199. Declarer won the ♡ 10 with the queen in dummy and finessed the ♠ Q successfully, but W gobbled the next spade finesse with the king, and declarer could never reach dummy again. W returned a heart to S. S laid down the ◊ A K, but the queen failed to drop. Next S led a low diamond, hoping W held the queen. But E got in with the ◊ Q and returned the ♣ Q, and ♣ A J x x x with W broke the contract.

Declarer was taken in by the defensive hold-up of the ♠ K at Trick 2. At Trick 3, with two spade tricks certain, S should quit spades and finesse diamonds to make game certain.

The safety play for an extra trick is to win the ♡ 10 opening in S and lay down the ◊ A to drop the possible lone queen in W, then lead a heart to the queen in dummy. Next comes the ♠ Q finesse. If it wins, shift to a *low* diamond and finesse the knave. This line ensures four diamond tricks if E holds the doubleton queen.

Deal 200. To Trick 3, S led a club to W's king, and E failed. W returned a heart which dummy had to ruff with his last trump lest E get in with the ♡ A and give W a ruff. Dummy had to score the ◊ A to let S ruff a diamond and get in to draw trumps. Diamonds

261

split badly and dummy had no side entry to set up the suit for enough discards and the contract was broken.

Declarer needs eleven tricks, not twelve; and the safety play at Trick 3 is to lead a diamond. Let opponents score both their remaining trumps and welcome, while you make sure of setting up, and bringing home, the great diamond suit.

Deal 201. Four trumps in E and four diamonds in W give the main theme, to prevent E from ruffing a top diamond until the third round.

S ruffs the heart opening and N wins a top trump. Then:

1. If W fails, N leads a diamond. E fails, else there is no problem, and must discard. N re-enters via a top club and leads another diamond. Again E must discard and S wins. S leads his last top diamond which E ruffs. S ruffs E's heart return, N ruffs high a diamond, N must win a top trump. (If N leads a low trump, E injects the ten.) S draws trumps and scores his diamonds.

Trap: If S plays a top diamond at Trick 4, E ruffs and forces S to ruff a heart. Now S must draw trumps lest E ruff another diamond. . . .

Variations : If E with 9–4 shape ruffs the first club lead and returns a heart, S ruffs. N then S draw trumps, N takes the marked club finesse, and scores the last trump to squeeze W.

2. If E fails in trumps at Trick 2, S lays down a top diamond. Then:

(a) If W ruffs, S ruffs W's heart return, S draws trumps, and N leads twice through ◇ J 10 x marked in E.

(b) If E fails again, N ruffs the fourth diamond lead. Next S must win the third trump lead, making W's trump a master card, then S pushes diamonds to force it.

Trap: If S draws trumps before testing diamonds, ◇ J 10 8 2 in W wins a trick and the hand collapses.

Deal 202. After winning the ♣ A, S draws trumps in three leads, plays the ♠ K, ruffs the club, and ruffs the third spade lead in dummy, leaving:

North:	♡ 9	◇ A 5 3 2
South:	♡ 4	◇ Q J 9 4

N leads a low diamond, E plays low, and the knave wins with W following suit also. If S makes the error of going to the ◇ A, E fails and W gets two diamond tricks. The sure trick is to lead the ◇ Q.

262

If W covers, dummy ducks and W is end-played or diamonds split 3–2. If W fails, the queen is run to the king in E who is end-played Neat, eh? The deal comes from Iain Macleod, M.P., author of *Bridge is an Easy Game* (Falcon Press).

Captain Wayne G. Barker offers a superior line. Begin with ♠ Q and finesse. If queen wins, the position above develops. If W covers, N wins with ace and finesses ◊ 9 on return, but ducks completely if E fails. If E wins queen with king, he is endplayed. Barker's method offers many chances to win all four diamond tricks.

Deal 203. S wins the club opening and wins three diamond tricks. A 3–3 split solves the problem. But:

1. If E stops diamonds, N wins three spade tricks and S wins two more clubs. S cashes the ♠ J, forcing W to keep a club stopper hence not more than two hearts. N sheds his now useless club, and E is squeezed. E is known to hold the top diamond, and must also pare down to two hearts. The ♡ K, ♡ A then ♡ J win the last three tricks.

2. If W stops a diamond and a club, N wins three spade tricks and S two more club tricks as in Line 1, creating this position:

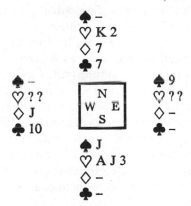

S lays down his last spade, forcing W to keep a diamond and a club stopper, hence only one heart; and N keeps two hearts. N wins his top heart to draw W's last known heart, and S takes the marked ♡ J finesse.

This ending is a version of the famous Harvard Coup, described on page 123 of *Endplays*.

File T

TEMPO

T stands for Tempo. In bridge, a tempo is the time value of a lead. A player uses his tempo, or time-unit, when he leads an honour from a sequence in order to drive out an enemy stopper. A tempo is a unit in the march of time to set up a trick or tricks in a suit. An early writer used to refer to the 'invisible shadow of the time factor' cast upon the play of the hand. This 'invisible shadow' is not so difficult to see if you take the trouble to measure it in terms of lead values by the *N plus 1* formula. This means that bringing home your suit requires one lead more than the number of enemy stoppers.

In bridge, the play for time is diametrically opposed to the play for position, characterized by the waiting game when you lead a trickless suit in order to let the enemy lead up to your tenaces.

In war, and in games of war such as bridge and chess, time so often presses, and a lead is a vital time unit. As Confederate General Nathan Bedford Forrest said, when asked for the formula by which he won his battles: 'I git thar fustest with the mostest. . . .'

Basic manifestations of the time factor are the first elements taught beginners, and tempo pervades many deals of other files. Hence tempo is often taken for granted. File T is devoted to deals in which tempo is the primary feature. Before reading further, turn back and study Deal 1, Section I, of the Introduction. It is an interesting mutate in tempi.

TEMPO

Matrix pura

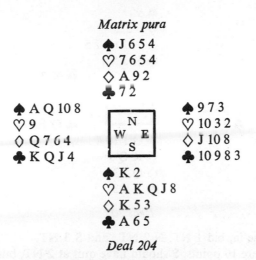

```
              ♠ J 6 5 4
              ♡ 7 6 5 4
              ◇ A 9 2
              ♣ 7 2
♠ A Q 10 8              ♠ 9 7 3
♡ 9            N       ♡ 10 3 2
◇ Q 7 6 4   W   E     ◇ J 10 8
♣ K Q J 4      S       ♣ 10 9 8 3
              ♠ K 2
              ♡ A K Q J 8
              ◇ K 5 3
              ♣ A 6 5
```

Deal 204

S bid 1 ♡, W doubled, N 2 ♡; and S 4 ♡.

W led the ♣ K. Should S take it with the ace?

S made the mistake of holding up the ♣ A. He would have been right—if W had led another club; but W saw E play the ♣ 3 and shifted to the ◇ 4, forcing the ten and king. S drew trumps. Placing the missing spade honours in W for his take-out double, S led a low spade to set up dummy's knave for a diamond discard—but he was too late. W won with the queen and returned another diamond, prematurely driving out declarer's second stopper, dummy's ace. W finally collected a club trick, two spades, and a diamond to break the contract.

An immediate diamond opening also breaks the contract, but the natural club opening gave S his chance—time control—which he overlooked.

The correct play is to win the ♣ K with the ace, draw trumps, and lead the ♠ K or ♠ 2—it doesn't matter which. W wins and returns a diamond to your king. You push another spade to promote dummy's knave for a diamond discard, *before* the second diamond stopper is knocked out. In this hand, the club ruff can wait: the spade establishment requires priority.

On the opening club lead E could play the nine to begin a Foster echo to show four cards. But the danger is that W supposedly might continue with the ace from ace-king and so establish ♣ Q in S for a diamond discard from dummy.

265

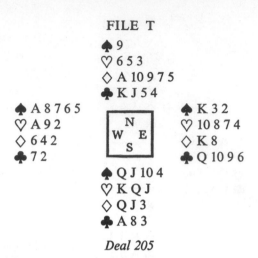

Deal 205

S, at game-in, bid 1 NT, N 2 NT; and S 3 NT.

With a bare 16 points, S should have quit at 2 NT, but the play is the real point of interest in the deal.

W led the ♠ 6 to the king, and W ducked E's spade return.

Declarer figured that game was in the bag if the diamond finesse was on, and erred by losing it to the king in E at once. E returned a spade which W won with the ace and W pushed another spade to clear the suit.

With only eight tricks on top, declarer led the ♡ J, hoping to sneak a trick, but W stepped in with the ace and scored his long spade to break the contract.

Declarer failed to perceive the positional character of his tempi. At Trick 2 he should first attack his shorter suit, hearts. If W holds up the ♡ A once, declarer can then shift to diamonds and go game. If W wins the ♡ A at once and resumes spades, S gets in and can finesse diamonds into E, now harmless with no spade left.

The general key to recognition of this situation is this: knock out *first* that entry which functions on both sides; and only *secondly* the entry which functions in the non-danger hand.

TEMPO

Carte Blanche Trumps

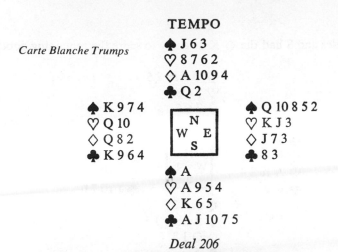

```
                    ♠ J 6 3
                    ♡ 8 7 6 2
                    ◇ A 10 9 4
                    ♣ Q 2
   ♠ K 9 7 4                      ♠ Q 10 8 5 2
   ♡ Q 10          N              ♡ K J 3
   ◇ Q 8 2       W   E            ◇ J 7 3
   ♣ K 9 6 4        S             ♣ 8 3
                    ♠ A
                    ♡ A 9 5 4
                    ◇ K 6 5
                    ♣ A J 10 7 5
```

Deal 206

S bid 1 ♣, N 1 ◇; S 1 ♡, N 2 ♡; and S 4 ♡.

After the heart raise, S felt that trumps were secure with eight cards despite his miserable *carte blanche* suit, for a sound partner rarely raises a 'reversed' or secondary suit on fewer than four trumps.

At several tables in a duplicate game W opened the ♠ 4 against 4 ♡, dummy ducked, and the ten dropped the ace. From here on the play varied.

At one table S played ace then low in trumps, and E overtook W's queen to play his knave also, reducing S to one trump. This E player forced S with a spade resumption. Dummy won the ◇ A to let S finesse clubs. W scored his ♣ K and cashed the ♠ K to break the contract.

At another table dummy won Trick 2 with the ◇ A and S lost the club finesse. W returned a diamond, driving out S's king. S cashed the ace of trumps and pushed clubs to get diamond discards in dummy, but E ruffed the third club lead and scored a diamond to break the contract.

Declarer at the third table fulfilled his contract, because he realized that he had *two jobs* to do: to draw trumps while controlling spades and diamonds; *and* to score clubs.

To Trick 2 S led a *low* trump to W's ten. S ruffed W's ♠ K return and S next led a low club to W's king, disdaining (rightly) the finesse, as taking out the ◇ A prematurely could wreck the hand if W returned a diamond when he won the ♣ K. S ruffed another spade return with his last low trump, laid down the ace of trumps, then pushed clubs to force E's master trump. At this point *dummy* could

267

ruff spades and S had the ◇ K as entry to score the remaining good clubs.

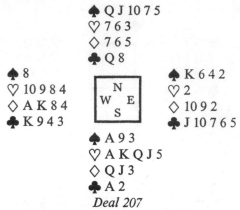

♠ Q J 10 7 5
♡ 7 6 3
◇ 7 6 5
♣ Q 8

♠ 8
♡ 10 9 8 4
◇ A K 8 4
♣ K 9 4 3

♠ K 6 4 2
♡ 2
◇ 10 9 2
♣ J 10 7 6 5

♠ A 9 3
♡ A K Q J 5
◇ Q J 3
♣ A 2

Deal 207

S bid 1 ♡, N 1 ♠; and S 4 ♡.*

W led the ◇ K, ◇ A, then ◇ 4 to S's queen.

How does S get round his two natural black losers?

S drew trumps in four leads and led a *low* spade to dummy's ten. If E scores his king and returns a club, S 'flies' with the ace, and spades furnish discards. So E must lay off the ♠ 10, which wins. Now dummy is on lead to take the spade finesse! All S loses finally is two diamonds and a club.

The threat of that long spade suit in dummy forces E's king to abdicate!

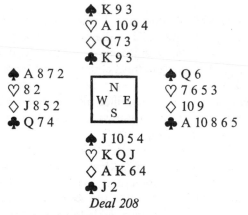

♠ K 9 3
♡ A 10 9 4
◇ Q 7 3
♣ K 9 3

♠ A 8 7 2
♡ 8 2
◇ J 8 5 2
♣ Q 7 4

♠ Q 6
♡ 7 6 5 3
◇ 10 9
♣ A 10 8 6 5

♠ J 10 5 4
♡ K Q J
◇ A K 6 4
♣ J 2

Deal 208

* An alternative bid, giving N a chance to play in spades if he had, say, a void heart and six indifferent spades, is 3 NT.—Editor.

TEMPO

With all vulnerable S bid 1 NT, and N 3 NT.*

W led the ♠ 2. Should dummy duck?

S noted his seven red tricks on top and thought that it would be a soft touch to go game with two more spade tricks, but it didn't work out that way.

S ducked the spade opening, which E's queen won. Had E returned a spade, S would have chalked up game and forgotten the deal, but E saw little nourishment in W's spades, marked as only four cards long by W's opening of the two. Therefore, E shifted to the ♣ 6, forcing the knave, queen and king. S tried to scamper home with eight more red tricks but diamonds failed to split. S led a low spade which W grabbed with his ace, and a club return let E win the balance to break the contract.

Note the difference if dummy 'flies' with the ♠ K at Trick 1. It is Trick No. 8 with seven red winners, and S now has time to set up his ninth trick in spades, or else force the defence to set up a club trick for him.

The tempo principle here is best described by the Japanese word *sente*, from the national Japanese game of *Go*. *Sente* has no exact translation; it implies a combination of initiative and tempo and describes the position above exactly.

Playing ♠ K, even if the ace is with E, has a psychological advantage: E is (unless a master player) likely to be so delighted at declarer's 'wrong view' that he may well—however wrongly—return spades at once!

If the position of the enemy spade honours is reversed, the duck in dummy forces the ace, to yield game. If either opponent holds *both* spade honours, no play makes any difference. However, the ♠ 2 opening marks four spades in W, and it is slightly more probable that he led from the ace than from the queen. The reason is that a modern player sitting W with such an anaemic spade suit as Q-8-7-2 would look for a better opening lead such as from a stronger suit if he held one or from the top of nothing in the other unbid major, hearts.

*Comment: N could bid 2 ♣ instead of 3 NT in order to ask S to bid a four-card major. But even if S rebid 2 ♡, the hands will probably play better in 3 NT than in 4 ♡ on account of N's Cavendish (4 3 3 3) shape, offering no ruffing trick.

File U

UNBLOCKING

U stands for Unblocking. It is defined as the play of high cards that would otherwise block partner's suit. Note the three basic *Matrices purae* below:

1	2	3
Q J 10 6 5	K J 10 6 5	Q J 10 6 5
A K	A Q	K 2

In Matrix 1 the ace and king must be played as early as possible in order to let partner score the rest of the suit later without interruption. In Matrix 2 N has no entry in another suit, hence S lays down the ace first to unblock then N overtakes the queen with the king to score the suit. If an opponent leads the ace in Matrix 3, S must make the unblocking play of the king.

4

$\diamondsuit$ Q J 10

$\clubsuit$ K Q J 10 9

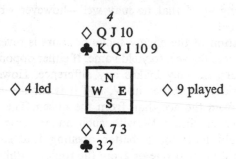

$\diamondsuit$ 4 led $\diamondsuit$ 9 played

$\diamondsuit$ A 7 3

$\clubsuit$ 3 2

Here, at no-trumps, N has no possible entry in spades and hearts. W leads the $\diamondsuit$ 4 and E plays the nine. If S lets the ten win and pushes clubs, the defence will hold up the ace once to kill the suit; hence S must get rid of his cumbersome ace at once by playing it on the first trick. After S drives out the $\clubsuit$ A, he can force entry to dummy in diamonds to score clubs.

From the above we see that unblocking plays preserve entries, as

270

in Matrix 1, or create entries. Unblocking plays constitute one of the five tribes of Entry plays. The especial preculiarity of Unblocking is that an obstructing card is played while following suit, for the *discard* of a high card on the lead of another suit is filed under J for Jettison, a sister tribe (q.v.).

Unblocking honours as above is easy, but during the hurly burly of play a player often overlooks troublesome small cards and fails to get rid of them

<table>
<tr><td align="center">5</td><td align="center">6</td></tr>
<tr><td align="center">A K Q 3</td><td align="center">A K Q 7 2</td></tr>
<tr><td align="center">6 5 4 2</td><td align="center">9 8 3</td></tr>
</table>

Matrix 5 contains two automatic unblocking plays, the six and five on the king and queen leads. If the suit splits 3–2, declarer can next play the four or the deuce on the ace, depending upon whether he wishes to win the fourth round with the three in dummy or with the four in his own hand. Matrix 6 is really a safety play based on an unblock. When N wins two honours, S must get rid of his nine and eight in case W started life with J 6 5 4 or 10 6 5 4. This precautionary unblocking lets S lead the three and finesse dummy's seven on the third round to take the lead—vital if dummy has no other entry.

Tandem Threats

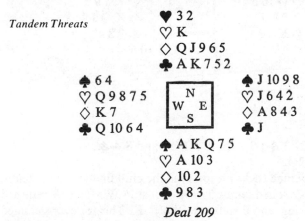

Deal 209

N bid 1 ◇, S 1 ♠; N 2 ♣, and S 3 NT.
W led the ♡ 7. How do you play on clubs?

This deal is something of a hangover from File T for Tempo. S lacks time to establish diamonds, for the heart opening makes diamonds one trick too late by the *N plus 1* formula.

Declarer used progressive threats in two suits—a two-pronged fork. The chances are 2–1 against a 3–3 spade split for nine tricks on top. Hence, S attacked clubs first, taking care to deposit his eight on the king.

Next he led low to his nine. He must lose a trick in clubs however they split, and four club tricks are a cinch for game if the suit splits 3–2 or if W takes the nine in the actual deal. The club unblock lets dummy finesse the seven next, but W blocked clubs by refusing, wisely, to take the nine.

Now, S still had time control, and simply shifted suits. He lost a spade trick to ensure four spade tricks against the probable 4–2 split.

The position is a mutate, because the threats shift during play: in this case, from clubs to spades.

Matrix typica

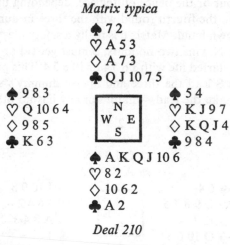

Deal 210

S bid 1 ♠, N 2 ♣; S 2 ♠, N 2 NT; and S 4 ♠.
W led the ♡ 4.

Declarer saw nine tricks on top plus the club finesse for the tenth, so he won the ♡ A in dummy. The ♣ Q lost to W's king. W returned a heart to E's king, and E shifted to the ◊ K. This for ever slammed the door shut on dummy's good clubs, for it drove out the ◊ A prematurely before S had a chance to unblock clubs.

Declarer's plan was half-baked, for simple routine play ensures eleven tricks.

Win the ♡ A, draw trumps, then play ace then low in clubs. Let W make his ♣ K and welcome while you preserve the ◊ A in dummy as entry to score clubs for plenty of discards. You can afford this play—unblocking the clubs—since the opening lead has bared only *one* heart loser. Even if W led ◇ 9, the play should be the same: 'fly' with ◇ A, draw trumps and play the ace and another club. E and W can cash two diamonds, but the losing heart goes away on the clubs and the contract is safe.

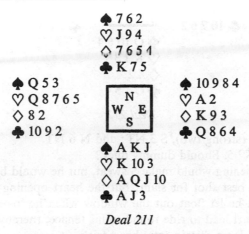

Deal 211

S bid 2 NT on his twenty-three points and N made it 3 NT on his four points. Acol bidding would be S 2 ♣, N 2 ◇; S 2 NT to show twenty-three points, and N 3 NT.

W led the ♡ 6 to E's ace and E returned the deuce which S won with the king.

S entered dummy with the ♣ K to win a diamond finesse, and next the ◇ A play failed to drop E's king. S continued diamonds but wound up with only eight tricks and an annoyed partner.*

The key play is to rid S of the ♡ K under E's ♡ A. This unblock creates a second entry to dummy with the ♡ J or ♡ 9 for an additional diamond finesse.

* Because S muffed his second chance to score game by a squeeze strip against W.

273

FILE U

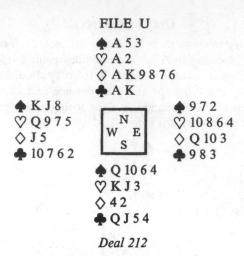

♠ A 5 3
♡ A 2
◇ A K 9 8 7 6
♣ A K

♠ K J 8   ♠ 9 7 2
♡ Q 9 7 5   ♡ 10 8 6 4
◇ J 5   ◇ Q 10 3
♣ 10 7 6 2   ♣ 9 8 3

♠ Q 10 6 4
♡ K J 3
◇ 4 2
♣ Q J 5 4

Deal 212

N bid 2 ◇ (strong two),'S 3 NT; and N 6 NT.
W led the ♡ 5. Should dummy duck?

A spade opening would make S sweat, but he would be forced to
finesse as his best shot for slam; but the heart opening gave S his
chance which he let float out the window when he 'naturally' permitted the heart lead to ride round to his tenace, thereby (in theory
only) establishing a certain extra heart trick.

He won two clubs in dummy, two diamonds, lost the next diamond
to E; and awoke to the fact that he now had no way to gain the lead
himself again to score his club pictures. E returned a heart to the
ace, and after scoring diamonds, dummy laid down the ♠ A in the
forlorn hope that it would drop the lone king from W.

Declarer did his thinking too late. The unblocking play occurs on
Trick 1. Win it with the ♡ A in dummy, clear clubs and diamonds;
later, the ♡ K lets S in to collect two more club tricks, to dispose of
N's losing spades. You do, in fact, sacrifice a heart trick (which you
can never make!) to score two club tricks which you can. (Cf. G for
Gambit.)

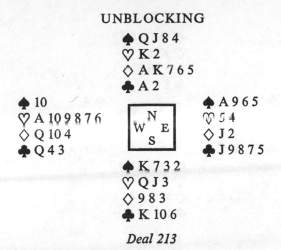

Deal 213

N bid 1 ◇, S 1 ♠, W 2 ♡; N 3 ♠ and S 4 ♠.

W led the ♡ A. How do you play it?

The deal requires careful unblocking technique, and the first un-block is to throw the ♡ K on W's ace lead. This lets S win the heart continuation in order to lead a low trump toward dummy's honours. The ten forces the knave and ace. E returns a club to the ♣ A in dummy.

Dummy wins the ♠ Q, showing the bad trump split when W dis-cards a heart. S wins, the ♣ K and takes care to ruff a club with dummy's *eight* to unblock trumps. S finesses the ♠ 7 and draws trumps. S loses a trump, a heart and a diamond.

The trap is a low trump lead to the king at Trick 2, for it lets E get two trump tricks. A primary low lead toward dummy's *two* trump honours is essential—and should be routine—hence the heart un-block. The bidding suggested that E was more likely to be long in trumps than W, who had bid hearts on a very few points and was therefore likely to be long in the suit and, consequently, short in spades—even if he held ♠ A. The second unblock is ruffing the third club lead far-sightedly with dummy's eight to permit the overtaking finesse.

FILE U

Obscure Defense

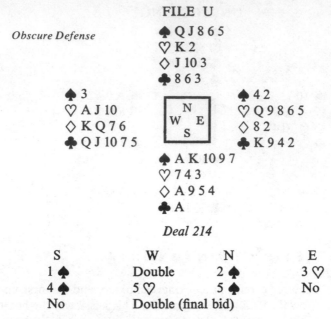

♠ Q J 8 6 5
♡ K 2
◇ J 10 3
♣ 8 6 3

♠ 3
♡ A J 10
◇ K Q 7 6
♣ Q J 10 7 5

N W E S

♠ 4 2
♡ Q 9 8 6 5
◇ 8 2
♣ K 9 4 2

♠ A K 10 9 7
♡ 7 4 3
◇ A 9 5 4
♣ A

Deal 214

S	W	N	E
1 ♠	Double	2 ♠	3 ♡
4 ♠	5 ♡	5 ♠	No
No	Double (final bid)		

W led the ♣ Q. S won and returned a heart.

Should W 'fly' with his ace?

W did 'lest the rats get it', and S ruffed W's club return. S drew trumps, cashed the ♡ K, and ruffed the club and the heart to strip these suits from his two hands.

Next declarer finessed the ◇ J to lose, and W was end-played. S lost a heart and a diamond, but marched home with his doubled 5 ♠ contract.

At Trick 2 W must unblock hearts by ducking and let dummy's king win. W *must* give E a chance to get on lead with the ♡ Q later to push a diamond which S must finesse. Later, S loses another diamond finesse and the contract with it.

If N returns ♡ 2 immediately after winning ♡ K, E—a difficult play—must go up with ♡ Q at once, leading—another difficult shot —not a club but a diamond.

276

UNBLOCKING

♠ K Q 3
♡ K 10 3
◇ A 9 7 6 5
♣ 10 2

♠ 10 8
♡ Q 8 7 4
◇ J 10
♣ K J 9 7 5

♠ J 9 5 2
♡ J 9 6 5
◇ K Q 2
♣ Q 3

♠ A 7 6 4
♡ A 2
◇ 8 4 3
♣ A 8 6 4

Deal 215

N bid 1 ◇, S 1 ♠; N 2 ♠, and S 3 NT.

S's *carte blanche* hand with three aces and no filler looks thin for
3 NT, but the N and S hands have a fair play for nine tricks despite
it—as they should with a twelve count opposite an opener.

W led the ♣ 7 to E's ♣ Q which S let win. E returned the club.
How do you play for nine tricks?

Declarer's only play is Avoidance, to keep W off lead while S sets
up diamonds. S won Trick 2 with the ♣ A and led a diamond, and
the ten forced the ace. A diamond return went to E's queen. S won a
heart return and lost another diamond to E, making dummy's two
diamonds stiff to fulfil the contract.

This all looks simple, but the deal is a *defensive* problem. On the
first diamond lead, E must give his diamond 'marriage' a quick
divorce and deposit the king or queen upon the ace. This play lets W
win *the second diamond lead* and, with it, the stiff clubs to break the
contract. A mere count of points should guide E to the proper
course. S must have 11–12 points for his two responses; N has 12;
E has 9. Giving W ♣ K J, he can have no 'quick' entry, and the
potential sacrifice of *one* diamond against the chance of three clubs
should be routine . . . if only E thinks of it.

277

File V

VARIETY

V stands for Variety. Declarer is faced with a variety of plays, specifically with two (or more) *good* plans of the strategy detailed in other files, with no choice of superiority. If one plan of play does offer superior odds, however slight, the deal should be advanced to File W for Winning Line. However, there is one difference. If the superior line of play happens to be a loser—and the inferior line a winner—the deal is a 'sport'. It does not deserve publication—except to illustrate for amusement how inferior (or even downright poor) play sometimes wins: a fact only too well known, but rarely mentioned. Such a deal at best belongs in File Q for Quandary.

The student is referred to the opening discussion in File M for Mêlée for the classification and position of Variety play among its sister files, Mêlée, New Plan, Quandary and Winning Line.

Technically, the plans of strategy covered in Variety occur in parallel arrangement. However, we get a vertical pattern in a deal offering declarer a second chance, a second line of play, if he overlooks the best plan. This simply goes to *dis*prove the old axiom that 'cards never forgive'. 'Never' and 'always' are misleading words in bridge axioms, and are best replaced by 'rarely' and 'usually' respectively; and modern, careful writers so temper these time-worn absolutes.

Technically, a playing deal qualifying for File V is best discarded. Any bridge problem with two equally good different lines of play, independent of the defence, is unsound, especially if double dummy; and it is called 'cooked', a term borrowed from Chess.

Only a purist frowns upon a minor variation or 'dual' in the main theme of a problem. A dual is not a genuine cook, but it is a small blemish. The spade suit in Deal 204 offers a dual in play, because S may 'lead the ♠ K or ♠ 2 and it doesn't matter which'.

A cooked deal is the bane of a bridge columnist's professional existence. He spends a lot of time and effort collecting, and writing up, a beautiful play to bring home a difficult contract; only to have a flock of disgruntled readers write in and show him a better or easier line of play which the writer overlooked. Here is a typical example from a top-ranking American newspaper.

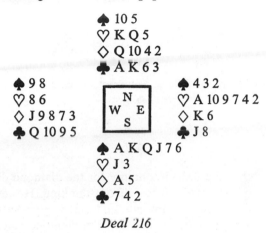

♠ 10 5
♡ K Q 5
♦ Q 10 4 2
♣ A K 6 3

♠ 9 8
♡ 8 6
♦ J 9 8 7 3
♣ Q 10 9 5

♠ 4 3 2
♡ A 10 9 7 4 2
♦ K 6
♣ J 8

♠ A K Q J 7 6
♡ J 3
♦ A 5
♣ 7 4 2

Deal 216

N bid 1 ♣, E 1 ♡; and S wound up at 6 ♠.

W led the ♡ 8 to E's ace and E returned a heart to the queen in dummy.

How do you play it?

A quick look at E's unchaperoned king shows the method. Draw trumps. Play the ◇ A, K ♣, ♡ K for the diamond discard, and ruff out the ◇ K to promote the ◇ Q for a club discard.

The writer made a lot of work for himself and his readers by an involved transfer squeeze.

S draws trumps, noting three with E. Dummy wins a club and the heart on which S shed a *club*. It looks as if E started with six hearts and three spades: hence four minor suit cards, including the K for the 1 ♡ overcall. If E holds ◇ K x or ◇ K x x without the knave, the transfer squeeze works. Dummy leads the ◇ Q, forcing E to cover (S ducks if E does) which *transfers* diamond control to W, and S wins with the ace. Finally S runs all his trumps, squeezing W in the minors.

If E started with ◇ K J x, no play wins. If E started with ◇ K J or ◇ K alone, the transfer squeeze fails. The simple ruff-out play caters for both these last two events; and an improved variation also

sets up a possible ruffing squeeze. After drawing trumps and laying
down the ◇ A, *cash only two more trumps,* leaving:

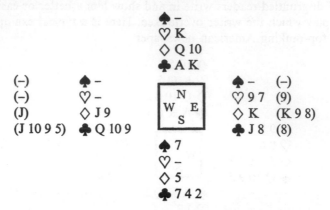

```
                    ♠ –
                    ♡ K
                    ◇ Q 10
                    ♣ A K
(–)        ♠ –                      ♠ –      (–)
(–)        ♡ –           N          ♡ 9 7    (9)
(J)        ◇ J 9    W       E       ◇ K      (K 9 8)
(J 10 9 5) ♣ Q 10 9     S          ♣ J 8    (8)
                    ♠ 7
                    ♡ –
                    ◇ 5
                    ♣ 7 4 2
```

Win a club and a heart in dummy for the diamond discard. Then
you can still lead the ◇ 10 to ruff out the king. However, you can
be counting how many diamonds and clubs opponents give up. If
opponents keep only two diamonds, the diamond ruff-out is automatic; if they keep three diamonds and two clubs, you have a choice.
Dummy can lead the ◇ Q for a scoop ruff-out against the distribution shown in parentheses, or dummy can cash another club for a
final 1–1 split.

An advantage of this line of play is that you give the enemy a
chance to make wrong, or revealing, discards.

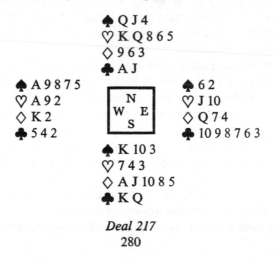

```
                    ♠ Q J 4
                    ♡ K Q 8 6 5
                    ◇ 9 6 3
                    ♣ A J
♠ A 9 8 7 5                        ♠ 6 2
♡ A 9 2           N                ♡ J 10
◇ K 2        W        E            ◇ Q 7 4
♣ 5 4 2          S                 ♣ 10 9 8 7 6 3
                    ♠ K 10 3
                    ♡ 7 4 3
                    ◇ A J 10 8 5
                    ♣ K Q
```

Deal 217

S bid 1 ◊, W 1 ♠, N 2 ♡; S 2 NT, and N 3 NT.

W led the ♠ 7. How do you plan the play?

S let the ♠ 7 ride to his king in order to lead a heart toward dummy's honours, W ducked and the ♡ Q won. S returned to his own hand via a club while E played the ten to show club length topped by a ten-high sequence. S led another heart, which W won with the ace.

If W had resumed spades, S would have got home; but W shifted to a club instead to knock out S's last stopper before S could set up his game-scoring trick in spades.

At Trick 3 S should re-enter his own hand via the ◊ A instead of the club. This play sets up both the king and queen for opponents, but they get in addition to ◊ K Q only their two major-suit aces, and S goes game.

Declarer has an alternative red suit to develop for game. The variation at Trick 3 is to finesse a diamond to W's king. No return hurts S, for he has time to set up another spade trick *and* finesse diamonds to run them. In all, he scores two spade tricks, a heart, four diamonds and two clubs.*

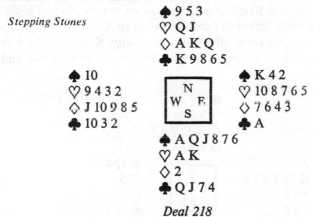

Stepping Stones

```
                    ♠ 9 5 3
                    ♡ Q J
                    ◊ A K Q
                    ♣ K 9 8 6 5
  ♠ 10                             ♠ K 4 2
  ♡ 9 4 3 2          N             ♡ 10 8 7 6 5
  ◊ J 10 9 8 5    W     E          ◊ 7 6 4 3
  ♣ 10 3 2          S              ♣ A
                    ♠ A Q J 8 7 6
                    ♡ A K
                    ◊ 2
                    ♣ Q J 7 4
```

Deal 218

S bid 1 ♠, N 2 ♣; S 3 ♡, N 4 ♠; and S 6 ♠.

N's jump to 4 ♠ on only three trumps is based on S's jump rebid, showing a powerful two suiter (S has a big hand with considerable club support—hence the phoney secondary force in hearts). Such

---

* Since E must drop an honour on the first round of hearts, the diamond switch is, though technically identical, psychologically more attractive.—Editor.

bidding is never made on a 4–4 two suiter, but only on a good primary suit (spades in this case) of at least five cards.

W led the ◇ J to the queen in dummy. How do you manage the red suits?

Obviously the spade finesse must be 'on' to give S a chance. S made the hand prettily and easily. He immediately jettisoned a heart on a second diamond trick, finessed a trump, cashed his heart, and led the ♣ J to E's ace. Dummy had only one direct entry and S's plan forced E to return a red suit to dummy, an indirect entry to let S repeat the trump finesse; or to lead a trump for an immediate second finesse. Now trumps are drawn and the hand is a pianola.

The same plan also wins against a 2–2 club split. If an opponent wins the ♣ A immediately, the ♣ K becomes a natural second entry to dummy. S's chief worry was ♣ A x x with W who might win the first club lead and give E a club ruff.

S's plan is as safe as possible; but there is an equally safe alternative play in the red suits, both aimed at holding the chance of an enemy red suit ruff to a minimum. Finesse a trump at Trick 2 and cash the ♡ A K *before* leading a club. Declarer has four cards of each red suit, so it is 50–50 whether he cashes two hearts and a diamond or vice versa before the club throw-in to E.

Here early red suit plays offer multiple duality. S can cash four or five red winners in a variety of ways before the club throw-in and still get home.

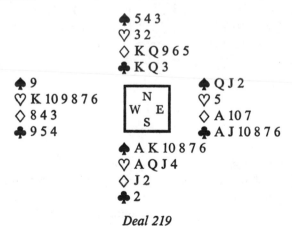

Deal 219

VARIETY

S	W	N	E
			1 ♣
Double	1 ♡	2 ◇	No
3 ♠	No	4 ♠ (final bid)	

W led the ♣ 9 to the queen and ace, and E switched to the ♡ 5. How many clubs did E hold? How many hearts?

S rightly decided that W started with six hearts and little else for his heart call and that E held one heart and six clubs. If E held five clubs, W would have four and might well have given E a club raise over S's spade bid.

S wins the heart switch with the ace and lays down the ♠ A.

S counts E with six cards in spades and diamonds and plans to cater both for their 3–3 or 4–2 division. To Trick 3 S leads the ◇ J and over-plays with the queen in dummy to force E to win with the ace, lest S shed his last diamond on the ♣ K. E returns the ♣ J which S ruffs, still uncertain of E's pattern in diamonds and spades. Next S lays down the ♠ K, and W's failure marks E with three spades and three diamonds. Dummy wins the ◇ K, S ruffs a diamond, and S loses a trump to E to force a return to dummy's good minor suit cards.

An equally good and less fancy line (without the diamond over-take) is to win both trumps at once. If trumps split 2–2, you have no worry about how clubs split, for dummy can ruff the ♡ 4 after conceding a trick to ♡ K. If E holds three trumps, S runs the ◇ J which E must let win. E takes the next diamond play, the queen, but E must now resign to dummy's good cards. (*Please turn to top of next page.*)

S bid 1 ♡, N 4 ♡; and S 6 ♡.*

W led the ♠ J to E's ace, and E switched to the ◇ K.

How do you play for twelve tricks?

Without a 2–2 club split the hand is hopeless, so we must assume that the clubs lie favourably. Another complication is S's third-round blocking card in clubs.

---

*SAB: S opened 1 ♡, N 4 ♡; S 4 NT Blackwood, N 5 ♣ denying an ace (!) temporarily; S 5 ♡ to sign off, then N 6 ◇ to show his ◇ void plus one ace. This is a new Blackwood void-showing convention. Then S bid 6 ♡.

FILE V

Nasty Little Trap

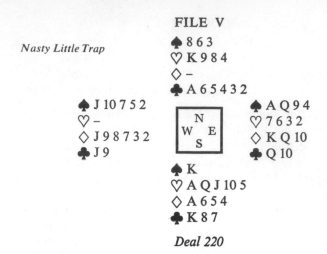

♠ 8 6 3
♡ K 9 8 4
◇ –
♣ A 6 5 4 3 2

♠ J 10 7 5 2
♡ –
◇ J 9 8 7 3 2
♣ J 9

♠ A Q 9 4
♡ 7 6 3 2
◇ K Q 10
♣ Q 10

♠ K
♡ A Q J 10 5
◇ A 6 5 4
♣ K 8 7

Deal 220

In a twelve-table duplicate most S players made 6 ♡ as easily as rolling off a log by a variety of methods.

At five tables S passed E's ◇ K to let dummy ruff. S won a trump revealing the 4–0 split, N ruffed another diamond, S won the ♣ K, and dummy ruffed S's last losing diamond. S ruffed a spade and drew trumps, and claimed the balance after the ♣ A dropped enemy clubs.

At three tables S adopted the dual line of winning the ◇ K with the ace on which dummy shed a spade, and dummy ruffed a diamond at once before any trump was led.

The Unlucky Expert (who wasn't so unlucky this time) also made 6 ♡, but he made a lot of hard work for himself by a difficult, yet beautiful, reverse-dummy play and jettison. He won the ◇ K with the ace and took care to discard a *club* from dummy. Next he laid down the ♡ A, to discover the bad split.

Dummy won a trump and S ruffed a spade. Dummy won the ♣ A and S ruffed the last spade. S won the ♣ K, dummy overtook S's last trump and dummy cashed the fourth trump to draw E's last while S jettisoned the blocking club.

What then, is the value of this 'cooked' deal? The point is: there is a nasty little trap lurking in the hand which caught several declarers. S took the ◇ K with the ace on which dummy shed a spade, S laid down the ace of hearts. Now the hand was ruined. S lacked entries to ruff three diamonds in dummy *and* to draw all E's trumps; and that fatal spade discard from dummy killed the reverse dummy plan.

The easy way is to ruff a diamond before touching trumps.

File W

WINNING LINE

W stands for Winning Line. Every deal in this file offers a choice between two (or more) lines of play stemming from different files. The key character separating Winning Line from its sister files (see File V) is a close or obscure decision facing declarer to avoid an alluring, but losing, line of play.

Solomon's Sluff

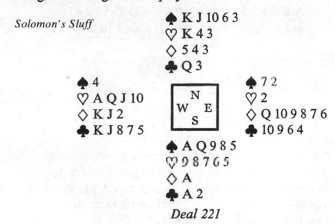

♠ K J 10 6 3
♡ K 4 3
◇ 5 4 3
♣ Q 3

♠ 4
♡ A Q J 10
◇ K J 2
♣ K J 8 7 5

♠ 7 2
♡ 2
◇ Q 10 9 8 7 6
♣ 10 9 6 4

♠ A Q 9 8 5
♡ 9 8 7 6 5
◇ A
♣ A 2

Deal 221

S bid 1 ♠, W doubled, N (pre-emptively) 3 ♠; and S, on shape and controls, 4 ♠.

W led the ♡ A and continued with the ♡ Q.

At rubber bridge, should dummy cover?

This deal was shown us by Charles J. Solomon of Philadelphia. W might have opened a trump, a waiting lead to avoid opening a tenace suit; but his actual play proved lucky for his side. Dummy covered the ♡ Q, E ruffed, and returned the ♣ 10, forcing S to risk the finesse which lost to the ♣ K; and the ♡ J broke the contract.

N crimed his partner for not ducking the ♡ Q at Trick 2. This would let E ruff the third heart (instead of the second), but S wins

285

the balance. On a club return, S 'flies' with the ace, draws trumps, and dummy ruffs a heart. This sets up S's fifth heart for a club discard in dummy.

The wise Solomon pointed out that covering the ♡ Q at Trick 2 may be right at match-point duplicate in order to chase a valuable extra trick for five odd against a normal 3–2 heart split favoured by the 2–1 odds. But in rubber bridge, the Safety Play to ensure ten tricks for game is to duck the ♡ Q even though it courts an enemy ruff.

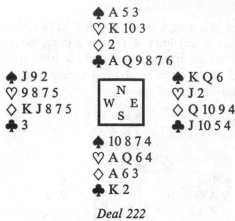

Deal 222

N bid 1 ♣, S 1 ♡; N 2 ♣, and S 3 NT.

W led the ◇ 7 to E's queen. How do you play?

Declarer grunted when he inspected N's fine dummy, for 6 NT is 'on' if both clubs and hearts split. S won the ◇ A at once, although a repeated hold-up would protect S against six diamonds in W. This detail had no bearing on the real point.

Declarer went after his clubs like a hound after a fox, but the second lead showed the bad split. Next, he tried the ♡ Q and ♡ K which dropped E's doubleton knave, but the suit was blocked with no side entry to S. S began and ended equally: with eight tricks on top.

In this Long Suit deal S should *try hearts first*. The knave's fall makes game frigid without any long clubs. The clubs will always keep and produce three extra tricks later if they split 3–2.

Compare with *Deal 160* on page 203.

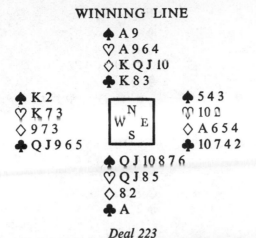

♠ A 9
♡ A 9 6 4
◇ K Q J 10
♣ K 8 3

♠ K 2   ♠ 5 4 3
♡ K 7 3   ♡ 10 2
◇ 9 7 3   ◇ A 6 5 4
♣ Q J 9 6 5   ♣ 10 7 4 2

♠ Q J 10 8 7 6
♡ Q J 8 5
◇ 8 2
♣ A

Deal 223

N bid 1 ◇, S 1 ♠; N 2 NT, S 3 ♠; and N 4 ♠.*
W led the ♡ 3.
Do you finesse? Why?
The ♡ 3 looked like a singleton, so S played the ace from dummy followed by the ace, then low, in trumps to avert an enemy heart ruff. E played the four, then three of spades, the trump echo to show a third trump in hand plus a desire to ruff. W won the second trump lead, the ♡ K, and gave E a heart ruff. Later the ◇ A broke the contract.

Mr. William F. Field of Portland, Maine, showed us this dilemma hand. The deal is a finessing frolic. If you take every finesse in sight, you wrap up twelve tricks!

A difficult decision faced declarer, with whom we sympathize. However, analysis points to taking the heart finesse initially! If W has a singleton heart, *he* is most likely (on simple mathematics) to hold the three trumps; so that the play of ace then low in trumps lets opponents in, and W will get his heart ruff anyway.

If E wins the heart finesse and W follows suit on E's heart return, declarer's better play is to finesse trumps in order to draw all low spades quickly.

* S should bid 4 ♠ over 2 NT.—Editor.

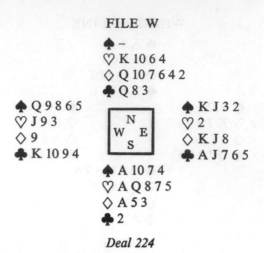

♠ –
♡ K 10 6 4
◇ Q 10 7 6 4 2
♣ Q 8 3

♠ Q 9 8 6 5
♡ J 9 3
◇ 9
♣ K 10 9 4

♠ K J 3 2
♡ 2
◇ K J 8
♣ A J 7 6 5

♠ A 10 7 4
♡ A Q 8 7 5
◇ A 5 3
♣ 2

Deal 224

S bid 1 ♡, N 3 ♡; and S 4 ♡. If W happens to stick in a mangy 1 ♠ over-call, his side will discover a good sacrifice of 4 ♠—which might even be on if W takes the right view of clubs—*not*, this time, 'queen over knave'—and plays trumps carefully (Cf. File S).

W led the ♠ 5. What is your plan?

S let the ♠ 5 come to the king and ace. S succumbed to the charm of the long diamond suit. He cashed two trumps, and played ace then low in diamonds. E won and returned a spade to force dummy, who led a third diamond to E. This stiffened the diamonds. E returned another spade to force the last trump from dummy, the last entry there. S got one discard on a good diamond which W ruffed, but S had to lose a fourth trick, a spade or a club according to his discard on the previous trick.

S's long suit plan wins if trumps or diamonds split 2–2, but a cross-ruff is the true winning line. On the spade opening dummy discards a diamond and S loses the club at once. S wins a trump return, but scores his side aces plus eight tricks in trumps including three spade ruffs in dummy.

WINNING LINE

Investigate Early

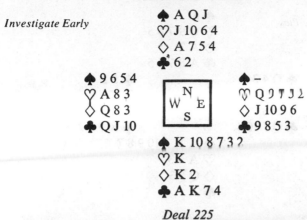

♠ A Q J
♡ J 10 6 4
◇ A 7 5 4
♣ 6 2

♠ 9 6 5 4
♡ A 8 3
◇ Q 8 3
♣ Q J 10

♠ –
♡ Q 9 7 3 2
◇ J 10 9 6
♣ 9 8 5 3

♠ K 10 8 7 3 2
♡ K
◇ K 2
♣ A K 7 4

Deal 225

S bid 1 ♠, N 3 ♠; and S 6 ♠. The calling lacked science but it was brief and to the point.

W led the ♣ Q. What is your diagnosis?

S won the ♣ Q with the ace, and chased club ruffs in dummy like a dog after a cat. S won another top club, dummy ruffed a club, S re-entered via the ◇ K, and dummy ruffed S's last club. S laid down dummy's last trump, only to discover the horrible 4–0 split of the trumps and the power of W's nine.

The dummy ruffing plan is good against a 3–1 or 2–2 trump split. To Trick 2 declarer should win a trump lead in dummy. This discovers the 4–0 split early and points to the necessity of promoting a heart trick. The ♡ K goes to W's ace. W returns the ♣ J to S. Dummy ruffs a club and returns the ♡ J, intending to let S shed a club if E passes. But E covers and S ruffs to make the ♡ 10 good for a club discard later.

S should investigate the hand early—by a trump lead in this case—and once spades show up 4–0, making the use of two of dummy's honours for ruffing purposes disastrous, the best hope is to play for the heart queen with East if you do not snatch the bare king.

Neat Double Play

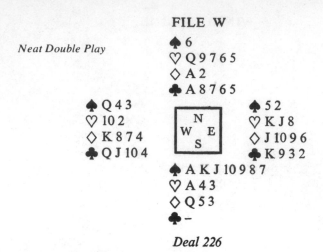

♠ 6
♡ Q 9 7 6 5
◇ A 2
♣ A 8 7 6 5

♠ Q 4 3
♡ 10 2
◇ K 8 7 4
♣ Q J 10 4

♠ 5 2
♡ K J 8
◇ J 10 9 6
♣ K 9 3 2

♠ A K J 10 9 8 7
♡ A 4 3
◇ Q 5 3
♣ −

Deal 226

S bid 1 ♠, N 2 ♡; and S 4 ♠.
W led the ♣ Q. What line of play wins?

Dummy won the ♣ Q with the ace on which S parked a diamond. The Long Suit game appealed to declarer, so he banged down both top trumps which failed to drop the queen. Next he played ace then low in hearts and E won the queen with the king. E returned the ◇ J, forcing the queen, king and ace. Declarer finally lost two heart tricks, a diamond, and a trump. The trump finesse at Trick 2 is equally futile.

Declarer has a neat double play here. Win the club and let S discard a *heart*. Next play ace, then low in diamonds. If E plays the king, your losers are a heart, a diamond and a trump. This is the hypothetical part of the double play.

The other part actually occurs against W because the ◇ Q loses to W's king. Now W cannot stop the diamond ruff in dummy by leading trumps without sacrificing his side's natural trump trick.

WINNING LINE

```
                    ♠ 5 4 3 2
                    ♡ 10 2
                    ◇ A Q J 4
                    ♣ A 8 3
    ♠ 10 8 6          ┌─────────┐          ♠ 9 7
    ♡ 7               │    N    │          ♡ K J 9 8
    ◇ 10 9 7 5        │  W   E  │          ◇ 8 6 3 2
    ♣ Q 10 7 6 5      │    S    │          ♣ K 9 4
                      └─────────┘
                    ♠ A K Q J
                    ♡ A Q 6 5 4 3
                    ◇ K
                    ♣ J 2
```

Deal 227

S bid 1 ♡, N 2 NT (Acol); S 3 ♠, N 4 ♠; S 4 NT, N 5 ♡ (Blackwood) or 5 NT (Culbertson);* and S 6 ♠.†

W led the ♣ 6.

What course do you pursue?

Dummy won the ♣ A and S drew trumps in three leads. Dummy overtook the ◇ K with the ace to let S park his dead club on another top diamond. S won the heart finesse and the ♡ A, but the bad 4–1 split left S short of entries to set up his hearts.

The winning line is to win the ♣ A in dummy and to take the heart finesse immediately—a necessary, calculated risk. Draw trumps and cash the ◇ K. Next score the ♡ A and ruff a heart in dummy. Finally, you get *three* discards on dummy's diamonds. S has to lose one trick but bags his slam. He gets four trump tricks, two hearts and a heart ruff, the ♣ A, and *four* diamonds.

---

* When N raises the reverse spade bid, it is clear he has four cards in the suit. Yet he did not bid 1 ♠. Why? Clearly because his spades were woeful; his hearts indifferent from failure to raise, and his minor suit cards compensatingly good. This is a nice piece of I for Inference.—Editor.

†*SAB:* S 1 ♡, N 2 ◇; S 2 ♠, N 4 ♠; S 4 NT Blackwood, N 5 ♡ to show two aces; S 5 NT, and N 6 ♣ to deny any king; so S settled for a contract of 6 ♠.

Echelon Three Plays

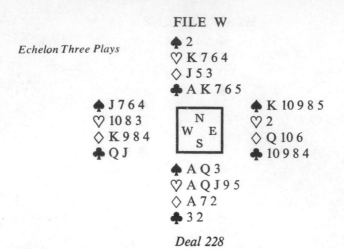

♠ 2
♡ K 7 6 4
◇ J 5 3
♣ A K 7 6 5

♠ J 7 6 4
♡ 10 8 3
◇ K 9 8 4
♣ Q J

♠ K 10 9 8 5
♡ 2
◇ Q 10 6
♣ 10 9 8 4

♠ A Q 3
♡ A Q J 9 5
◇ A 7 2
♣ 3 2

Deal 228

S bid 1 ♡, N 2 ♣; S 2 NT, N 4 ♡; S 5 ◇, and N 6 ♡.*
W led the ◇ 4, Where is Trick No. 12?

S played the hand for twelve tricks by properly echeloning three
different plays: a ruff in dummy, a finesse, and a long suit play.

Dummy ducked the ◇ 4 opening, and the ten forced S's ace. S
won the ♡ A Q and discovered the annoying 3–1 split. Next dummy
won a club and S finessed the ♠ Q despite dummy's singleton.
Dummy won another club and S ruffed a club with ♡ J. Dummy
scored the ♡ K drawing W's last, and S ruffed another club. Next
the ♠ A and a spade ruff put dummy in to score the twelfth trick
with the fifth club.

If trumps split 2–2, risking the spade finesse is unnecessary. Also,
odds are 2–1 against a 3–3 club split, substantiated by the early fall
of W's club honours.

The next and final deal in File W straddles Files W and X.

SAB: S 1 ♡, N 3 ♡; S 4 NT Blackwood, N 5 ◇ on one ace; S 5 NT, N 6 ♡ on
two kings, end.

Ripe for Endplay

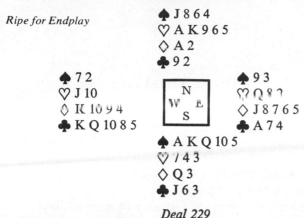

♠ J 8 6 4
♡ A K 9 6 5
◇ A 2
♣ 9 2

♠ 7 2
♡ J 10
◇ K 10 9 4
♣ K Q 10 8 5

♠ 9 3
♡ Q 8 7
◇ J 8 7 6 5
♣ A 7 4

♠ A K Q 10 5
♡ 7 4 3
◇ Q 3
♣ J 6 3

Deal 229

Playing Acol S bid 1 ♠ and N 4 ♠.* †

W led the ♣ K. E played the encouraging seven so W next led the ♣ 8 to E's ace. E switched to the ◇ 6.

What is S's winning play at Trick 3?

With two potential red losers, S tried to eliminate one immediately by playing the ◇ Q to Trick 3, but W covered and dummy won. S drew trumps and won two top hearts, but S could not eat his two red losers which broke the contract.

The contra defence to the diamond shift at Trick 3 is for S to play his LOW diamond. S draws trumps, ruffs the club in dummy, takes two top hearts, and exits to W via the ◇ Q to the ◇ K. W, now dry of spades and hearts, has to return a minor suit card which lets S park his heart loser while dummy ruffs.

Superficially it appears that this elimination play offers only about a 50% chance to win, depending upon W's holding fewer than three hearts, whereas the ◇ Q play at Trick 3 also offers 50%. However, E's diamond switch to Trick 3 strongly indicates that he does NOT hold the ◇ K. Therefore, S's best hope is that W, with his presumed ◇ K, holds only a doubleton heart and is ripe for the end-play.

* S was playing Acol, perhaps; N was certainly not! He is worth 2 ♡ and, over 2 ♠, 4 ♠—the 'delayed game raise' at least; and some Acolytes would sooner bid 3 ♡ at once.—Editor.

†*SAB:* S 1 ♠, N 3 ♠; S 4 ♠.

Files X, Y and Z

ENDPLAYS

Before delving into the three files separately, let us pause for a general view of the entire subject.

Modern students of bridge are fortunate to have available a rich source of reference material on Eliminations (File X), Coups (File Y) and Squeezes (File Z). Their elements and tactics are well covered in two current texts, my own *Endplays* and Raphael Cioffi's *Bridge Endings*. Hence Files X, Y and Z will be confined to an advanced treatment of end-plays.

When I was at Harvard only too long ago (1924–28), no good text-book on play existed. Skimpy popular books on auction bridge exemplified elementary elimination plays and the flashy, but rare, grand coup. Milton C. Work's books of that period mentioned the squeeze without explanation or illustration.

Since these early days when Contract Bridge was in its swaddling clothes, the fascination of end-plays, both in practical bridge and at double dummy, has inspired the publication of more than a dozen special monographs.

During my last college years *Judge Magazine* awarded fabulous cash prizes ranging up to 2,000 guineas each for double-dummy problem-solving contests conducted by Sidney S. Lenz. He used several problems from a curious little old book, *Double Dummy Bridge* by Ernest Bergholt (1906!). After these contests ended, the interest in double dummy exercises waned. In 1944 Albert H. More-head, then editor of *The Bridge World*, told me that he received so many complaints from readers that he was forced to discontinue double dummy problems. In America to-day they have almost vanished from bridge columns, the reflection of an unfortunate trend.

The modern antipathy to double dummy problems is not well founded from the instructional point of view. It must be admitted, of course, that many complex and compound endings in double dummy problems rarely occur during the rub of the green or are impossible of diagnosis in actual play—which is often needlessly slow and sometimes much too fast. But the fact remains that all end-plays capable of analysis and execution in practical play appear in double dummy problems, and therefore solving these problems will sharpen one's playing acumen at the bridge table.

File X

ELIMINATION

X is the assigned file letter for Elimination. The family of elimination plays consists of four natural tribes, as follows:

Tribe 1. Basic Eliminations

Simple Strips. At the end an opponent is forced to lead a specific suit (usually) at the cost of a trick.

Squeeze Strips. Before the throw-in play occurs, an opponent is forced to discard a winner, or a vital exit card, in order to guard his tenace. (Sometimes a bluff discard from the tenace defeats the elimination play.)

Trump Tenace Strips. In the end an opponent is forced to lead up to a tenace in trumps. These plays are closely related to the true coups in File Y.

Tribe 2. Combination Eliminations

Repeating Strips. After scoring an extra trick by an end-play, declarer throws the enemy into the lead again to develop a second extra trick. Such positions are curiosities.

Double Strips. Either opponent may win declarer's final exit play, but the return causes a natural defensive trick to evaporate.

Compound Strips. The opponent finally thrown on lead has a choice of suicide in two or three suits.

Tribe 3. Imperfect Eliminations

False Strips. The opponent can make a harmless discard, or ultimately lead a harmless suit.

Bluff Strips. Declarer induces the opponent to make a fatal lead instead of a harmless one.

Unblocking Strips. The opponent avoids the fatal throw-in by getting rid of a high card or cards during the stripping process.

296

ELIMINATION

Tribe 4. Preparatory Eliminations

These are not strictly true end-plays, because they *prepare* the position for declarer's final play, a finesse or suit establishment otherwise impossible for lack of entry.

Before examining specific examples in this arrangement of tribes, let us look at three deals requiring a strategic choice according to the Winning Line technique.

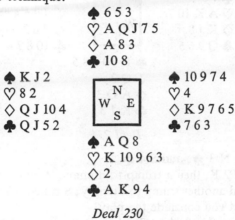

Deal 230

S bid 1 ♡, N 3 ♡; and S 6 ♡.*

S saw no point in fooling around with ace-showing bids, for at Acol the 3 ♡ raise by N limited his hand and S lacked the values for a grand slam.

W led the ◇ Q which dummy won, trumps were drawn and S ruffed a diamond, N ruffed the third club lead, S the last diamond, and N the last club. N led a spade and S intended to insert the eight, but E injected the nine to block this play, and the queen finesse lost to W's king. W returned a spade and another enemy spade trick finally broke the contract.

If S had held the NINE of spades instead of the eight, or if W had held ♠ K J 10 9, S would have got home; but the eight proved to be one rank too weak.

N (how wise is dummy!) pointed out the winning line, solid against any defence. Win the ◇ A, ruff a diamond, play a trump to dummy, ruff the last diamond, and play another trump to dummy. Next, let dummy lead the ♣ 10 and let it ride to the knave in W. Now W is

*SAB: S 1 ♡, N 3 ♡; S 4 NT Blackwood, N 5 ♡; S 5 NT, N 6 ♣ to show no king; and S 6 ♡.

end-played in three suits! He has no saving return—no reasonable exit. If E covers the ♣ 10, S wins and pushes clubs by straight leads to drive out the second enemy club honour. The next deal was the next deal in the same rubber.

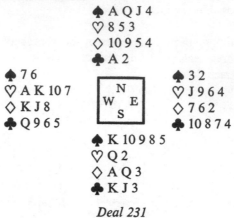

♠A Q J 4
♡8 5 3
◇ 10 9 5 4
♣A 2

♠7 6
♡A K 10 7
◇K J 8
♣Q 9 6 5

♠3 2
♡J 9 6 4
◇7 6 2
♣10 8 7 4

♠K 10 9 8 5
♡Q 2
◇A Q 3
♣K J 3

Deal 231

S bid 1 ♠, N 3 ♠; and S 4 ♠.*

W led the ♡ K, then a trump to dummy. W won dummy's heart return and led another trump to dummy; S ruffed N's last heart.

How would you conclude the play?

Dummy won the ♣ A at Trick 6. S remembered N's lecture on the previous deal, and finessed the ◇ 10 to W's knave.

'It's your lead', crowed S to W. But W simply returned a club up to S's king-knave, and dummy's diamond discard on S's third club trick was worthless. Another diamond finesse lost the game.

This deal is the contratype of the previous one. Here declarer should ruff out the third club before taking a diamond finesse. The key to the difference is that in this hand, N and S have between them A Q 10 9 of the throw-in suit—not A Q 8 only.

Incidentally, S played the deal incorrectly as a bluff strip (although he did not realize this at the time) instead of properly as a compound strip.

SAB: S 1 ♠, W double, N redouble, E 2 ♡; S 2 ♠. W 3 ♡, and N 4 ♠.

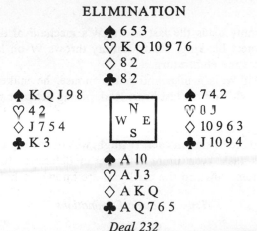

Deal 232

This deal from a pairs' duplicate game was reported by Alphonse Moyse, Jr., editor of *The Bridge World*. At most tables N bid and made 6 ♡, although thirteen tricks are 'on' if you gamble on a 2–2 heart split.

At one table S bid 2 NT, N 4 ♡; and S 6 NT, W double.

W led the ♠ K. Do you take this trick?

S huddled long and squirmed agonizedly in his chair; finally, he played his ten; so W continued with his eight to drop the ace. S cashed three diamonds and dummy discarded a club, then S ran dummy's hearts, expecting to squeeze W in clubs and spades. But W could count and shed all his spades while E clung grimly to his seven, the biggest card in North America. At Trick 12, in desperation, S finessed the ♣ Q, going down one.

Declarer selected the wrong family of end-plays, a squeeze instead of a squeeze strip. Win the ♠ K at once and run all the diamonds and hearts. Before the final heart lead the position is:

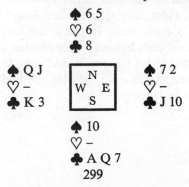

When dummy leads the last heart, W's mechanical discard is a spade to protect his king. Next, dummy throws W on lead with a spade to force the club return.

However, if W is a man and not a mouse, he makes the bluff discard of his ♣ 3 on the last heart lead, posing declarer with a difficult guess. Declarer might easily go wrong by finessing to W's now bare ♣ K or by throwing him in with a spade to let W collect another spade trick to break the contract. W might well discard ♠ Q (not ♠ J) to make S's task even more difficult, in deference to the good defensive axiom: 'discard the card you are known to hold'.

Tribe 1. Basic Eliminations

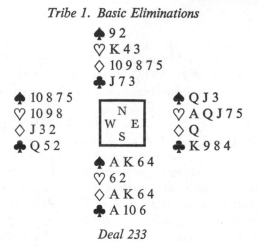

```
              ♠ 9 2
              ♡ K 4 3
              ◇ 10 9 8 7 5
              ♣ J 7 3
♠ 10 8 7 5              ♠ Q J 3
♡ 10 9 8      N        ♡ A Q J 7 5
◇ J 3 2     W   E      ◇ Q
♣ Q 5 2       S        ♣ K 9 8 4
              ♠ A K 6 4
              ♡ 6 2
              ◇ A K 6 4
              ♣ A 10 6
```

Deal 233

N and S have 60. S bid 1 ◇, N 2 ◇, E 2 ♡; S 2 ♠, and N 3 ◇.

W led the ♡ 10 and S ruffed the third heart lead. S laid down the ◇ A and the fall of the queen from E made S suspect a trump loser. This with two hearts lost and probably two clubs still to lose, threatened game. How do you avoid one loser?

Declarer has no true finesse in clubs, for he lacks the nine. He assumed that enemy club honours were divided and played accordingly. Hence he cashed his top spades and ruffed a spade in dummy. S won the top trump to re-enter, proving the bad split, and dummy ruffed the last spade, leaving:

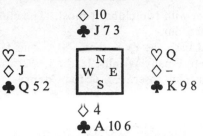

```
              ◇ 10
              ♣ J 7 3
♡ -            ┌─────┐        ♡ Q
◇ J           │  N  │        ◇ -
♣ Q 5 2       │W   E│        ♣ K 9 8
              │  S  │
              └─────┘
              ◇ 4
              ♣ A 10 6
```

Dummy lost the diamond to the knave in W, and E shed a club. W returned the ♣ Q which S let win, a type of Bath Coup, to force another club lead. If, instead, W returns a low club to E's king, S wins it and returns a club.

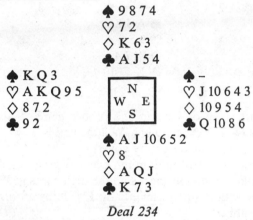

```
              ♠ 9 8 7 4
              ♡ 7 2
              ◇ K 6 3
              ♣ A J 5 4
♠ K Q 3        ┌─────┐        ♠ -
♡ A K Q 9 5   │  N  │        ♡ J 10 6 4 3
◇ 8 7 2       │W   E│        ◇ 10 9 5 4
♣ 9 2         │  S  │        ♣ Q 10 8 6
              └─────┘
              ♠ A J 10 6 5 2
              ♡ 8
              ◇ A Q J
              ♣ K 7 3
```

Deal 234

At rubber game S bid 1 ♠, W 2 ♡, N 2 ♠, E 3 ♡; and S 4 ♠.

W led the ♡ K, then ♡ Q which S ruffed. Dummy won the ◇ K and led a trump for S to finesse, but E discarded so S took the ace. How do you play from here?

With a heart trick lost and two trump losers, S laid down the ♣ K then tried the ♣ J finesse which lost and the hand was dead.

S was a card pusher who played without fear or analysis.* The trump break was bad luck, but W's hand yields nicely to a count.

After S wins the trump ace, he should cash two more diamond tricks, which reveals three diamonds with W. Now, W has shown three trumps and he must have five hearts for his vulnerable over-

---

* *Sans peur*, no doubt; but with plenty of *reproche* . . . from his partners!
—Editor.

call, marking him with two clubs at most. The club finesse, held in reserve, is counted out.

Next S should cash the ♣ K then ♣ A, and throw W into the lead with a trump. Finally W must lead a heart which dummy ruffs while S parks his club loser. (Cf. C for Count.)

Either-Or Play

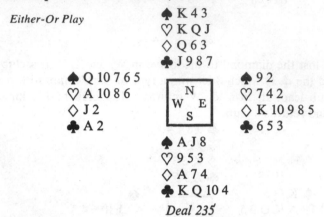

```
              ♠ K 4 3
              ♡ K Q J
              ◇ Q 6 3
              ♣ J 9 8 7
♠ Q 10 7 6 5              ♠ 9 2
♡ A 10 8 6      N        ♡ 7 4 2
◇ J 2        W   E       ◇ K 10 9 8 5
♣ A 2           S        ♣ 6 5 3
              ♠ A J 8
              ♡ 9 5 3
              ◇ A 7 4
              ♣ K Q 10 4
```

Deal 235

With a part score of sixty in the rubber game, S bid 1 ♣, W doubled, N 2 ♣, E 2 ◇ ; S no bid, W 2 ♠, and N 3 ♣.

W led the ◇ J. Should dummy cover?

Before touching a card in dummy, declarer reviewed the auction. Clearly the take-out double marks all the high cards in W except the ◇ K, shown with diamond length by E's desperate diamond bid 'to save the rubber'.

Hence declarer ducked in dummy and held up the ace, which card took the second diamond lead. This hold-up is essential to exhaust W of diamonds. The ♣ K forced the ace and W returned a trump; S drew E's last. S led a heart which W won with the ace, exiting with a heart. Dummy won two heart tricks, the ♠ K, and S the ♠ A. Now, S exited with his knave of spades to throw W on lead. W had to return a spade which dummy ruffed while S parked his diamond loser. S lost one trick in each suit, but scored game.

Alternately, at Trick 11, S can exit in diamonds instead of in spades in order to endplay E instead of W.

ELIMINATION

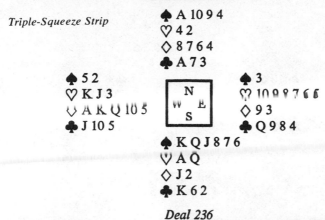

♠ A 10 9 4
♡ 4 2
◇ 8 7 6 4
♣ A 7 3

♠ 5 2
♡ K J 3
◇ A K Q 10 5
♣ J 10 5

♠ 3
♡ 10 9 8 7 6 5
◇ 9 3
♣ Q 9 8 4

♠ K Q J 8 7 6
♡ A Q
◇ J 2
♣ K 6 2

Deal 236

At rubber game W bid 1 ◇, S 2 ♠; and N 4 ♠.

W led the ◇ K, ◇ Q, then shifted to the ♣ J.

Who holds the high cards? How do you play?

Two lost diamond tricks, a club and the ♡ K indicated with W by his opening bid threatened the contract, so S played for a squeeze strip.

S won the ♣ K at Trick 3, entered dummy with a trump, and ruffed high a diamond in case E started with three diamonds. Next S ran all his trumps but one to this ending:

♡ 4 2
◇ 8
♣ A 7

♡ K J
◇ A
♣ 10 5

♡ 10 9 8
◇ -
♣ Q 9

♠ 7
♡ A Q
◇ -
♣ 6 2

S led the last trump, squeezing W in three suits. W must keep the ◇ A. W cannot shed the ♡ J lest he reveal the nakedness of his king. Hence W must shed a club, his vanishing exit card. Next dummy wins the ♣ A to draw W's last club, and dummy's diamond return throws W in to the lead to force the heart return.

303

Deal 237

The bidding: *N and S game in*

S	W	N	E
		(dealer)	
–	–	1 ◇	No
1 ♠	No	3 ◇	No
4 ♣	No	4 ♠	No
4 NT	No	5 ♡ (B)	Double
6 ♠	Double (final bid)		

Writes Mr. Alexander G. Spencer of Fanwood, New Jersey: 'I enjoyed playing this hand. E, desperate because of the impending vulnerable slam, doubled 5 ♡ to indicate a lead (a true "informatory" double). W thought then that his double of the slam was justified. Why aren't players ever satisfied just to beat the slam? The double gave the show away and let me make the hand.

'W opened the ♡ 6, covered by 8, 9 and knave. Club ace, club ruff, ♡ A, club ruff. Ruff a heart, ◇ A, ◇ K, ruff a diamond. Cash ♠ K. . . .' This play leaves:

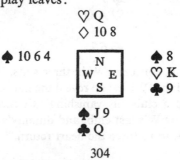

ELIMINATION

S leads the club which W trumps, and E cannot over-ruff because he must follow suit! Now S's trump tenace wins the last two tricks.

Tribe 2. Combination Eliminations

Double Endplay

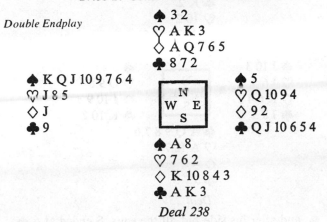

```
                    ♠ 3 2
                    ♡ A K 3
                    ♢ A Q 7 6 5
                    ♣ 8 7 2
♠ K Q J 10 9 7 6 4              ♠ 5
♡ J 8 5          ┌─────────┐   ♡ Q 10 9 4
♢ J             │   N     │   ♢ 9 2
♣ 9             │ W   E   │   ♣ Q J 10 6 5 4
                │   S     │
                └─────────┘
                    ♠ A 8
                    ♡ 7 6 2
                    ♢ K 10 8 4 3
                    ♣ A K 3
```

Deal 238

S bid 1 ♢, W 4 ♠, and N 5 ♢.

W led the ♠ K. How do you win eleven tricks?

Declarer's problem is to 'evaporate' one of his three natural losers. W's spade pre-empt showed a huge suit: *ergo*, very short side suits; so a ruff-and-discard elimination seemed logical.

S wins the ♠ A, two trumps, and two clubs. W's minor suit singletons revealed that he had no possible defence against the endplay. S cashed dummy's top hearts, leaving:

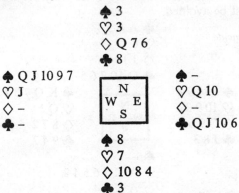

```
                    ♠ 3
                    ♡ 3
                    ♢ Q 7 6
                    ♣ 8
♠ Q J 10 9 7              ♠ —
♡ J             ┌─────────┐   ♡ Q 10
♢ —            │   N     │   ♢ —
♣ —            │ W   E   │   ♣ Q J 10 6
               │   S     │
               └─────────┘
                    ♠ 8
                    ♡ 7
                    ♢ 10 8 4
                    ♣ 3
```

S led the heart to cut liaison between E and W. If W wins the heart, he gets a spade trick; but then another spade lead lets dummy

305

ruff while S parks his club loser. If E overtakes the heart, he gets club trick then is similarly hedged by trumps. The end-play is double because it operates against both adversaries.

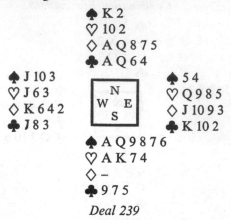

♠ K 2
♡ 10 2
◇ A Q 8 7 5
♣ A Q 6 4

♠ J 10 3　　　　　　　　♠ 5 4
♡ J 6 3　　　　　　　　♡ Q 9 8 5
◇ K 6 4 2　　　　　　　◇ J 10 9 3
♣ J 8 3　　　　　　　　♣ K 10 2

♠ A Q 9 8 7 6
♡ A K 7 4
◇ –
♣ 9 7 5

Deal 239

S bid 1 ♠, and after his side bid all the suits, S ended at 6 ♠. W led the ♠ J. How do you play it?

Dummy's king won the ♠ J. S won the ♡ A K and dummy ruffed a heart. S ruffed a low diamond and drew trumps.

The contract succeeds if the club finesse is 'on', or if E holds a fourth heart with S. So S tried the heart play first, holding the club finesse in reserve in case W wins the heart. E had to win the heart and he was forced to lead up to one of dummy's ace-queens.

A trap in the hand is to cash the ◇ A early for a club discard. This play must be avoided.

Three-Way Suicide

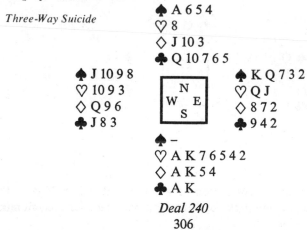

♠ A 6 5 4
♡ 8
◇ J 10 3
♣ Q 10 7 6 5

♠ J 10 9 8　　　　　　　♠ K Q 7 3 2
♡ 10 9 3　　　　　　　　♡ Q J
◇ Q 9 6　　　　　　　　◇ 8 7 2
♣ J 8 3　　　　　　　　♣ 9 4 2

♠ –
♡ A K 7 6 5 4 2
◇ A K 5 4
♣ A K

Deal 240

S bid 2 ♡, N 2 ♠; S 3 ◇, N 3 NT; and S 6 ♡.

W led the ♠ J. How do you secure the slam?

S chucked quickly. He won the ♠ A for a diamond discard and, since he thought that he was in dummy for the last time, he tried the ◇ J finesse which lost the slam.

Apparently dummy has no second entry, but as the enemy cards lie, dummy has three entries by elimination play! The winning technique is to duck the spade opening in dummy and ruff. Lay down two top trumps and two top clubs, then lead a trump to W's only trick. W had a threefold choice of suicide to put dummy on lead.

If E wins the third trump lead, he must return a diamond lest dummy's top spade and top club give S two diamond discards, so S still has the diamond finesse in reserve to try for slam.

S's early diamond finesse wins only if E holds the ◇ Q while the proper attack (with W holding the trump winner) wins wherever she is.

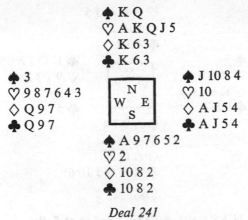

♠ K Q
♡ A K Q J 5
◇ K 6 3
♣ K 6 3

♠ 3
♡ 9 8 7 6 4 3
◇ Q 9 7
♣ Q 9 7

♠ J 10 8 4
♡ 10
◇ A J 5 4
♣ A J 5 4

♠ A 9 7 6 5 2
♡ 2
◇ 10 8 2
♣ 10 8 2

Deal 241

N bid 1 ♡, E doubled for a take-out, S 1 ♠; N 2 NT, S 3 ♠; and N 4 ♠.

W led the ♡ 9. What plan do you adopt?

E has the typical modern 'cream-puff' double with eleven points in high cards plus two dummy points for the singleton heart.

S drew the valuable inference of the take-out double—that it was aimed at the other major, spades; hence, S played E for four spades.

Dummy won the heart opening with his knave, and two top trumps. Next dummy led the ♡ 5, E shed a diamond, and S ruffed.

S played the ♠ A, then a low spade to throw E on lead to force his return to a king in dummy, an entry for the good hearts.

A far-sighted E can attempt to avoid the end-play by getting rid of his best spades on top spade leads, but S should counter this by keeping the ♠ 2 for the fourth spade lead, playing higher cards under dummy's honours.

If W happens to open either minor, E can take three tricks in clubs and diamonds (A and J of the suit led, plus the other ace), and then sit back and wait for his natural trump trick to break the contract.

W, with six hearts, has a superficially attractive lead from the suit; but N, on the 2 NT bid, is virtually marked with the quart major. If E had been void of hearts he would probably have bid his five-suit —or, at least, doubled the final contract. Hence the heart opening was contra-indicated.

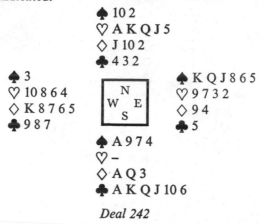

Deal 242

S bid 1 ♣, N 1 ♡, E 1 ♠ ; and S ended at 6 ♣.
W led the ♠ 3.
How do you get to dummy to score the hearts?

S won the spade opening with the ace, drew trumps, and laid down the ◇ Q, hoping to coax out the king immediately and promote a diamond entry to dummy. But W had been round bridge tables long enough to know what was what and grimly clutched his king. S was defeated by two tricks.

The spade bid by E coupled with the ♠ 3 opening lead by W with ♠ 2 in dummy marked the ♠ 3 a singleton.

After winning two trumps, lead the ♣ 6 to W's nine! W is forced to

return a heart or a diamond to let dummy in to score the hearts. This
♣ 6 play is a gambit to create an entry to dummy: giving up a need-
less trump trick to get four heart tricks in return. (Cf. File G.)

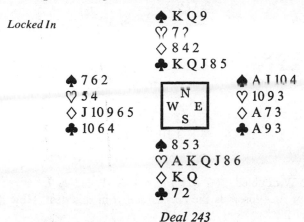

Locked In

♠ K Q 9
♡ 7 ?
◇ 8 4 2
♣ K Q J 8 5

♠ 7 6 2
♡ 5 4
◇ J 10 9 6 5
♣ 10 6 4

♠ A J 10 4
♡ 10 9 3
◇ A 7 3
♣ A 9 3

♠ 8 5 3
♡ A K Q J 8 6
◇ K Q
♣ 7 2

Deal 243

S bid 1 ♡, N 2 ♣; and S 4 ♡.

W led the ◇ J to the ◇ A in E, who made a very fine play by
returning the knave of spades. What is your plan?

E was vulnerable and his flat shape is too dangerous for aggressive
action despite his thirteen points. If E doubles and W bids hearts on
a blank hand, E and W will lose a lot of tricks. E has a good defensive
hand for wait-and-see tactics.

Dummy won the ♠ J return at Trick 2 and S drew trumps and
cashed his high diamond; then he led a club to dummy's knave. E
was forced to duck lest the entire club suit swamp him, so S ruffed
away E's last diamond, an essential manœuvre. S returned a club to
the queen which E won, but E was locked in in the black suits. S
must pray E holds only three diamonds.

Work's Favorite Strip

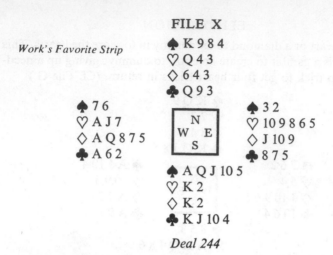

                  ♠ K 9 8 4
                  ♡ Q 4 3
                  ◇ 6 4 3
                  ♣ Q 9 3

  ♠ 7 6   ♠ 3 2
  ♡ A J 7   N   ♡ 10 9 8 6 5
  ◇ A Q 8 7 5   W   E   ◇ J 10 9
  ♣ A 6 2   S   ♣ 8 7 5

                  ♠ A Q J 10 5
                  ♡ K 2
                  ◇ K 2
                  ♣ K J 10 4

Deal 244

S bid 1 ♠, W doubled, N 2 ♠; and S 4 ♠. W led ♠ 7.

One of your four losers is the *corpus delicti* in this deal. How do you get rid of it?

The take-out double marks W with most of the unseen high cards, and S planned accordingly. Clearly the ◇ K is a goner if anyone but W leads a diamond.

S drew trumps and pushed clubs. W won the second club lead and S won W's club return: W's only safe exit at this point.

Next S made the key play. He led a LOW heart. If W wins, he sets up the ♡ Q for a diamond discard; so W ducked and the queen won. S won a trump to get back into the lead, and cashed the last club on which dummy ditched a heart. S led the ♡ K which W won, but W was trapped in the classic end-play popularized by the late Milton C. Work. It is called the cross-ruff fork strip, because W must lead a heart to yield a cross-ruff, i.e. ruff and discard; or up to S's fork (or tenace) position in diamonds.

Old examples of this end-play were called 'baby eliminations' because they were simple to play. The deal above requires careful analysis of the calling and proper use of the threat in hearts in order to develop the end-play.

ELIMINATION

```
               ♠ 8 7 3
               ♡ 10 9 7 6 5
               ◇ K 6 2
               ♣ A J
    ♠ A 2              ┌─────────┐       ♠ K J 10
    ♡ Q 4 3           │    N    │       ♡ –
    ◇ 10 9 7 4        │ W     E │       ◇ Q 8 5
    ♣ K Q 9 4         │    S    │       ♣ 10 8 7 6 5 3 2
                      └─────────┘
               ♠ Q 9 6 5 4
               ♡ A K J 8 2
               ◇ A J 3
               ♣ –
```

Deal 245

With E and W vulnerable S bid 1 ♠, N 1 NT; S 2 ♡, and N 4 ♡.
W led the ♣ K. Should dummy's ace win it?

It is good tactics to keep a choice of discards open, so dummy
ducked the ♣ K and S ruffed. S won the ♡ K, discovering a sure
trump loser. Prospects looked dim with the threat of three spade
losers also.

S played for the chance of the ♠ A or ♠ K being alone, or being
doubleton in W. S played the ◇ A, ◇ K, ♣ A for a diamond discard, and S ruffed the diamond, leaving:

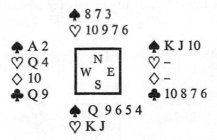

```
               ♠ 8 7 3
               ♡ 10 9 7 6
    ♠ A 2              ┌─────────┐       ♠ K J 10
    ♡ Q 4             │    N    │       ♡ –
    ◇ 10              │ W     E │       ◇ –
    ♣ Q 9             │    S    │       ♣ 10 8 7 6
                      └─────────┘
               ♠ Q 9 6 5 4
               ♡ K J
```

S led a low spade and the suit was blocked defensively. E won the
♠ 10, W won the ♠ A, then he had to return a minor suit card which
let dummy sluff the spade while S ruffed. S lost a trump trick but
won game.

The spade lead is maddening for the defenders for, however they
play, they cannot collect *three* spade tricks and the trump.

311

Tribe 3. *Imperfect Eliminations*

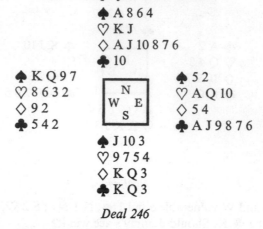

♠ A 8 6 4
♡ K J
◇ A J 10 8 7 6
♣ 10

♠ K Q 9 7   ♠ 5 2
♡ 8 6 3 2   ♡ A Q 10
◇ 9 2   ◇ 5 4
♣ 5 4 2   ♣ A J 9 8 7 6

♠ J 10 3
♡ 9 7 5 4
◇ K Q 3
♣ K Q 3

Deal 246

N bid 1 ◇, E 2 ♣, S 2 NT; and N 3 NT.
W led the ♣ 5.
What is your best play for game?

School is out if E wins the club opening with the ace, but E covers the ten with the knave, which loses to S's queen. Declarer has eight tricks on top with no club for dummy to lead and promote Trick No. 9, so he ran five diamond tricks to put the squeeze on E. The 2 ♣ overcall located most of the missing strength in E, who was forced down to this ending:

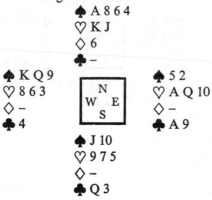

♠ A 8 6 4
♡ K J
◇ 6
♣ –

♠ K Q 9   ♠ 5 2
♡ 8 6 3   ♡ A Q 10
◇ –   ◇ –
♣ 4   ♣ A 9

♠ J 10
♡ 9 7 5
◇ –
♣ Q 3

On the final diamond lead E shed his precious deuce of spades, which looked worthless; but this discard proved to be a fatal chuck. Dummy won the ♠ A to draw E's last spade and switched to a heart to let E collect three heart tricks. But in the two-card ending E's ♣ 9 lost to the queen, S's Trick No. 9.

In the matrix F must discard the ♣ 9 to avoid this end-play and give himself a safe exit in spades. If W does not hold as good as K J x in the black major, school is still out!

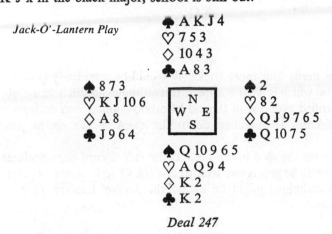

Jack-O'-Lantern Play

```
              ♠ A K J 4
              ♡ 7 5 3
              ◇ 10 4 3
              ♣ A 8 3
  ♠ 8 7 3                      ♠ 2
  ♡ K J 10 6      N            ♡ 8 2
  ◇ A 8       W       E        ◇ Q J 9 7 6 5
  ♣ J 9 6 4       S            ♣ Q 10 7 5
              ♠ Q 10 9 6 5
              ♡ A Q 9 4
              ◇ K 2
              ♣ K 2
```

Deal 247

S bid 1 ♠, N 3 ♠; and S 4 ♠.
W led the eight of spades.

The four threatening red suit losers were declarer's hex. Anyway, S had a sure heart loser, which should be yielded early, and S must keep E off lead lest he lead the ◇ Q to let W chop the king.

S won the trump opening and another trump, the ♣ K, ♣ A, and a club ruff. Dummy won a third trump, drawing W's last; and then led a heart and S inserted the nine which W's ten won in the situation shown on the next page.

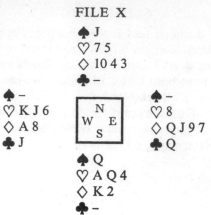

♠ J
♡ 7 5
◇ 10 4 3
♣ —

♠ —
♡ K J 6
◇ A 8
♣ J

♠ —
♡ 8
◇ Q J 9 7
♣ Q

♠ Q
♡ A Q 4
◇ K 2
♣ —

Declarer needs four more tricks. W would be completely boxed if out of clubs, which is what S hoped. But although he still held a club, W was petrified with fear of the old bugaboo about giving declarer a ruff-and-discard. He planked down the ◇ A, which ended proceedings.

If W returns the ♣ J in the matrix, the ruff discard does declarer no good, for all he gets is two trumps and the ♡ A, however he plays. Declarer's technique might be called the Jack-o'-Lantern play: a shadow-threat.

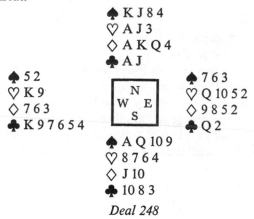

♠ K J 8 4
♡ A J 3
◇ A K Q 4
♣ A J

♠ 5 2
♡ K 9
◇ 7 6 3
♣ K 9 7 6 5 4

♠ 7 6 3
♡ Q 10 5 2
◇ 9 8 5 2
♣ Q 2

♠ A Q 10 9
♡ 8 7 6 4
◇ J 10
♣ 10 8 3

Deal 248

This is another deal from 'Sonny' Moyse 'at the sign of' *The Bridge World*. N bid 1 ◇,* S 1 ♠; N 5 ♠, and S 6 ♠. You probably won't like the bidding; nor do we. But that's the way it happened.

* N must have been playing Roth-Stone—a popular new U.S. system which possesses no opening forcing bid. A 23-count qualifies under any other system, either for a forcing bid or, at the very least, for 2 NT.—Editor.

W led the ♣ 5. How do you avoid two heart losers?

S hoped W held the ♡ K Q x, or a doubleton heart picture for a bluff strip ending. Dummy won the ♣ A, then led a trump to S who immediately led a heart. In a bluff strip it is important to play a top card early in opponents' exit suit before, catching on to your plan, they frustrate it by unblocking. W followed low (the play of the king breaks the contract) and dummy won with the ace.*

Next, S won another trump, leaving the seven with E, and S won four diamonds for club discards. S ruffed dummy's last club. Again W might have saved the day if he had jettisoned the ♡ K on the fourth diamond lead, but he chucked again, shedding a club. S lost a heart to W's now bare king, and W had to return a club which let dummy sluff the heart while S ruffed.

Observe a peculiar feature of this elimination position. S drew only TWO rounds of trumps, hoping that E held the outstanding trump. Declarer cannot afford three trump leads, because he must finish with two trumps in both hands, in order to score all four trumps separately by cross-ruffing. A hand requiring both luck and skill plus bad defence: in fact, not a slam to be in!

Tribe 4. Preparatory Eliminations

Stepping-Stone Strip

```
              ♠ 9 7 6 5
              ♡ K Q 3
              ◇ 8 7 3
              ♣ J 7 3
  ♠ -                        ♠ Q 10 4 2
  ♡ A J 10 8 7 6    N        ♡ 9 5 4
  ◇ J 10 9       W     E     ◇ 6 5 2
  ♣ A K 9 4         S        ♣ 8 6 2
              ♠ A K J 8 3
              ♡ 2
              ◇ A K Q 4
              ♣ Q 10 5
```

Deal 249

S bid 1 ♠, W doubled, N 2 ♠; and S 4 ♠.

W led the ♣ K then ♣ A, and shifted to the ◇ J.

If E shows four trumps, how do you trap them?

* Actually W *should* play ♡ K, for if S holds ♡ Q and others, it is bound to fall under the ace.—Editor.

S took care to ditch the queen on the second club lead, and won the diamond switch at Trick 3. Next S laid down the ♠ A and learned the bad news—the 4–0 trump split. Dummy needs two entries to let S finesse trumps twice.

S led a club to dummy's knave and N returned the ♠ 9, covered by the ten and knave. Next S cashed two more top diamonds luckily escaping a ruff, leaving this ending:

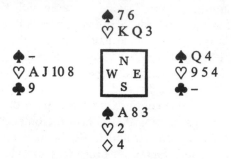

```
                    ♠ 7 6
                    ♡ K Q 3

    ♠ -          ┌───────┐      ♠ Q 4
    ♡ A J 10 8   │   N   │      ♡ 9 5 4
    ♣ 9          │ W   E │      ♣ -
                 │   S   │
                 └───────┘
                    ♠ A 8 3
                    ♡ 2
                    ◇ 4
```

S led the heart and W had to score his ace or lose it. A heart return is hopeless, so W tried the ♣ 9 which dummy trumped. Declarer can win the balance whether E discards or over-trumps.

The purpose of this end-play is to prepare a second entry to dummy for S's vital second trump finesse for game.

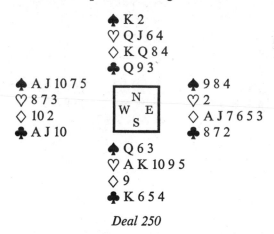

```
                    ♠ K 2
                    ♡ Q J 6 4
                    ◇ K Q 8 4
                    ♣ Q 9 3

    ♠ A J 10 7 5  ┌───────┐      ♠ 9 8 4
    ♡ 8 7 3       │   N   │      ♡ 2
    ◇ 10 2        │ W   E │      ◇ A J 7 6 5 3
    ♣ A J 10      │   S   │      ♣ 8 7 2
                  └───────┘
                    ♠ Q 6 3
                    ♡ A K 10 9 5
                    ◇ 9
                    ♣ K 6 5 4
```

Deal 250

At rubber game S bid 1 ♡, W 1 ♠, N 3 ♡; and S 4 ♡.

W led the ◇ 10 to queen and ace and E returned the ♠ 9 which, W properly ducking, was won by the king in dummy.

316

ELIMINATION

With nine tricks icy, how do you develop the vital tenth?

S's best chance is to play W for two aces for his 1 ♠ overcall.
S ruffed high a low diamond for Trick 3. Next S won a trump, then
dummy a trump, and S ruffed high another low diamond, and dummy
won another trump, leaving:

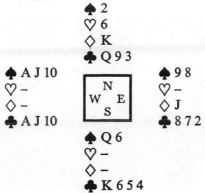

Dummy cashed the ♦ K, S shed a club and W a spade. Next
dummy led the trump, S shed another club, and W was squeezed.
Another spade discard would let S duck a spade to the bare ace, so
W shed the ♣ 10. Next the ♣ K drove out the ace and W got only
one more trick, the ♠ A.

Strip Double Ruffout

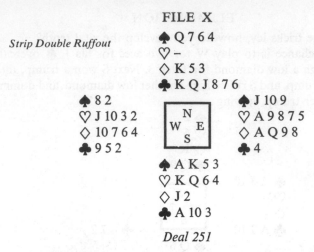

♠ Q 7 6 4
♡ –
◇ K 5 3
♣ K Q J 8 7 6

♠ 8 2
♡ J 10 3 2
◇ 10 7 6 4
♣ 9 5 2

♠ J 10 9
♡ A 9 8 7 5
◇ A Q 9 8
♣ 4

♠ A K 5 3
♡ K Q 6 4
◇ J 2
♣ A 10 3

Deal 251

The bidding:			Rubber game
W	N	E	S
		(dealer)	
—	—	1 ♡	Double
No	2 ♡!	No	2 ♠
No	3 ♠	No	4 ♣
No	4 ♡ !!	No	4 ♠
No	6 ♠ (final bid)		

N's 2 ♡ call is the famous 'kick-back', announcing great strength and implying an equal choice of trump suit. Later N rebid 4 ♡ to show a genuine heart void.

Against a heart opening the slam is easy to make. Dummy ruffs, wins the trump queen, S wins a trump, dummy ruffs another heart, and S re-enters via the ♣ A to draw trumps then run clubs.

A diamond opening breaks a contract, but that is not our story. But W led the ♠ 8. What is wrong with the plan above?

The trump opening gives S entry trouble, for the odds are about even that a second club lead to get S on lead will be ruffed. Hence S, placing the red aces and ◇ Q with E for his opening 1 ♡ bid, adopts a safer plan. Dummy wins the trump opening, S draws trumps and runs clubs, squeezing E down to this position:

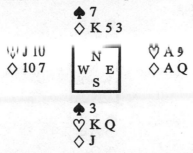

♠ 7
♦ K 5 3

♥ J 10   ♥ A 9
♦ 10 7   ♦ A Q

♠ 3
♥ K Q
♦ J

Dummy leads a low diamond to E's queen! If E returns the ♦ A, S ruffs to set up and score dummy's king; if E returns the ♥ A, dummy ruffs to set up and score S's king.

Note that if declarer ruffs a heart in dummy before running trumps and clubs, he cannot develop this end-play.

Double Squeeze Scoop

♠ A 6 3
♥ K 6 3
♦ A 7 6 4 3
♣ 8 2

♠ Q J 10 7 5   ♠ 9 8 4
♥ A 4 2   ♥ J 10 8 7
♦ 10 2   ♦ 8
♣ Q J 10   ♣ 7 6 5 4 3

♠ K 2
♥ Q 9 5
♦ K Q J 9 5
♣ A K 9

Deal 252

S bid 1 ♦, W 1 ♠, N 3 ♦; S 4 ♣ (ace), N 4 ♠ (ace); and S 6 ♦. W led the ♠ Q.

What can you do about the two natural heart losers?

S won the spade opening with the king and drew trumps. To Trick 4, S led a low heart, W ducked, and dummy's king drew the seven from E. This led S to suspect ♥ J 10 8 7 in E, and the spade overcall marked all other high cards in W.

Next came the top clubs and a club ruff in dummy, and the fall of ♣ Q J 10 from W exposed his hand to a count. W showed three clubs and two diamonds, and probably three hearts, corroborated by his 1 ♠ overcall indicating five spades. S won two trumps, leaving this marked ending:

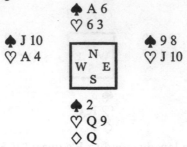

```
                    ♠ A 6
                    ♡ 6 3
     ♠ J 10                      ♠ 9 8
     ♡ A 4         ┌─────┐       ♡ J 10
                   │  N  │
                   │W   E│
                   │  S  │
                   └─────┘
                    ♠ 2
                    ♡ Q 9
                    ◊ Q
```

S needs three more tricks. He led the diamond, squeezing W first. If W sheds the low heart, dummy sheds the low spade and S leads his low heart to drop W's now bare ace. So W must instead shed a spade, dummy sheds a now useless heart, and E is squeezed. E cannot throw a spade also, for W has only one spade left; hence E must give up a heart. Next dummy wins the ♠ A to draw W's last spade, and the ♡ Q covers the knave from E, and S comes to a trick with ♡ 9!

COUP

Y is the assigned file letter for the True Coups, the trump tenace pick-up plays. At times they are preceded by trump reduction. When declarer ruffs dummy's winners for this end, the position becomes the classic, but astronomically rare, grand coup.

It should be pointed out that many so-called 'coups' are not true coups at all but plays belonging to altogether different families. Such are the cases of the Bath Coup and Deschapelles Coup which both stem from Whist and of such modern plays as the Coffin Coup, Dewey Coup, Kempson Coup and Harvard Coup.

File Y is closely related to trump tenace strips in File X and to some types of ruffing plays in File R. Hence it is not always clear whether a deal involving over-ruffs should be referred to File R, X or Y. Below is such an ambiguity.

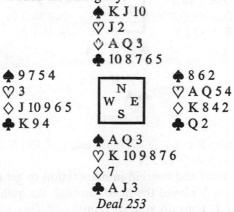

```
              ♠ K J 10
              ♡ J 2
              ◇ A Q 3
              ♣ 10 8 7 6 5
♠ 9 7 5 4         ┌─────┐      ♠ 8 6 2
♡ 3               │  N  │      ♡ A Q 5 4
◇ J 10 9 6 5      │W   E│      ◇ K 8 4 2
♣ K 9 4           │  S  │      ♣ Q 2
                  └─────┘
              ♠ A Q 3
              ♡ K 10 9 8 7 6
              ◇ 7
              ♣ A J 3
```

Deal 253

S opened 1 ♡ third hand, N 2 NT; and S 4 ♡.

W led the ◇ J which dummy won with the ace. Dummy finessed the ♡ J which won, and S won the ♡ 7 finesse next. W discarded a diamond, marking E with ♡ A Q.

321

How do you confine E to one trump trick?

For the coup ending, declarer must reduce his trumps to equal E's trumps in number and trap them, by leading at Trick 12 from the table. Hence at Trick 4 dummy won a spade, S ruffed a diamond; dummy won another spade, and S ruffed another diamond. S cashed both black aces, and cut himself adrift by a club lead and simply waited for his king of trumps to float home for his tenth winning trick.

If W wins Trick 11, S can over-ruff the queen of trumps in true coup fashion; otherwise E is caught in a losing trump finesse or end-play. Declarer has no interest in the academics of whether the deal belongs in File R, X or Y; only in scoring his king of trumps for game.

If E 'flies' with his ace of trumps on dummy's first or second trump lead, S still rids himself of two surplus trumps lest he get stuck on lead via a side suit at the end and be forced to lead away from his major tenace in hearts.

Matrix Typica

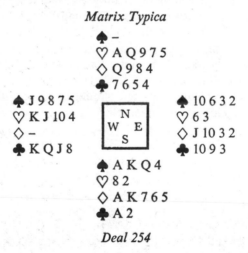

Deal 254

At rubber game S bid 1 ◇, W doubled, N 1 ♡; S 2 ♠, N 4 ◇; S 4 NT, N 5 ◇; S 6 ◇ and N 7 ◇.

N was a big loser and overbid in desperation to get even quickly. He was lucky, for S played the hand 'through the quill'.

W led the ♡ J. How do you get home?

Declarer was compelled to finesse the ♡ Q—a seven based on a first trick finesse—ugh! It won. Next S made the safety play of the ◇ Q* which proved wise, and continued with the ◇ 9, which E and

_____
* The rare case when the first trick is won by the single-honour hand.

S covered. S cashed three top spades for three club discards in dummy, and dummy ruffed the low spade.

For Trick 8 declarer won the ♡ A, then ruffed a heart, cashed the ♣ A and ruffed the club with dummy's last trump for Trick 11. These carefully timed plays put dummy into the lead for Trick 12 with S holding A 7 in trumps over E's J 3 for the over-ruff finesse or true coup.

W failed to explain why he did not open the ♣ K instead of the ♡ J, but the final result would have been the same as the heart finesse was right.

In the next deal, declarer pulled a fast finesse and got away with murder.

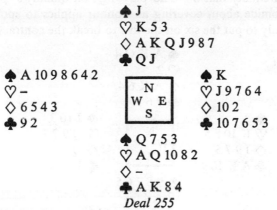

Deal 255

S bid 1 ♡, W 1 ♠, N 3 ◇; S 4 ♣, N 4 NT (Blackwood); S 5 ♡, N 6 ♡, and E doubled.

W led the ♠ A, dropping E's king; and W continued with the ten.

W's 1 ♠ overcall was dangerous on only one defensive trick, for it may encourage a fatal penalty double by E, as, in the event, it did. Actually, E was a fish to double for three reasons: first, his double requested W to lead something other than spades, the 'normal' lead: probably dummy's first bid suit, diamonds, according to the Lightner Slam Lead-Directing Double—although W ignored it! Second, it warned S of something rotten in trumps and offered a chance to shift to 6 NT, which is frigid on the fortunate spade distribution. Third, and fatally, it located the missing trumps with E. In defending against a slam, the crucial aim is to defeat it: not to jeopardize your chance of stopping 1,000 points or more for the sake of chasing a possible measly 50 or 100.

When E doubled 6 ♡, he thought that he had declarer over a barrel, which was a fact; but E made a slip in defending and the barrel shifted its position.

When W led another spade at Trick 2, dummy ruffed with the ♡ K and led the ♡ 5, E played his four and was horrified when S put on the deuce! S gave E a meaning look while he scooped in Trick 2 with the ♡ 5, and S led dummy's last heart and finessed the eight.

Dummy re-entered with a club and pushed the great diamond suit to coup E's trump tenace and bag the slam.

S took advantage of his only chance to score his impossible contract—E's credulity that S would play high on dummy's ♡ 5 lead. The old bromide about covering an honour applies to spots here; for E has only to put the six on the five to break the contract!

En Passant

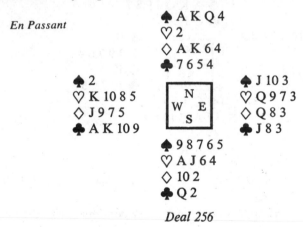

          ♠ A K Q 4
          ♡ 2
          ◇ A K 6 4
          ♣ 7 6 5 4

♠ 2   ♠ J 10 3
♡ K 10 8 5   ♡ Q 9 7 3
◇ J 9 7 5   ◇ Q 8 3
♣ A K 10 9   ♣ J 8 3

          ♠ 9 8 7 6 5
          ♡ A J 6 4
          ◇ 10 2
          ♣ Q 2

Deal 256

N bid 1 ◇, S 1 ♠; and N 4 ♠.

W led the ♣ K, ♣ A, then shifted to the ◇ 5.

How do you get home if E holds three trumps?

The ◇ K won Trick 3, and dummy won two top trumps, revealing the bad 3–1 split. A third trump would impoverish S with two heart losers, so instead dummy won the ◇ A and S ruffed a diamond. Next S won the ♡ A and dummy ruffed a heart, leaving:

COUP

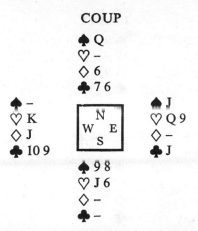

♠ Q
♡ –
◇ 6
♣ 7 6

♠ – ♠ J
♡ K ♡ Q 9
◇ J ◇ –
♣ 10 9 ♣ J

♠ 9 8
♡ J 6
◇ –
♣ –

S ruffed a club and dummy ruffed a heart; and dummy's return let S score his last trump by the classic *en passant* play. If E ruffs, S sluffs his heart loser; otherwise S scores his last trump immediately.

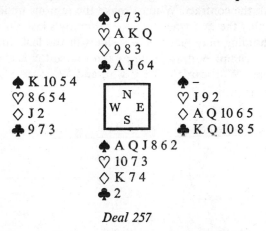

♠ 9 7 3
♡ A K Q
◇ 9 8 3
♣ A J 6 4

♠ K 10 5 4 ♠ –
♡ 8 6 5 4 ♡ J 9 2
◇ J 2 ◇ A Q 10 6 5
♣ 9 7 3 ♣ K Q 10 8 5

♠ A Q J 8 6 2
♡ 10 7 3
◇ K 7 4
♣ 2

Deal 257

At rubber game E bid 1 ◇, S 1 ♠, N 3 ♠; and S 4 ♠.

W led the ◇ J to E's ace, and E returned the ◇ Q which S won with his king, W dropping the deuce, showing no more diamonds. Dummy won the ♣ A and returned his bottom trump on which E discarded to show the dreadful division.

How do you play for game?

S won Trick 4 with his ace and decided that his best chance was to bail out the hands. Dummy won a heart and S ruffed a club, dummy won another heart and S ruffed another club, and dummy won the last heart, leaving:

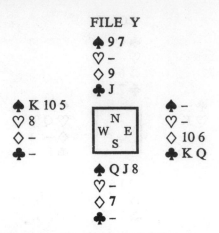

♠ 9 7
♡ –
◇ 9
♣ J

♠ K 10 5
♡ 8
◇ –
♣ –

♠ –
♡ –
◇ 10 6
♣ K Q

♠ Q J 8
♡ –
◇ 7
♣ –

Dummy led the club which S trumped high and W impatiently over-ruffed with the king. Later, W scored his ten of trumps but S got two of the last four tricks for game.

To break the contract, W must make the famous under-trumping coup and play the ♠ 5 when S trumps dummy's last club with ♠ Q. This is a holding play that lets W's side win the last three tricks. If S returns a trump, W draws trumps and scores the heart; if S leads the diamond, W discards to let E win, and W coups S's trumps on E's return.

File Z

SQUEEZE

Z is the assigned file letter for the Squeezes. They are plays to force an opponent to discard a winner or an essential guard to one.

For years a squeeze play was considered something difficult and mysterious—something strictly for the inner sanctum of a handful of world's top bridge experts. Recently I made a remark along these lines to Albert H. Morehead, Bridge Editor of the *New York Sunday Times*. His prompt rebuttal was, 'Why, George, I consider squeeze plays easy.'

He was referring, primarily, to the common, simple types: the automatic and one-way squeezes of one opponent in two suits. To-day, a working knowledge of these positions is standard equipment of thousands of experienced players. Years ago we saw John Campbell (who played Deal 191) announce a double squeeze and spread his hand as declarer without playing it out. The squeeze was there.

However, a few simple, rare squeezes and a host of compound and complex squeezes are difficult or impossible to diagnose in the heat of ordinary play. A rich variety of complex mutates exists only in double dummy problems, which is beyond the realm of this work.

Four natural tribes may be erected in the family of squeezes as follows:

Tribe 1. Basic Squeezes

Automatic Squeezes. Leading the final forcing card breaks up the hand of either opponent who happens to hold all the key cards. These include the simple squeezes, triple squeezes, ruff-out squeezes, true trump squeezes, and others.

One-Way Squeezes (positional). Leading the final forcing card squeezes second hand only, for the leader's partner cannot discard until second-hand has made his choice. These squeezes include simple one-way squeezes, triple squeezes, jettison squeezes, and others.

FILE Z

Tribe 2. Compound Squeezes

The Double Squeezes. Leading the final forcing card squeezes both opponents.

The Progressive Squeezes (Split Squeezes). A preparatory squeeze against one opponent leaves his partner vulnerable to a true squeeze on a later trick. Essentially these are a variety of the double squeeze.

The Repeating Squeezes. These are triple squeezes in which the forced discard establishes a second forcing card which is led to win and squeeze the same opponent again. (Some of the Super Squeezes are also Repeaters.)

Tribe 3. Imperfect Squeezes

Pseudo Squeezes (False Squeezes). No true squeeze position exists unless an opponent makes a wrong discard.

Vulnerable Squeezes. These are true squeezes of any classification which the enemy can break up early in the play by attacking a vital entry or a threat card.

Tribe 4. Super Squeezes

Compound Squeezes. One opponent is squeezed in three suits and his partner in two or three suits. These are sometimes called pentagon squeezes and hexagon squeezes respectively. Penta- refers to five, a squeeze of one defender in three suits and the other in two. Hexa- refers to six, squeezes on both opponents in all three suits outside the one led.

Mutate Squeezes. In these, a preparatory squeeze creates shifting threats according to the enemy discard which uncovers one or two or more different latent squeeze endings.

Mutates are usually too complex to recognize during actual play, but they occur in great variety in double dummy problems. However, Dr. Clyde E. Love and others have demonstrated the possibilities of actual mutate squeeze play in regular bridge.

In passing, we should point out that many types of preparatory squeezes occur which set the stage for the final play of other files, such as the squeeze long-suit in which declarer has to establish his long suit AFTER forcing an opponent to weaken it by a discard; the squeeze finesse, the squeeze strip, etc. Technically, such plays do not belong in File Z.

Before we offer a formal series of deals exemplifying the four

328

tribes of squeezes, let us pause to examine the technique of how to play to discover, and develop, a squeeze position. The most important aspect is when NOT to look for a squeeze. Dr. Love's book covers this phase completely and space here permits only a brief résumé.

Every top-notch player has gone through a phase of chasing phantom squeezes (and other non-existent endings) which has cost many games and slams makeable by routine play. Here is a case where an old campaigner out-smarted himself.

Deal 258

S bid 1 ♣, N 1 ◇; S 3 NT, and N 6 NT.

N was brazen to bid slam on a combined count of twenty-nine or thirty points, for he utterly lacks 'pushers'—supporting cards—outside his diamond suit.

W led the ♠ Q to E's ace, and E returned the ♠ 6 which S won with the king. With eleven tricks on top, No. 12 seemed to depend on a finesse or a squeeze, and declarer chucked. He ran his diamonds at once to this ending:

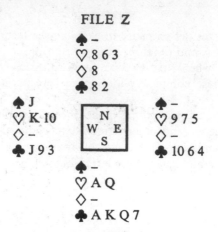

♠ –
♡ 8 6 3
◇ 8
♣ 8 2

♠ J
♡ K 10
◇ –
♣ J 9 3

♠ –
♡ 9 7 5
◇ –
♣ 10 6 4

♠ –
♡ A Q
◇ –
♣ A K Q 7

On dummy's last diamond lead E shed a heart. Declarer huddled long enough to check his odds. The heart finesse had a 50% chance while a 3–3 club split offered only one chance in three. Hence S discarded his low club and next finessed the ♡ Q, which W delightedly stepped on with his king to break the contract.

Looking at all four hands makes all this seem so silly, and you wonder how an expert can go so wrong on a simple hand that any rabbit would probably bring home without thought.

The squeeze position sought is simply out of this world. If E holds four clubs and the ♡ K, the finesse wins anyway; whereas, if W holds these cards, the last diamond lead squeezes the S hand first!

The correct play is to lay down three top clubs at once. The only play is to try to drop clubs 3–3 and, if this fails, to finesse the ♡ Q. The deal is a simple long suit affair with the finesse in reserve. The squeeze is out.

SQUEEZE

Tribe 1. Basic Squeezes

The ensuing deals shows basic squeezes in various trappings.

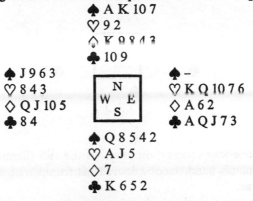

```
                    ♠ A K 10 7
                    ♡ 9 2
                    ◇ K 9 8 4 3
                    ♣ 10 9
    ♠ J 9 6 3       ┌─────────┐       ♠ —
    ♡ 8 4 3         │    N    │       ♡ K Q 10 7 6
    ◇ Q J 10 5      │ W     E │       ◇ A 6 2
    ♣ 8 4           │    S    │       ♣ A Q J 7 3
                    └─────────┘
                    ♠ Q 8 5 4 2
                    ♡ A J 5
                    ◇ 7
                    ♣ K 6 5 2
```

Deal 259

The bidding: Rubber Game

W	N	E	S
Oswald	Harold S.	Samuel M.	John
Jacoby	Vanderbilt	Stayman	Crawford
No	No	1 ♡	No
No	Double	3 ♣	3 ♠
No	4 ♠	No	No
Double	No	No	No

W led the eight of clubs, which E won with the ace. E returned the ♣ Q to S's king.

Which suit do you lead to Trick 3?

The deal was played in Mr. Vanderbilt's flat in New York City, and the four greats were not playing for bottle-caps. Vanderbilt practically invented Contract Bridge in 1926 and he has always loved the game. Note his re-opening take-out double which enables Crawford to bid and make the spade game. Jacoby's penalty double smacks of the sucker, but Jacoby had every right to expect to smear Crawford for a huge penalty in view of Stayman's jump rebid of 3 ♣, showing great power.

To Trick 3 Crawford led the diamond, W played the ten, but dummy and E ducked. W returned the ♠ 3 which dummy took with the ten. S ruffed a low diamond and returned a club, W shed a heart, and dummy ruffed low. S ruffed another diamond, dropping Stayman's ace.

331

Next Crawford cashed the top trumps in dummy and the ◇ K, leaving:

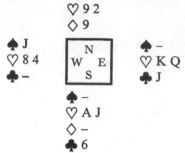

In this one-way squeeze, dummy led the stiff diamond, wrecking poor Stayman's hand. Jacoby scored his trump trick but Crawford scored game.

Another way to make the hand without the squeeze is to cash the ♡ A at Trick 8, to win a trump in dummy, the ◇ K, then score the two top trumps separately by ruffs. Why Crawford did not adopt this line was not explained. It is prosaic and practical, but not so artistic as the squeeze. The deal is one of Albert Morehead's, quoted in *The New York Times*.

Vienna Coup

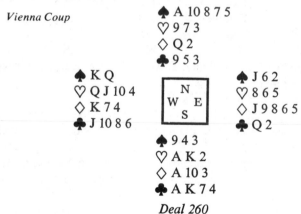

Deal 260

S bid 1 ♣, N 1 ♠; S 2 NT, and N 3 NT.

N should have dropped the 2 NT call like a hot brick, but declarer's problem was to collect nine tricks.

W led the queen of hearts.

How do you develop spades? If W holds only four hearts, what chances have you for Trick No. 9?

S won the ♡ Q and ducked a spade to W. W returned the ♡ J, which S passed; and W pushed another heart to the ace. S was happy to discover the 4–3 heart split. S ducked another spade to W, who collected his fourth heart, and switched to the ♣ J which S won, leaving:

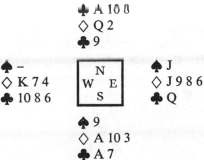

Before touching spades again S must lay down the ◇ A, establishing the king for W. This vital unblocking play for the squeeze is the famous preparatory Vienna Coup.* Finally, on the last spade lead S keeps two clubs and W with ◇ K and ♣ 10 8 is automatically squeezed.

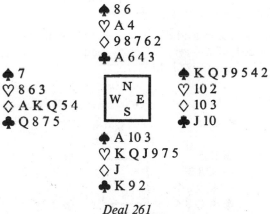

Deal 261

In a duplicate game reported by W. Howard Woolworth, Bridge Editor of the *Buffalo Courier-Express*, some years ago, all were vulnerable.

* So called, curiously enough, because the first recorded example of this 'un-block-for-discard, menace-erecting' manœuvre occurred (at whist) in Vienna. —Editor.

E opened 1 ♠ third hand, S bid 2 ♡, W 3 ◇, N 3 ♡; and S 4 ♡.*
At all tables W led the ◇ K on which E played the ten, and at
many tables W continued with the ◇ Q which let S ruff and gave
him time to set up a spade ruff in dummy to get home.

But at a few tables W took the view that S, not E, started with a
single diamond, and found the glittering defence of shifting to a
trump to stop dummy's spade ruff. Declarer played the ace then low
in spades and the defence returned another trump to clean all trumps
off the board. Exit the spade ruff in dummy—and the game with it.

One skilled declarer countered this line with an automatic squeeze.
At Trick 6 declarer lost the spade to E, ruffed the diamond return,
and cashed two trumps, leaving:

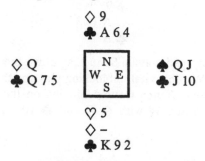

On the last trump lead dummy shed a club, and W was automatically squeezed. If E—very difficult—leads a club when in with the
third spade, the squeeze is broken.

Endings in Series

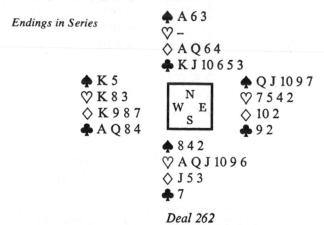

Deal 262

SAB: E opens 3 ♠ third hand, S says 4 ♡ end.

SQUEEZE

At rubber game W bid 1 ♣, N doubled, E 1 ♠, S 2 ♡; N 3 ♣, and S 4 ♡.

W led the king of spades.

How do you plan to circumvent two of your five top losers?

Dummy ducked the ♠ K then won the ♠ 5 continuation. The ♠ 4, 3 and 2 in view coupled with E's 1 ♠ bid marked W now out of spades. Also W's opening 1 ♣ bid marked most missing honours with W, so dummy led the ♣ K to improve chances of keeping E out of the lead, and W's ace won. Partially end-played, W exited safely with a low trump to S's ten. S played ace then queen of trumps, totally end-playing W this time. W returned a low diamond, which S let ride round to the knave. S drew trumps and finessed the ◇ Q in dummy; he then ruffed a club, leaving:

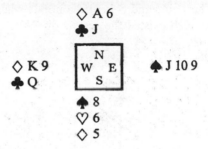

```
              ◇ A 6
              ♣ J

    ◇ K 9        N        ♠ J 10 9
    ♣ Q       W     E
                  S
              ♠ 8
              ♡ 6
              ◇ 5
```

S led the heart to squeeze W one way. In this deal, S both end-played and squeezed, each manœuvre netting him an extra trick.

Probably the most obscure simple squeeze to uncover is one hiding behind the screen of reverse dummy play, as below:

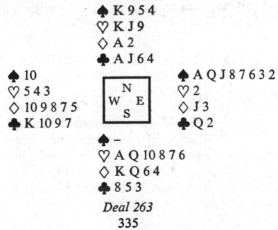

```
                  ♠ K 9 5 4
                  ♡ K J 9
                  ◇ A 2
                  ♣ A J 6 4

    ♠ 10                          ♠ A Q J 8 7 6 3 2
    ♡ 5 4 3            N          ♡ 2
    ◇ 10 9 8 7 5    W     E       ◇ J 3
    ♣ K 10 9 7          S         ♣ Q 2

                  ♠ -
                  ♡ A Q 10 8 7 6
                  ◇ K Q 6 4
                  ♣ 8 5 3
```

Deal 263

335

FILE Z

At rubber game N bid 1 NT, E 4 ♠, and S 6 ♡.

E's pre-emptive 4 ♠ overcall crowded S, but he was not the type to be pushed around so he decided to have a go at slam. If N has little or nothing in spades, his advertised sixteen points should put fur on those bare spots of S's suits.

W led the ♠ 10. How do you play it?

S ruffed the ♠ 10, won the ♡ 9 in dummy, and ruffed another spade. Next S finessed dummy's ♣ J to the queen in E, primarily to 'rectify the count' of tricks for a possible squeeze. E returned a club to the ace in dummy, to try to break up the impending disaster. S ruffed a third spade, re-entered dummy via the ♡ J, and S ruffed the last spade with his last trump. W heroically under-trumped to avoid the squeeze in the minors, but his escape was only temporary. Dummy won the ◇ A, and S kept diamonds when dummy cashed the last trump which twisted the screws on W.

True Trump Squeeze

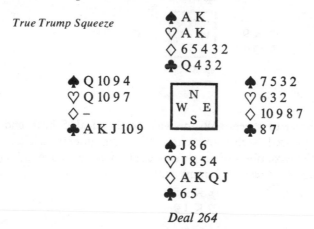

♠ A K
♡ A K
◇ 6 5 4 3 2
♣ Q 4 3 2

♠ Q 10 9 4
♡ Q 10 9 7
◇ –
♣ A K J 10 9

♠ 7 5 3 2
♡ 6 3 2
◇ 10 9 8 7
♣ 8 7

♠ J 8 6
♡ J 8 5 4
◇ A K Q J
♣ 6 5

Deal 264

W opened 1 ♣, N doubled, S bid 2 ♡; N 2 NT, S 3 ◇; and N 5 ◇. W led his king, ace, then knave of clubs.

Should dummy cover the knave of clubs?

Dummy *must* cover (lest, as happens, E holds all four unseen diamonds). E trumps and S over-ruffs. S wins a trump to test the split. It proves the worst possible so that S cannot ruff dummy's club loser lest he promote a natural trump trick for E. So dummy cashes his hearts, S wins a trump to re-enter, and dummy ruffs a low heart without dropping the queen. Finally dummy cashes his spades to develop the *true trump squeeze* on the next page.

SQUEEZE

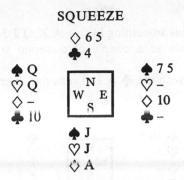

```
              ◇ 6 5
              ♣ 4
   ♠ Q                    ♠ 7 5
   ♡ Q        N           ♡ –
   ◇ –      W   E         ◇ 10
   ♣ 10       S           ♣ –
              ♠ J
              ♡ J
              ◇ A
```

S draws E's trump, *squeezing W in three singletons*! If W sheds a queen, S scores the knave of her suit; otherwise dummy ruffs a knave and scores the four of clubs. The squeeze is automatic.

Squeeze Jettison

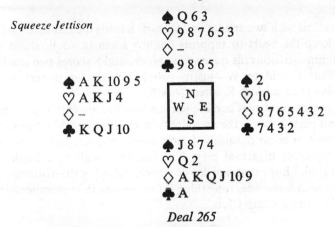

```
                    ♠ Q 6 3
                    ♡ 9 8 7 6 5 3
                    ◇ –
                    ♣ 9 8 6 5
   ♠ A K 10 9 5                    ♠ 2
   ♡ A K J 4          N            ♡ 10
   ◇ –              W   E          ◇ 8 7 6 5 4 3 2
   ♣ K Q J 10         S            ♣ 7 4 3 2
                    ♠ J 8 7 4
                    ♡ Q 2
                    ◇ A K Q J 10 9
                    ♣ A
```

Deal 265

S bid 3 NT (Acol) and W doubled.

E (reading S for a solid club suit for the specialized bid) may think he has good cause to rescue the double by calling 4 ◇ ; but if he does, his side will contract for a bushel of trouble.

W led the ♠ K, ♠ A, ♡ K and ♡ A, dropping S's queen, and E discarded clubs. Next W shifted to the ♣ K at Trick 5.

How do you win nine tricks against any defence and distribution?

W can, of course, break the contract by taking his knave of hearts at Trick 5, but—greedy or ambitious or imaginative—he had visions of bigger things. W wanted to stifle dummy's hearts until he had set up three club tricks. This play *seems* safe despite the great diamond suit advertised (to W at least) by S's opening 3 NT bid. W and dummy are both void of diamonds, placing E with all the missing ones, and if S holds something like ◇ A K Q J 3 2, W reckons that E will surely come to a couple of diamond tricks. Even one is enough!

S wins Trick 5 with the ♣ A and runs five diamonds, leaving:

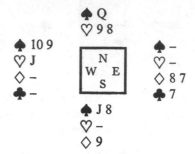

W is marked with two spades and a heart. S leads the last diamond. W must keep the heart to suppress dummy's hearts, so W sheds a spade, dummy jettisons his queen to unblock, and S scores two spade tricks. What E said to W—justly—would scorch the paper! W's correct play is to lead ♣ K after ♡ A K.

The true trump squeeze and the jettison squeeze are extremely rare in practical play, because they require such exacting combinations of circumstance to occur naturally. I have never seen a report of either of these squeezes in actual play. The last two deals are, frankly, manufactured. I hope that one day someone will enjoy the distinction of playing such a squeeze, something far more rare than membership in the *élite* Grand Coup Club.

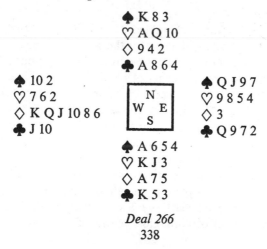

Deal 266

SQUEEZE

Not vulnerable S bid 1 NT (Acol) and N 3 NT.

W leads the ◇ K and you hold up the ace. W continues with the ◇ 10 on which E sheds a heart.

Do you win the second diamond lead?

Clearly the deal is one of those affairs with eight tricks on top, requiring a 3–3 black suit split or a squeeze for Trick No. 9.

W's long diamond suit suggests that E is long in the black suits. S lets the ◇ 10 win to rectify the count for a squeeze. S wins the third diamond lead and E sheds another heart.

S wins three heart tricks and the last one does the business on E, who is now down to two four-card black suits and no saving discard. He elected to shed a spade, so declarer played the king, ace then low in spades to set up his fourth spade.

The squeeze in this case is not a true end-play but a *preparatory play*, which paves the way for declarer to set up a long suit trick in the end.

Tribe 2. Compound Squeezes

Double Squeeze

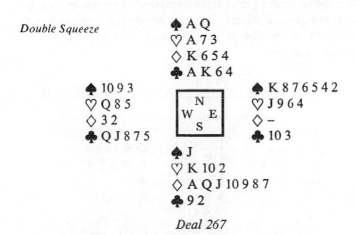

Deal 267

S bid 3 ◇, N 4 NT; S 5 ◇, N 5 NT; S 6 ◇ and N 7 ◇.

S has too good a hand for an opening three-bid, for modern preemption is usually based on trash.

W led the ♠ 10. Do you finesse?

Captain Edwin G. Davis showed us this hand. Declarer has a heart loser which may go off on the ♠ A after the spade finesse wins. But declarer strongly suspected that the ♠ K was wrong and estimated that the chances for a squeeze were better than those for the finesse. So declarer 'flew' with the ♠ A in dummy, drew trumps, and ruffed the third club lead to establish a club threat against W in case he held four or more clubs. Next S ran trumps to this position:

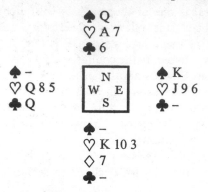

When S led his last diamond, W had to shed a heart to stop dummy's club; dummy threw the club, now useless, and E was squeezed. Note that the squeeze against both opponents operates on one lead.

When the two forced-discard elements of a double squeeze occur on different tricks, the double squeeze becomes a progressive squeeze as shown in the next deal.

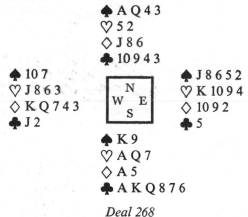

Deal 268

S bid 1 ♣, N 1 ♠; and S 6 NT.
W led the ◇ K.
Mr. Ransford M. Smith of Augusta, Maine, won top score on this board in the Puritan Pairs of 14th June 1953 at Scituate, Massa-

chusetts. He collected an extra trick for thirteen tricks in all by finding the ♡ K right plus a squeeze.

If E holds the ♡ K, how do you do likewise?

Writes Mr. Smith, 'I admit it was a plunge to call 6 NT.' However, his play eclipsed his calling here. He won the ◇ K with the ace, won five club tricks and the ♠ K, leaving:

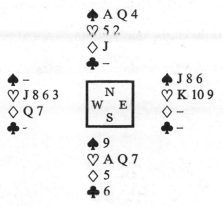

```
                    ♠ A Q 4
                    ♡ 5 2
                    ◇ J
                    ♣ —
    ♠ —                         ♠ J 8 6
    ♡ J 8 6 3       N           ♡ K 10 9
    ◇ Q 7        W     E        ◇ —
    ♣ —             S           ♣ —
                    ♠ 9
                    ♡ A Q 7
                    ◇ 5
                    ♣ 6
```

When Mr. Smith led his last club, W and N shed hearts. This preparatory squeeze forced E to shed a heart also, in order to guard spades. Next, dummy won a top spade on which W shed a diamond. Dummy won another spade on which S discarded his diamond and W was in great pain. W had to hold the top diamond against the knave so, perforce, he shed another heart. S finessed the ♡ Q to win and collected three heart tricks.

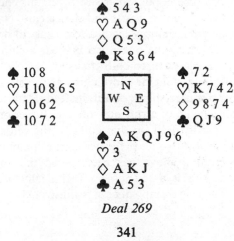

```
                    ♠ 5 4 3
                    ♡ A Q 9
                    ◇ Q 5 3
                    ♣ K 8 6 4
    ♠ 10 8                        ♠ 7 2
    ♡ J 10 8 6 5     N            ♡ K 7 4 2
    ◇ 10 6 2      W     E         ◇ 9 8 7 4
    ♣ 10 7 2         S            ♣ Q J 9
                    ♠ A K Q J 9 6
                    ♡ 3
                    ◇ A K J
                    ♣ A 5 3
```

Deal 269

341

S bid 2 ♠, N 3 NT; S 4 NT, N 5 ◇; S 5 NT, N 6 ◇; and S 7 ♠.
When N's Blackwood responses showed the missing ace and a king which let S count eleven tricks on top, S reckoned that N must also have a queen or two as part of his early jump response of 3 NT.

W led the knave of hearts.

If the ♡ J opening is from the top of the imperfect sequence, J 10 8, how can you wrap up thirteen tricks against any defence and distribution?

The ending is the classic 'double trump squeeze' based on a scoop threat against W.

Dummy's ace wins the heart opening. S wins five trump tricks and two top diamonds, leaving:

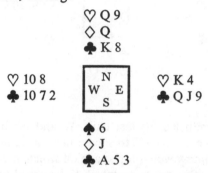

```
            ♡ Q 9
            ◇ Q
            ♣ K 8

  ♡ 10 8      N      ♡ K 4
  ♣ 10 7 2  W   E    ♣ Q J 9
                S
            ♠ 6
            ◇ J
            ♣ A 5 3
```

Dummy wins the diamond, which automatically ruins both defenders. If W sheds a heart, dummy next leads the ♡ Q to scoop W's now blank ten simultaneously forcing E's king. If E covers, S ruffs to make N's nine good; otherwise S gets his club discard at once. Hence W must keep two hearts and shed a club. Now E cannot shed a heart! If he does, dummy leads a low heart to drop the king which S ruffs, establishing the queen, so E sheds a club also. These club discards give declarer three club tricks.

Note that if W holds four or more clubs at the start, only W is caught in the scoop-squeeze play; and if, instead, E started with four clubs, E is the sole victim of a ruff-out squeeze. Either of these plays can, and does, occur by itself on the scuffle of the verdant baize. In the deal just studied, the two plays formed a true compound squeeze.

Although the ending above has been called the double trump squeeze for years, this is a misnomer. Technically it is a double squeeze *ruffout*. The *true* trump squeeze is illustrated by *Deal 262*.

SQUEEZE

Tribe 3. Imperfect Squeezes

False Triple Squeeze

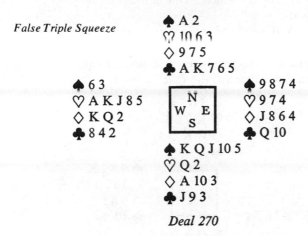

```
              ♠ A 2
              ♡ 10 6 3
              ◇ 9 7 5
              ♣ A K 7 6 5
♠ 6 3                          ♠ 9 8 7 4
♡ A K J 8 5      N             ♡ 9 7 4
◇ K Q 2        W   E           ◇ J 8 6 4
♣ 8 4 2          S             ♣ Q 10
              ♠ K Q J 10 5
              ♡ Q 2
              ◇ A 10 3
              ♣ J 9 3
```

Deal 270

N bid 1 ♣, S 1 ♠, W 2 ♡; S 3 ♠ and N 4 ♠.

W led the ♡ K, ♡ A, then shifted to the ◇ K on which E deposited the eight to show the knave also. S won with his ace.

If you are a declarer, how do you manage clubs?

S wins five trump tricks at once. If you are W, what cards do you keep?

S drew trumps, developing this ending:

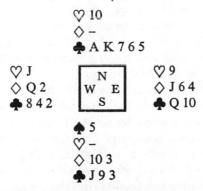

```
              ♡ 10
              ◇ -
              ♣ A K 7 6 5
♡ J                            ♡ 9
◇ Q 2           N              ◇ J 6 4
♣ 8 4 2       W   E            ♣ Q 10
                S
              ♠ 5
              ♡ -
              ◇ 10 3
              ♣ J 9 3
```

At this point S could do nothing but pray successfully. S must drop doubleton club honours AND coax a club discard, so S led his last trump to 'squeeze' W in three suits. W discarded a club without fear or imagination, and dummy parked the heart. S took care to

343

lead the ♣ 9 to unblock, and dummy's king won. Next dummy laid down the ♣ A, dropping the queen on which S completed his un-block by contributing the knave. This let dummy run clubs for S's diamond discards.

When W chucked a club, his only thought was that his clubs were typical of the usual trash he holds. He failed to consider that his eight—out-ranking dummy's highest non-honour card—might be a stopper. W had a safe discard, the ◇ 2 (or even ◇ Q!).

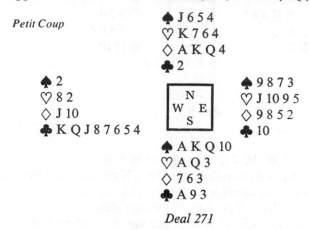

Petit Coup

	♠ J 6 5 4	
	♡ K 7 6 4	
	◇ A K Q 4	
	♣ 2	
♠ 2		♠ 9 8 7 3
♡ 8 2	N	♡ J 10 9 5
◇ J 10	W E	◇ 9 8 5 2
♣ K Q J 8 7 6 5 4	S	♣ 10
	♠ A K Q 10	
	♡ A Q 3	
	◇ 7 6 3	
	♣ A 9 3	

Deal 271

At rubber game S bid 1 ♠, W 4 ♣, N 4 ♠; S 5 ♣ (ace), N 5 ◇ (ace); S 5 ♡ (ace), and N 7 ♠.

W led the ♣ K and E dropped the ♣ 10.

How do you go after thirteen tricks?

S won the ♣ A and ruffed a club with dummy's knave to shut out an over-ruff by E, indicated by W's vulnerable 4 ♣ pre-empt, and E chucked a diamond. S drew trumps and later dummy scored FOUR diamond tricks because E had unguarded the suit.

At Trick 2 a heart discard by E instead of a diamond would only be swopping horses in mid-stream; but E *can* break the contract by the Petit Coup—under-trumping! This play uncovers the one-way squeeze for declarer—with E sitting the wrong way for declarer, because dummy, who holds both red suit threats, must finally discard before E. The position is a pseudo- or false squeeze.

SQUEEZE

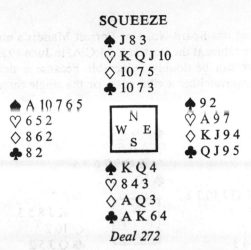

```
              ♠ J 8 3
              ♡ K Q J 10
              ◇ 10 7 5
              ♣ 10 7 3
♠ A 10 7 6 5              ♠ 9 2
♡ 6 5 2       N          ♡ A 9 7
◇ 8 6 2    W   E         ◇ K J 9 4
♣ 8 2         S          ♣ Q J 9 5
              ♠ K Q 4
              ♡ 8 4 3
              ◇ A Q 3
              ♣ A K 6 4
```

Deal 272

At game-all, S bid 1 NT, N 2 NT; and S 3 NT.

W led the ♠ 6, which ran to the nine and queen.

Where do you dig up nine tricks?

S shifted to hearts at Trick 2 and E held up his ace. S finessed the ◇ Q which won, and shifted back to hearts. E held up his ace again but he had to win the third heart lead. E returned the ♠ 2 and S played the king, hoping to coax out the ace but W ducked lest dummy's knave serve as entry to score the fourth heart. S led another spade which W won, and W won another spade, leaving:

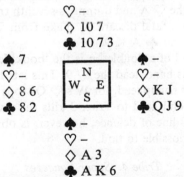

```
              ♡ –
              ◇ 10 7
              ♣ 10 7 3
♠ 7                      ♠ –
♡ –           N          ♡ –
◇ 8 6      W   E         ◇ K J
♣ 8 2         S          ♣ Q J 9
              ♠ –
              ♡ –
              ◇ A 3
              ♣ A K 6
```

W led his last spade and dummy shed a club. Caught in the throes of the induced (or 'suicide') squeeze, E got noisy and justifiably crimed W for not leading a diamond or a club instead of taking his last spade.

Give opponents enough chance to commit *hara-kiri*, and often they will accommodate you.

345

FILE Z

The next deal was Board No. 1 at Forrest Maddix's master point night of sixteen tables at the Boston Y.M.C.A. in June 1953. It shows how a squeeze can be doubly vulnerable because a defender can prematurely remove either a vital entry or the single threat card.

Two-Way Defence

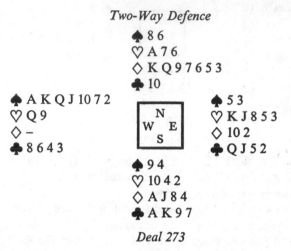

Deal 273

S bid 1 ◇, W 1 ♠, N 3 ◇; S 4 ♣, W 4 ♠, and N 5 ◇.

W led the ♠ K, and the ♠ 10; and shifted to the ♡ Q.

With ten tricks on top, how do you promote No. 11?

Dummy won the ♡ A and dummy's seventh trump lead squeezed E, then down to a fatal discard to make from ♡ K and ♣ Q J 6 under S's ♡ 10 and ♣ A K 9.

The higher card of a doubleton is the 'book' lead, but at Trick 3, W should, on this hand, lead the ♡ 9! This lets E later shed his last heart on the final trump lead, for W's ♡ Q stops the suit.

Alternately, a club lead to Trick 3 kills the pivotal entry to S for the squeeze. This line of defence, however, is obscure, questionable and virtually impossible to find.

Tribe 4. Super Squeezes

The deal below occurred at a duplicate game *chez* Mrs. J. Herbert Mead in Arlington, Massachusetts, back in the spring of 1949.

SQUEEZE

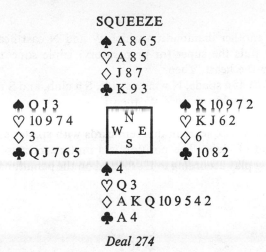

♠ A 8 6 5
♡ A 8 5
◇ J 8 7
♣ K 9 3

♠ Q J 3   ♠ K 10 9 7 2
♡ 10 9 7 4   ♡ K J 6 2
◇ 3   ◇ 6
♣ Q J 7 6 5   ♣ 10 8 2

♠ 4
♡ Q 3
◇ A K Q 10 9 5 4 2
♣ A 4

Deal 274

I sat S and pushed my partner, Mrs. Harold B. Wood of Arlington, into an impossible 7 NT contract, which she made against soft defence. The optimum contract is 7 ◇ which cannot be defeated against perfect play by declarer. Acolites (if Blackwooding) would probably bid the hand thus: S 2 ◇, N 3 NT; S 4 NT, N 5 ♡; S 5 NT, N 6 ◇; and S 7 ◇; *or* 2 ◇ – 3 ◇; 4 ♣ – 4 NT (Culbertson); 5 NT (2 aces) – 6 ◇; 7 ◇.

If W opens the ♠ Q, N wins. S ruffs a spade, draws trumps, cashes the ♣ A, and runs all but one trump to develop a ruff-out squeeze against E holding ♠ K 10 and ♡ K J with a fatal discard still to make after dummy wins the ♣ K. Any other opening, except a heart, lets S develop the same squeeze.

If W opens the ♡ 10 (or any heart), declarer can develop one of Dr. Love's pet mutates. Dummy takes the ♡ A, and S plays off six trumps, leaving:

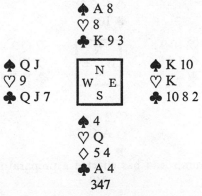

♠ A 8
♡ 8
♣ K 9 3

♠ Q J   ♠ K 10
♡ 9   ♡ K
♣ Q J 7   ♣ 10 8 2

♠ 4
♡ Q
◇ 5 4
♣ A 4

S wins another diamond on which W and N cast hearts and immediately puts the super (or preparatory) triple squeeze on E. He must keep the heart. Then:

A. If E casts a spade, N wins a spade, S a club, and S plays his last diamond to double-squeeze W, then E.

B. If E casts a club, N then S each win a club to arrive at the same double one-way squeeze in different cards with spades as the middle suit instead of clubs. The position is a mutate, because the threats shift during play according to E's discard on the penultimate diamond lead.

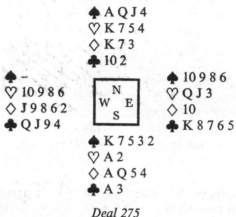

```
              ♠ A Q J 4
              ♡ K 7 5 4
              ◇ K 7 3
              ♣ 10 2
  ♠ -                          ♠ 10 9 8 6
  ♡ 10 9 8 6      N            ♡ Q J 3
  ◇ J 9 8 6 2   W   E          ◇ 10
  ♣ Q J 9 4       S            ♣ K 8 7 6 5
              ♠ K 7 5 3 2
              ♡ A 2
              ◇ A Q 5 4
              ♣ A 3
```

Deal 275

In this deal, Deal 188 from File R for Ruff, S made his contract of 6 ♠ by reverse dummy play. An alternate line is a complex squeeze.

W led the ♣ Q to the ace. Declarer wins four trump tricks and the ♡ A on which E plays his knave to unblock, leaving:

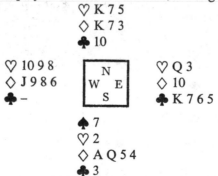

```
              ♡ K 7 5
              ◇ K 7 3
              ♣ 10
  ♡ 10 9 8                     ♡ Q 3
  ◇ J 9 8 6      N             ◇ 10
  ♣ -         W   E            ♣ K 7 6 5
                S
              ♠ 7
              ♡ 2
              ◇ A Q 5 4
              ♣ 3
```

The fourth trump lead has effected a preparatory triple squeeze on W. He had to shed his last club in order to protect diamonds against the drop and hearts against the ruff-out.

In the matrix above, N wins the ♡ K. Then:

A. If E plays low, N loses a heart to E, and S sheds the club. S ruffs a club return (or wins a diamond return and plays the trump), squeezing W automatically in the red suits.

B. If E unblocks the ♡ Q on the king play, dummy loses the club to E, and W sheds a heart in comfort with the ruff-out threat gone. However, this threat forces E to return a club which S ruffs, squeezing W; or to return a diamond which S wins and S leads the last trump to squeeze W.

Trap. If S loses the club immediately to rectify the count, W sheds a heart and E wins. *E must return a club* to force S's trump and destroy the heart ruff-out threat on W, and W sheds another heart safely.

The next deal illustrates a bizarre mutate squeeze which Frank K. Perkins reported in *The Boston Herald*. The preparatory play squeezed W in three suits and E in two, and the final squeeze again squeezed W in three suits and E in two!

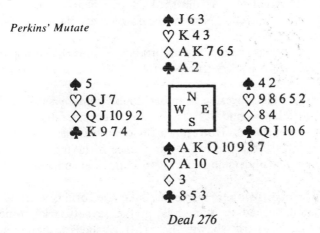

Perkins' Mutate

♠ J 6 3
♡ K 4 3
◇ A K 7 6 5
♣ A 2

♠ 5
♡ Q J 7
◇ Q J 10 9 2
♣ K 9 7 4

♠ 4 2
♡ 9 8 6 5 2
◇ 8 4
♣ Q J 10 6

♠ A K Q 10 9 8 7
♡ A 10
◇ 3
♣ 8 5 3

Deal 276

Acol bids with Blackwood would be S 2 ♠, N 3 ◇; S 4 ♠, N 4 NT; S 5 ♡, N 5 NT; S 6 ◇, and N 7 ♠.

W leads the ◇ Q. Map out a plan.

Dummy wins the ◇ K. S then dummy each win a trump, dummy cashes the ◇ A for a club discard, and S ruffs a diamond in hopes of setting up the suit, but E discards a heart to prove the long suit game futile. Hence declarer makes himself a discard nuisance by cashing two more trumps to this ending:

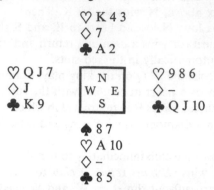

S leads a trump and N sheds the low club. Then:

A. If W sheds a heart, E must shed a club. Note the full range of this preparatory '3–2' squeeze, in three suits against W and in two suits against E. S plays his last trump, again squeezing W in three suits and E in two. W cannot shed another heart lest S score both the ace then ten (in actual play W did shed another heart, ending the game); hence W sheds a club, N sheds the now useless diamond, and E is done in.

B. If W sheds a club, so can E comfortably. N wins the club and S a heart, and S leads his last trump in the one-way double-squeeze ending.

Admittedly all this squeezing is rather double dummyish, and if W does not shed his second heart, S has to do considerable guess-work about enemy shapes. However, if S closely watches both dis-cards and enemy squirms, he has a fair chance of taking the right view—but only if he understands the complications of super-squeeze technique.

Mr. H. Nelson Brown, Jr. of China Lake California, wants to know, "What happened to diamonds on the seventh trick (one previous to that in matrix shown above)? If W sheds a diamond, S can ruff out and set up a diamond trick in N without further ado."

A probe revealed that a double chuck occurred. In the heat of play, W then N each shed a diamond in a momentary lapse. How-ever, if W keeps diamonds, other mutates occur.

A CATALOGUE OF SELECTED DOVER
BOOKS IN ALL FIELDS OF INTEREST

CONDITIONED REFLEXES, Ivan P. Pavlov. Full translation of most complete statement of Pavlov's work; cerebral damage, conditioned reflex, experiments with dogs, sleep, similar topics of great importance. 430pp. 5⅜ x 8½.   60614-7 Pa. $4.50

NOTES ON NURSING: WHAT IT IS, AND WHAT IT IS NOT, Florence Nightingale. Outspoken writings by founder of modern nursing. When first published (1860) it played an important role in much needed revolution in nursing. Still stimulating. 140pp. 5⅜ x 8½.   22340-X Pa. $2.50

HARTER'S PICTURE ARCHIVE FOR COLLAGE AND ILLUSTRATION, Jim Harter. Over 300 authentic, rare 19th-century engravings selected by noted collagist for artists, designers, decoupeurs, etc. Machines, people, animals, etc., printed one side of page. 25 scene plates for backgrounds. 6 collages by Harter, Satty, Singer, Evans. Introduction. 192pp. 8⅞ x 11¾.   23659-5 Pa. $5.00

MANUAL OF TRADITIONAL WOOD CARVING, edited by Paul N. Hasluck. Possibly the best book in English on the craft of wood carving. Practical instructions, along with 1,146 working drawings and photographic illustrations. Formerly titled *Cassell's Wood Carving*. 576pp. 6½ x 9¼.
                                      23489-4 Pa. $7.95

THE PRINCIPLES AND PRACTICE OF HAND OR SIMPLE TURNING, John Jacob Holtzapffel. Full coverage of basic lathe techniques—history and development, special apparatus, softwood turning, hardwood turning, metal turning. Many projects—billiard ball, works formed within a sphere, egg cups, ash trays, vases, jardiniers, others—included. 1881 edition. 800 illustrations. 592pp. 6⅛ x 9¼.   23365-0 Clothbd. $15.00

THE JOY OF HANDWEAVING, Osma Tod. Only book you need for hand weaving. Fundamentals, threads, weaves, plus numerous projects for small board-loom, two-harness, tapestry, laid-in, four-harness weaving and more. Over 160 illustrations. 2nd revised edition. 352pp. 6½ x 9¼.
                                      23458-4 Pa. $5.00

THE BOOK OF WOOD CARVING, Charles Marshall Sayers. Still finest book for beginning student in wood sculpture. Noted teacher, craftsman discusses fundamentals, technique; gives 34 designs, over 34 projects for panels, bookends, mirrors, etc. "Absolutely first-rate"—E. J. Tangerman. 33 photos. 118pp. 7¾ x 10⅝.   23654-4 Pa. $3.00

A CATALOGUE OF
SELECTED DOVER BOOKS
IN ALL FIELDS OF INTEREST

DRAWINGS OF WILLIAM BLAKE, William Blake. 92 plates from Book of Job, *Divine Comedy, Paradise Lost,* visionary heads, mythological figures, Laocoon, etc. Selection, introduction, commentary by Sir Geoffrey Keynes. 178pp. 8⅛ x 11. 22303-5 Pa. $4.00

ENGRAVINGS OF HOGARTH, William Hogarth. 101 of Hogarth's greatest works: *Rake's Progress, Harlot's Progress, Illustrations for Hudibras, Before and After, Beer Street and Gin Lane,* many more. Full commentary. 256pp. 11 x 13¾. 22479-1 Pa. $7.95

DAUMIER: 120 GREAT LITHOGRAPHS, Honore Daumier. Wide-ranging collection of lithographs by the greatest caricaturist of the 19th century. Concentrates on eternally popular series on lawyers, on married life, on liberated women, etc. Selection, introduction, and notes on plates by Charles F. Ramus. Total of 158pp. 9⅜ x 12¼. 23512-2 Pa. $5.50

DRAWINGS OF MUCHA, Alphonse Maria Mucha. Work reveals draftsman of highest caliber: studies for famous posters and paintings, renderings for book illustrations and ads, etc. 70 works, 9 in color; including 6 items not drawings. Introduction. List of illustrations. 72pp. 9⅜ x 12¼. (Available in U.S. only) 23672-2 Pa. $4.00

GIOVANNI BATTISTA PIRANESI: DRAWINGS IN THE PIERPONT MORGAN LIBRARY, Giovanni Battista Piranesi. For first time ever all of Morgan Library's collection, world's largest. 167 illustrations of rare Piranesi drawings—archeological, architectural, decorative and visionary. Essay, detailed list of drawings, chronology, captions. Edited by Felice Stampfle. 144pp. 9⅜ x 12¼. 23714-1 Pa. $7.50

NEW YORK ETCHINGS (1905-1949), John Sloan. All of important American artist's N.Y. life etchings. 67 works include some of his best art; also lively historical record—Greenwich Village, tenement scenes. Edited by Sloan's widow. Introduction and captions. 79pp. 8⅜ x 11¼. 23651-X Pa. $4.00

CHINESE PAINTING AND CALLIGRAPHY: A PICTORIAL SURVEY, Wan-go Weng. 69 fine examples from John M. Crawford's matchless private collection: landscapes, birds, flowers, human figures, etc., plus calligraphy. Every basic form included: hanging scrolls, handscrolls, album leaves, fans, etc. 109 illustrations. Introduction. Captions. 192pp. 8⅞ x 11¾. 23707-9 Pa. $7.95

DRAWINGS OF REMBRANDT, edited by Seymour Slive. Updated Lippmann, Hofstede de Groot edition, with definitive scholarly apparatus. All portraits, biblical sketches, landscapes, nudes, Oriental figures, classical studies, together with selection of work by followers. 550 illustrations. Total of 630pp. 9⅛ x 12¼. 21485-0, 21486-9 Pa., Two-vol. set $15.00

THE DISASTERS OF WAR, Francisco Goya. 83 etchings record horrors of Napoleonic wars in Spain and war in general. Reprint of 1st edition, plus 3 additional plates. Introduction by Philip Hofer. 97pp. 9⅜ x 8¼. 21872-4 Pa. $3.75

THE EARLY WORK OF AUBREY BEARDSLEY, Aubrey Beardsley. 157 plates, 2 in color: *Manon Lescaut, Madame Bovary, Morte Darthur, Salome,* other. Introduction by H. Marillier. 182pp. 8⅛ x 11. 21816-3 Pa. $4.50

THE LATER WORK OF AUBREY BEARDSLEY, Aubrey Beardsley. Exotic masterpieces of full maturity: *Venus and Tannhauser, Lysistrata, Rape of the Lock, Volpone,* Savoy material, etc. 174 plates, 2 in color. 186pp. 8⅛ x 11. 21817-1 Pa. $4.50

THOMAS NAST'S CHRISTMAS DRAWINGS, Thomas Nast. Almost all Christmas drawings by creator of image of Santa Claus as we know it, and one of America's foremost illustrators and political cartoonists. 66 illustrations. 3 illustrations in color on covers. 96pp. 8⅜ x 11¼. 23660-9 Pa. $3.50

THE DORÉ ILLUSTRATIONS FOR DANTE'S DIVINE COMEDY, Gustave Doré. All 135 plates from Inferno, Purgatory, Paradise; fantastic tortures, infernal landscapes, celestial wonders. Each plate with appropriate (translated) verses. 141pp. 9 x 12. 23231-X Pa. $4.50

DORÉ'S ILLUSTRATIONS FOR RABELAIS, Gustave Doré. 252 striking illustrations of *Gargantua and Pantagruel* books by foremost 19th-century illustrator. Including 60 plates, 192 delightful smaller illustrations. 153pp. 9 x 12. 23656-0 Pa. $5.00

LONDON: A PILGRIMAGE, Gustave Doré, Blanchard Jerrold. Squalor, riches, misery, beauty of mid-Victorian metropolis; 55 wonderful plates, 125 other illustrations, full social, cultural text by Jerrold. 191pp. of text. 9⅜ x 12¼. 22306-X Pa. $6.00

THE RIME OF THE ANCIENT MARINER, Gustave Doré, S. T. Coleridge. Dore's finest work, 34 plates capture moods, subtleties of poem. Full text. Introduction by Millicent Rose. 77pp. 9¼ x 12. 22305-1 Pa. $3.50

THE DORE BIBLE ILLUSTRATIONS, Gustave Doré. All wonderful, detailed plates: Adam and Eve, Flood, Babylon, Life of Jesus, etc. Brief King James text with each plate. Introduction by Millicent Rose. 241 plates. 241pp. 9 x 12. 23004-X Pa. $6.00

THE COMPLETE ENGRAVINGS, ETCHINGS AND DRYPOINTS OF ALBRECHT DURER. "Knight, Death and Devil"; "Melencolia," and more—all Dürer's known works in all three media, including 6 works formerly attributed to him. 120 plates. 235pp. 8⅜ x 11¼. 22851-7 Pa. $6.50

MAXIMILIAN'S TRIUMPHAL ARCH, Albrecht Dürer and others. Incredible monument of woodcut art: 8 foot high elaborate arch—heraldic figures, humans, battle scenes, fantastic elements—that you can assemble yourself. Printed on one side, layout for assembly. 143pp. 11 x 16. 21451-6 Pa. $5.00

THE COMPLETE WOODCUTS OF ALBRECHT DURER, edited by Dr. W. Kurth. 346 in all: "Old Testament," "St. Jerome," "Passion," "Life of Virgin," Apocalypse," many others. Introduction by Campbell Dodgson. 285pp. 8½ x 12¼. 21097-9 Pa. $6.95

DRAWINGS OF ALBRECHT DURER, edited by Heinrich Wolfflin. 81 plates show development from youth to full style. Many favorites; many new. Introduction by Alfred Werner. 96pp. 8⅛ x 11. 22352-3 Pa. $5.00

THE HUMAN FIGURE, Albrecht Dürer. Experiments in various techniques—stereometric, progressive proportional, and others. Also life studies that rank among finest ever done. Complete reprinting of Dresden Sketchbook. 170 plates. 355pp. 8⅜ x 11¼. 21042-1 Pa. $7.95

OF THE JUST SHAPING OF LETTERS, Albrecht Dürer. Renaissance artist explains design of Roman majuscules by geometry, also Gothic lower and capitals. Grolier Club edition. 43pp. 7⅞ x 10¾ 21306-4 Pa. $3.00

TEN BOOKS ON ARCHITECTURE, Vitruvius. The most important book ever written on architecture. Early Roman aesthetics, technology, classical orders, site selection, all other aspects. Stands behind everything since. Morgan translation. 331pp. 5⅜ x 8½. 20645-9 Pa. $4.00

THE FOUR BOOKS OF ARCHITECTURE, Andrea Palladio. 16th-century classic responsible for Palladian movement and style. Covers classical architectural remains, Renaissance revivals, classical orders, etc. 1738 Ware English edition. Introduction by A. Placzek. 216 plates. 110pp. of text. 9½ x 12¾. 21308-0 Pa. $8.95

HORIZONS, Norman Bel Geddes. Great industrialist stage designer, "father of streamlining," on application of aesthetics to transportation, amusement, architecture, etc. 1932 prophetic account; function, theory, specific projects. 222 illustrations. 312pp. 7⅞ x 10¾. 23514-9 Pa. $6.95

FRANK LLOYD WRIGHT'S FALLINGWATER, Donald Hoffmann. Full, illustrated story of conception and building of Wright's masterwork at Bear Run, Pa. 100 photographs of site, construction, and details of completed structure. 112pp. 9¼ x 10. 23671-4 Pa. $5.00

THE ELEMENTS OF DRAWING, John Ruskin. Timeless classic by great Viltorian; starts with basic ideas, works through more difficult. Many practical exercises. 48 illustrations. Introduction by Lawrence Campbell. 228pp. 5⅜ x 8½. 22730-8 Pa. $2.75

GIST OF ART, John Sloan. Greatest modern American teacher, Art Students League, offers innumerable hints, instructions, guided comments to help you in painting. Not a formal course. 46 illustrations. Introduction by Helen Sloan. 200pp. 5⅜ x 8½. 23435-5 Pa. $3.50

CATALOGUE OF DOVER BOOKS

THE ANATOMY OF THE HORSE, George Stubbs. Often considered the great masterpiece of animal anatomy. Full reproduction of 1766 edition, plus prospectus; original text and modernized text. 36 plates. Introduction by Eleanor Garvey. 121pp. 11 x 14¾. 23402-9 Pa. $6.00

BRIDGMAN'S LIFE DRAWING, George B. Bridgman. More than 500 illustrative drawings and text teach you to abstract the body into its major masses, use light and shade, proportion; as well as specific areas of anatomy, of which Bridgman is master. 192pp. 6½ x 9¼. (Available in U.S. only) 22710-3 Pa. $3.00

ART NOUVEAU DESIGNS IN COLOR, Alphonse Mucha, Maurice Verneuil, Georges Auriol. Full-color reproduction of *Combinaisons ornementales* (c. 1900) by Art Nouveau masters. Floral, animal, geometric, interlacings, swashes—borders, frames, spots—all incredibly beautiful. 60 plates, hundreds of designs. 9⅜ x 8-1/16. 22885-1 Pa. $4.00

FULL-COLOR FLORAL DESIGNS IN THE ART NOUVEAU STYLE, E. A. Seguy. 166 motifs, on 40 plates, from *Les fleurs et leurs applications decoratives* (1902): borders, circular designs, repeats, allovers, "spots." All in authentic Art Nouveau colors. 48pp. 9⅜ x 12¼. 23439-8 Pa. $5.00

A DIDEROT PICTORIAL ENCYCLOPEDIA OF TRADES AND IN-DUSTRY, edited by Charles C. Gillispie. 485 most interesting plates from the great French Encyclopedia of the 18th century show hundreds of working figures, artifacts, process, land and cityscapes; glassmaking, paper-making, metal extraction, construction, weaving, making furniture, clothing, wigs, dozens of other activities. Plates fully explained. 920pp. 9 x 12. 22284-5, 22285-3 Clothbd., Two-vol. set $40.00

HANDBOOK OF EARLY ADVERTISING ART, Clarence P. Hornung. Largest collection of copyright-free early and antique advertising art ever compiled. Over 6,000 illustrations, from Franklin's time to the 1890's for special effects, novelty. Valuable source, almost inexhaustible.
Pictorial Volume. Agriculture, the zodiac, animals, autos, birds, Christmas, fire engines, flowers, trees, musical instruments, ships, games and sports, much more. Arranged by subject matter and use. 237 plates. 288pp. 9 x 12. 20122-8 Clothbd. $13.50

Typographical Volume. Roman and Gothic faces ranging from 10 point to 300 point, "Barnum," German and Old English faces, script, logotypes, scrolls and flourishes, 1115 ornamental initials, 67 complete alphabets, more. 310 plates. 320pp. 9 x 12. 20123-6 Clothbd. $15.00

CALLIGRAPHY (CALLIGRAPHIA LATINA), J. G. Schwandner. High point of 18th-century ornamental calligraphy. Very ornate initials, scrolls, borders, cherubs, birds, lettered examples. 172pp. 9 x 13. 20475-8 Pa. $6.00

ART FORMS IN NATURE, Ernst Haeckel. Multitude of strangely beautiful natural forms: Radiolaria, Foraminifera, jellyfishes, fungi, turtles, bats, etc. All 100 plates of the 19th-century evolutionist's *Kunstformen der Natur* (1904). 100pp. 9⅜ x 12¼.   22987-4 Pa. $4.50

CHILDREN: A PICTORIAL ARCHIVE FROM NINETEENTH-CENTURY SOURCES, edited by Carol Belanger Grafton. 242 rare, copyright-free wood engravings for artists and designers. Widest such selection available. All illustrations in line. 110pp. 8⅜ x 11¼.
23694-3 Pa. $3.50

WOMEN: A PICTORIAL ARCHIVE FROM NINETEENTH-CENTURY SOURCES, edited by Jim Harter. 391 copyright-free wood engravings for artists and designers selected from rare periodicals. Most extensive such collection available. All illustrations in line. 128pp. 9 x 12.
23703-6 Pa. $4.50

ARABIC ART IN COLOR, Prisse d'Avennes. From the greatest ornamentalists of all time—50 plates in color, rarely seen outside the Near East, rich in suggestion and stimulus. Includes 4 plates on covers. 46pp. 9⅜ x 12¼.   23658-7 Pa. $6.00

AUTHENTIC ALGERIAN CARPET DESIGNS AND MOTIFS, edited by June Beveridge. Algerian carpets are world famous. Dozens of geometrical motifs are charted on grids, color-coded, for weavers, needleworkers, craftsmen, designers. 53 illustrations plus 4 in color. 48pp. 8¼ x 11. (Available in U.S. only)   23650-1 Pa. $1.75

DICTIONARY OF AMERICAN PORTRAITS, edited by Hayward and Blanche Cirker. 4000 important Americans, earliest times to 1905, mostly in clear line. Politicians, writers, soldiers, scientists, inventors, industrialists, Indians, Blacks, women, outlaws, etc. Identificatory information. 756pp. 9¼ x 12¾.   21823-6 Clothbd. $40.00

HOW THE OTHER HALF LIVES, Jacob A. Riis. Journalistic record of filth, degradation, upward drive in New York immigrant slums, shops, around 1900. New edition includes 100 original Riis photos, monuments of early photography. 233pp. 10 x 7⅞.   22012-5 Pa. $6.00

NEW YORK IN THE THIRTIES, Berenice Abbott. Noted photographer's fascinating study of city shows new buildings that have become famous and old sights that have disappeared forever. Insightful commentary. 97 photographs. 97pp. 11⅜ x 10.   22967-X Pa. $5.00

MEN AT WORK, Lewis W. Hine. Famous photographic studies of construction workers, railroad men, factory workers and coal miners. New supplement of 18 photos on Empire State building construction. New introduction by Jonathan L. Doherty. Total of 69 photos. 63pp. 8 x 10¾.
23475-4 Pa. $3.00

THE DEPRESSION YEARS AS PHOTOGRAPHED BY ARTHUR ROTH-STEIN, Arthur Rothstein. First collection devoted entirely to the work of outstanding 1930s photographer: famous dust storm photo, ragged children, unemployed, etc. 120 photographs. Captions. 119pp. 9¼ x 10¾.
23590-4 Pa. $5.00

CAMERA WORK: A PICTORIAL GUIDE, Alfred Stieglitz. All 559 illustrations and plates from the most important periodical in the history of art photography, Camera Work (1903-17). Presented four to a page, reduced in size but still clear, in strict chronological order, with complete captions. Three indexes. Glossary. Bibliography. 176pp. 8⅜ x 11¼.
23591-2 Pa. $6.95

ALVIN LANGDON COBURN, PHOTOGRAPHER, Alvin L. Coburn. Revealing autobiography by one of greatest photographers of 20th century gives insider's version of Photo-Secession, plus comments on his own work. 77 photographs by Coburn. Edited by Helmut and Alison Gernsheim. 160pp. 8⅛ x 11.
23685-4 Pa. $6.00

NEW YORK IN THE FORTIES, Andreas Feininger. 162 brilliant photographs by the well-known photographer, formerly with Life magazine, show commuters, shoppers, Times Square at night, Harlem nightclub, Lower East Side, etc. Introduction and full captions by John von Hartz. 181pp. 9¼ x 10¾.
23585-8 Pa. $6.00

GREAT NEWS PHOTOS AND THE STORIES BEHIND THEM, John Faber. Dramatic volume of 140 great news photos, 1855 through 1976, and revealing stories behind them, with both historical and technical information. Hindenburg disaster, shooting of Oswald, nomination of Jimmy Carter, etc. 160pp. 8¼ x 11.
23667-6 Pa. $5.00

THE ART OF THE CINEMATOGRAPHER, Leonard Maltin. Survey of American cinematography history and anecdotal interviews with 5 masters—Arthur Miller, Hal Mohr, Hal Rosson, Lucien Ballard, and Conrad Hall. Very large selection of behind-the-scenes production photos. 105 photographs. Filmographies. Index. Originally Behind the Camera. 144pp. 8¼ x 11.
23686-2 Pa. $5.00

DESIGNS FOR THE THREE-CORNERED HAT (LE TRICORNE), Pablo Picasso. 32 fabulously rare drawings—including 31 color illustrations of costumes and accessories—for 1919 production of famous ballet. Edited by Parmenia Migel, who has written new introduction. 48pp. 9⅜ x 12¼. (Available in U.S. only)
23709-5 Pa. $5.00

NOTES OF A FILM DIRECTOR, Sergei Eisenstein. Greatest Russian filmmaker explains montage, making of Alexander Nevsky, aesthetics; comments on self, associates, great rivals (Chaplin), similar material. 78 illustrations. 240pp. 5⅜ x 8½.
22392-2 Pa. $4.50

HOLLYWOOD GLAMOUR PORTRAITS, edited by John Kobal. 145 photos capture the stars from 1926-49, the high point in portrait photography. Gable, Harlow, Bogart, Bacall, Hedy Lamarr, Marlene Dietrich, Robert Montgomery, Marlon Brando, Veronica Lake; 94 stars in all. Full background on photographers, technical aspects, much more. Total of 160pp. 8⅜ x 11¼.   23352-9 Pa. $5.00

THE NEW YORK STAGE: FAMOUS PRODUCTIONS IN PHOTO-GRAPHS, edited by Stanley Appelbaum. 148 photographs from Museum of City of New York show 142 plays, 1883-1939. *Peter Pan, The Front Page, Dead End, Our Town,* O'Neill, hundreds of actors and actresses, etc. Full indexes. 154pp. 9½ x 10.   23241-7 Pa. $6.00

MASTERS OF THE DRAMA, John Gassner. Most comprehensive history of the drama, every tradition from Greeks to modern Europe and America, including Orient. Covers 800 dramatists, 2000 plays; biography, plot summaries, criticism, theatre history, etc. 77 illustrations. 890pp. 5⅜ x 8½.
20100-7 Clothbd. $10.00

THE GREAT OPERA STARS IN HISTORIC PHOTOGRAPHS, edited by James Camner. 343 portraits from the 1850s to the 1940s: Tamburini, Mario, Caliapin, Jeritza, Melchior, Melba, Patti, Pinza, Schipa, Caruso, Farrar, Steber, Gobbi, and many more—270 performers in all. Index. 199pp. 8⅜ x 11¼.   23575-0 Pa. $6.50

J. S. BACH, Albert Schweitzer. Great full-length study of Bach, life, background to music, music, by foremost modern scholar. Ernest Newman translation. 650 musical examples. Total of 928pp. 5⅜ x 8½. (Available in U.S. only)   21631-4, 21632-2 Pa., Two-vol. set $10.00

COMPLETE PIANO SONATAS, Ludwig van Beethoven. All sonatas in the fine Schenker edition, with fingering, analytical material. One of best modern editions. Total of 615pp. 9 x 12. (Available in U.S. only)
23134-8, 23135-6 Pa., Two-vol. set $15.00

KEYBOARD MUSIC, J. S. Bach. Bach-Gesellschaft edition. For harpsichord, piano, other keyboard instruments. English Suites, French Suites, Six Partitas, Goldberg Variations, Two-Part Inventions, Three-Part Sinfonias. 312pp. 8⅛ x 11. (Available in U.S. only)   22360-4 Pa. $6.00

FOUR SYMPHONIES IN FULL SCORE, Franz Schubert. Schubert's four most popular symphonies: No. 4 in C Minor ("Tragic"); No. 5 in B-flat Major; No. 8 in B Minor ("Unfinished"); No. 9 in C Major ("Great"). Breitkopf & Hartel edition. Study score. 261pp. 9⅜ x 12¼.
23681-1 Pa. $6.50

THE AUTHENTIC GILBERT & SULLIVAN SONGBOOK, W. S. Gilbert, A. S. Sullivan. Largest selection available; 92 songs, uncut, original keys, in piano rendering approved by Sullivan. Favorites and lesser-known fine numbers. Edited with plot synopses by James Spero. 3 illustrations. 399pp. 9 x 12.   23482-7 Pa. $7.95

PRINCIPLES OF ORCHESTRATION, Nikolay Rimsky-Korsakov. Great classical orchestrator provides fundamentals of tonal resonance, progression of parts, voice and orchestra, tutti effects, much else in major document. 330pp. of musical excerpts. 489pp. 6½ x 9¼.   21266-1 Pa. $6.00

TRISTAN UND ISOLDE, Richard Wagner. Full orchestral score with complete instrumentation. Do not confuse with piano reduction. Commentary by Felix Mottl, great Wagnerian conductor and scholar. Study score. 655pp. 8⅛ x 11.   22915-7 Pa. $12.50

REQUIEM IN FULL SCORE, Giuseppe Verdi. Immensely popular with choral groups and music lovers. Republication of edition published by C. F. Peters, Leipzig, n. d. German frontmaker in English translation. Glossary. Text in Latin. Study score. 204pp. 9⅜ x 12¼.
23682-X Pa. $6.00

COMPLETE CHAMBER MUSIC FOR STRINGS, Felix Mendelssohn. All of Mendelssohn's chamber music: Octet, 2 Quintets, 6 Quartets, and Four Pieces for String Quartet. (Nothing with piano is included). Complete works edition (1874-7). Study score. 283 pp. 9⅜ x 12¼.
23679-X Pa. $6.95

POPULAR SONGS OF NINETEENTH-CENTURY AMERICA, edited by Richard Jackson. 64 most important songs: "Old Oaken Bucket," "Arkansas Traveler," "Yellow Rose of Texas," etc. Authentic original sheet music, full introduction and commentaries. 290pp. 9 x 12.   23270-0 Pa. $6.00

COLLECTED PIANO WORKS, Scott Joplin. Edited by Vera Brodsky Lawrence. Practically all of Joplin's piano works—rags, two-steps, marches, waltzes, etc., 51 works in all. Extensive introduction by Rudi Blesh. Total of 345pp. 9 x 12.   23106-2 Pa. $14.95

BASIC PRINCIPLES OF CLASSICAL BALLET, Agrippina Vaganova. Great Russian theoretician, teacher explains methods for teaching classical ballet; incorporates best from French, Italian, Russian schools. 118 illustrations. 175pp. 5⅜ x 8½.   22036-2 Pa. $2.50

CHINESE CHARACTERS, L. Wieger. Rich analysis of 2300 characters according to traditional systems into primitives. Historical-semantic analysis to phonetics (Classical Mandarin) and radicals. 820pp. 6⅛ x 9¼.
21321-8 Pa. $10.00

EGYPTIAN LANGUAGE: EASY LESSONS IN EGYPTIAN HIERO-GLYPHICS, E. A. Wallis Budge. Foremost Egyptologist offers Egyptian grammar, explanation of hieroglyphics, many reading texts, dictionary of symbols. 246pp. 5 x 7½. (Available in U.S. only)
21394-3 Clothbd. $7.50

AN ETYMOLOGICAL DICTIONARY OF MODERN ENGLISH, Ernest Weekley. Richest, fullest work, by foremost British lexicographer. Detailed word histories. Inexhaustible. Do not confuse this with Concise Etymological Dictionary, which is abridged. Total of 856pp. 6½ x 9¼.
21873-2, 21874-0 Pa., Two-vol. set $12.00

A MAYA GRAMMAR, Alfred M. Tozzer. Practical, useful English-language grammar by the Harvard anthropologist who was one of the three greatest American scholars in the area of Maya culture. Phonetics, grammatical processes, syntax, more. 301pp. 5⅜ x 8½.   23465-7 Pa. $4.00

THE JOURNAL OF HENRY D. THOREAU, edited by Bradford Torrey, F. H. Allen. Complete reprinting of 14 volumes, 1837-61, over two million words; the sourcebooks for *Walden*, etc. Definitive. All original sketches, plus 75 photographs. Introduction by Walter Harding. Total of 1804pp. 8½ x 12¼.   20312-3, 20313-1 Clothbd., Two-vol. set $50.00

CLASSIC GHOST STORIES, Charles Dickens and others. 18 wonderful stories you've wanted to reread: "The Monkey's Paw," "The House and the Brain," "The Upper Berth," "The Signalman," "Dracula's Guest," "The Tapestried Chamber," etc. Dickens, Scott, Mary Shelley, Stoker, etc. 330pp. 5⅜ x 8½.   20735-8 Pa. $3.50

SEVEN SCIENCE FICTION NOVELS, H. G. Wells. Full novels. *First Men in the Moon, Island of Dr. Moreau, War of the Worlds, Food of the Gods, Invisible Man, Time Machine, In the Days of the Comet.* A basic science-fiction library. 1015pp. 5⅜ x 8½. (Available in U.S. only)
20264-X Clothbd. $8.95

ARMADALE, Wilkie Collins. Third great mystery novel by the author of *The Woman in White* and *The Moonstone*. Ingeniously plotted narrative shows an exceptional command of character, incident and mood. Original magazine version with 40 illustrations. 597pp. 5⅜ x 8½.
23429-0 Pa. $5.00

MASTERS OF MYSTERY, H. Douglas Thomson. The first book in English (1931) devoted to history and aesthetics of detective story. Poe, Doyle, LeFanu, Dickens, many others, up to 1930. New introduction and notes by E. F. Bleiler. 288pp. 5⅜ x 8½. (Available in U.S. only)
23606-4 Pa. $4.00

FLATLAND, E. A. Abbott. Science-fiction classic explores life of 2-D being in 3-D world. Read also as introduction to thought about hyperspace. Introduction by Banesh Hoffmann. 16 illustrations. 103pp. 5⅜ x 8½.
20001-9 Pa. $1.75

THREE SUPERNATURAL NOVELS OF THE VICTORIAN PERIOD, edited, with an introduction, by E. F. Bleiler. Reprinted complete and unabridged, three great classics of the supernatural: *The Haunted Hotel* by Wilkie Collins, *The Haunted House at Latchford* by Mrs. J. H. Riddell, and *The Lost Stradivarius* by J. Meade Falkner. 325pp. 5⅜ x 8½.
22571-2 Pa. $4.00

AYESHA: THE RETURN OF "SHE," H. Rider Haggard. Virtuoso sequel featuring the great mythic creation, Ayesha, in an adventure that is fully as good as the first book, *She*. Original magazine version, with 47 original illustrations by Maurice Greiffenhagen. 189pp. 6½ x 9¼.
23649-8 Pa. $3.50

UNCLE SILAS, J. Sheridan LeFanu. Victorian Gothic mystery novel, considered by many best of period, even better than Collins or Dickens. Wonderful psychological terror. Introduction by Frederick Shroyer. 436pp. 5⅜ x 8½. 21715-9 Pa. $6.00

JURGEN, James Branch Cabell. The great erotic fantasy of the 1920's that delighted thousands, shocked thousands more. Full final text, Lane edition with 13 plates by Frank Pape. 346pp. 5⅜ x 8½. 23507-6 Pa. $4.50

THE CLAVERINGS, Anthony Trollope. Major novel, chronicling aspects of British Victorian society, personalities. Reprint of Cornhill serialization, 16 plates by M. Edwards; first reprint of full text. Introduction by Norman Donaldson. 412pp. 5⅜ x 8½. 23464-9 Pa. $5.00

KEPT IN THE DARK, Anthony Trollope. Unusual short novel about Victorian morality and abnormal psychology by the great English author. Probably the first American publication. Frontispiece by Sir John Millais. 92pp. 6½ x 9¼. 23609-9 Pa. $2.50

RALPH THE HEIR, Anthony Trollope. Forgotten tale of illegitimacy, inheritance. Master novel of Trollope's later years. Victorian country estates, clubs, Parliament, fox hunting, world of fully realized characters. Reprint of 1871 edition. 12 illustrations by F. A. Faser. 434pp. of text. 5⅜ x 8½. 23642-0 Pa. $5.00

YEKL and THE IMPORTED BRIDEGROOM AND OTHER STORIES OF THE NEW YORK GHETTO, Abraham Cahan. Film *Hester Street* based on *Yekl* (1896). Novel, other stories among first about Jewish immigrants of N.Y.'s East Side. Highly praised by W. D. Howells—Cahan "a new star of realism." New introduction by Bernard G. Richards. 240pp. 5⅜ x 8½. 22427-9 Pa. $3.50

THE HIGH PLACE, James Branch Cabell. Great fantasy writer's enchanting comedy of disenchantment set in 18th-century France. Considered by some critics to be even better than his famous *Jurgen*. 10 illustrations and numerous vignettes by noted fantasy artist Frank C. Pape. 320pp. 5⅜ x 8½. 23670-6 Pa. $4.00

ALICE'S ADVENTURES UNDER GROUND, Lewis Carroll. Facsimile of ms. Carroll gave Alice Liddell in 1864. Different in many ways from final Alice. Handlettered, illustrated by Carroll. Introduction by Martin Gardner. 128pp. 5⅜ x 8½. 21482-6 Pa. $2.00

FAVORITE ANDREW LANG FAIRY TALE BOOKS IN MANY COLORS, Andrew Lang. The four Lang favorites in a boxed set—the complete *Red, Green, Yellow* and *Blue* Fairy Books. 164 stories; 439 illustrations by Lancelot Speed, Henry Ford and G. P. Jacomb Hood. Total of about 1500pp. 5⅜ x 8½. 23407-X Boxed set, Pa. $14.95

HOUSEHOLD STORIES BY THE BROTHERS GRIMM. All the great Grimm stories: "Rumpelstiltskin," "Snow White," "Hansel and Gretel," etc., with 114 illustrations by Walter Crane. 269pp. 5⅜ x 8½.
21080-4 Pa. $3.00

SLEEPING BEAUTY, illustrated by Arthur Rackham. Perhaps the fullest, most delightful version ever, told by C. S. Evans. Rackham's best work. 49 illustrations. 110pp. 7⅞ x 10¾. 22756-1 Pa. $2.50

AMERICAN FAIRY TALES, L. Frank Baum. Young cowboy lassoes Father Time; dummy in Mr. Floman's department store window comes to life; and 10 other fairy tales. 41 illustrations by N. P. Hall, Harry Kennedy, Ike Morgan, and Ralph Gardner. 209pp. 5⅜ x 8½. 23643-9 Pa. $3.00

THE WONDERFUL WIZARD OF OZ, L. Frank Baum. Facsimile in full color of America's finest children's classic. Introduction by Martin Gardner. 143 illustrations by W. W. Denslow. 267pp. 5⅜ x 8½.
20691-2 Pa. $3.50

THE TALE OF PETER RABBIT, Beatrix Potter. The inimitable Peter's terrifying adventure in Mr. McGregor's garden, with all 27 wonderful, full-color Potter illustrations. 55pp. 4¼ x 5½. (Available in U.S. only)
22827-4 Pa. $1.25

THE STORY OF KING ARTHUR AND HIS KNIGHTS, Howard Pyle. Finest children's version of life of King Arthur. 48 illustrations by Pyle. 131pp. 6⅛ x 9¼. 21445-1 Pa. $4.95

CARUSO'S CARICATURES, Enrico Caruso. Great tenor's remarkable caricatures of self, fellow musicians, composers, others. Toscanini, Puccini, Farrar, etc. Impish, cutting, insightful. 173 illustrations. Preface by M. Sisca. 217pp. 8⅜ x 11¼. 23528-9 Pa. $6.95

PERSONAL NARRATIVE OF A PILGRIMAGE TO ALMADINAH AND MECCAH, Richard Burton. Great travel classic by remarkably colorful personality. Burton, disguised as a Moroccan, visited sacred shrines of Islam, narrowly escaping death. Wonderful observations of Islamic life, customs, personalities. 47 illustrations. Total of 959pp. 5⅜ x 8½.
21217-3, 21218-1 Pa., Two-vol. set $12.00

INCIDENTS OF TRAVEL IN YUCATAN, John L. Stephens. Classic (1843) exploration of jungles of Yucatan, looking for evidences of Maya civilization. Travel adventures, Mexican and Indian culture, etc. Total of 669pp. 5⅜ x 8½. 20926-1, 20927-X Pa., Two-vol. set $7.90

AMERICAN LITERARY AUTOGRAPHS FROM WASHINGTON IRVING TO HENRY JAMES, Herbert Cahoon, et al. Letters, poems, manuscripts of Hawthorne, Thoreau, Twain, Alcott, Whitman, 67 other prominent American authors. Reproductions, full transcripts and commentary. Plus checklist of all American Literary Autographs in The Pierpont Morgan Library. Printed on exceptionally high-quality paper. 136 illustrations. 212pp. 9⅛ x 12¼. 23548-3 Pa. $7.95

YUCATAN BEFORE AND AFTER THE CONQUEST, Diego de Landa. First English translation of basic book in Maya studies, the only significant account of Yucatan written in the early post-Conquest era. Translated by distinguished Maya scholar William Gates. Appendices, introduction, 4 maps and over 120 illustrations added by translator. 162pp. 5⅜ x 8½.
23622-6 Pa. $3.00

THE MALAY ARCHIPELAGO, Alfred R. Wallace. Spirited travel account by one of founders of modern biology. Touches on zoology, botany, ethnography, geography, and geology. 62 illustrations, maps. 515pp. 5⅜ x 8½.
20187-2 Pa. $6.95

THE DISCOVERY OF THE TOMB OF TUTANKHAMEN, Howard Carter, A. C. Mace. Accompany Carter in the thrill of discovery, as ruined passage suddenly reveals unique, untouched, fabulously rich tomb. Fascinating account, with 106 illustrations. New introduction by J. M. White. Total of 382pp. 5⅜ x 8½. (Available in U.S. only)   23500-9 Pa. $4.00

THE WORLD'S GREATEST SPEECHES, edited by Lewis Copeland and Lawrence W. Lamm. Vast collection of 278 speeches from Greeks up to present. Powerful and effective models; unique look at history. Revised to 1970. Indices. 842pp. 5⅜ x 8½.   20468-5 Pa. $8.95

THE 100 GREATEST ADVERTISEMENTS, Julian Watkins. The priceless ingredient; His master's voice; 99 44/100% pure; over 100 others. How they were written, their impact, etc. Remarkable record. 130 illustrations. 233pp. 7⅞ x 10 3/5.   20540-1 Pa. $5.00

CRUICKSHANK PRINTS FOR HAND COLORING, George Cruickshank. 18 illustrations, one side of a page, on fine-quality paper suitable for watercolors. Caricatures of people in society (c. 1820) full of trenchant wit. Very large format. 32pp. 11 x 16.   23684-6 Pa. $5.00

THIRTY-TWO COLOR POSTCARDS OF TWENTIETH-CENTURY AMERICAN ART, Whitney Museum of American Art. Reproduced in full color in postcard form are 31 art works and one shot of the museum. Calder, Hopper, Rauschenberg, others. Detachable. 16pp. 8¼ x 11.
23629-3 Pa. $2.50

MUSIC OF THE SPHERES: THE MATERIAL UNIVERSE FROM ATOM TO QUASAR SIMPLY EXPLAINED, Guy Murchie. Planets, stars, geology, atoms, radiation, relativity, quantum theory, light, antimatter, similar topics. 319 figures. 664pp. 5⅜ x 8½.
21809-0, 21810-4 Pa., Two-vol. set $10.00

EINSTEIN'S THEORY OF RELATIVITY, Max Born. Finest semi-technical account; covers Einstein, Lorentz, Minkowski, and others, with much detail, much explanation of ideas and math not readily available elsewhere on this level. For student, non-specialist. 376pp. 5⅜ x 8½.
60769-0 Pa. $4.50

CATALOGUE OF DOVER BOOKS

AMERICAN ANTIQUE FURNITURE, Edgar G. Miller, Jr. The basic coverage of all American furniture before 1840: chapters per item chronologically cover all types of furniture, with more than 2100 photos. Total of 1106pp. 7⅞ x 10¾.   21599-7, 21600-4 Pa., Two-vol. set $17.90

ILLUSTRATED GUIDE TO SHAKER FURNITURE, Robert Meader. Director, Shaker Museum, Old Chatham, presents up-to-date coverage of all furniture and appurtenances, with much on local styles not available elsewhere. 235 photos. 146pp. 9 x 12.   22819-3 Pa. $5.00

ORIENTAL RUGS, ANTIQUE AND MODERN, Walter A. Hawley. Persia, Turkey, Caucasus, Central Asia, China, other traditions. Best general survey of all aspects: styles and periods, manufacture, uses, symbols and their interpretation, and identification. 96 illustrations, 11 in color. 320pp. 6⅛ x 9¼.   22366-3 Pa. $6.95

CHINESE POTTERY AND PORCELAIN, R. L. Hobson. Detailed descriptions and analyses by former Keeper of the Department of Oriental Antiquities and Ethnography at the British Museum. Covers hundreds of pieces from primitive times to 1915. Still the standard text for most periods. 136 plates, 40 in full color. Total of 750pp. 5⅜ x 8½.

23253-0 Pa. $10.00

THE WARES OF THE MING DYNASTY, R. L. Hobson. Foremost scholar examines and illustrates many varieties of Ming (1368-1644). Famous blue and white, polychrome, lesser-known styles and shapes. 117 illustrations, 9 full color, of outstanding pieces. Total of 263pp. 6⅛ x 9¼. (Available in U.S. only)   23652-8 Pa. $6.00

Prices subject to change without notice.

Available at your book dealer or write for free catalogue to Dept. GI, Dover Publications, Inc., 180 Varick St., N.Y., N.Y. 10014. Dover publishes more than 175 books each year on science, elementary and advanced mathematics, biology, music, art, literary history, social sciences and other areas.